The Italian American Table

The Italian American Table

Food, Family, and Community in New York City

SIMONE CINOTTO

UNIVERSITY OF ILLINOIS PRESS
Urbana, Chicago, and Springfield

Manufactured in the United States of America

1 2 3 4 5 C P 5 4 3 2 1
∞ This book is printed on acid-free paper.

Library of Congress Control Number: 2013948292

This book is dedicated to the memory
of Maria and Anna Spinelli,
immigrant women workers.

Contents

Illustrations

13. "Italian bakery of First Avenue between Tenth and Fourteenth Streets," February 1943.

14. "How could you become so fat in just a few weeks?" Ad from *Il Progresso Italo-Americano*, April 24, 1921.

15. "Don't waste the pleasure of a good meal!" Ad from *Il Progresso Italo-Americano*, November 23, 1930.

16. "She drinks milk to improve her complexion." Ad from *Il Progresso Italo-Americano*, November 6, 1935.

17. The Queens-based Ronzoni Macaroni Company constructs an imagined heritage rooted in Italian cities known for their food. Ad from *Il Progresso Italo-Americano*, May 15, 1921.

18. With its packaged spaghetti, the La Rosa and Sons Macaroni Company promised a modern version of traditional ethnic food. Ad from *Il Progresso Italo-Americano*, November 23, 1930.

19. Cans of tomato products evoke the natural Italian origins, while the text boasts that the products are "prepared in compliance with the most modern and effective methods of vacuum packing." Ad from *Il Progresso Italo-Americano*, September 7, 1930.

20. Ali d'Italia peanut oil is claimed to be an equal of olive oil. Ad from *Il Progresso Italo-Americano*, January 4, 1935.

21. Gem Packing Corporation, maker of Gemma brand olive oil, announces its sponsorship of a popular Italian music radio show. Ad from *Il Progresso Italo-Americano*, August 6, 1939.

22. Cheese importer Mattia Locatelli asks Italians in New York to "buy and defend" Italian-imported foods as a way to "respond to the vile boycott that evil interests declared against the Motherland." Ad from *Il Progresso Italo-Americano*, November 3, 1935.

23. On Columbus Day, 1942, the day the classification of six hundred thousand nonnaturalized Italian Americans as "enemy aliens" was repealed, food manufacturers professed their patriotism, as shown by this advertisement from the Atlantic Macaroni Company. Ad from *Il Progresso Italo-Americano*, October 12, 1942.

24. By the end of the 1930s, leading Italian restaurants in New York used the ethnic press to reach the many Italian American customers who had deserted them. Ad from *Il Progresso Italo-Americano*, June 4, 1938.

Maps

Tables

Acknowledgments

Looking back over the long time that this book has been in the making, I can see how many people have contributed so importantly to it.

An early three-month period of research in New York was made possible through an Alberto Aquarone prize for the best Italian thesis in U.S. history awarded by the American Studies Department of the University of Rome III, the National Republican Committee, and the Lois Roth Endowment. Between 1998 and 2008, I conducted further research as a visiting scholar in the history department of Columbia University, and I am very grateful to the chairs Alan Brinkley and Alice Kessler-Harris for their invitations. Also at Columbia, I did research and presented early parts of my work as a Fellow of the Italian Academy for Advanced Studies in America in 2004. My sincerest thanks go to the academy's director, David Freedberg, and to all the staff, especially Allison Jeffrey. Much of the research for the first section of the book was done at the Balch Institute for Ethnic Studies of the Historical Society of Pennsylvania in Philadelphia, which generously offered me resident fellowships in 1998, 2000, and 2009. Finally, some of the ideas in this book sprang from the graduate seminar "Italian Signs, Italian Values: Producing and Consuming Italian American Identities," which I taught in 2008 as a Tiro a Segno Visiting Professor in Italian American Culture in the Department of Italian Studies at New York University. I want to thank the Tiro a Segno Foundation for their generosity as well as the graciousness with which they welcomed me. At NYU, the chair of the Department of Italian Studies, Ruth Ben-Ghiat, and the director of Casa Italiana Zerilli-Marimò, Stefano Albertini, were also incredibly supportive. The director of undergraduate studies, Chiara Ferrari, worked to arrange for the summer course I taught in the department in 2010.

The first to believe in this project at a time when the cultural history of food (and especially its application to migration studies) was a barely existent—even bizarre—scholarly field was my PhD advisor, Maurizio Vaudagna. Maurizio was tremendously helpful in allowing me to join the international research teams in U.S. and transatlantic history that he worked so actively to create. He has followed my work since then and provided essential advice and support. I owe him much.

Another early and long-time supporter of this book is Donna Gabaccia. At a lecture in Turin in 1997, she first told me about some of the sources (the archives of the WPA Federal Writers' Project) that became critical to my research. She read my dissertation and offered the invaluable comments one would expect from a leading scholar in migration studies. When the dissertation became a book, she first brought it to the attention of the University of Illinois Press.

I am also grateful to Carole Counihan, who read the entire manuscript and offered terrific feedback.

At the 1998 annual conference in New York of the American Italian Historical Association, I was introduced to a group of excellent scholars in Italian American studies who have given me a helpful sense of community, starting with Richard Juliani, Gerald J. Meyer, John Paul Russo, and the late founding father of the field, Rudolph J. Vecoli. Rich and his wife, Sandra, were caring and hospitable every time I did research in Philadelphia; Jerry—to whom I am united by passion for the history of Italian Harlem and the belief in its scholarly and political value—has been incredibly generous with his time, reviewing, commenting, and discussing with me most of what I have done, including the entire manuscript of this book.

The field of Italian American studies has recently been blessed by an eruption of fresh scholarly perspectives, the incorporation of a progressive activism that has rejuvenated the idea of Italian ethnicity, and the emergence of institutions and spaces that showcase the intellectual production of the field. Among these, I want to mention the John D. Calandra Italian American Institute at Queens College–CUNY, which is brilliantly directed by Anthony J. Tamburri. The Calandra Institute's associate director for academic and cultural programs, Joseph D. Sciorra, has performed the exceptionally useful work of disseminating the results of this "new" Italian American scholarship and, personally, has been of tremendous help to me in many different ways.

I am indebted in many ways to the Italian American studies circle at large: Helen Barolini (who granted me a wonderful interview), Nancy Carnevale, Teresa Fiore, Fred Gardaphé, Edvige Giunta, Jennifer Guglielmo, Tom Guglielmo, George Guida, Chiara Mazzucchelli, James Periconi, the late Nunzio Pernicone, Stanislao Pugliese, Laura Ruberto, Joan Saverino, and Robert Viscusi. I thank also the contributors to my forthcoming edited collection on consumer culture

(Danielle Battisti, Marcella Bencivenni, Giorgio Bertellini, Vittoria Caratozzolo, John Gennari, Ervin Kosta, Dominique Padurano, Fabio Parasecoli, Courtney Ritter, Stefano Luconi, Maddalena Tirabassi, Donald Tricarico, and Elizabeth Zanoni), and many others too numerous to mention here.

For the important help they offered at some point along the road, or—more often—over and over again, special thanks are due to Patrizia Audenino (University of Milan), Alberto Capatti, Andrea Carosso (University of Turin), Paola Corti (University of Turin), Sarah DeMott (NYU), Hasia Diner (NYU), Ferdinando Fasce (University of Genoa), Pietro Frassica (Princeton University), David Gentilcore (University of Leicester), Allen Grieco (Harvard University), Franco La Cecla, Priscilla Parkhurst Ferguson (Columbia University), Mario Maffi (University of Milan), Martino Marazzi (University of Milan), Massimo Montanari (University of Bologna), Mark Naison (Fordham University), Marion Nestle (NYU), Mae Ngai (Columbia University), Fraser Ottanelli (University of South Florida), Silvana Patriarca (Fordham University), Jeffrey Pilcher (University of Minnesota), Krishnendu Ray (NYU), Nick Salvatore (Cornell University), Matteo Sanfilippo (University of Tuscia), Lisa Sasson (NYU), Daniel Soyer (Fordham University), Tom Sugrue (University of Pennsylvania), Arnaldo Testi (University of Pisa), John Torpey (CUNY Graduate Center), Angelo Torre (University of Eastern Piedmont and *Quaderni Storici*), Elisabetta Vezzosi (University of Trieste), Richard Wilk (Indiana University), and Jennifer Wilkins (Cornell University). To those I have failed to mention, please blame my brain, not my heart.

At the University of Gastronomic Sciences, I want to thank the president of the university and international president of the Slow Food association, Carlo Petrini, and Dean Piercarlo Grimaldi for their support.

I have presented parts of this book at too many conferences and public lectures to list here. I thank collectively those who attended and offered important feedback and criticism. I also thank my students in the United States and Italy with whom I discussed, tested, and refined much of the material.

I am also very thankful (how could I not possibly be?) to the chefs and masters of Italian American Italian cuisine in America who have been kind enough to meet me for an interview, a fabulous meal, or both: Lidia Bastianich, Johnny "Meatballs" DeCarlo, Marcella Hazan, Pino Luongo, and Tommaso Verdillo. On the business side of Italian American food, Tom Ammirati, Lavazza U.S.A.'s Ennio Ranaboldo, and Gustiamo's Martina Rossi Kensworthy, Beatrice Ughi, and Stefano Noceti were extremely helpful. Two New York friends—filmmaker Gianfranco Norelli, who documents the Italian American experience, and performing artist LuLu LoLo Pascale—have also helped me many times and in several ways. Many thanks to Marc Fasanella for granting permission to use Ralph Fasanella's painting *Family Supper*, now on permanent display in the Great Hall at the Ellis Island Immigration Museum, for the cover art of the book. No other piece of art could have better represented the contents of my book.

Some of the protagonists of the events that I narrate in the book and whom I interviewed are now among us only in spirit. I am always happy to remember Rose Pascale and Father Peter Rofrano of Italian Harlem, who generously shared their memories of the beloved community where they were born and had been a part of all of their lives. I hope that this book will help keep their memory alive.

The former editor in chief at the University of Illinois Press, Joan Catapano, first saw potential in this book. Upon her retirement in 2011, she recommended it to the press's director, Willis G. Regier. Bill has been the best editor I could ever dream to find, and I am very grateful to him and to Joan.

I kept for last the person without whom this book *really* would not be in your hands. Sometime in 2008, Robert Oppedisano read the Italian edition upon which this book is loosely based and almost single-handedly revived a long-stalled project of publishing an entirely new, improved, and updated English edition. Thanks to his long experience with some of the leading university presses in the country, Bob was crucial in securing a contract for the book and then in meticulously overseeing the entire process of polishing my English, editing, and cutting the manuscript to the length requested by the publisher. The secret of the success of our collaboration is that Bob is at the same time a talented and skilled publishing professional, a connoisseur of New York history and Italian Americana, a more-than-fluent Italian speaker, an enthusiastic lover of Italian and Italian American food, and the son and grandson of a first-generation Italian American family that made its way in the food business in New York City. He is also one of the most tactful and charming gentlemen I have ever met. That in the process of creating this book we also became friends is a collateral effect of which I am happy and proud.

To my family—Valeria, Pier Ferdinando, and Cristina—all my appreciation for the patience with which they tolerated time and again the inconvenience this new book meant for them. I wish them all my love—as always.

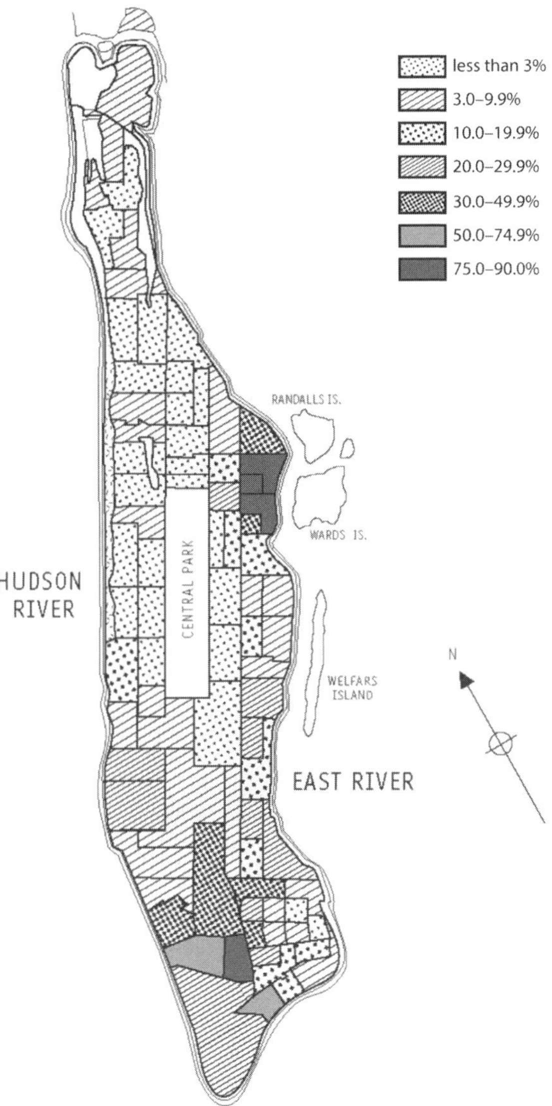

Map 1. Percentage of Italian population (first- and second-generation) in Health District Areas of Manhattan, 1930. Source: William B. Shedd, *Italian Population in New York* (New York: Casa Italiana Educational Bureau, 1934).

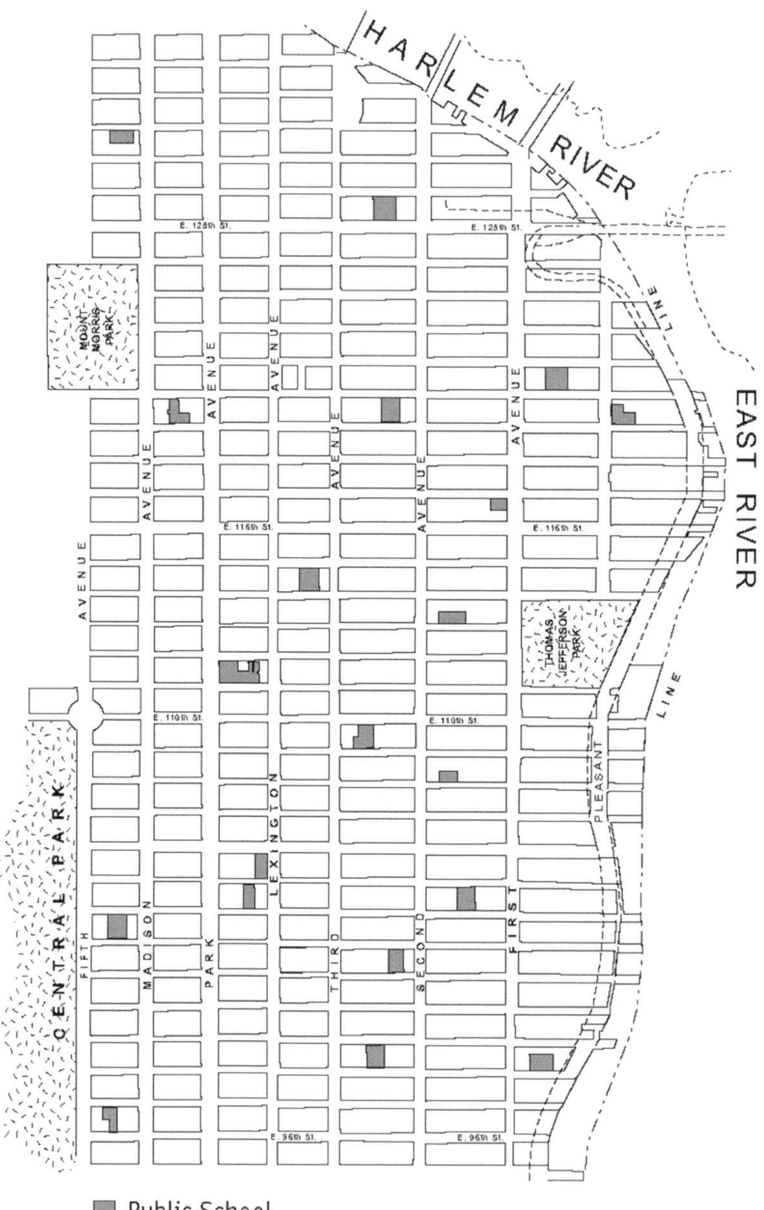

Map 2. East Harlem, ca. 1937. Source: Leonard Covello Papers, Pennsylvania Historical Society, Philadelphia, "Housing," box 43, folder 11.

The Italian American Table

Introduction

Even a perfunctory look at the representations of Italian Americans in film and on TV reveals the centrality of food in Italian American culture. In *The Sopranos* David Chase (born De Cesare) created at once one of the most sophisticated historical narratives about America at the turn of the millennium and a hyperreal description "from the inside" of Italian American life. Throughout the series, Tony Soprano makes nightly visits to the fridge for ethnic comfort food like capocollo and eggplant parmigiana, usually to deal with his depression—a consequence of the unresolved emotional relationship with his mother. Tony regularly reaffirms his family leadership by asserting his power over food rituals like the careful grilling of sausages and the preparation of braciole. Tony's wife, Carmela, plays the same food game, drawing her dysfunctional family around the table with dishes of baked ziti. Substituting food for an impossible love, Carmela treats the young parish priest with her special rigatoni, only to find out that Father Intintola has been "cheating" on her by accepting as a gift the pasta made by one of Carmela's closest women friends. In Arthur Bucco's Vesuvio restaurant, the other Soprano family feasts on high-end Italian food and wine in a display of conspicuous consumption and ethnic conviviality, pleasure, and pride. In an early episode, two of Tony's middle-aged wiseguys, Paulie "Walnuts" Gualtieri and Salvatore "Pussy" Bonpensiero, find themselves in a fancy coffee shop where everyone orders lattes, caramel macchiatos, and decaf cappuccinos. Perplexed by the scene around him, Paulie, a memory keeper of old-school Italian America, begins a tirade against "the rape of the culture" by Anglo-Americans. He rants that these Americans ate "pootsie" before Italians gave them the gift of their cuisine and now reap the benefits of the immense popularity of Italian food—

"pizza, calzone, buffalo moozarell, olive oil." "But this, this espresso shit, this is the worst," Paulie concludes, defiantly stealing an Italian coffeemaker on the way out as his protest against cultural colonialism.[1]

A generation earlier, *The Godfather* used food as a force that kept the Americanizing Corleone family anchored to *Italianità*. The Italian-born mobster Peter Clemenza, who orders his associate to "leave the gun, take the cannoli" after killing a suspected traitor, also teaches the young Godfather-to-be Michael Corleone how to make real Italian Sunday gravy, so that he will one day be able to feed his own (personal and crime) family. Food is everywhere in Martin Scorsese's *Goodfellas*, where family dinners, barbecues, and impromptu midnight meals make up much of the everyday life of the criminal community. *Fatso*, written and directed by Anne Bancroft (born Anna Maria Louisa Italiano in the Bronx), wryly explores the ways food, more than anything else, defines the most "Italian" of human relationships—the mother-son bond. Finally, in *Big Night*, Stanley Tucci's film two recent immigrants who own a struggling restaurant on the New Jersey shore in the 1950s, food is the fullest expression of the craving for security and social redemption that drove immigrants to America *and* of their longing for what was lost in the process.

Not only has food been the most eloquent symbol of collective identity for Italian Americans throughout memoirs, literature, poetry, and the visual arts, but generations of social workers, sociologists, anthropologists, and other observers have also described the way eating becomes an act of self-identification and pride for Italians and an occasion for asserting cultural and political claims. It has become a truism that distinctive "Italian" food habits persist long after language and other cultural features have vanished.[2]

Why has this happened? Why has the food of immigrants and their children continued to serve as an extraordinarily powerful means of identification across different generations of Italian Americans, both within the community and in the eyes of outsiders? Why, and how, have Italian food and foodways come to define Italian America? What accounts for the immense and nearly universal popularity of Italian food—in many varieties, forms, and declensions—in American society, and, indeed, around the world? What does the persistence of Italian foodways tell us about the character and meaning of the Italian experience in America and, more broadly, about the function of consumption in the racial and ethnic formation of minority groups in the United States?

Novelist Mario Puzo was born in 1920 in the Italian Hell's Kitchen section of Manhattan. In 1970, asked to explain what was at the core of his ethnic experience, the author of *The Godfather* and *The Fortunate Pilgrim* confessed:

> I had every desire to go wrong but I never had a chance. The Italian family structure was too formidable. I never came home to an empty house; there was always

> the smell of supper cooking. My mother was always there to greet me. . . . During the great Depression of the 1930s, though we were the poorest of the poor, I never remember not dining well. Many years later as a guest of a millionaire's club, I realized that our poor family on home relief ate better than some of the richest people in America. My mother would never dream of using anything but the finest imported olive oil, the best Italian cheeses. My father had access to the fruits coming off ships, the produce from railroad cars, all before it went through the stale process of middlemen; and my mother, like most Italian women, was a fine cook in the peasant style.[3]

Puzo's memory vividly frames the arguments of this book. In 1920s and 1930s New York City, cuisine took on its central role in defining Italian American identities because of three reasons: first, the power of food to create and support family and community in a world of cultural and material stress; second, the importance of the food trade in the Italian immigrant economy; and, third, the symbolic value of food in the self-representations that helped Italians understand who they were and whom they aspired to be. As this book demonstrates, food—its production, distribution, consumption, rituals, protocols, symbolic values, and imaginative and material effects—shaped Italian identity and made a diasporic Italian nation by embodying a distinctive pattern of domesticity and intimacy. The interwar years, marked by the emergence of American-born generations and the transformation of Italian migrants into American ethnics, were crucial moments for this process to take hold. It was then that New York's Italians developed a collective *taste* (as a way to judge things and make sense of the world based on subjectivity, culture, memory, and social class) that they used to define themselves in opposition to "others" and to project their distinctive political claims. However, the long, complex process of nation making would not have advanced simply as a symbolic project without an abundant supply of the material "stuff" that fueled it ("the finest imported olive oil, the best Italian cheeses") or the economic interests that promoted diasporic Italian food and a diasporic Italian identity. Articulated through food and eating, Italian American ethnicity was as much a social and physical construction as a cultural, narrative, and symbolic one.

Among immigrants, the equation of food and family—an Italian-inflected notion of *the family that eats together*—produced nation by circulating the values of a distinctive domesticity that eventually strongly identified diasporic Italians in private as well as public arenas. That relationship also gave purveyors of Italian food a metaphor for presenting their products and services to their diasporic consumers and for establishing their participation in the same diasporic community of taste. The vision of a family eating together was best exemplified in the Italian restaurants of New York as the most valuable self-representation Italians were able to craft in the diaspora—that of the authentically spontaneous, warm, and artistic Italian—which dialectically mirrored white middle-class self-control and restraint and echoed familiar overtones of authenticity and style for black and white working-class audiences.

The Italian American Table argues that the Italian American food system in New York City offers a model for understanding the ways in which other U.S. migrant and racial groups have used their own domesticities, commodities, and marketplaces to create and redefine their identities. Indeed, to ask why food, of all possible cultural artifacts, became so pivotal to Italian Americans is to illuminate the complicated role of consumption in the production of race, ethnicity, and nation. Scholars of popular culture have suggested that collective identities are produced in relation to commodities and commercial images.[4] The creative, and even subversive, use of consumerism for collective identity making can reveal the limits of bloodlines and descent as sources of ethnic identity, illuminating instead the powers of narrative, ritual, and style in a group's response to its experience of social and economic life. "It is not any a priori cultural difference that makes ethnicity," Werner Sollors has noted. "'The Chinese laundryman does not learn his trade in China; there are no laundries in China.' . . . It is always the specificity of power relations at a given historical moment and in a particular place that triggers off a strategy of pseudo-historical explanations that camouflage the inventive act itself."[5] Embodied in the most intimate of relations, food is a living source for the construction of consumer subcultures and ethnic groups. Although any cuisine is the product of change and contamination—through migration, imperialism, commerce, technological innovation, and interclass borrowing—food offers convincing narratives of identity, difference, and "tradition."[6] The story of Italian American food in the interwar years in New York City explores the dynamics at work in the construction of diasporic identities via consumption and lifestyle and the formation of an ethnic/transnational economy that provided immigrants the raw material for meaningful, racialized, and gendered self-representations.

Making Taste and Identity in the Diaspora: The Literature on Consumption, Class, and Ethnicity

The historical literature on food and immigration has offered only a partial view of the role of food in the creation of an Italian American community. Restricting its focus to the period of mass migration from Europe, roughly 1890–1924, it has mostly failed to account for the experiences of more than one or two immigrant generations. By not fully distinguishing among the varied experiences of Italians in the United States—rural and urban, East and West Coasts—and by juxtaposing sources from different circumstances, times, and places, these studies did not fully explore the relationship between consumption and identity, either in American or transnational contexts. Finally, by concentrating narrowly on the effect of assimilation on immigrant culture, these studies did not address the power struggles within the community over the meaning of ethnic food and the role of ethnic food in the interactions between Italians and other (especially non-European) migrants. As a result, the existing scholarship does not fully acknowledge Italian American food as a part of transnational American culture, the many exchanges and interactions of which it was a product, and the creative agency of immigrants in producing it.[7]

Indeed, the history of Italian American food suggests that migrant subjects like Puzo's mother and father, and countless unknown others, can better be described as *inventive creators* rather than as cultural conservatives. When the first great wave of Italians arrived in New York in the 1890s, they brought with them neither a sense of nation nor any single concept of "Italian" cooking. There was no such thing as a national cuisine in Italy, but rather a patchwork of local food habits that reflected divides between the diets of the well-off and the working poor, and those in the cities and in the countryside. The staples of the *contadino* (peasant) diet were corn polenta and chestnuts in the north, and black bread and vegetable soup in the south. These foods were sometimes complemented with small amounts of durable proteins—cheese, salami, dried cod, and salted sardines—and fats, mostly lard, rarely butter or olive oil. What are now praised as regional cuisines were recent creations, the result of the adoption of a few festive or popular dishes by rural elites and the urban middle class during the nineteenth century. Even so quintessential an Italian American specialty as spaghetti and tomato sauce (with or without meat) has a shaky national pedigree. Industrially produced durum-wheat pasta was a fairly rare commodity in the Italy of 1900, and even Neapolitans, by far the world's largest consumers of pasta at the time, had only in the 1830s begun to sauce their macaroni with tomatoes.

In America, an army of immigrant cooks, mostly women, used the city's unprecedented variety of foods (including pasta, canned tomatoes, olive oil, and other products imported from Italy) to create many new dishes. These were based broadly on "time-blessed" recipes—some of them inspired by the cooking of the rich in the old *paese* (hometown)—so that *novelty* took on the appearance of *tradition*. Culinary invention was fostered by intermarriage and daily interactions with neighbors from different backgrounds. Rosa, a Lombard migrant to a labor camp where she did housework for single men, first heard about "Italian food" when she arrived: "Never in my life had I made coffee, and I would have to learn if I was going to cook for these men in America. 'But it is easy, Rosa,' Gionin [one of the immigrant men] said. 'Just make the water boil and grind the coffee and put it in like this. And always we have plenty of sugar and cream to go in. . . . Angelina [a Sicilian woman] will teach you everything—even to make the spaghetti and ravioli like the people in South Italy.'"[8] Puzo's mother might have learned to be "a fine cook in the peasant style" in similar circumstances.

In New York, Italian food merchants and restaurateurs and non-Italian observers alike labeled as "Italian" the style of cooking that immigrants were synthesizing in the diaspora. Restaurants codified this newly invented cuisine, because they needed familiar, standardized menus that would serve both a multiregional Italian immigrant clientele and a mainstream American public. Many of the dishes that immigrant cooks contributed to the New York foodscape as Italian fare were elaborations of older recipes, enhanced with high-value ingredients like meat and sugar that acknowledged the importance of "American abundance." These included such classic dishes as veal parmigiana, clams Posillipo, spaghetti and meatballs, veal Marsala, and Italian cheesecake, which differed radically from what was eaten in Italy.[9] Immigrants in New York developed a taste for their diasporic cuisine and adopted its hybrid flavors as distinctive and meaningful signs of an emerging identity. Middle-class Italian travelers, on the other hand, usually dismissed the food that Puzo found so delicious and comforting as too garlicky, spicy, greasy, and rich. Their dislike of the food matched their views of the migrants who cooked it for them.

An inventive style of consumption and taste, informed by social class, came to characterize Italian identity in New York by the end of World War I. And as Puzo's memory of his "poor family on home relief [eating] better than some of the richest people in America" during the Depression indicates, food continued to define immigrants' *class-conscious* representations of taste, respectability, and ethnicity. The two most important histories of American ethnic food, Donna R. Gabaccia's *We Are What We Eat* and Hasia R. Diner's *Hungering for America*, however, insist on the importance of assimilation and cultural persistence in the Italian culinary experience, while skating over the issues of generational conflict and the production of place, race, and class that are central to this book. Gabaccia, who is mostly interested in cross-cultural food consumption as an enduring feature of American history, describes the emergence of food in ethnic identity building among Italian immigrants as a generally consensual affair in a dichotomous Italian and American world: "Food celebrated Italians' connections to friends, neighbors, and kin," Gabaccia writes. "Bountiful food symbolized Italians' satisfaction with American life," but "eating bountifully did not mean eating like Americans," for "to abandon immigrant food traditions for the food of Americans was to abandon community, family, and religion, at least in the minds of many immigrants."[10] Writing from the perspective of the immigrant encounter with American plenty as an exceptionalist experience (although Italian migrants also traveled to Argentina, France, and, later, Canada and Australia with similar expectations of prosperity), Diner traces a linear path of eating habits from one side of the Atlantic Ocean to the other. Diner's presentation of Italy and the United States as disjointed realities (here, modernity and abundance; there, timeless scarcity), though, limits her understanding of class and ethnicity. Although Diner does not discuss race, class figures prominently in her interpretation of food consumption in postunification Italy, where peasants and laborers, although they ate poorly, had frequent contact with the food of the upper classes—in public spaces, during celebrations, through domestic service. These contacts created food envy and a sense of social inferiority. Describing how immigrants redefined their identities in their encounters with American food, Diner replaces class with ethnicity. As consumers in the rich American marketplace, immigrants transformed festive food into the everyday, in the process reorganizing their ethnic identity: Old World class differences were replaced with social differences based on ethnicity. For Diner, the terrain of food remained conflict free across generations. While acknowledging that children of immigrants experienced some "shame at eating Italian food," she maintains that those experiences "were rare and limited to the public sphere. Children ate, with appreciation, the foods in their homes." Indeed, "the harmony in Italian homes in America over food contrasted with a deep generational chasm between immigrant parents and American children over much else in their cultural repertoire."[11]

I build on the notion of the sharing of "bountiful food" as the material foundation of the Italian American family as presented by Gabaccia and Diner (and Puzo). However, I expand the frame and the analysis. I argue that food emerged as a nation-building symbol among Italian Americans not only because the wide availability of food in America was the prize won by migrants driven by hunger, but also because food was at the center of consumer choices that articulated the languages of class, race, gender, and generational relations of power. In particular, food was not an exception to the rule of generational conflict between Italian-born parents and New York–born children over the meaning of *Italianità* and Americanization but was consistent with it, since many second-generation children saw immigrant food as a detested reminder of their parents' social inferiority. "The harmony in Italian homes in America over food" was the result of a negotiation that set the terms for an ideological separation between a diasporic private domain for acting "Italian" and an acceptable domain outside the home that was unsupervised, public, and "American." Through these intrafamilial negotiations, domestic rituals centered on food created private spaces for the building of group ideology and the cultural transmission of values. Learned around the table, these values distinguished the public behavior, presentation, and identification of Italian Americans.

As Puzo's memory suggests, the success of the ideology of the "Italian family," shaped and transmitted through food-sharing rituals, was largely rooted in class. First, as powerful as the "Italian family" narrative could be for building solidarity and controlling the desire of younger members for freedom and mobility, it could also be ineffective if it were not grounded in the fact that family ties remained critical to the survival of members of the urban working class, before and especially during the Depression. Second, the development of Italian American versions of such concepts as home, domesticity, and privacy signaled an early move by Italians in New York toward middle-class values and behaviors. The quest for whiteness that characterized Italian New York in the 1920s and 1930s, as a response to the migration of people of color from the American South, the Caribbean, and Puerto Rico, would also be an important dimension of that social mobility, both around and away from the family table. Finally, the attachment of Italians in New York to their distinctive food patterns was at once the cause and the consequence of the disproportionate Italian presence in virtually every kind of food business, from pushcart peddlers and grocers to manufacturers, importers, and restaurateurs. While providing material for community self-sufficiency, the food business also created a unique pathway for the formation of an immigrant middle class.

The Italian American Table argues that although Italian Americans have been much studied as producers, as labor migrants in the working class, they have created their identities, personal and public, at least as much as *consumers*, through the creative use of goods. Of those many goods, nothing has been more important than food, which maintained the bodies of men, women, and children; defined family life; and produced meanings and values within and outside the community. Immigrants did the work of group identification with the tools they acquired in the encounter with the goods, markets, and material culture of their host country and with the continuing circulation of foods, people, capital, ideas, and imaginaries between Italy, the United States, and the rest of the world (with an intensity that, albeit measuring against less-advanced transportation and communication technologies compared to today's global world, did not differ from contemporary examples of migrant transnational consumerism).[12] This process did not stop in the 1930s with the end of mass migration, the formation of a multiethnic white working class, the social policies of the New Deal, or the decline of immigrant institutions in the Depression.[13] On the contrary, the creation of an Italian American food culture illustrates how even poor immigrants exercised their choices as consumers and defined the notions of taste, distinction, and lifestyle that were passed down as habitus to subsequent generations of "ethnics."[14] The close connection of Italian immigrants to food was not a "natural" result of living in relatively uniform urban enclaves, but was rather a property immigrants crafted for themselves through an array of innovative consumer behaviors that often juxtaposed "old" and "new" material cultures. Inventiveness and flexibility made this syntax of taste pattern successful, as a means of identification and self-representations in changing historical contexts.

The Book's Structure

The Italian American Table explores the emergence of Italian American food in New York City, in the years between the two world wars. Analyzing the years between 1920 and 1940 extends the time frame beyond the experience of migration to include the process of cultural reproduction and change over subsequent generations. Also by 1940 Italians in New York had been in contact, and reworked their identity against, many different others, including newly urbanized "nonwhite" migrants. The choice of New York enables an exploration of the meaning of food within *specific* political contexts and local environments that were key nodes of national and transnational networks. In the 1930s, New York was not only the world's largest Italian city, with a population of more than one million first- and second-generation Italian Americans, but also an enormous market for the global trade in "Italian" commodities and imaginaries.

The 1920s and 1930s were pivotal years for both New York and its Italian community. In the 1920s, the ripening of urban consumer culture transformed the city into the most cosmopolitan cultural capital of the world. In the Depression years, under the administration of Mayor Fiorello La Guardia, first- and second-generation ethnic New Yorkers—Jews, blacks, and Italians in particular—were asked to participate to an unprecedented degree in a citywide project of modernization. Even the commodification of racial difference (to be consumed in restaurants, dancing halls, and other public sites) became for the first time an evident phenomenon in the interwar years. Italian New York experienced dramatic changes. After the racist 1924 Immigration Act restricted further large immigration from Italy, New York–born Italians surpassed in number their immigrant parents, while the arrival of many black migrants gradually changed the racial status of Italians from suspect and threatening to respectably "Caucasian."[15] Many Italians left areas of first immigration in Manhattan for homes in the outer boroughs. On an international scale, the new Italian fascist state sought to mobilize the patriotism of New York Italians in the "successes" of its authoritarian and imperialist regime, by urging them, among other things, to buy imported food in support of the "homeland" economy. The outbreak of war between the United States and Italy by the beginning of the following decade, however, would change almost everything for Italians in New York.

The book is organized in two parts. The first, "The Social Origins of Ethnic Tradition: Food, Family, and Community in Italian Harlem," focuses on the largest "Little Italy" in New York in the 1920s and the 1930s—and the largest Italian community in the Western Hemisphere. In the interwar years, East Harlem was home to some eighty thousand Italian immigrants and their children, representing between 75 percent and 90 percent of the area's population. Italians shared

Harlem with an unparalleled—for the time—diversity of other groups, including the second-largest Jewish community in New York and, later, Puerto Ricans, African Americans, and other black migrants.[16] The chapters in this part draw heavily on a remarkable archive: the collected papers of the Italian American educator, public leader, scholar, and longtime East Harlem resident Leonard Covello. Covello's interviews with the Italian immigrants of East Harlem and the written assignments of his students offer a unique picture of domestic food practices, the bond between eating habits and ethnic identity in the community, and, more broadly, the culture of the people of Italian Harlem over several decades. The second part of the book, "Producing and Consuming Italian American Identities: The Ethnic Food Trade," analyzes the Italian food trade and market in New York and their national and transnational ramifications. These chapters draw widely on the manuscripts, oral histories, and photographs collected in the late 1930s by the Federal Writers' Project of the Works Progress Administration on New York City, its food scene, and the local Italian community.

Chapter 1 illuminates the conflict over food that, through the 1920s, pitted New York–born Italians against their immigrant parents. This conflict was in large measure the result of campaigns waged by public schools and other institutions against Italian food habits, using Italian American pupils to introduce "correct," "rational," and "wholesome" dietary notions to their homes. These new habits would help change the lives of newly urbanized people as "ignorant" about modern homemaking as they were about democratic citizenship. The fascination of Italian American children for a modern popular culture that disregarded immigrant ways of life as backward and inferior fueled the clash of values and tastes. But domestic conflicts also stemmed from the inside of the immigrant household and mostly involved the guiding light of immigrants' consumer behavior: hunger for property. The majority of the Italians who arrived in New York between 1890 and 1924 were rural workers from southern Italy, then one of the poorest areas of Europe. In Harlem, nearly all of them were southerners from Campania, Sicily, Calabria, Basilicata, and Puglia. Before World War I, many migrants were men employed in low-skilled occupations who intended to return to Italy to purchase a house and land. In the meantime, these men and their families abroad lived transnational lives, and returns to Italy were very frequent. Only the availability of jobs for women and children in the city's garment and other light industries turned Italian seasonal migration into permanent settlement: by 1930, one-third of New York households with an Italian-born head of family owned their homes, nearly all of them in outer boroughs. But owning a home meant mobilizing all of a family's resources—including children's paychecks—and sacrificing other investments in social mobility, such as education. Immigrant children had reasons to believe that the organization of the immigrant family endangered their prospects of upward mobility.[17]

Chapter 2 illustrates how at this stage immigrants articulated new food-based strategies aimed at controlling the mobility of immigrant children by delaying their embrace of middle-class values. Immigrants invested heavily in this solidarity- and nation-building process, and the share of Italian family budgets marked for food surpassed by a wide margin that of other ethnic groups of comparable income. Italians spent extravagantly to ensure proper feasting at occasions like baptisms, confirmations, weddings, wakes, and funerals. The investment made sense to immigrants not only because food-centered conviviality reinforced family and community ties but also because food was one of the few spheres in which they thought they could fully exercise their taste and "traditional" knowledge about health and body care in the face of "American" norms. To people who had suffered hunger because of class oppression, the relative abundance of inexpensive foods in the American marketplace offered an opportunity for overcoming class barriers and attaining the full humanity and self-respect that they had always been denied. Knowing how to turn cheap ingredients into appetizing and nutritious dishes was an important advantage for working people struggling to make ends meet.

By the 1930s, the patterns of domesticity, conviviality, respectability, and solidarity based on food had become vital for the identification of Harlem's Italians, both first and second generation. Rich, celebratory Sunday dinners of familiar "Italian" foods gave immigrants an occasion to nurture family relations that had been crucial for survival. The circle of solidarity created by the sharing of food was especially important as immigrants' children had begun to achieve significant autonomy in the world of school, work, and leisure and to adopt "American" public values and behaviors that traditionally coercive methods of discipline were unable to control. Family food rituals like the Sunday dinner created a distinctive domestic sphere where anyone, especially younger family members, could act "Italian" and reaffirm group membership with no risk to the new public identities they were creating as Americans. Had the immigrant family table not become a place for negotiating generational conflicts and a stage for the production of *Italianità*, it is doubtful that Italian food as a marker of ethnic identity would have survived the passing of the Italian-born generation.

Chapter 2 argues that the construction of Italian American food culture was a heavily gendered process, resulting in a *feminization* of the ethnic domestic sphere and in women's specialized roles as supervisors of food preparation and consumption. As immigrant men expressed increasing anxieties about the loyalty of the second generation, the solidity of the diasporic family, and the sexuality of their wives, sisters, and daughters, the new ideal of domesticity based on a clear separation of the home and the outside world meant an expanding role for women as self-sacrificing guardians of the hearth and skilled providers of well-prepared food for the increasingly important family meal. The "good Italian woman" started out as a girl trained to cook in the "Italian tradition" and became a wife and mother who used her skills to please her family in an "Italian" expression of dedication and care, in return for which she expected affection, recognition, and respect. In New York, the nurturing *and* virginal Madonna popular in southern Italy became the object of immigrants' most intimate devotion.[18] Skill in cooking became synonymous with a woman's irreproachable sexual behavior.[19] Still, though many first- and second-generation Italian women often felt ambivalent about the identification of food and value, and some resisted the new identity altogether, most embraced the power, authority, and chance for creativity and sociability that this form of unpaid work made possible inside and *outside* the home. Some Italian women even used their culinary skills to create private havens of solidarity for circles of radical militants.[20]

The newly invented Italian American food culture could indeed be consistent with community mobilization, progressivism, and radical movements for social reform. Even as the development of a rich family life and private sphere—spurred by racial and political marginalization—led Italians to later take a predominantly conservative political stance, Italian American consumerism never fully functioned as a consensus-producing machine.[21] Often distant from and skeptical of the American urban commercialism that they were learning to master, Italian immigrant consumers were creating first and foremost an original working-class project of survival and self-representation.[22] Left-wing Italian American artists such as the painter Ralph Fasanella and the novelist Pietro di Donato used the sharing of food and wine among immigrant construction workers and their families as a recurrent expression of class solidarity, sociability, and community.[23]

The study of place and race in East Harlem—the subject of chapter 3—demonstrates that the immigrant community was also a race-inflected geography of food consumption. Italian immigrants transformed East Harlem's monotonous tenement landscape into a Little Italy by surrounding themselves with a sensual universe of Italian foods, colors, tastes, names, and smells, provided by "ethnic" restaurants, shops, and street markets. The distinctive Italian foodscapes that immigrants so successfully carved into "their" neighborhood provided the community with a secure sense of place. And it created *locals* at the same time that it created *place*.[24] In Italian Harlem, as well as in other Italian neighborhoods in the city, food shaped a distinctive, sustaining Italian urban working-class culture by locating people and their history in spaces that were, literally, consumable.

Chapter 3 shows how immigrants in Harlem ended up shaping *many* places with food. These included the imaginary "Italy" they recreated when they ate or when they talked about Italian food in New York. As diasporic nationalists, they narrated "Italy" to their American-born children, who had never seen it, as a negative "American space" where the domestic order was naturally unchallenged, children deferred to their parents' authority, and *the family always ate together*. Food also mapped another elusive place—the "Old Neighborhood"—a vanished world that immigrants and their children fashioned in nostalgia in their new homes in Brooklyn and the Bronx. In the "Old Neighborhood," Italian restaurants, food shops, and street stands at annual religious feasts were shrines of the past, Italian islands in a sea no longer very much "Italian," but one that returnees could visit to repair in the most direct, sensual way possible the wounds they endured in abandoning a community.

Chapter 3 details how food has been central to the Italian experience of race in America, starting with the way representations of race were linked to cooking and eating in the creation of Italian and Italian American identities. In the nineteenth century, the bourgeoisie at the helm of a new Italian nation constructed poorer southern Italians as an inferior race, blaming the dietary deprivation of southern peasants for problematic "innate" traits such as short stature, weakness, and irrationality. Southern Italian foodways were dismissed with metaphors of dirt and contamination. In New York, southern Italians were often racialized as undisciplined and ignorant eaters, unfit for modern urban life and democratic citizenship, their inborn flaws exacerbated by an inferior diet. Resisting this characterization, immigrants kept consuming "Italian" food and celebrating the role of women as makers of food in an effort to counter the experience of oppression and solidify group membership. By the 1930s, more frequent encounters with migrants of color helped establish food as a source of self-identification and pride for Italians in Harlem. Nowhere else in the city did the arrival of Puerto Ricans and black migrants from the American South so transform the city's "racial problem," previously concerned with the Americanization of Italian, Jewish, and other European immigrants, into a matter of color. The arrival of migrants of color "whitened" Italian Harlemites, who used their once despised foodways as a strategy to define themselves against the darker "others" who were now their neighbors. Italians in East Harlem compared their "superior" food habits and stronger consumer power to those of the Puerto Rican and African American "invaders" of "their" neighborhood to confirm that they possessed a superior family culture, to construct much of their sense of working-class respectability, and to reclaim their stake in American cultural citizenship.

The political ecology of food was also racialized in Harlem. Before World War I, East Harlem and the other overpopulated areas of Italian settlement topped all other districts in the city for rates of tuberculosis and other diseases. Social workers and other observers constantly denounced the unsanitary conditions under which Italian food was prepared, sold, and consumed. By the late 1920s and 1930s, however, even those Italians remaining in the old neighborhood ate better than their new Puerto Rican and African American neighbors, thanks to their greater citywide political power. In East Harlem, while Italians took pride in their capacity to use their traditional foodways and open food markets to cope with Depression-era scarcities, the nearby segregated foodscapes of black and Spanish Harlems seemed to them to generate "sick, emaciated, TB-looking, starving" Puerto Ricans and blacks.[25] Now it was the turn of these darker newcomers, against whom Italians fought to prove their whiteness, to suffer from the accusation by "white" Americans that they had innate proclivities for consuming unhealthy food.

Chapter 4 explores the layered worlds of the Italian food business and consumer marketplace. For New York Italians, all the emotional and material investments in food described in chapters 1 through 3 developed another level of connection between Italian American culture and the dynamics of social class: the centrality of food created an entrepreneurial ethnic middle class based in the food trade. This new class nurtured and was in turn supported by the symbolic connection between the consumption of Italian food and the construction of diasporic Italian identities. Unlike other elites, the new food entrepreneurs were welcomed by immigrants because their businesses were essential to their struggle to control the adoption of middle-class "American" values.

Successful food merchants existed in New York before the "great migration" at the turn of the twentieth century and helped make food and wine important Italian exports to the United States. However, only with mass migration and the formation of Little Italies did a mature ethnic economy burgeon around Italian food, dramatically reinforcing the centrality of food in creating a sense of nationhood among Italian immigrants. Chapter 4 shows that World War I was a crucial turning point in this area. Interrupting imports from Italy, the war helped domestic manufacturers of Italian food (themselves overwhelmingly Italian) to win an increasing share of the immigrant market. Using modern techniques of production, packaging, marketing, and advertising, they gained an edge over their competitors. "Made in America" Italian foods increasingly satisfied the tastes of immigrants and their children. Italian American manufacturers offered foods that both celebrated *Italianità* and met the evolving preferences of Italian American consumers for standardized, high-quality products. Combining the features of industrialism and consumer culture with the their "ethnic" advantage, Italian American producers thus *constructed* the diasporic taste of fellow Italian American eaters. Local Italian grocers, butchers, bakers, and peddlers provided immigrants a sense of identity and place, sponsoring community activities, policing the streets, and providing jobs to younger residents.

Chapter 5 illustrates how the business of importing food was aggressively supported by the Italian state (especially in its fascist version after 1922) and its representatives in New York in order to use the vast Italian immigrant population to expand Italian economic and political influence in the United States. Supplying immigrants with "authentic" Italian food helped strengthen relations between Italy and America, creating a tangible economic dimension that complemented ideological and emotional diasporic nationalism. Until World War I, Italian immigrants were receptive to this nationalism of the table, spending large shares of their food budgets on expensive imported foodstuffs. By the interwar years, though, when Italian American food manufacturers became more competitive and U.S tariffs heavily penalized imports, Italian entrepreneurs had to play the nationalist card more assertively, for example, asking New York Italians during the Italo-Ethiopian War of 1935–36 to prove their patriotism by using Italian imports.

The successful immigrant entrepreneurs in the food trade were instrumental in unifying a community deeply divided by class, politics, and loyalties to home villages in Italy. Although competing for the same consumers, Italian importers, domestic producers, and merchants shared a strong interest in shaping a single *Italian* market for their products. They *explicitly* connected consumption and diasporic Italian nationalism, making sure that immigrants understood that food shopping was an act of deference to traditional culture, ethnic pride, and patriotism.

Chapter 6 describes how one group of ethnic businesspeople—restaurateurs—used food to represent Italian identity and nation outside the community. After World War I, when restrictionist laws reduced both the number of new migrants from Italy and the related fear of an "immigrant menace," most Italian restaurants in New York had grown from rough taverns serving the single men who comprised the early immigrant community to more respectable, but still exotic, locales where middle-class natives and tourists could experience a romantic "culture." Using cheap immigrant and family labor and inexpensive ingredients like macaroni and meatballs, Italian restaurateurs attracted non-Italian customers by offering popular food (and during Prohibition, illegal wine) in an appealing atmosphere. In the early 1920s, Italian cooking, which nutritionists and social workers had once criticized as unhealthy, started to enjoy an increasingly good press, in part because the discovery of vitamins affirmed the value of cereals (pasta) and vegetables, and in part because middle-class America had become more comfortable with cultural diversity. Prohibition and an emerging ethnic tourism also made Italian restaurants necessary stops in the middle-class urban tour of the city's "safe dangers." But it was the skill of restaurateurs and their staffs in crafting an irresistible narrative of *Italianità*, mixing images of "black Italy" (primitivism, maternalism, and Mediterranean sensuality) with those of "white Italy" (Rome, the Renaissance, and opera), that lured crowds of middle-class Americans into their restaurants. New York's Italian restaurants were important sites for the creation and consumption of Italian identities and for interethnic encounters that complicated notions of taste, social position, and racialized desire. The experience of "eating the other" in Italian restaurants can shed fresh light on the way Italian American identity was constructed in race as it was in class and gender.

I argue that food assumed its vital role in Italian American culture and life not so much as a transplanted Old World heritage but more as a cultural and material presence that was, and is, central to the experience of migration and to the processes of racialization, Americanization, and nationalism. New York City, the cultural capital of Italian America, provides a unique vantage point for exploring these topics. In the early twentieth-century city, food—its production, importing, trade, preparation, and consumption—was essential in the shaping of a distinctive diasporic Italian working-class culture. Much of the group's life in public, its relationships with the many others sharing urban space, was articulated through a language of food. The domestic and transnational business interests of the Italian American community also converged around food.

The Italian American Table shows how in the often ingenious responses of Italian migrants and their children to the social worlds around them, food became a persistent feature of Italian American ethnicity, a toolkit that helped New York Italians, immigrant and American-born, work their own way through the realities of class, gender, race, and nation, in the process shaping Italian American accents of all those notions. From the history of Italian American food and of Italian Americans as consumers, ethnicity emerges less as a calcified set of traditions at odds with the homogenizing forces of commodification and the capitalist marketplace than as a rich, flexible, and instrumental source of symbols, meanings, solidarities, and power.

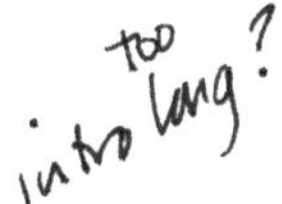

PART I

The Social Origins of Ethnic Tradition

Food, Family, and Community in Italian Harlem

1

The Contested Table

Food, Gender, and Generations in Italian Harlem, 1920–1930

Food, Domesticity, and Italian American Familism

The proposition that family has been socially and psychologically central to the Italian American experience has become an axiom, as three generations of immigration historians have demonstrated: the realms of domesticity and family intimacy have been the most significant venues in which an Italian American identity has developed.

In her early classic study of the Italians of Buffalo in the peak years of immigration between 1890 and 1930, Virginia Yans-McLaughlin set the tone for discussion to follow: "All provide evidence for the cohesion of both nuclear and extended [Italian immigrant] families. . . . On the whole, they maintained strict sex role definitions and an adult-centered family structure. Most of these families also resisted outside pressures toward independence and individualization of their members."[1] Forty years later, most scholars still insist on the domestic core of Italian American identity and identify in family life, rather than work or politics, the main source of migrants' feeling of belonging to a diasporic nation of Italians. "Among the descendents of Italians living abroad," conclude Loretta Baldassar and Donna Gabaccia in a recent anthology, "a connection to Italy is often expressed through identification with particular friends and family and particular local home places and deeply felt obligations to stay connected with them, as well as with the pleasures of kinship, domestic life, and cuisine, while the nation and the nation-state remain objects of suspicion when not of outright scorn and contempt."[2] The power of family ideology to define Italian American identity persists. Italian Americans have often interpreted social reality, presented themselves in the public sphere, and claimed their place in U.S. society almost more than anything else as a family-oriented people.

This strong family ethos is deeply connected to and often used to explain the importance of foodways and the rituals of eating and the table in Italian American culture. The private ideal of a rich family life, represented by the consumption of food, has been located at the core of Italian American ethnicity in works of scholarship, public and personal memory, imaginative literature, and popular culture. In Richard Gambino's *Blood of My Blood*, a widely quoted defense of Italian American culture published in the midst of the white ethnic revival of the 1970s, the pivotal relationship between family life and traditional food is stressed at length. Recollecting his growing up in Brooklyn in the 1950s, Gambino notes:

> In the tradition, each meal is significant. The noontime meal, *colazione*, was taken whenever possible by the entire family. . . . *Pranzo*, dinner, was a gathering of the entire family. . . . To all Mediterranean people, food is the symbol of life, of all that is good and nourishing. Thus, these people find the attitude of some Americans toward food worse than barbarous. This attitude, characterized in the extreme by the American food stand where one eats bland mass-prepared food on the run, is seen as sacrilegious. To the Italian-American, food is symbolic both of life and of life's chief medium for human beings, the family. I remember the attitude conveyed to me as a child by the adults in my family, immigrants and second generation, that the waste or abuse of food was a sin. I was made to feel that food was the host of life, and not in any remote or abstract sense. It was the product of my father's (or grandfather's, or uncle's, etc.) labor, prepared for us with care by my mother (or grandmother, or aunt, etc.). It was in a very emotional sense a connection with my father and my mother, an outreach by them toward me. In a very poignant way, meals were a "communion" of the family, and food was "sacred" because it was the tangible medium of that communion.[3]

Gambino's revivalist celebration of food and family life has been taken up by more recent scholars, including those in queer and feminist studies. Gay and lesbian Italian Americans have confronted their exclusion from that same family table, while women writers have shed light on the misogyny and unequal relations of power involved in the ethnic family dinner. Yet critical studies do not deny the magic of the family table as the site where expressions of solidarity, bonds of affection, storytelling, humor, material culture, and taste have produced an original Italian American identity.[4]

The bond between food and family in Italian American life appears to be especially strong because it is presented as a cultural trait rooted in an immemorial past and transplanted untouched by immigrants in their new homeland.[5] Scholars (again, across the political and analytical spectrum) have regularly interpreted the intimate connection between food and family culture, and the persistence of distinctive food habits among Italian Americans, as a legacy of the traditional southern Italian peasant culture that has endured in America because it was passed successfully to younger generations. In his classic study of an Italian American working-class community in Boston in the late 1950s, Herbert Gans observes that "generally speaking, the Italian and Sicilian cultures that the immigrants brought with them to America have not been maintained by the second generation. A number of Italian patterns, however, have survived, the most visible ones being food habits. The durability of the ethnic tradition with respect to food is probably due to the close connection of food with family and group life."[6]

The first three chapters of this book offer another perspective. For different generations of Italian Americans, the important role of food in family life and ethnic identity was less the result of cultural entropy than it was a dynamic process that took place in modern America and one that needs to be historicized as a significant dimension of the Italian experience in the United States. The history of the Italian American community of East Harlem, New York City, in the 1920s and 1930s shows that the role of food habits in Italian American culture was strongly influenced by the different ways that immigrant and American-born generations constructed their sense of self in an interaction between the family in both generations and a rapidly changing social and economic world. The Italian American family of the interwar years was not a place where minority ethnic traditions could be easily preserved and protected against the influence of social workers, nutrition experts, and the lures of mass consumption. It was, rather, a place where ethnic traditions were *created* by family members drawing *selectively* on and recasting old values and cultural features as a result of new economic and social realities, including relations with neighboring ethnic groups and emerging ideas about race and morality.

The meaning of food culture in the Italian American family cannot be separated from the Americanization of immigrants and their children and their political, social, and cultural integration into the host society. An important factor in this process was the fascination of younger Italian Americans with a popular culture that they viewed as a pathway to autonomization and integration at the same time that this exciting urban culture scorned the un-American customs of unrefined immigrants struggling with English and performing unskilled labor with no hope of social advance. The "Italian" food many immigrant children refused to eat embodied all these negative social implications, laying the origins of a "contested table" in the immigrant family. Eventually, in the midst of two generations' conflicting views about American life and its rewards, food and food rituals acquired a leading role in constructing an ideology of the ethnic private sphere that emphasized devotion, solidarity, responsibility, the work ethic, and the suspicion of the outside world. This food-based ideology became the moral foundation on which many Italian Americans structured a large part of their ethnic experience and identity.

The food culture that shaped the rituals of family gatherings of working-class Italian immigrants in Harlem was at base an investment in family and community ties, aimed as it was at maintaining group solidarity against the appeals of middle-class values and behaviors, even as family members began to earn more at better jobs. In order to do that, paradoxically, Italian immigrants made use of and ultimately internalized a distinct version of such middle-class "American" notions as home, domesticity, respectability, privacy, and secrecy. Italian Americans in East Harlem redefined the boundaries between the public and the private in their lives, concepts and values that often held little meaning in the rural societies from which most immigrants came. In building a family ideology—which in turn created an Italian American ethnicity—they abandoned the solidarity of the *paese*, which often collapsed individual and family into the community. In its place, they began to embrace the contemporary middle-class ideal of the family as a distinct cell of social life. The Italian American domesticity that many contemporary observers defined as traditional was itself largely an American invention and an important step toward the acquisition of American cultural citizenship.

How did food become a symbol of both domesticity and ethnicity for Italian Americans in East Harlem?

Domestic Conflicts in Italian Harlem

Located in the northeastern section of Manhattan, East Harlem is a rough triangle bound by the Harlem and the East Rivers to the north and east, the neighborhood of Yorkville to the south at East Ninety-Sixth Street, and Fifth Avenue and Central Park to the west. Since the 1960s, the entire area has been known as Spanish Harlem or El Barrio because of its predominantly Puerto Rican and Latino population. But throughout the twentieth century, the neighborhood experienced an impressive succession of ethnic groups moving into and out of its boundaries. Unlike Central Harlem, which had originally been an upper middle-class community, East Harlem had always been a working-class neighborhood home to transient immigrants attracted by its low-rent housing stock. Poorer immigrant newcomers typically replaced earlier residents who, having attained some economic mobility, left for more desirable areas. Ethnic hostility dominated East Harlem history, illustrating how in twentieth-century New York racial interactions and conflicts always reproduced class and power relations.[7] Understanding the development of eating patterns and the meanings they held in the Italian American family demands a sense of time and space within the Italian settlement—and its changing social, political, and economic status, and its relation to the many other groups living in the neighborhood.

The first Italian immigrants to East Harlem were workers hired as strikebreakers by J. D. Crimmins, an Irish American contractor laying the tracks of the First Avenue Trolley in the 1870s. They settled in a shantytown along the East River around 106th Street. East Harlem became urban only after the elevated rails of the New York Central Railroad along Second and Third Avenues were completed in 1879 and 1880. The laborers who laid those tracks created the first nucleus of Little Italy around East 113th Street and First Avenue, where the first Italian food shops appeared.[8] In the 1880s, churches, schools, police stations, and firehouses were built to serve an overwhelmingly German and Irish American population of some two hundred thousand. By the end of the century, cheap rents and easy transportation to the garment industry downtown attracted sizable contingents of Jewish and Italian immigrants, some of whom were leaving overcrowded enclaves on the Lower East Side (the Mulberry Bend slum was cleared in 1895). Heavy chain migrations from Europe would follow. In 1917, East Harlem was home to a Jewish population of ninety thousand. Along with eighty thousand Jews living farther west in Central Harlem, Harlem as a whole was the second largest Jewish community in the country after the Lower East Side. In the meantime, as construction of the Lexington Avenue subway line (completed in 1919) provided Italian immigrants with more job opportunities, entire families and villages from Italy's Mezzogiorno landed in East Harlem. By 1910, the area delimited by the East River, Third Avenue, East 116th Street, and East 100th Street had become Italian Harlem.[9]

Two-thirds of the Italian immigrants to East Harlem were unskilled laborers from southern Italy and Sicily. Half of the men and more of the women were illiterate. They occupied the least desirable housing on the eastern fringe of the neighborhood and the most exhausting and poorly paid jobs in construction and in the clothing, candy, and artificial flower industries; peddling fruit, vegetables, fish, ice, and coal; and picking rags.[10] Most girls worked in the garment industry, either in the shops or at home "finishing" pieces: many of the workers who died in the terrible Triangle Shirtwaist Factory fire on March 25, 1911, came from Italian Harlem. The arrival of southern Italians and eastern European Jews in the neighborhood at the start of the century spurred the exodus of the Germans and the Irish.[11] Less than half of the sixty thousand Irish and German Americans who had called East Harlem home in 1910 were there in 1920. Despite the mass influx of Jews and Italians, between 1910 and 1920 the neighborhood experienced a net loss of 7,224 residents as the city grew outward.[12]

Until the mid-1920s, Italians were East Harlem's poorest and most disparaged ethnic group. The Irish in particular harbored deep prejudices against Italians, variously deeming them ignorant, superstitious, dirty, and lazy. The local Tammany Hall political clubs, as well the many Irish police officers and teachers, discriminated against the southern European newcomers. In the early years of the Italian community, the Irish clergy condemned immigrants' popular Catholicism as a form of residual paganism, sometimes refused to offer them pastoral care, and forced them to celebrate mass in the basement of churches.[13] Many reasons for conflict arose in the labor market. The Irish, who had just won a fragile socioeconomic security, feared the newcomers as a threatening supply of cheap labor.[14] Blacks resented the fact that Italians had stolen jobs that they had previously monopolized, such as barber, porter, waiter, and shoe shiner.[15] That Italian immigrant sometimes served as strikebreakers earned them the hostility of the more unionized Jewish immigrants.[16]

Between 1920 and 1930, the ethnic composition of the neighborhood shifted again. Italian Americans became East Harlem's predominant group just as its Jewish community almost completely vanished, from 128,000 in 1919, to 28,000 in 1930, and to 4,000 in 1937. Jews moved out in search of better housing, schools, and streets, but their flight was also accelerated by a significant influx of Puerto Ricans who began to occupy the once heavily Jewish sections between Third and Fifth Avenues and around East 104th Street at the borders of Italian Harlem. East Harlem began to change its skin color in this decade, as African American and new West Indian immigrants also settled in the northwestern part of the neighborhood on the edge of Central Harlem.[17]

The 1930 U.S. Census marked the era's greatest expansion of the Italian community. In 1930, some 80,000 first- and second-generation Italian Americans lived in East Harlem, out of a total population of 233,400, of which 69,519 were of foreign stock. The other largest groups included African Americans (29,000), Jews (28,000), Irish (19,000), Puerto Ricans (14,000), and Germans (11,000).[18] In Health Areas 21, 22, and 26—delimited by Third Avenue, the East River, East 119th Street, and East 104th Street—Italian Americans represented respectively 79.6 percent, 78.6 percent, and 84.3 percent of the population.[19] Ironically, though, East Harlem became the largest Italian enclave in the United States and in the Western Hemisphere just as the neighborhood lost population and the passage of a racist immigration law (the Johnson-Reed Act of 1924) blocked new arrivals from Italy. Racial tensions, a decaying housing stock, and burgeoning rates of crime and disease pushed not only most Jewish, Irish, and German Americans, but also many Italian American skilled workers and second-generation families out of the neighborhood and into newly developed areas in the Bronx, Queens, Brooklyn, and New Jersey.[20] By the end of the 1920s, a researcher investigating the high rates of juvenile crime in the neighborhood drew a dismally graphic picture of Italian Harlem:

> Old brick buildings, row on row, dingy, dreary, drab; wash flying like stings of pennants from the fire-escapes, garments of none-too-selective choice; streets

> littered with rubbish from pushcarts, busy curb markets of the district; "mash" in dark heaps in the gutter, silent evidence of a flourishing illegal industry [winemaking]; garbage in piles, thrown from kitchens where heavy, oily fare is prepared for gluttonous gourmands; penciled or chalk lines on walls and sidewalks, indecent expressions of lewd minds; ground-floor shops, unattractive warehouses of dusty stocks, cellar pool rooms, "drink parlors," many curtained or shuttered, suggestive of their real business; human traffic busy about nothing in this squalid congestion.[21]

Although slowed somewhat by the Depression, the linked trends of increasing impoverishment, quickening racial change, and growing Italian control over the neighborhood continued in the 1930s. As better-off Italians left, more brown and black faces were seen in the streets. Whatever interracial tolerance or cooperation existed, in particular between Italians and Puerto Ricans, was due mostly to the progressive political leadership of two prominent Italian Americans and champions of Italian Harlem: Fiorello La Guardia (1882–1947) and Vito Marcantonio (1902–54). Italian Harlem elected La Guardia to Congress between 1922 and 1932 and gave him landslide support in the elections that made him mayor of New York City from 1934 to 1945. La Guardia reciprocated by bringing power and recognition to Italian Harlem, ensuring that the neighborhood benefited from New Deal public works and welfare programs. His protégé Marcantonio, a lifelong Italian Harlemite, succeeded him in Congress and represented the district for seven terms between 1934 and 1950. Marcantonio adopted a more radical agenda, relentlessly supporting the needs of his poor Italian constituents and organizing Puerto Ricans, then the most powerless community in the city, for the first time. In the 1930s, after decades of discrimination and poverty at the bottom of the racial and socioeconomic hierarchy, Harlem's Italians achieved political control over the neighborhood. And for the first time they also experienced the presence among them of a large "nonwhite" unprivileged population.[22]

In the interwar years, social and demographic changes also affected the Italian community from within. As the doors on immigration closed, the American-born became more numerous than first-generation Italians. It was at this turning point that immigrants began to express anxiety about their family life, disappointed by their children's departure from long-standing ideals of deference and "respect." Immigrant mothers and fathers blamed the influence of American life on their children's abandonment of the "tradition." A unique opportunity to understand the everyday life and culture of Italian Harlem during this time of change is found in the interviews and life stories gathered among immigrants and their children by Leonard Covello (1887–1982). Born to a family of cobblers in Avigliano, in the Basilicata region of Italy, Covello emigrated in 1896 to join his father, Pietro, in East Harlem. As a young man, Covello was influenced by the Protestant progressivism of Anna C. Ruddy, the evangelist who founded one of the first settlement houses in uptown Manhattan, the Home Garden (later Haarlem House), and who devoted herself to Italian immigrants. Covello converted to Protestantism and, with Ruddy's help, received a BA in literature from Columbia University in 1911. In 1922, he taught the first course in Italian language and culture in New York's public schools at DeWitt Clinton High School. In 1934, his commitment to developing curricula that met the special needs of students of immigrant background culminated in the opening of Benjamin Franklin High School in the heart of Italian Harlem. As principal, Covello devoted all his life to transforming Benjamin Franklin into a "community-centered school," one that worked with the local community to help solve the many problems that Italians and other East Harlemites suffered because of poverty and alienation.

Covello's groundbreaking work defined Italian American studies as a legitimate scholarly field: he was the first to theorize extensively about the Italian American *famiglia*. In his 1944 PhD dissertation, *The Social Background of the Italo-American School Child*, Covello described the peasant family of southern Italy as a network of nuclear and extended families linked tightly by bonds of blood and marriage.[23] Covello thought that the totalizing power of these intact family structures, the result of economic deprivation and centuries of foreign rule, had survived immigration and the shift from a rural to an urban society. In New York, "just as in Italy, all social control was based on no other moral categories than those of family, so any social consciousness of Italo-Americans within 'Little Italys' appertain[ed] primarily to sharing and adhering to the family tradition as the main motif of their philosophy of life. . . . The Italo-American family continue[d] to be the repository of the old-world cultural inheritance and the locus of a cultural transfer upon the American-born generation."[24]

Covello's analysis was influenced by classic sociological theories positing a linear evolution of the traditional extended family into the nuclear family that fitted the needs of industrial society. He was also influenced by Robert Park's theme of the "marginality" of the immigrant second generation socialized under the influence of two contrasting cultures.[25] Covello believed that the main reason for the high truancy, drop-out, and maladjustment rates among second-generation schoolchildren in Italian Harlem was the conflict between the norms learned in the public school and those with which children were socialized in the immigrant family. In New York, too many forces encouraged an individualism that threatened the family: public institutions, popular culture, and the mass media. The scorn of the children for immigrant culture, which public schools instilled and fostered, had weakened and disoriented their parents' authority. Covello agreed with the immigrants who felt that Americanization pitted their children against them. He argued that the generational conflict he witnessed daily originated in the determination of American-born children to act as individuals who fulfilled their own needs and interests rather than solely those of the family. Covello thought that although the aspirations of the younger generation were legitimate, the melting-pot agenda served by the school and other institutions could only produce frustrated parents and alienated children. Only a bilingual and multicultural education (pioneered at Benjamin Franklin) that provided immigrants the tools to participate in American society and taught their children to respect and even love the best in Italian culture would close the generation gap and transform Little Italy's residents into responsible democratic citizens.[26]

Conflicts within Italian Harlem's families had a number of sources: turning children's wages over to the family, choices in marriage, girls' request to go out unchaperoned, and the use of leisure time all helped create a divide of suspicion and disdain between the generations. A student of Covello noted, "It is a common occurrence in Italian families to find a break between the immigrant parents and their American-born children. . . . Sometimes children would poke fun at anything Italian. The parents in turn would call their children, '*stupidi, imbecilli*.' Children left their homes, sometimes the parents demanded that they leave. Intolerance made life unbearable for the family."[27] A social worker at the East Harlem Health Center reflected, "[Italian immigrants are] an honest, hard-working people still largely ignorant of the laws, customs, and traditions of the country in which they live. This ignorance is a severe handicap in the struggle for existence and a tragic source of discontent. It undermines the stability of the home, on which everything depends, and creates between parent and child a social gap which contributes immensely to the prevailing anarchy of youth."[28] In her research on Italian Harlem's girls in the late 1920s, Dorothy Reed also noted "the lack of understanding between the girl and her parents, the lack of confidence in each other, the inability of the older generation to grasp the meaning of the new world so strange to them in its differing customs and attitudes. . . . Observation of juvenile court session [was] convincing proof of the breach that [was] ever widening, and case histories and arrest cards innumerable [told] the same story, 'conflict of the old-world traditions and American customs.'"[29] Writing in 1934, Covello noted that there were "still two distinct groups in Italian communities in America—the immigrant group and the second generation—and each sees life with different eyes."[30] Benjamin Franklin High School advertised its English and citizenship classes with flyers in Italian that encouraged immigrants to "learn English so your children will respect you." As its principal, Covello met weekly with parents to discuss students' problems. The problems were monotonously alike: "It might be . . . an Italian woman with a black shawl tied over her head looking for her son who had not been home for a week. Or a father wanting his son to quit school, to go to work in his grocery store or shoe shop, and questioning [the school's] moral right to hold him there."[31]

The critical state of the immigrant family may have been a cause of the skyrocketing rates of juvenile delinquency in the 1920s. In 1926, the Italian section of East Harlem topped any other neighborhood in New York in that department.[32] In the mid-1930s, police and social workers linked the area's high level of juvenile crime to "the lack of authority of non-English speaking parents" and the "children crowding the streets long after midnight."[33] In response to perceived threats to their status and to the survival of the family, many immigrant fathers resorted to violent physical discipline. Asked by a student for help in ending daily fights with his father, Covello decided to meet the abusive man. After a short conversation, "Pappa D'Angelo . . . extended a massive paw. 'With this instrument I have taught him right from wrong. Respect for his elders. For those who instruct him in school. In the old tradition. . . . Where is the harm in a father correcting his son? This is something new. Something American. I have heard of it but I do not understand.'"[34]

Second-generation Italian Americans were in fact likely to be attracted to the values and lifestyles of urban America. On the streets of the neighborhood, they reinterpreted through the filters of class and ethnicity a version of an emerging youth subculture that emphasized autonomy from parental control, camaraderie in the peer group, and participation in consumer culture.[35] American-born Italian Americans, who spoke English fluently, became avid consumers (if only in desire) of spectator sports, fashion, cosmetics, and commercial leisure in motion picture theaters, dance halls, and amusement parks. It was in this geography of fantasy and pleasure, in school and the workplace—where official culture praised patriotism, nationalism, and capitalism's promises of material comfort—that youth groups constructed their own values and behaviors.[36] In the idiom of immigrants and their children, these values and behaviors were "American"—a definition that conveyed desirability or undesirability depending on the speaker and the situation.

The other side of this urge to embrace and be embraced by American life was the determination to be free of the burden of an immigrant background synonymous with social inferiority. At the turn of the century, southern Italian immigrants had been racialized as a primitive, irrational, and suspiciously dark people; men were hard working but quick tempered and dull witted; women were submissive, superstitious, and hyperprolific. Not until the 1924 law reduced immigration from Italy to a trickle, and racially darker groups moved into the city in large numbers, did this stigma slowly lift. Some of the most dispossessed immigrants clustered in Italian Harlem, giving the neighborhood a bad name. Young Italian Americans routinely lied about where they lived when they ventured outside the neighborhood, since a Harlem address was likely to raise a policeman's suspicion or cause a job application to be rejected.[37] Their hostility toward *Italianità* harbored significant shame and self-hatred, feelings derived from personal insecurity as well as the recognition that an Italian identity damaged their prospects for upward mobility and self-realization.

As the director of the Boys' Club of Italian Harlem, A. Warren Smith, argued, "The outstanding problem in connection with the Italian boys of this neighborhood is to arouse a greater sense of responsibility and to help them to overcome an inferiority complex which is prevalent. The average Italian feels he is looked down upon by other races."[38] Mimicry and passing were frequent survival strategies for younger Italian Americans, only adding to a widening and painful generation gap. A social worker noted:

> The Italian girl, as she comes through her school work and her employment into contact with girls of other nationalities and standards, begins to compare her home and her life with theirs, and resents the difference. She meets here a certain intolerance and misunderstanding of her race; its members are called "wops" and "dagoes" and are spoken of as "our criminal class." She begins to feel ashamed of her heritage and incurs the bewildered anger of her parents by refusing to speak Italian even at home and by insisting on adopting American customs. I shall never forget the pained indignation of one father when he learned that his daughter, instead of enrolling herself at her place of employment under her own unmistakably Italian name of Augusta Solamoni, had called herself Gussie Solomon.[39]

Many second-generation Italian Americans thought they could achieve a new American identity and belong to the larger "white" society by discarding everything Italian in them. Covello noted that many Italian Harlem youths reasoned: "The native-born Americans are American because they speak English; the foreign-born can only become good Americans by forgetting everything their parents brought along with them: language, habits, culture, dress, festivals, song, dance and even food."[40] The fact that immigrants' children rejected or derided so many features of parental culture did not necessarily challenge loyalty, solidarity, or affection within the family. However, parents' ability to instruct and discipline their children through example was seriously crippled. In the intimate space of the home, parents began to lose control over their children's physical and emotional development. Many younger Italian Americans began to dismiss their parents' food habits as embarrassing expressions of an inferior culture. In the eyes of younger Italian Harlemites, immigrant foodways were symptoms of ignorance, backwardness, and poverty. Just as there were many children who refused to reply to parents when addressed in Italian, there were, Covello observed, "many cases where children refused to eat Italian food because it was called by an Italian name."[41]

Food Conflicts in the Immigrant Home

Because it is a cultural code learned early in life, food is a powerful means for building and reinforcing ethnic bonds and identities; like language, food habits leave indelible marks on one's sense of self. But food culture may also be quickly abandoned as a marker of difference in exchange for the rewards of conformity and integration. Helen Barolini remembers her childhood in Syracuse, New York, in the 1930s: "Once in a while my mother would have me accompany her to get cheese in an import store which I hated to enter because of the smells—smells that were Italian and which intensified my own determination not to be. I hated the fish store because of the revolting un-American eels and squid that were displayed there." Barolini points to the effects of traditional foods on the standards of attractiveness set for the body in a consumer culture: "I even hated Josie's pastry shop because Josie, who made all those foreign-looking cookies, was fat and foreign looking herself, with black circles under her eyes and an uncorseted figure—not at all the image of life I was seeing each Saturday afternoon at the movies."[42]

In *Mount Allegro*, his novel set in Rochester, New York, in the early 1920s, Jerre Mangione describes how his family's noisy conviviality and unapologetic display of the appetites of the body were for him embarrassing sources of painful cultural difference. "I had a particular dread of picnics in public parks," Mangione remembered. "Spaghetti, chicken, and wine were consumed with pagan abandon then and the talk and laughter of my relatives filled the park like a warm summer breeze. A few feet away would be an American family quietly munching neatly cut sandwiches that came out of neatly packed baskets—and drinking, not wine of course, but iced tea with trim slices of lemon stuck into the brims of their glasses to make them look pretty. It would make me blush to realize how shocked these subdued, well-mannered Americans must be by the circus din of our Sicilian eating festival."[43]

The feelings of shame and the ridicule that immigrant food habits provoked had particularly strong consequences in the school. In Italian Harlem, the school was crucial in setting the stage for, and actually promoting, food conflicts in the Italian immigrant family. During the 1920s, schools were problematic in two ways. On the one hand, the school fostered the sense of inferiority of children of Italian origin by stressing the gap between their own domestic reality (including patterns of food preparation and consumption) and middle-class ideals of cleanliness, body maintenance, discipline, citizenship, and whiteness. On the other, the school destroyed the family's monopoly on the care of its members, threatening the credibility and authority of domestic rules, practices, and hierarchies—especially those regarding eating.

In East Harlem's elementary schools, Italian schoolchildren were confronted for the first time with hierarchies of class and cultural difference. They were widely singled out as "problematic" in terms of both discipline and education, and as a group were the most socially disadvantaged.[44] The children's feelings of fear and resentment of and fascination with the outer world represented by teachers and students of different backgrounds often found expression in the idioms of food. "Lunch at elementary school was a difficult problem for me," remembered one of Covello's students.

> To have a bite I either stole some money from home or took it from my shoe shining on Saturdays and Sundays. With this money I would buy the same stuff that non-Italian boys were eating. To be sure, my mother gave me each day an Italian sandwich; that is half a loaf of bread filled with fried peppers and onions, or with one half dipped into oil and some minced garlic on it. Such a sandwich would certainly ruin my reputation; I could not take it to school. My God, what a problem it was to dispose of it, for I was taught never to throw away bread.[45]

The dislike of his immigrant culture compelled this boy to control outside access to his private world. Since smelly and messy foods like garlic, onions, peppers, and homemade bread were seen as foreign snacks, the schoolchild responded by buying proper food, exchanging his labor for the avoidance of shame, while struggling to minimize conflict with family norms and authority. By hiding and throwing away his sandwich, the boy defended his privacy as the realm of the secret and the unknown. For second-generation Italian Americans in East Harlem, using secrecy to deal with the conflict between public and private was a recurring strategy.

The choice of secrecy, to be sure, can frustrate opportunities for discovery and adjustment. Many children hesitated to make friends outside the Italian circle. They feared that having to reciprocate an invitation would lead to the embarrassment of introducing classmates to their parents, their home, and their foodways. In East Harlem, racial differences were especially significant because they reproduced class differences. A student told Covello:

> "I . . . made friends with a boy who was on the football team with me and he invited me to his home. I only went twice and then found some excuse not to go. They lived in a private house, had a fine dining room and I felt that I could not ask him to come to Little Italy. I was ashamed to do so. . . . Then one fine day I plucked up enough courage to invite him. He came. You can be sure I watched him carefully to see what impression all that he saw and heard was making upon him. I was relieved when the whole thing was over. I had done my duty—but I made up my mind that it was best to carry on my social life at the school—and stop there.[46]

Italian American schoolchildren learned from an early age to carefully navigate the boundaries between home, community, and the outer world.

The elementary school years marked children's separation from the family, as they faced for the first time alone experiences that the immigrant family did not fully understand or control. As a result, Italian children gradually felt the fracture between the private realm of the family and the public realms of the school, the peer group, consumer culture, and leisure. Understanding the need to keep these realms separate, schoolchildren often turned to a strategy of distancing, similar to that used to defend family foodways against the school's relentless campaign for "proper" eating and nutrition. From the moment the Italian child enters school, Covello noted, "the world to which he renders sincere allegiance—his family—is shown to him to be a source of grossly improper conduct. The methods of keeping house, feeding of children, clothing that parents provide are pointed out unfavorably. The mother comes in for a great deal of criticism for allowing as a lunch meal a sandwich of gargantuan proportions, instead of a 'balanced repast.'"[47]

In early twentieth-century New York City public schools, food education was not a marginal or extracurricular activity. It was an essential part of the public school's mission to forge loyal American citizens out of immigrant children.[48] Inspired by Progressive thought, the "New Education" that emerged at the turn of the twentieth century as the dominant pedagogical movement was heavily influenced by the overrepresentation in U.S. schools of Chicano, Asian, and especially southern and eastern European immigrant children, who did not speak English and lived in very different cultures. Public school was to be at the forefront of Americanization, not only because the character of future generations depended on effective assimilation but also because schoolchildren would become agents of assimilation, able to introduce to their families the ideas and values learned in school. The New Education focused on the public school's lead role in dealing with issues that had up until then been the charge of the family, settlement houses, social workers, and an array of charities: the overall health, hygiene, and psychophysical development of children.[49]

School reformers and teachers were heavily influenced by the debates that, reflecting scientific racism, judged new immigrants to be morally and culturally inferior. If not assimilated, these dispossessed masses would become a serious threat to America's democratic institutions, its middle-class way of life, and even the very existence of the Anglo-Saxon race.[50] In the classroom, ethnocentrism and social conservatism prevailed. Hygiene and nutrition classes were designed to improve the health of immigrant schoolchildren and families and prevent the spread of disease outside immigrant neighborhoods. Home economics classes prepared immigrant girls for their future as mothers and housewives in a proletarian family to which no alternative could likely be imagined.[51]

After the discovery early in the century of high rates of malnutrition among immigrant children spurred food programs in many city schools, Italian schoolchildren were regularly exposed to "balanced meals" of cereals, juice, toast, and milk.[52] As early as 1908, charities such as the New York Association for the Improvement of the Condition of the Poor (NYAICP) operated free or low-cost lunch programs in public schools. While such programs initially emphasized relieving undernourishment rather than the quality of the diet, these programs were explicitly designed to improve the discipline and the performance of immigrant schoolchildren and hasten their Americanization.[53] By now, students were being tested in racial groups for average IQ and academic performance as well as for their diet and nutrition. In 1908, Italian Americans had the highest percentage (36 percent) of pupils repeating a year in a sample of New York elementary schools, while in 1911 less than 1 percent of Italian American students graduated high school, the lowest rate in the city.[54] In 1907, 22.3 percent of Italian American elementary school children were found to be malnourished, more than in any other racial group.[55]

During World War I, new discoveries in the field of nutrition—notably vitamins—spurred food education in New York public schools and sharpened the focus on reforming immigrant food habits. At the same time, wartime nativist sentiments and calls for the forced Americanization of immigrant children further encouraged an assimilationist nutritional agenda in schools.[56] By 1919, experts of the National Tuberculosis Association, the American Child Health Association, and the American Red Cross all volunteered to provide nutrition classes, while teachers were asked to take nutrition classes taught at hospitals and universities.[57] That same year, the New York City Board of Education extended lunch to all public schools of the city.[58] Dental clinics were established in schools, where oral hygienists instructed children about correct dietary habits.[59] New dietary theories tended to blame parents' ignorance, lack of control, and ethnic foodways rather than poverty for children's malnutrition.[60] The different ethnic food cultures of the city were considered important influences on the development of younger generations.

The food education taught in school connected Americanism as an ideology to what was believed to be a scientifically correct diet. As Diane Ravitch has noted, the basic charge of the public school in Americanizing the children of the new immigration was "teaching them how to speak English; inspecting their heads for lice; lecturing them on cleanliness and hygiene; teaching them to salute the flag, to recite the Pledge of Allegiance, to sing the national anthem, and to revere American heroes"; and each single part was critical to the whole task.[61] Teachers in East Harlem schools were mostly lower middle-class, second- and third-generation Irish and German Americans who were often unsympathetic toward their difficult Italian American pupils. Italian American students would hear daily criticism of family habits and be singled out as antipatriotic and un-American, which deepened a sense of nonbelonging.[62] In the classroom, as one observer recalled,

> His father, whom heretofore he has regarded as omnipotent and ideally self-reliant, is pointed out unfavorably for his speech, his dress, his wine drinking, and perhaps his winemaking; His mother—for her methods of keeping house, her feeding of her children, and for the clothing she provides them. . . . The basic habits of food, shelter, hygiene, etc., of the family all come in for their share of criticism and complaint. . . . The usual meal likewise, is preached against, since the breakfast is seldom likely to be exactly recommended by the pink faced cherub of the cereal advertisements. Hot cereals are a nuisance to prepare, while the beverage of the breakfast remains, since the parents find it impossible to forego the pleasure of their own drink, and since conditions do not generally permit the brewing of two drinks, coffee, for both young and old. As a substitute for the piping hot lunch which is strongly recommended to him in the class, the boy buys instead a sandwich of gargantuan proportions.[63]

Sometimes, food education was introduced in support of the civic culture of immigrant children. In 1925–26, the NYAICP and the School of Education of New York University teamed up to conduct experimental classes at PS 106 on Lafayette Street, whose students were nearly all southern Italian immigrant children. The entire project rested on the notion that good health and proper diet represented "one of the prime requisites of good citizenship."[64] The preliminary report found that 93 percent of students followed a poor diet. The high rates of infant mortality and malnourished children were said to be consequence of "food practices . . . on the whole inimical to health," imported from a country where "cereals [were] unknown; coffee and wine form[ed] an invariable part of the regular diet; and sleeping with the bedroom windows open [was] a positive menace to health."[65] Researchers recorded all students' meals on a daily basis. Large placards with the captions "DRINK – EATING HABITS – WHAT TO EAT EVERY DAY" were posted on classroom walls; and students were taught to prepare shows titled "The Little Girl Who Didn't Like Tea or Coffee" or "The Girl Who Taught Her Mother a Lesson about Health Milk." All students had to memorize a list of dietary rules: "1. Drink one quart of milk every day; 2. Eat plenty of vegetables; 3. Drink four or five glasses of water every day; 4. Eat at regular hours; 5. Do not drink coffee or tea; 6. Eat a dark cereal every morning; 7. Eat plenty of fruit; . . . ; 26. Think clean thoughts; 27. Always be happy and never worry; 28. Keep smiling."[66]

After a year, however, the coordinators admitted that the project had largely failed. As usual, they blamed the students' social environment for its stubborn rejection of scientifically supported food reform.[67] Indeed, Italian immigrants became notorious among nutrition experts for their resistance to change in their children's diet.[68] A frustrated social worker remembered how, after many attempts to convince the parents of a malnourished girl to give her milk for breakfast, the mother brusquely interrupted the conversation by saying: "Louisa eats what the family eats!"[69] Even by the early 1930s, studies showed that the presence of young children in Italian American families had no influence on food choices. On the contrary, "the menus were selected on the basis of the likes and dislikes of the parents, and the children were given free choice of all dishes upon the family."[70]

Desdemona L. Heinrich examined a large sample of "the three most represented groups in New York elementary schools, Americans, Jews, and Italians" and concluded that Italian food habits lagged behind those of the other two in households with elementary school–aged children. "In the evening meals the Italians alone have a poor report, for only fifty-four per cent of the cases have approved or acceptable evening meals."[71] Among children, Heinrich identified such dietary deficiencies as an insufficient or negligible consumption of milk and breakfast cereals and the excessive drinking of wine and coffee. Other incorrect Italian food habits included the eating of dessert between meals and the unhealthy reliance on pasta, white bread, and overcooked vegetables drenched in olive oil. Unlike in other groups, Heinrich noted, class was not an important variable in determining food behavior among Italians, who shared similar food patterns across social classes.[72] The determining factors were, again, the dynamics of cultural assimilation and the persistence of Italian food habits that diverged widely from middle-class patterns. Heinrich ranked Jewish schoolchildren's diet closer to the American ideal, thanks to quicker rates of acculturation: "Comparing the three nationalities it is found that the American children have the best food consumption in each food class and the Italian children have the poorest, with the Jewish children nearer to the American standards than to the Italians. In cereals, in milk, in vegetables and fruits, the Jewish children are almost parallel with the American, with a poor showing for the Italians."[73]

In the heat of the public debate that would lead to the passage of the Immigration Act of 1924, which curtailed new arrivals from Italy, the alleged widespread malnutrition of Italian children reflected even more explicit racist discourses that, despite growing scientific evidence, continued to deny the influence of the environment on the formation of individual character. Research commissioned by NYAICP compared the physiological development of Italian children in New York unfavorably to the national average, concluding that, as important as malnutrition was, it was not the decisive issue. Italian American children, the researchers proclaimed, were much shorter and more malformed than average because of congenital (racial) defects, which pervasive malnutrition only exacerbated.[74]

In the most widely circulated manifesto of Anglo-Saxon racial supremacy, *The Passing of the Great Race*, Madison Grant wrote: "Exceedingly adverse economic conditions may inhibit a race from attaining the full measure of its growth and to this extent environment plays its part in determining stature, but fundamentally it is race, always race, that sets the limit. The tall Scot and the dwarfed Sardinian owe their respective sizes to race and not to oatmeal or olive oil. . . . The Mediterranean race is everywhere marked by a relatively short stature, sometimes greatly depressed, as in South Italy and Sardinia, and also by a comparatively light body framework and feeble muscular development."[75]

Through the 1920s, second-generation Italian American schoolchildren in East Harlem for the most part accepted the ideological and rhetorical link between correct nutrition and citizenship. They accepted the school's view that to become Americans and enjoy the promises of social mobility, they needed to discard their immigrant background as soon as possible. In this way, they also accepted the existence, and to a certain extent the legitimacy, of racist and discriminatory elements in American public discourse, elements they would later use to construct their own racial position as whites in the face of new, "nonwhite" neighbors. The social disadvantage and segregation from larger society that second-generation Italians experienced in East Harlem made school the most significant window on a "dominant culture" with which they were anxious to identify. Italian Harlem schoolgirls admired their middle-class teachers as models of femininity and appropriate behavior in domestic life.[76] In his autobiography, Covello illustrates time and again the fascination that an imagined and yearned-for "America" exercised on Italian Harlem youth and on the construction of hybrid identities. He recalls that at PS 83, on East 110th Street between Second and Third Avenues, "our teachers impressed us mainly because they did not live in the neighborhood. They dressed better and spoke differently and seemed to come from somewhere beyond the horizon. Somehow we tried to measure up to this outer world which we knew was American, though we have no conception of what it was. Only its people had a life far easier and with greater luxuries than ours. But in trying to make a good impression on our teachers, it was always at the expense of our family and what was Italian in us."[77]

This was especially true for the rules of body care and discipline, including diet. Rules learned at school often met puzzlement or hostility at home. "At elementary school I was thrilled with everything that was taught about America: its history, geography, and what it stands for. It was very pleasant to hear about it," remembered another Italian Harlem boy.

> But when I came home in the afternoon, I felt a painful contrast between what I saw at home and what [I] had been taught during the day. The teacher had said,

> for instance, that clean hands, clean clothing, and a toothbrush are essentials. And that plenty of milk should be taken in the morning. I felt so ashamed, so inferior, when I realized that my parents do not exemplify such things at home. My mother showed even opposition to the teacher's recommendation about food. She began ridiculing all my teachers for their ideas, and this made me very sad, for she ruined my dreams of becoming a real American. I felt that I needed milk in the morning more than anything else. But my mother, and so my father, insisted that this was not according to the good customs; that American milk was poison. "These teachers of yours are driving us crazy," they told me. I realized that everything I learned at school was met by my parents with disapproval.[78]

The equation *American food = American citizenship* was reinforced by another symbolic equivalence: *American food = American body*. The body was the canvas onto which immigrant children could inscribe their new identities and social relations most easily; food and diet were the most effective means for (re) constructing their hybrid identities. As echoed by Helen Barolini, young Italian Americans elaborated a notion of their bodies as a modifiable form that diet could shape to match the aesthetic models projected by popular consumer culture. By the 1920s, some of the sports heroes and movie stars who embodied the canons of the attractive body were endorsing mass-produced foods and drinks. Magazines insisted that dieting was necessary for girls who wished to attain the new ideal of white feminine beauty personified by the slim flapper.[79] Dieting permitted Italian American children to control their body shape more easily than trying to change skin or hair color. In this effort, the substantial peasant food of their parents was almost certain to fare much worse than the "balanced," vitamin-powered meals praised by school and corporate food advertisements alike. For "The Boys' Club Study," Italian American young people were interviewed about their food habits: "To what extent is there a conflict between the health standards inculcated in school and that at home?" asked a researcher. "'American foods ruin your stomach,'" "Nick" answered. "One afternoon I was sent home from the clinic because I had something in my head. . . . The woman at the clinic had given me pamphlets, showing red-cheeked boys who eat carrots, spinach, etc. I got home and told them about fresh air at night. My mother said that's bad, but I was all excited and wanted to be like [bodybuilders] Bernarr Macfadden and Earl Lederle."[80]

Overall, in the 1920s, Italian Harlem's younger generation identified in food, as well as in other features of their immigrant culture, an expression of their parents' cultural conservatism; their food was an un-American symptom of backwardness and superstition that crippled prospects of social emancipation and assimilation into "white" society. "This attitude on the part of our elders discourages us because it makes us think that because we are of the under-class there is no chance for us to rise, to become something better," another boy told to the researchers of "The Boys' Club Study." "We are in the gutter and we must stay there. Who are we that we should try to learn to control our voices, to act like gentlemen, to have lady friends, to become cultured, to understand music, to appreciate poetry, and to love the works of nature? The boys are mocked when they are seen cleaning themselves too often, when they try to learn to dance, when they refuse food that will make them too fat or too thin or that it will stop their growth."[81]

Immigrant Italians in Harlem resisted the increasing exposure of an area of family life—food—that had once been managed in private. The reasons for this resistance were not limited to widely noted suspicions about the state, the school, and other public institutions. The food habits of Italian immigrants certainly changed fairly soon after their arrival in America. But these dietary changes were mostly affected by new and different market conditions, by the changing supply and quality of ingredients, and by methods of cooking in Harlem tenements as opposed to houses in the rural villages of southern Italy. In New York, the local food patterns that immigrants had brought with them were gradually blended, sometimes as a result of intermarriages that joined spouses of different regions, into a hybrid cuisine. Foods that in Italy were only consumed regularly by the upper classes were in the United States often available to poorer families, in what a food historian would call a "carnival come true."[82] Meat, pasta, canned tomatoes, white bread, coffee, sugar, and actual wine (as opposed to the poor Italian farmer's diluted *vinello*)—what social workers and food reformers identified as the staples of the Italian immigrant diet in New York—were recent additions. In southern Italy, these foods, which needed to be bought in the marketplace, were, as such, often out of the *contadino*'s reach. Although food experts, teachers, social workers, and immigrants themselves seemed to believe it, there was no single thing as traditional Italian cooking.

Still, southern Italian immigrants retained distinctive food habits. They were openly skeptical of or indifferent to mass-culture food advertisements as well as the food programs that schools, settlement houses, and charity organizations directed at them, because they powerfully disagreed with the evaluation of their foodways as inferior. In the rural culture of the Mezzogiorno, strong beliefs in the link between food and health created a rich oral tradition of food-related norms, practices, and taboos, despite the constant preoccupation with hunger and scarcity. By the time of mass migration, southern Italians "knew, or thought they knew, the effects deriving from the use, abuse, and lack thereof of specific food and drinks."[83] Immigrants to New York continued to rely on this knowledge. In 1942, the federal wartime Committee on Food Habits coordinated by Margaret

Mead found that many Italian New Yorkers retained long-standing beliefs about the beneficial and harmful combination of ingredients and the proper format, weekly cycle, and seasonal pattern of meals.[84] Parents transmitted these beliefs as expert knowledge to their children. Richard Gambino remembered that his father insisted that endive be served once a week "to cleanse the intestines."[85] A second-generation immigrant was introduced to chicory by his Sicilian grandmother. "She boiled it, then sautéed it in garlic and olive oil. It was strong and slightly bitter. 'Eat!' she said. 'Is good for your blood!'"[86] Some Italians thought that drinking milk caused "worms" in children.[87] The deeply rooted belief in the nutritional and curative value of wine encountered the strongest disapproval in school and among food reformers. When Maria Sermolino was caught in school with a bottle of wine diluted with water, she was sent home with a reprimand stating that the school prohibited alcoholic beverages on the premises. After that, Sermolino remembered, "grandma would bring us white wine diluted with water and my teacher who saw us drinking it mistook it for ginger ale, even though it did not sparkle, because grandma would bring it in a ginger ale bottle. In doing this grandma's interest lay not in defying the teacher but in aiding our digestion."[88] Jerre Mangione also refers to the Sicilian immigrant's habit of giving their children "sips of wine, on the remarkable theory that wine-drinking not only stimulated the appetite but actually created blood. '*Vivi, figlio mio*,' a mother would urge her youngest child. '*U vinu ti fa sangu*.'"[89]

Gang members in Italian Harlem, who dropped out of school early, believed that "all judges, policemen, lawyers, and politicians are crooked," as well as that "the people who have color in their cheeks drink a lot of wine" and "the people who season their food with red hot peppers will eventually become very strong."[90] To the mothers of Italian Harlem, it was a matter of pride to show off plump, red-cheeked children, who bore the sign of good health and good blood.[91] The association of fat with beauty, good health, and well-being was a heritage of peasant culture and the history of scarcity it confronted daily. In that southern Italian context, a fleshy figure reflected social status: it identified those who could afford to eat much and well.[92]

Immigrants thought that they could offer their children a credible food alternative to the mandates of educators and experts. Immigrants emphasized the value of fresh, simple, and "natural" foods, which they seemed to obsess about. They also taught their New York–born children a hierarchy of taste that assigned significance to foods and ingredients based on rural Italian standards. For immigrants, achieving victory over hunger was one of the most significant outcomes of their migration experience. Whatever the experts might have thought, the relatively liberal consumption of foods like pasta, white bread, wine, coffee, sugar, and especially meat had a special social value: it represented the fulfillment of deeply felt desires and the rupture of hated class barriers. In East Harlem, immigrant cooks added unknown ingredients to their diet, experimented with new combinations, and ate foods that in Italy they could very rarely afford. They did so within a relatively rigid *culinary structure*, with persistent normative ideas about the order and compatibility (or incompatibility) of flavors, ingredients, and dishes. Thanks to residential segregation, a dense community life, and the development of a food marketplace that catered to their preferences and needs, a shared food pattern developed that was labeled "Italian." Although specific practices varied widely, this popular culinary pattern resembled neither the *contadino* diet nor the cuisine of the Italian urban middle class. This was the food structure that Italian Harlem immigrants defended from "foreign" ingredients and practices. Covello recalled his own experience as a student: "Once at . . . school I remember the teacher gave each child a bag of oatmeal to take home. This food was supposed to make you big and strong. You ate it for breakfast. My father examined the stuff, tested it with his fingers. To him it was the kind of bran that was fed to pigs in Avigliano. 'What kind of school is this?' he shouted. 'They give us the food of animals to eat and send it home to us with our children! What are we coming to next?'"[93]

Insisting on the value of continuity, memory, and tradition, immigrants tried above all to safeguard their parental role in such a challenging environment. Food had a central socializing role in the household, and creating the proper diet for their children posed difficult choices for parents. Their children's health was just one issue: the control parents exercised over the family diet was closely related to the control they exercised over the affective and personality development of their children. For many mothers, regulating their children's diet meant fully assuming the maternal role.[94] In this new domestic context, the move from the rural Mezzogiorno to a complex industrial and consumer society was a critical turning point for immigrant women. Class was also a decisive factor. For working-class mothers, being skilled housekeepers and cooks was intimately linked to morality and social respectability. Competence and power as the person in charge of the domestic sphere were basic to immigrant mothers' identity, which found its most telling expression in the regulation of children through food. A teacher remembered the case of an angry immigrant mother who unexpectedly showed up at school and told her: "I came to find out whether Tony eats his sandwich I give him each morning or whether he throws it away. You people in school have no interest in that. You will probably tell him that he does not have to listen to his mother. You have different customs here; and if I let Tony do as you tell him, I cannot control him."[95] Another woman wrote to the principal challenging the legitimacy of the school's interference with the family: "Forgive my writing but the matter is important. Perhaps I shall have to come and see how my son Joseph behaves in school. He is now seventeen years old and therefore, independent, so I cannot talk to him much. When he comes home he does nothing but eat and drink; he bathes every night. He drinks mostly milk."[96]

Many Italian Harlem immigrants energetically rejected the food practices that the school and other institutions taught their children. Their resistance was a result of their culture, history, and memory, but also of the realities they faced in America. In southern Italian rural society, children began to contribute to the family economy as wage earners after only a few years of elementary school and often during school. Truancy was informally tolerated, allowing poorer peasant families to send their children to work in fields, pastures, and mines.[97] In America, the encounter with compulsory mass education—and the truant officer—changed the lives of turn-of-the-twentieth-century immigrants. For poorer immigrants, the forced separation of children from family by the school, along with the ban on child labor, were costly impositions. Furthermore, the shift of some socializing tasks from family to school weakened the control of parents, especially fathers, over their children. The separation between home and workplace undermined patriarchal authority. In New York, children went to work for a wage after completing their school years. They took a large step toward personal autonomy and experienced aspects of American life not open to their parents. They were now able to wield an unprecedented influence on family decisions. Fathers increasingly depended on their children's willingness to contribute their wages to the family, a shift that clashed with gendered cultural standards that once defined the father's unconditional power within the family.[98] For immigrant fathers, the stresses of migration increased their worries about the behaviors, mores, and sexuality of women in the family, especially as their daughters and sometimes even their wives went to work outside the home.[99] In 1925, 61 percent of unmarried second-generation Italian American women in New York worked (63.6 percent among women between sixteen and twenty-one years old).[100]

Family meals, with their complex ritual of menu selection, kitchen roles, order of service, and size of portions, created a stage for the symbolic representation of this problematic phase in the history of the Italian American family in East Harlem. In its tenement apartments, dinners were dramas of generational conflicts. Of the immigrants interviewed by Marie Concistré in the late 1930s, 96 percent agreed that their family unity was best expressed by the entire family gathering at the dinner table.[101] Family meals continued to provide essential opportunities for parents to communicate with their children. Immigrants struggled to keep their children around the table, and criticized the practice of dining out. "The American custom of children regularly visiting at their friends' homes for dinner was unknown in my neighborhood," Gambino remembered. "Whenever one of us (influenced by the media) would broach the idea with parents, the response was always an unyielding: 'You come home for dinner!'"[102] Being absent for dinner was sometimes punished by forcing the transgressor to eat the leftovers the day after.[103] Italian Harlem immigrants used to call their children *Americani* when they did not defer to parental authority, lacked respect for "family values," or simply put on airs.[104] Immigrants also used the word *mangiacake*—cake-eaters—to reproach younger people about eating fast food in the streets, a practice that stood in contrast to the formal family meal and as a symbolic revolt against familial demands.[105] The use of *mangiacake* to reproach children suggests that the common practice of eating snacks on the street bought in the neighborhood's many candy stores was indeed a form of rebellion against family pressures.[106] For a twenty-year-old woman, the sense of liberation after the death of her tyrannical father had the taste of the forbidden food. "Never shall I forget the enjoyment derived from the ambrosian taste of pancakes eaten at 2 A.M. and flavored with strange excitement and dare-devilness," she confessed to Covello.[107]

In most descriptions of Italian family meals, the father is the domineering figure. At the same time, his power appears to be mostly fictional, a ceremonial reminder of his dramatically receding authority. Seated at the head of the table, the father assumed the position of the head of the family, organizing domestic space and setting the rules of the food ritual. He was generally served first by his wife or one of his daughters. After the meal, he did not clear or wash the dishes, which would have degraded his masculinity and patriarchal status.[108] The choice of food also largely depended on him as the actual or alleged family breadwinner. All domestic chores, including shopping and cooking, were on women's shoulders, and the father usually managed to get the food he wanted to eat. A settlement-house employee working with Italians noted, "The Italian woman . . . cooks one meal a day, and that at night. Pot or pan may be placed in the middle of the table and each helps himself from it, but the food is up to the standard of her husband. It is what he wants."[109] The male dominance in food choices was reproduced in newly formed households when the wife, to please her spouse, accepted her mother-in-law as her cooking instructor. The notion that men, and in particular fathers, deserved the best and most nutritious food conflicted with the American idea that children's diet came first, designed for the particular needs of each developmental stage. Lucy Gillett, a NYAICP nutrition expert who worked in Italian Harlem, sharply criticized the habit of putting fathers first, denouncing Italian mothers who did "not appreciate this wave of enthusiasm that [was] sweeping the land in the interest of child welfare. According to Gillett, "The man that earns the money for their daily bread must have the best there is so that he may keep in good condition. They frequently say, 'Oh my man must have meat because he works, but the children, they can eat anything.'"[110]

Social workers were equally disturbed by the degree of conflict they experienced in Italian immigrant homes at mealtimes. "Whatever the cause, a family of Italian children seldom eats its meals in peace," Gillett noted. "Someone is nagging, scolding, or, in their phraseology, someone is 'yelling' at them all the time."[111] Many children dreaded family meals and their ritual shows of patriarchal power. The Italian father was described by many observers in Freudian tones as the enforcer of symbolic control and discipline; he seemed an oppressive *and* grotesque, even ridiculous, figure. One of Covello's students remembered that around the table, children's jokes and laughter ceased when they heard the sound of father's approaching steps. "No one had the right to touch the food. If one made too much noise or attempted to reach for a morsel of food the mother could warn with 'Accorte, ca mo vene l'erba c'abrusce!' (careful, here comes the grass that bites!)" From the head of the table, the father, making sure to maintain his haughty dignity, began to give orders to the mother on ways to distribute food, "in a manner a ruler would dispose his favors or wrath over his subjects. . . . First he took his portion. The next best pieces (usually the largest) went to the sons; the daughter received the smallest and worst pieces. If there was fruit to be eaten, the father would—in an unemotional tone—disburse it. 'Three figs to Carmine! Give two figs to Paolo, no give him also three. Tonio and Luigi two a piece. Carmela two figs, no not that, the one next to it. One fig to Angelina!'" After that, the family ate in complete, tension-filled silence, which was torture for the children. "But the meal was finally over, the acting unnecessary; the father went into the street and suddenly again behaved as his real self."[112]

In the early American years of one Neapolitan family, "the supper table was fraught with ceremonious forms. The father would sit at the head of the table to the left of his wife. All the children sat around quietly and waited until served. No one made a grab for the food. Each child was served individually according to age. Only Italian could be used at the table and conversation had to be sparing and confined to the limits of necessity. The father acted as disciplinarian." Over time, however, such formalism was impossible to maintain: "Later when many of the children [nine girls and two boys] grew up, it was difficult for the parents to stop the use of English at the table. The children became more voluble and Yiddish, which was learned in the factories, developed into a useful tool to avoid the parent's knowledge of their social plans and activities. After a time Francesco stopped trying to insist upon quiet or the exclusive use of Italian at the supper table."[113] The familiarity of the children with the features of multiethnic urban life (the Yiddish spoken on the shop floor, for example) resulted in a kind of Americanization from the bottom up that threatened relations within the immigrant family as powerfully as the Americanization from the top down preached by the school and other institutions. Gradually, immigrant fathers found it impossible to pretend that a complete separation of the public from the domestic sphere existed when the lines between them were ever more insecure and porous. In the interaction between the two spheres of immigrant experience, the public sphere caused a profound transformation of private life, influencing habits, languages, roles, and hierarchies. The everyday life of the immigrant family was being redefined from its foundations by the domestic effects of social change.

A classic photograph by the celebrated founding father of social photography, Lewis Hine, *An Italian Family Has Supper, East Side, New York City*, graphically represents the generational drama that was staged every night around the immigrant family table in Italian Harlem between 1910 and 1930. The father's position in the picture is especially critical. Hine's perspective pushes him into the background, in the corner of the image, making him smaller than he actually is. He is still the formal head of the household, for he occupies the head of the table, but other clues clearly speak of a crisis: his heavy moustache, undershirt, and suspenders; the beer he is drinking; and his uncomfortable, averted gaze in the presence of the camera. The father's appearance betrays that his traditionally dictated role of uncontested patriarch is challenged by the social reality he has encountered in the American city; his partial or complete inability to speak English has relegated him to low-paid, unskilled work, while his habits are regarded as an indelible mark of backwardness and permanent social inferiority. The older son, sporting a clean shirt and a grin, probably earns more money than his father because of his better command of English and familiarity with urban culture. The other children also have easier access to "American culture" through school and the peer group—an impression conveyed by how relaxed they appear, in contrast to their father, in the presence of the photographer; the child to the right of the father chuckles and looks into the camera regardless of the fact that she or he was told not to do so. In Hine's photograph, the very epicenter of family life appears to be the mother. Even her figure, in the foreground of the picture, is imposing, for she embodies the entire power of the household. She *is* the home: her position beside the equally imposing cooking stove symbolically makes her the person in charge of family meals and the survival and welfare of the family as a whole. The older girl's place on the side of the mother speaks of her readiness to take on the same role in terms of both the material culture required to nurture her own family and the cultural apparatus necessary to fulfill the role of the "proper Italian woman."[114]

When social change altered the father's status within the family, family meals reproduced the change. Often, as in the examples cited here, the ritual behaviors symbolizing the father's supreme power over the family continued to be accepted by the other family members, for the sake of family unity, its tensions repressed. Sometimes the growing detachment between the symbolic and the actual role of the father in the family exploded in confrontations between father and children. Either way, in this period in Italian Harlem history, the patriarchal family structure was in deep crisis, contested, and eventually subjected to redefinition. Immigrant food culture also did not survive untouched by the widespread generational conflict that Italian Harlem experienced in the 1920s: immigrants and their children argued about not only *what* to eat but also *how* to eat. The family table was the site where social change was staged and conflicts formalized. It was also where immigrant parents realized their growing helplessness to impose traditional authority on their children. Between the 1920s and the 1930s, Italian immigrants began to rethink and redefine their strategies for socializing their children to accept traditional parental authority. Since the usual techniques of discipline had become impracticable, they tried to craft new tools for influencing their children's choices and new forms of psychological manipulation to keep the American-born generation in their grasp.[115] The new strategies touched areas as diverse as gender relationships, courtship, sexuality, the selection of spouses, the approach to education, and the choice of a job or career. Immigrants were now resigned to the "Americanization" of their children in the public sphere: they stopped trying to impose values and behaviors that were untenable in a modern, urban, and bureaucratized consumer society. And they accepted the fact that outside the home the young generation "became American" all on their own. In return for recognizing these changes, first-generation Italian immigrants asked their children to declare their commitment and devotion to a *private ethnic sphere* through ritual and symbolic actions. Immigrants were convinced that family solidarity could be ensured only through subtle strategies of conditioning rather than coercive discipline—methods that the social disparagement of Italian immigrant culture had rendered unworkable.

It was at this turning point that immigrants began to employ food and food rituals in the construction of the Italian American *famiglia*, with its emphasis on solidarity, strong gender roles, a commitment to work, suspicion toward abstract ideas, and an appreciation of the effective limits of happiness. The ideology of *la famiglia* met the needs of a working-class culture—itself under development—that prepared individuals to the life of labor most of them were destined to live. Convincing though the narrative of *la famiglia* was, it could work only when family ties remained critical to survival for members of the urban working classes, a reality even more evident during the Depression years. The ceremonies through which each individual was socialized into the group culture were centered on the ritual consumption of food. Thanks to intergenerational compromises, "Italian" food, which the American-born generations had earlier rejected as a marker of social inferiority, became a central symbol of the group identity.

If the immigrant family had not made the rituals of organized conviviality the center of its strategies for socializing new generations, food would not have become such a vital part of Italian American culture. Immigrant food would probably have disappeared with the maturity of an American-born generation that had already discarded it as a stigma of social inferiority. In the end, cooking and conviviality became the most important aspects of the turn that immigrants made toward more complex forms of psychological and ideological control of their children.

2

"Sunday Dinner? You Had to Be There!"

Making Food, Family, and Nation in Italian Harlem, 1930–1940

The Generational Contract: Family Food Rituals and Eating Cultures

On a summer afternoon in the late 1940s, Orlando Guadalupe, a student who was preparing a paper on East Harlem street life for Leonard Covello's class, ventured deep into the Italian section of the neighborhood. Back then, that could be a dangerous trip for a dark-skinned Puerto Rican boy. Guadalupe briskly walked the streets of Italian Harlem, memorizing the images that struck him the most. He knew that "the Italians brought over with them their love of the opera, the most favorite games and sports of their dear Italy, customs and habits such as eating spaghetti, mourning their dead for months and months while dressed in black, religious processions, and the singing of Italian folk songs. [But] despite their well-ingrained folkways, the younger generation ha[d] discarded them with no difficulty and ha[d] assimilated the American way of life with surprising rapidity." Guadalupe noted more details: "My attention was focused on the large mustaches the old Italians wear. This is not common around the rest of the community. However, the middle-aged Italians and the younger ones did not have them. Coming back home I saw an Italian movie house advertising a film shown in their vernacular language. I stopped for a while to see what sort of people went in. Very soon I observed that mostly old people bought tickets. The younger generation mostly patronized the other American movie nearby."[1]

The rigid generational boundaries in the streets of Italian Harlem may have seemed strange to Guadalupe when compared to those of the Puerto Rican community just a few blocks away. The public spaces where food was consumed suggested the segregated worlds of Italian immigrants and their children. On one side of the street, young Italian Americans congregated at candy stores to sip sodas and chat about sports and girls in New York street slang, while on the other side of the street a group of immigrants sat talking in southern Italian dialect.[2] One of Covello's student researchers noted:

> In the matter of places where persons can go for a "good time," there is a saloon at 2123 Second Avenue, Italian owned, where friends in the neighborhood get together afternoons and evenings, to play cards, horses and no doubts "policy slips [illegal lottery]," as in the short time I "hung" around, I noticed evidence of all three. It has no dance floor, or music at any time, but a radio giving the results of the races, etc. There are 6 tables in the premises, with about 22/23 chairs, and the element there is noticeably of the gambling type of Italian Americans. No Italian spoken and to my address in Italian was answered in English. Another saloon is at 245 East 109th Street, where cards are also played and the element going there is exactly the opposite of that at 2123 Second Avenue. Here are all Italians of the old Italian ideas, hardly understanding any English. Cards of the Italian game similar to Casino, were played. No women go there on afternoons, but I was informed that at night they did go there. The first place is very clean and typically American; the latter European in most every respect.[3]

In the streets of Italian Harlem each generation claimed its own spaces and carefully avoided one another's territory. This distancing was a consequence of the generational shifts that defined the community between the 1920s and the 1930s, when immigrants started relinquishing direct control of their children's public life and discarding traditional methods of parental authority. Earlier in the century, immigrant parents had closely controlled their children, especially girls, following the patriarchal code of honor and shame of rural southern Italy, in which a girl's offense against a rigid sexual morality would jeopardize the respect (*rispetto*) of the community for the entire family—especially its males. But even boys' leisure time was seriously policed. Activities outside the home, like sports, were generally considered useless and detrimental to good upbringing. The idea of adolescence as an intermediate time between childhood and adulthood, when children had special needs, was foreign to immigrant *contadino* culture.[4]

However, immigrant parents soon realized that American life had so changed the balance of family power that any effort at preventing their children's independence and development outside the home was futile. In response, they relented, and granted an unprecedented degree of freedom to both boys and girls. By the late 1920s, Caroline Ware noted that among Greenwich Village Italians, "different aspects of the patriarchal family institution were breaking down at different rates, those which had been bound up with land and family estate—i.e., the arrangement of marriage by parents and the giving of dowries—going the fastest."[5] In Italian

Harlem of the 1930s, Marie Concistré found that 87 percent of immigrants agreed that a young woman should be allowed to choose her spouse. Many immigrants now accepted some "American" form of courtship and dating: the majority of Italian-born mothers, for example, would allow their daughter to go on a date with her fiancé if the couple was officially engaged.[6]

In many urbanizing societies of the twentieth century, parents were inventing new ways to deal with their increasingly independent children. In Italian Harlem negotiating the conflicts between immigrants and their American-born children resulted in a distinctive *generational contract.* The terms of this contract were fairly straightforward: immigrant parents would grant their children much greater autonomy in public in exchange for showing allegiance to the family through ritual and symbolic actions—most importantly the regular participation in the gatherings centered on ritual food consumption that brought families together. These convivial social occasions, centered always around food, offered a subtle, effective method for socializing the next generation. By accepting the terms of this diasporic, food-centered domesticity, young people could still act independently outside the home.

A second-generation adolescent told Covello that his Sicilian family had fractured along generational lines: "All the social activities of the parents are pretty well confined . . . to visits to relatives, Italian and American movies, Italian plays, and friends. The children prefer the American movies, the American newspapers, American dance steps, sports, and other activities. The Italian radio programs are listened to with greatest interest by the mother, but the children do not like them." Girls enjoyed an increasing degree of freedom outside the home, even though the Italian-born daughter did "not avail herself of it, and there ha[d] never been any dispute about going alone." The younger daughter fought to be allowed to join clubs and go on picnics. At home, parents spoke in Sicilian dialect to each other and to their children, who spoke exclusively in English. Food, however, was a different matter. While the parents had adopted "American" clothes and furniture, "cooking and the preparation of food [was] still purely Italian and supplemented by very little 'American food.'" Children, who enjoyed "American" food with their friends, did not object. "The children tend to break away from most of the Italian patterns, *except the foods.* When the children were younger the father was the supreme head of the family and his wishes were considered first. Now, there [was] no noticeable head of the family. Each member [was] fairly independent in many ways, and [was] not obliged to keep any of the rituals that [were] kept by the family, except *being present at the family gatherings.*"[7] This was the core of the generational contract: the symbolic act of submission immigrants obtained from their children in exchange for the right to engage with the autonomy of American life.

Why did immigrants insist on such a single ritualized form of commitment to family intimacy as a price for relinquishing control of their children's public life? And why did younger Italian Americans agree?

Most second-generation immigrant children agreed to "be present at ritual family gatherings" because taking part in them did not seriously conflict with their lives outside the home. In the interwar years, many younger Italian Americans articulated a sharp division between the public (peer group, school, and street) and the private (home and family) spheres, an adjustment that kept developmental conflicts at a minimum. "I never tried to change the home because of school," a Covello's student recalled. "I always considered them as two different worlds entirely. When I was home I was the typical Italian boy who did everything my mother told me. I helped her, went out, etc. In school I was a schoolboy. I never referred to my home. Just did what the teachers said."[8] As a successful demarcation between private and public spheres, this generational détente meant that children might at last avoid the embarrassing presence of their parents in their public life. Children were now free to criticize and even ridicule immigrant culture in the company of their peers, as long as they were receptive to family norms in private. Covello remembered the plight of the second generation of Italian Harlem:

> We were highly critical if not disrespectful of the many traditions that the old folks wanted us to live up to and conform to. . . . Many of my Italian friends would say, "They have lived their own lives in their own way. We want to live our lives in our own way and not to be tied down to fantastic customs that appear ridiculous not only to us but particularly to our 'American' friends." And I can assure you we were particularly keen about that ridicule. In fact so much so that we never invited our "American" friends to our home. And while "American" boys took their parents to some of the school functions, we not only did not take our parents but never told them they were taking place. That was our life—exclusively ours and that of the other boys. The deadline was the threshold of the door of the house or the tenement in which we lived. Beyond that the older folks went their way and we went ours.[9]

Younger generations discovered that taking part in family food rituals was consistent with a shared allegiance to different social groups, each requiring cooperation and commitment. Family food rituals, concealed behind a veil of domestic secrecy, did not conflict with values and behaviors accepted in the peer group. In 1938, a twenty-one-year-old man born in East Harlem told Covello: "I find the old custom of all relatives meeting together a very beautiful custom. It makes sense to me. So I accept it wholeheartedly. But there are other things which are trifle old-fashioned; these I don't follow, especially if they make me look ridiculous in other people's eyes."[10]

Maintaining the distinction between public and private performance required the use of multiple identities. Different "acts" in front of different audiences managed to avoid most contradictions—one could safely "be Italian" for the ritual feast, for example. These convivial occasions could be especially rewarding for girls, whose access to public space was limited. Dorothy Reed reported, "[On Sunday] the whole family goes to call on the relatives in some other block or another section of New York's Italian colonies, and this is the occasion for family celebration and feasting and merrymaking. There is as a rule a number of children at such a gathering and as several girls said, 'Gee, what a swell time we have!'"[11]

Yet, participating in festive family meals was almost always compulsory. "My parents are always keen to have family gatherings of some kind, [but] I don't like very much this kind of stuff," a student confessed to Covello. "I think it is old-fashioned, and it was good in Italy, but here in America life is different, and I don't see the reason why all this bother. I have nothing against [my family] coming together once in a while. I even enjoy it, for there is lots of fun on such occasions and plenty of good eats. But somehow, I would prefer to spend the time with my friends on the block. If I attend these gatherings it is because my parents drag me to them against my will."[12]

The immigrants' emphasis on family food rituals in the generational contract has a practical basis. The rites of the table reinforced the family dynamics that helped newcomers to Italian Harlem manage the experience of migration. Family meals not only deepened intimate bonds but also offered the chance to display, share, and celebrate the private rewards of hard work in America: victory over food scarcity and a rich and stable family life.

Being able to create and sustain a strong family was a powerful goal of southern Italian immigrants. Families in southern Italy were not typically the large, extended, cooperative units of popular myth, but rather highly localized, nuclear families with limited resources.[13] Family life in the Mezzogiorno could be deeply dysfunctional as well. The *Inchiesta Parlamentare Jacini*, a study of the conditions of the rural classes commissioned by the Italian parliament on the eve of the late nineteenth-century "great migration," reported very high rates of adultery, illegitimate births, incest, and rape. The *Inchiesta* found that for Neapolitan peasants "affection and love . . . [were] not either the purpose or the basis of their conjugal bond," while in Calabria "little or no respect of children for their parents and the very low regard of the latter for their children" prevailed.[14]

The historian Donna Gabaccia most profoundly revised the interpretation of the Italian American *famiglia* as an institution and moral world transplanted intact from southern Italy. In her account of a Sicilian community in New York in the early twentieth century, Gabaccia studied immigrants in their native town and on Elizabeth Street, where they clustered. Gabaccia demonstrated that the diasporic *famiglia* was an adaptive response to the demands of the migration experience rather than a static remnant of the Old World. In Sicily, Gabaccia showed, the nuclear family predominated, and children formed a distinct new unit when they married. Envy, jealousy, and distrust characterized relations with relatives, and the nuclear family often turned to neighbors and friends for support. The family as a cooperative, harmonious extended household existed only as an ideal.[15]

For these Sicilians, the conditions of immigrant life made family relations increasingly important. High rents forced the immigrants of Elizabeth Street to experiment with unprecedented forms of cohabitation, by taking in migrant boarders and by forming flexible and contingent households with extended family members. At the same time, high levels of residential mobility made it more difficult to rely on neighbors for support. In this fluid context, family networks became the most reliable source of solidarity (to find a job, a place to stay, credit, or childcare) and were idealized in a way they had never been before. In the settlement years, kin were now the center of social networks in the same way the nuclear family had been in Sicily; the gatherings based on the sharing of familiar food, held in small tenement kitchens or smoky restaurants, helped create and reinforce kin-based social networks: everyone ate together. In this setting, Sicilian traditions, like the male social networks that met around food and wine to make business deals and resolve local conflicts, could be reconfigured to meet new needs.[16] The early immigrant pattern of two or more families living under the same roof also helped establish the practice of extended family conviviality.

By the end of World War I, when many immigrant children started to work, making a permanent settlement and even buying property became the goal of most Italian migrants. As the boarding system faded because of laws restricting new arrivals, the nuclear family became the most common structure of Italian American households. Despite these changes, family networks continued to provide support, cooperation, and care. The familism of Italian immigrants, Gabaccia writes, was "a product of migration and life in the United States."[17] Because the *famiglia* was an ingrained if mostly unrealized ideal in the rural Mezzogiorno, immigrants could call on this ideal as a *tradition* that would help them navigate the changes they were facing.

Italian Harlem shared with Little Italy downtown the high rates of residential mobility that enhanced the value of an extended family circle. Although Italian Harlem residents remember the neighborhood as a self-sufficient urban village where "everyone knew everyone," in reality people traveled from and to Italy, moved frequently from one tenement to another, and, after World War I, left for better and safer areas.[18] The community continually reinvented itself in relation to the different groups that followed one another into the area. Table 1, covering a four-year period in Italian East Harlem, shows the high rate of population turnover and an exceptional ethnic complexity.

Table 1. Population change in Sanitary District 170 (from Third to First Avenues and from 109th to 114th Streets) between 1925 and 1929

	Outgoing	Incoming
Italians	1,619	875
Russians	348	54
Poles	80	26
Americans	283	180
English Speaking	54	110
Germans and Austrians	129	79
Puerto Ricans	10	48
American Negroes	0	8
Others	82	82
Total	2,605	1,462

Source: C. W. Leonard, "A Study of the Settlements of East Harlem," pp. 16–17, "Social World of East Harlem Street Boy," box 67, folder 17, LCP.

The insecurity of migrants' lives and the discrimination they faced suggested to Italian Harlem immigrants that family intimacy was the most dependable source of emotional and material strength. Immigrants learned that food sharing defined the social position of the family and created bonds with kin and community. The group's ceremonial consumption of food—one of the most significant *innovations* of their American experience—became, in Italian Harlem, the most significant expression of a new diasporic Italian culture of domesticity, articulated by immigrants as "traditional Italian family culture" and the most efficient means of conditioning the younger generation to the ideology of the *famiglia*.

Sunday dinner was the most frequent gathering of the *famiglia* and the key provision of the generational contract. The entire process of ritualizing a diasporic domesticity and socializing younger generations depended on the presence at the table of children and grandchildren. The centrality of Sunday dinner recurs constantly in the memories of second-generation Italian Americans in East Harlem. As an Italian American man explained to historian Robert Orsi: "We were taught two things: religion and we were taught family life. That was it, that was it. We weren't taught family—we just picked it up. We were very close. Sunday meal was the meal you had to be there."[19] Another son of immigrants remembered the idea of duty entangled in Sunday dinner: "For dinner, oh, we ate—and Sunday you had to eat together. Nobody got up until we were through. No bullshit like 'I'm goin' to the country.'"[20] The Sunday ceremonial had a detailed cultural geography and enforced a specific body discipline. Women started cooking and cleaning early in the morning, everyone dressed up, and some went to Mass. Later relatives would visit each other, and finally all would be seated at the table.

This moment coalesced many meanings, especially the importance Sunday dinner held for the generational contract. First, abundance and conviviality were in the meal the most tangible expressions of the dream of immigrants who had known only scarcity. The relatively frequent consumption of meat, pasta, white bread, coffee, and sugar, foods that immigrants had only dreamed of in Italy, had revolutionary implications, signaling the breakdown of a long-standing class barrier. Liberated from the chains of scarcity, cooking was the only feature of immigrant material culture that could fully blossom in the new urban world. Food rituals told success stories: in *Mount Allegro*, Uncle Nino explains immigrant America to young Jerre Mangione mostly in food terms, narratively creating a diasporic Italy as a private and domestic realm—as opposed to the public and the state:

> "Sicily is beautiful, yeah. So beautiful, in fact, that I should like nothing better than to return there. But it is also terribly poor. It lies at the end of the Italian boot and some government clique in Rome is always kicking it around. Some Sicilians got tired of that treatment and finally left. That, Gerlando, is the chief reason most of us are in this *maliditta terra* [damned country], where we spend our strength in factories and ditches and think of nothing but money. All that journeying and all that work just so that we might live and die with our bellies full." He dug his fork into another piece of sausage by way of punctuation.[21]

In other memories, food security becomes the promise that America has most fully kept: "In Italy we were poor, always on the verge of starvation," an immigrant told Covello. "Who could afford to eat spaghetti more than once a week? In America no one starved, though a family earned no more than five or six dollars a week. Don't you remember how our *paesani* here in America ate to their heart's delight till they were belching like pigs, and how they dumped mountains of uneaten food out of the windows? We were not poor in America; we just had a little less than the others."[22] Food rituals celebrated the victory of labor over need. A festive meal had several courses and proudly showcased foodstuffs with a high social status. Since the absence of meat on southern Italian peasant tables carried the stigma of social inferiority, in New York festive tables were overloaded with meat dishes of many kinds. "For weekday suppers a soup course, some spaghetti and meat, followed by a salad, was an ample meal," Mangione remembered.

> But on Sundays and holidays it was assumed that your appetite became gargantuan and, besides soup and salad, you were expected to stow away at least three different courses of meat, four or five vegetables, along with celery and fennel,

> all topped off with pastry, fruits, and nuts. One of my father's meat courses was usually *brusciuluna*, a combination of Roman cheese, salami, and moon-shaped slivers of hard-boiled eggs encased in rolls of beef that had been pounded into tenderness. All this was held together by an engineering feat involving many strings and toothpicks. The other meats served were chicken (two kinds usually—boiled chicken, from which the soup had been made—and roast chicken), lamb, and veal.[23]

The cult of family feasts was also nurtured among Italian immigrants in Harlem by the southern Italian social ideal of *bella figura*, a culture of hospitality and the accumulation and display of social capital, in which to offer food was to gain dignity, reputation, and respect. The southern Italian rural host was ashamed when he could offer only little food, as was the family that hid its bare cupboards. Covello remembered, "In Avigliano there were times when there was no food in the house. Then we bolted the door and rattled kitchen utensils and dishes to give the impression to our close neighbors that the noonday meal was going on as usual."[24] In Calabria, families shook the tablecloth from the window to make neighbors believe they had eaten a meal that never occurred.[25] The abundance or scarcity of food illustrates the central role that food security plays in the honor-and-shame-based interactions in the Mezzogiorno—and in the self-perception of the family in the community. Immigrants to East Harlem felt they could achieve *bella figura* through food events and display, adapting the old ideal to new narratives of respectability. Displaying an abundance of food and celebrating the cooking abilities of women were important in fulfilling another function of food rituals: expanding and reinforcing extended family relations. To achieve this goal, many immigrant families spared no expense on feasts that accompanied baptisms, confirmations, weddings, and funerals. Middle-class reformers were appalled by the money poor and working-class families spent on food, instead of using it for far more "urgent" or "useful" purposes.[26] From an immigrant's point of view, this heavy investment in family and community ties made enormous sense. The offering and sharing of food marked all the occasions that redefined the place of individuals within family and community—including death. A student of Covello suggested that death was dramatized in funeral rites as the most important social event in Italian Harlem, when resentments were to be forgiven and forgotten during the family reunion: "After the burial services are over, again a big meal is prepared for the bereaved family. This time the stomach really can accommodate a goodly amount of food because it undoubtedly must have been starved for the past three or four days of vigil, while this body was exposed to the friends and relatives."[27]

Immigrants created and re-created stories and myths about foods specific to certain occasions, like the feast of the seven fishes on Christmas Eve and the many ritual breads and cakes of Easter. Both religious feasts and life-cycle events were celebrated with particular dishes and menus.[28] Even for the American-born, the complexities of this food calendar defined their parents' culture and, as the code was learned and interiorized, the liturgy of a family religion. "I had learned early . . . that Mardi Gras, Easter, Christmas and New Year's Day did not have to do so much with things religious as with things to eat," a second-generation immigrant remembered. "The eating was done with many relatives. This feasting was so important that each holiday had its own menu. Mardi Gras I came to associate with gnocchi in tomato sauce and roasted peppers, Easter with manicotti and roast lamb, Christmas with lasagna and New Years' with macaroni in pesto and roast pork."[29] Religious festivities, along with Sunday dinners, provided immigrants with many opportunities to honor the *famiglia* with the sharing of food. Immigrants early on adopted Thanksgiving because they could easily domesticate it as another Italian family celebration—incorporating the turkey into a meal with antipasti, baked pasta, and wine.[30] Food rituals helped determine group membership, drawing boundaries between those who had to be invited and those not permitted to breach the limits of privacy. Strangers and acquaintances were not allowed in because private matters were not to be discussed in the presence of outsiders. Younger Italian Americans remembered their embarrassment when visiting friends were bluntly invited to leave by their friends' parents and relatives. "'We do not want a stranger knowing the business of our family,' they would say."[31] Within the family and kin group, hospitality and food sharing were the most frequently used ways to express, manage, and pacify conflicts. Mangione noted that "the impossibility of getting all the relatives together under one roof sometimes resulted in bitter family quarrels. Some relative would decide to take offense because he had not been invited to a family gathering and the quarrel would be on. The chances were that it would continue over a long period of months and get increasingly worse, eventually reaching the point where no one could recall the original cause of the quarrel and everyone would offer dozens of reasons to prove that it was entirely justified and should probably go on forever."[32]

Finally, food was the most effective means for re-creating a sense of communion in visits with relatives and *paesani* who lived far away in "America" or had just arrived from Italy. During the Feast of the Madonna of Mount Carmel in mid-July, Italian Harlem families welcomed into their home relatives and friends from New Jersey, Connecticut, Pennsylvania, Massachusetts, California, and overseas. Preparing food for such an occasion took weeks of work. Seated around the table with children, siblings, nephews, and cousins, immigrants ate, drank, talked, sang, and shared their emotions, memories, and appreciation for the food. The feast outside was an impressive public and private food event: a Sunday dinner transported to the streets and parks of the community, where for a week in the streets around the church on East 115th Street and inside nearby Jefferson Park, tens of thousands ate lavishly—and publicly. The food, purchased from vendors and pushcarts, featured *capozzelle* (lamb's head), *scungilli* (conch), and the other peculiar specialties that both recalled a world left behind and also domesticated the new world of Upper Manhattan. Late at night, in cramped tenement apartments, family reunions continued around the dinner table.[33]

The construction of a new diasporic domesticity based on ritual food consumption was also a heavily gendered process. Although the food served at family tables was designed to satisfy male demands, the family meal system also had a feminizing effect. Because of their special skills, women were in charge of supervising this emerging ethnic domesticity. In rural southern Italy, cooking and housework were less central than other female responsibilities such as working in the fields, tending animals, and making household objects (in addition to, of course, giving birth, mothering, and caring for the elderly). In Harlem, even wives and mothers who stayed home contributed to the family economy by managing family money and earning additional income through household labor, while providing extended childcare and performing chores under circumstances that were more demanding than those in Italy.[34] As a result, the prevalent image of the Italian immigrant mother in children's memories is that of a woman completely absorbed by her role, "always" busy in the kitchen and the home. "I come from a family of ten children," a second-generation woman remembered.

> My uncle lived with us so there were thirteen at the table and we always set up the dining room table for our Sunday meal and it was always a big spread. We had soup, and then we had macaroni and we had the meat in the sauce also. And we had a roast, either a lamb or a roasting chicken, with roasted potatoes and vegetables and salad and fruit. My mother did all the cooking and we set up the table and cleared the table. She always washed the dishes. My mother was always in the kitchen. She never had the time to do anything else.[35]

Such an identity—the Madonna-like, sacrificing, giving, and caring Italian mother—had tremendous psychological consequences for children as well as for the family life. As a result of their unpaid work, many Italian women, while lacking public power, ruled at home through domestic routines and rituals. Some elderly immigrant women, often uneducated and sheltered, were respected sources of tradition and symbolic guardians of family unity. This identity was often articulated in and projected through domestic skills. "Despite my grandmother's unworldly ways, she ruled the house," another second-generation man recalled. "Grandmother's expertise embraced when and what the family ate, what time they would go to sleep after eating whatever they ate, and bowel movements."[36]

As a rule, mothers decided who was to be invited to meals and other convivial events, regulating social interaction within family circles. The mother's role "as the family's center was celebrated by her culinary arts."[37] A man who grew up in Italian Harlem remembered the Easter feasts in his family: "*Pizza rustica*, *pizza dolce*, *struffoli* [small deep-fried balls of dough dipped in honey, a Neapolitan dish], etc. All were made with basically the same recipes. All with variations that identified each owner's end product just by taste. One taste and one could recall, 'This was made by *commara* Lucia or Nannina or Zia Rosa etc.'" The culinary ability of women cooks was highly valued by the group, with contested consequences. Women's obsession with food and their competitiveness about culinary excellence reflected the pressure placed on gender behaviors and values. "One woman informed me that it took her five hours to make the delicious sauce that she served with the spaghetti," a non-Italian student of Covello noted. "When I remarked on the time consumed she informed me that, if her family and guests liked it, it was very worth it. This seems to sum up [Italian women's] philosophy in cooking."[38]

Sunday dinners, weddings, baptisms, first communions, funeral banquets, and the meals that accompanied family reunions offered immigrants the unique opportunity to celebrate the most significant promises their migration had fulfilled: intense family life and freedom from hunger. The rituals of food sharing helped in creating and reinforcing family bonds and family ideology. Under the banners of communal eating and devotion to family, Italian immigrants in Harlem reclaimed their identity as Italians in America and established their relationship with their home overseas. In the ceremonies that focused on food as a symbolic act of communion, immigrants could create, reinforce, and share the ideology of the *famiglia* with their *Americani* children. Immigrant parents could set their children free to act "American" in public, as long as the younger generation participated in family food rituals. Struggling against what they felt to be the major threat to domestic life—their children's alleged individualism—immigrants turned to family food rituals as the only real way to socialize younger people into the ideology of the family. Around the spaghetti bowl, immigrants hoped their children's hearts could be won by a sensual web of symbols, stories, and imagination.

Food Memories and Ideology: Creating Nation in the Diasporic Private Sphere

Even a casual reading of classic narratives of Italian American life such as Mangione's and Gambino's suggests that the ritual Sunday dinner was as much about eating as it was the discursive articulation of family, authority, taste, and identity. "The major meal of the week was the one at which time and circumstances permitted the most leisurely and largest gathering of *la famiglia*," Gambino points out. "It was the Sunday *pranzo*, which began in midafternoon . . . and lasted until early evening, or even late into the evening. It is a relaxed social gathering of the clan, featuring intimate conversations as much as well-prepared courses."[39] "There were seldom less than fifteen men, women, and children at those Sunday sessions," Mangione recalled. "On the Sundays when it rained, there would be as many as thirty"; those Sunday sessions were obviously not only the most anticipated event of immigrant social life but also the most important drama of group definition—its identity, common past, and expectations for the future. Given immigrants' emphasis on "tradition" as the engine of collective identity, it was through narratives of the past and moral stories set in "the *paese*," "Sicily," or "Italy" that immigrants and their children absorbed the group's values—and felt them to be under mortal attack from American life.[40] Memory, deployed most instrumentally during convivial family gatherings, became vital for the production of the ideology of the *famiglia* in America.

Memory also divided the generations. The recollections of immigrants and their children were separated not only by time but also by space: the former remembered having grown up in Italy, and the latter in New York; most immigrant children could only imagine the distant *paese* through their parents' tales. These asymmetrical memories were crucial to the production of family ideology and in the discipline of American-born children. The historian Robert Orsi has argued that, contrary to what Covello believed, immigrants did not teach the *famiglia* tradition to their children to include them in that tradition but rather to *exclude them* from it. The "southern Italy" of Italian Harlem nostalgia was a place where family order and harmony reigned; parental authority went unchallenged; women knew their place; children took care of their elders; every relative cooperated for the common good; and the family ate "as a family." Their children, born in an America of individualistic values, could never know such a place. Immigrants in East Harlem, Orsi concludes, consciously used the past as a weapon against which their children were defenseless: the narration of the Italian family tradition was fundamentally a strategy of power and control enacted to contrast the crisis of parental authority.[41] Immigrants resorted to the weapon of memory in the most critical time of generational conflict (the interwar years), when other forms of discipline and socialization proved impracticable and inefficient.

Memory, as oral historians know well, "is not an exact and neutral recollection of the past; rather, it is often literally an invention of the past, or an escape from it."[42] It is the narrating act aimed at bestowing meaning on certain events or facts and hiding or downplaying others; memory is always a response to the needs, aspirations, and desires of the present. Remembering and narrating the past are acts that attempt to explain the world, performed with others and for others. For this reason, collective memory is fundamental in shaping a nation: the selection of symbolic elements from the past, typically enacted during rituals and commemorations, constructs a people's sense of belonging to the "imagined community" of the nation.[43]

Italian Harlem immigrants effectively created a nation around the family table, telling their American-born children tales of a different land, "Italy"—an "other side" where their ideals of family life and values, frustrated in America, finally came alive. This "Italy" was not the native village immigrants thought they remembered, frozen in time, but an imaginary place whose culture, character, and history were summoned to make sense of an American present. The identification of Italian Harlemites with this imagined place, "Italy," and their sense of belonging to the imagined community of the Italian nation were articulated most deeply through the code of food and the family—so much so that food and the family became in fact their diasporic national language. More than anything else, this symbolic geography of "Italy" as the realm of proper family life and eating defined Italians in America as a diasporic nation, as people who rallied around a superior family culture by celebrating it with food and conviviality.

Until World War I, the vast majority of Italian migrants thought themselves members of their small-town communities of origin. Very few spoke the national language. Few felt any sense of loyalty extending outside the close circle of relatives, friends, and fellow villagers. For most, the Italian state was little more than the soldier, the policeman, and the tax collector. This village-bound identity was often reflected in love for the food of one's own *paese*, which in America created a mosaic of local foodways and an energetic trade in foodstuffs between *paesi* in Italy and their "twins" in the United States. For migrants, the experience of working and living abroad with other Italians, the nationalist propaganda of ethnic leaders, and an American culture that defined them all generically as "Italians" were crucial in reconfiguring migrant identities in national terms.[44] However, a new diasporic family ethos, celebrated in the rites of the table and instilled in younger generations through storytelling, was at least as important a factor in creating an immigrant sense of self as an *Italian* American. Yet even as local foodways slowly merged into a pan-Italian cuisine (thanks to immigrant intermarriage across regional lines and an expanding ethnic food marketplace and Italian restaurants offering standardized menus to American customers) *Italian* food was defined by its incorporation into the immigrants' domestic rituals that transformed local villagers from Sicily or Calabria into Italians in New York.

In the Italy that immigrants talked about at the table, the family was the force that fully regulated the lives of individuals and provided the exclusive source of emotional and material gratification. A terrible fate awaited those who betrayed it.

"May my name be lost in your home!" screamed the father at the son who married without his approval, in an East Harlem immigrant's tale. Being expelled from the family meant social death and desperation: "Who disobeys his mother and father will die like a dog," a Basilicata proverb went.[45] In the immigrant's "Italy," it was taken for granted that children obeyed their parents. And unlike in New York, no public institution had the power to threaten family unity. School, in "Italy," taught children to dedicate themselves to the family and to respect their parents. Finally, in this Italy there were none of the forces that in America had divided the generations: not selfish individualism but cooperation and unity. "In our family, every member of the family worked for the family. There were no wages and there were no pay days. You didn't come home with the pay envelope on Saturday. . . . The family provided for everything. . . . We had no use for money as individuals. We ate as one family."[46]

In immigrant narratives of the Italian past, food and the family were symbols of cohesion. Older Italian Americans were most touched when they recalled themselves as young children being served dinner by Mother in the stone house in the little village, and their most vivid recollections were those of good food: fruit trees, vines, freshly pressed oil, the smell of homemade bread. Immigrants combined the memory of scarcity and hunger—"In Italy," one of them recalled, "we did not waste anything. If a crumb fell on the floor, we bent down, picked it up and kissed it, thanking God that we had it"—with the recollection of a place where food was good, healthy, and tasty and the family ate as a proper family.[47] "So when you marry we should have a house like my grandfather had in Italy," an immigrant woman told her children. "He had four sons and there were four houses all joined together. Each son and his family had his own place but it was one household—grandfather, of course, was *il padrone*, and grandmother *comandava tutte le nuore* (ruled over the daughters-in-law). *La famiglia* often ate together and in the cool autumn evenings or cold winter nights would gather around a tremendous fire-place and talk over the events of the day."[48]

Amid crisis and change, immigrants in Italian Harlem found in food, cooking, and table rituals those elements that most effectively could be co-opted to reconnect the Italian American family with an idealized past. During family gatherings around a well-laid table, immigrants looked into their children's faces, listened to their voices, scrutinized their gestures, and saw how much they all had changed; how Italy—both as a place and as an imaginary nonplace—was far away. Then came comforting recollections of a family reunited around the table, anecdotes about memorable feasts, and descriptions of the food of the *paese*. The summoning of an ordered, satisfying family life filled a sensual void, celebrated an elegiac past, and helped remind children of their duties in a problematic present. "In Molfetta," an immigrant recalled, reminiscing about his diasporic home,

> the relations between the various households of our whole family were in the main most cordial. Ours was a social existence as truly spontaneous and beautiful as

> it was natural. All the long line of relatives, uncles, aunts, and cousins of every degree lived in Molfetta. This gave an opportunity for much social intercourse. We had a custom of frequently getting together in the evenings for social good times. . . . Usually "eats" and drinks were served by the entertaining households; almonds, walnuts, raisins and stuffed dates or figs, with home-made cakes and candy. The best of the year's wine and *rosolio*—a delicate liquor—were served. . . . Christmas also was a time of real feasting. . . . The Christmas dinner in our home was a memorable occasion not alone because of the good things to eat, but also because of a special custom we had of showing our gratitude to our parents. For days before Christmas we would hunt high and low for letter paper with the best decorations and mottoes. Then we children would vie with one another in composing the best letter or little poem to express our love for mother and father. Before the Christmas dinner, we would hide these in some place on the table, perhaps folded in a napkin, under the plate of father and mother, and even under the tablecloth. Our parents would first pretend not to see them, and would feign surprise when they were found, and the best part of the Christmas dinner was to hear father and mother read the letters we had written, and then pronounce which one was the best.[49]

Narratives of this kind created the tradition of the *famiglia* for children born in America. Beyond their value as nostalgia, however, they created meanings that helped structure everyday immigrant life. First was the value of tradition as a source of normative knowledge and a corresponding suspicion of novelty. If proper family life was defined by the "Italian tradition," good food was "natural," either homemade or purchased in familiar, local markets. Second was the emphasis on the family as the sole producer of wealth and the bulwark against need, articulated during Sunday dinner and the other family gatherings through the sharing of food. In the social history of Italy as taught by immigrants, there was only *la miseria* (extreme poverty); outside the family circle were the local gentry, the church, and the state as oppressors of the *contadini* and the *famiglia*. Third was the close connection between the ideal of a proper meal and a proper family life. In reality, many immigrant families were remote from their own ideals. Deaths, desertions, or the common hardships of migration had often caused the absence of one of both parents for years.[50] Many Italians had come alone or accompanied by an uncle, aunt, or family acquaintance; some women came to be married to men they had never met. Others came to escape oppressive family bonds. Still, in immigrant narratives family meals always replicated family order. The performance of proper meals—eating as "Christians" were supposed to eat—reproduced the ideal of the entire family gathered at the table. The motherly image of the nurturing woman devoted to the *famiglia* also found a convincing representation in a proper family meal framed by talk of an imaginary diasporic past.

When pressed, Italians in Harlem acknowledged that migration had changed not only their lives but their worldview; that "in America it's different." They did not hesitate to say that they were "living better" materially.[51] But when it came to dealing with their "uncontrollable" children, their life in East Harlem was universally disturbing and bewildering. They clung to the ideal of the *famiglia* as anchor and guidepost as they tried to limit their children's violations by rhetorical and ritual, rather than repressive, means.

But if the *famiglia* was such a perfect organization, why, then, was it in crisis? The answer, of course, was outside its closed circle, in American life and American values. The Italy of immigrant food memories had its opposite in "America," where food was industrial, tasteless, and fit only to fill one's belly, where lonely people ate by themselves, and where families were damaged by indulgence and indifference. As always, immigrants judged "America" from limited contacts outside the boundaries of the community. In this America, experienced or imagined, the white, urban middle-class family—the post-Victorian, smaller, more affectionate, and egalitarian unit—granted some independence to women and children and even tolerated freer sexual conduct.[52] Many Italian Americans assumed this model to be the American norm, one also shared by the other white ethnic families they had come to know. "In America," a fifty-eight-year-old immigrant said to Covello, "children run wild and are taught not to have any respect for their parents. They do exactly what they please. Young married women no longer attend to their household duties but run here and there all day long and at night too. They think it's perfectly all right to be seen in public with men, other than their husbands, and to be alone with them. Here they get away with it. Such things were unheard of in Italy. Women stayed home and were only too happy to take care of their husbands and children."[53]

Because Italian immigrants claimed that a distinctive family ethos distinguished them from any other group, instructing their children in the canons of the "Italian family" drew on a set of moral norms; and foodways, the most effective way immigrants had found to communicate with their children, became inextricably intertwined with the normative nature of the "Italian family" in America. In the late 1930s, Marie Concistré asked immigrants which traits of *Italianità* they would love to keep. The replies were unanimous: "The home life, family unity, respect for parents, and love of cooking."[54] The convergence of food and family moral principles marked many immigrant testimonies. "It is difficult to bring up children in this country," a mother of seven, six of whom were born in New York, told Covello. "In the old country children somehow knew, without being taught, that they should help the family. In America all children are much younger; they have neither the understanding nor the physical strength that children in Italy have. Here a family has to wait a long time till the children get sense and make up their minds that there is nothing finer in the world than to take interest in the affairs of the family. Maybe it's the weather, maybe is the bad food."[55] The alleged demoralizing and debilitating influence of American food on immigrant children is in fact a recurring complaint in Italian Harlem oral histories. An immigrant father recriminated: "Our mistake was giving [our children] too much liberty and everything they wanted since they were small children, such as money, toys, candies, ice cream, cakes, and moving pictures."[56]

As hard as immigrants worked to build a familiar material environment around them—an astounding number of Italian restaurants, markets, and food shops dotted the neighborhood—some never felt completely at home in America. For them, the memory of "Italian food" was always opposed to the reality of "American food." Italy was a food paradise lost. "From the way my relatives usually talked about it, Sicily sounded like a beautiful park, with farmland around that produced figs, oranges, pomegranates, and many other kinds of fruit that refused to grow in Rochester," Mangione remembered. "The air was perfect in Sicily, neither cold nor damp as it was in Rochester most of the time. The wine tasted better, and you could pick almonds and olives off the trees. In the summer the men strummed guitars and sang in rich tenor voices, and the women went on picnics in the country. Everyone was much happier there."[57] The taste of America was strange: "You, the chemists, the doctors, the engineers, of America, you have made this country grey," one of them wrote in his memories. "Why do you handle grey things only, why does everything turn grey in your hands? Why do you want to take the joy out of oranges and peaches—kill fruits? . . . This is the complaint of a million Italians . . . ; '*America, donne senza colore e cibo senza sapore*'—America: women without color and fruits without taste."[58] A second-generation Italian immigrant to Queens remembered, "Pop [would mumble] the while on the strange blindness of the great American nation where the best of everything was available and the people were content with tasteless food. . . . The notion that food's function was 'to keep body and soul together' was to him a sacrilege meriting the wrath of the Almighty. . . . 'On the other side . . .' And he went on to repeat what I heard many times before. In even the meanest Italian homes or restaurants, his monologue went, there was great respect and love for God's food and for people's God-given stomachs."[59]

The identification of women, home, and family was central to the discourse of the honor-based "Italian family." Food symbols helped define these female roles and identities, while culinary competence, long one of the most important motherly virtues, took on added importance during the interwar years. The strict public-private divide that regulated most aspects of Italian Harlem life became especially important in constructing gender roles. In the streets of the neighborhood, women showed unquestioned deference to the men in the family, but in private the mother was a source of almost unquestioned power and authority.

Italian mothers influenced the most intimate areas of family life, evaluating their daughters' and sons' behaviors, friendships, and choice of spouse, and punished their children on their own or by way of their husbands or older sons. A Calabrian immigrant, describing the private power of mothers in "Italy," revealed what secrecy and gendered performance meant in Italian American domesticity:

> When my father got old, we [members of the family] obeyed our mother more than before. My brother, who became head of the family, had to take orders from her. But that was done only in our home. On the street he tried to impress everybody that he was the boss of the family. As I remember now it was laughable to see him give my mother commands in the presence of other people and then, five minutes later, to listen politely to what my mother had to say at home and to just puff when she would slap him in front of smaller sisters and brothers.[60]

Italian Harlem mothers, however strong at home, were obliged to conform to the community ideal of the respectable mother—devoted to family integrity, sexually irreproachable, unselfishly caring for husband and children, often silent. Even when women mobilized in grassroots politics—as they did in the 1930s campaign to bring low-rent public housing to East Harlem, led by Vito Marcantonio, Covello, and other progressive leaders—they did so mostly as "mothers," exploiting an Italian-inflected maternalism in order to join in public action and support a progressive cause without jeopardizing their primary identity.[61]

More difficult was the condition of unmarried young women, who did not enjoy the domestic power of their mothers while still having to meet very complicated social expectations. The protection of the honor of unmarried daughters and sisters was an obsession that affected the entire community. "A girl couldn't date more than three or four times with the same man, and if you dated five or six different men, you were no good," a man who grew up in Italian Harlem recalled. "'She doesn't know how to stay with one man.' It was much more difficult for a girl than a man. In the Italian mentality, a man could do anything. If she got a bad name, my God, you moved out, went to Pennsylvania, Jersey, and finally married and got away. I've heard many stories about that. Your reputation was everything."[62] In courtship, girls could not appear old-fashioned but still had to resist boys' sexual requests. Girls should be protected from any temptation or threat to their virginity, be prepared for marriage and maternity, and manage to remain an appealing spouse. For Italian Harlem families, an unmarried daughter was typically both a disgrace and an economic burden. As an immigrant mother told Covello, "Every girl's place sooner or later is in a man's home. The earlier she marries the less worries there are for her relatives."[63]

For immigrants, the "Italian way" was the only acceptable way for their daughters to fulfill these demands. Only "traditional" Italian educational practices could instill in girls the gifts of decency, devotion, and modesty that would make them good wives and mothers. Immigrants insisted on the values and skills of domesticity not only to prepare daughters for their own family life but also to shape their moral standing. "I came from Italy with my mother when I was fourteen years of age," an Italian Harlem woman noted.

> At fifteen I was married and in the course of my married life I had sixteen children, eleven of whom are still living. My daughters were married later than I was. In fact they married in their early twenties but I trained them in housework at an early age. At the age of thirteen I sent them to work so they could make a contribution to the family. So that then they were married, they really were grown up and had some sense in their heads. But my grandchildren, fourteen, fifteen, sixteen, and even seventeen years of age, . . . do not want to learn any of the household duties and their chief concern is playing, movies, and boy friends. It is a bad country where children, boys and girls, but particularly girls, are not trained to work with their mothers in the home.[64]

In Italy, in contrast, another immigrant woman claimed, "All the girls in my village worked as I did. We also did much housework, following our mothers around continuously. There was never an idle moment for girls or women. We all wanted to earn the reputation of being good workers."[65]

Italian Harlem girls actually spent much of their days in housework. After school, their daily routine consisted of washing dishes, cleaning up, spending some supervised time with girlfriends on the stoop of their tenement, and cooking. Even older women working in offices or factories were expected to do the same work when they returned home. For much of their "leisure time," Italian Harlem single women were busy looking after younger siblings, shopping, doing the laundry, sewing, and cooking. Saturday afternoon was for cleaning and Sunday morning for helping mothers prepare the lavish Sunday dinner. Girls did these chores because they would "have to keep [their] own houses one day."[66]

From a very early age, girls in Italian Harlem were channeled into distinctly gendered behaviors that were constantly articulated inside the home. A boy told Covello, "When father is around I become domineering over my sister, and I know that father is pleased to see me assert my masculinity. He always protests my washing dishes, claiming it as below the dignity of a man."[67] As late as 1940, a college student who had grown up in Italian Harlem complained, "The girls have a much harder time as boys. The boys were and still are the favored ones in Italian families. They are catered to, hand and foot. With regard to education, again the boys are favored. Girls are meant to take care of the home, cook, and get married."[68]

The primacy of women's skills in housework and cooking was consistent with this strong separation of gender roles. Close to 90 percent of the immigrant mothers interviewed by Concistré said "good housework skills" were the main reason for a son's choice of a bride: love, intelligence, family reputation, dowry, and physical beauty followed far behind.[69] A girl able to cook Italian food well was said to have been taught the proper moral values of a good wife, and possessing these skills was thought to increase this "good Italian girl's" odds of marrying a man from a "good family." For Italian Harlem's immigrants, the love for Italian food and a woman's ability to prepare it were signs that a tradition had been successfully transmitted across generations, something to be praised and protected. In practice, it meant that the new bride was ready to serve her new husband the food his mother used to cook.

The connection that immigrants imagined to exist between a woman's commitment to culinary traditions and morality is clear in many testimonies. A forty-year-old immigrant believed that his daughter was a good housewife in the Italian tradition because of her preference for Italian cooking: "She likes Italian cooking and knows herself how to cook. She is 18 years old now, and by now has made up her mind what her own home should look like. And I bet, she knows that is safer to marry an Italian, because she knows in advance what to expect; and she knows—she learned it from her mother—how to go around one's husband."[70] Another father shared the same belief: the desire and ability to "cook Italian" were an expression of the moral integrity and respect for tradition that only the Italian family could convey. "Our daughter is much more Italian than the boy," the man claimed.

> The girl, for instance, likes Italian cooking; she goes eagerly with my wife to see the Italian *comares* [women friends associated with kin] . . . and once a month they go for a visit to my wife's family in Brooklyn. Call it Italian custom or call it any other custom, no one will point at our girl disapprovingly. She has a good reputation among the people here, and I know, even the boys respect her. And she will be a desirable bride. I feel very proud when people tell me how well Italians bring up their girls. Yes, I say to them, that is a good "Italian custom."[71]

It did not matter how "Americanized" girls might seem on the outside, or if they wore cosmetics or went out unaccompanied. Their socialization into the ideology of the Italian family—loyalty to Italian food and the expertise in the kitchen its important features—was believed to safeguard tradition and morality. A young man from Brindisi had been pleasantly surprised to notice that many Italian Harlem girls, although fashionable and quick to disagree with their mothers in public, still kept good Italian domestic traditions. "I was proud to see families gather together on Sundays; their preference for the good old Italian cooking," he said. "And when I saw how industrious the Italian girls in the community were, how they brought reverently the weekly paycheck to the mother, how politely, but with masculine dignity, the boys treated the girls, and how well mannered the girls showed in all their dealings with men—I was willing to forgive their layers of lipstick and marry one of the American Italians."[72]

Finally, the love for cooking and a good appetite gave the "good Italian girl" the strength and health necessary to succeed as mother and wife. Italians thought that the slender profile of "American" girls betrayed physical frailness, while a fleshy body promised better chances for marriage and maternity. Girls were encouraged to eat, especially in the presence of family and potential spouses, while dieting, for any reasons, was considered a sign of weakness. Yet young women often resisted this bodily imperative with an ingenious appropriation of "tradition": they used the period of Lent as a socially approved cover for fasting to attain the slim figure dominant in consumer culture.[73]

Praising a potential spouse for having this quality of *Italianità* was a sign of the strong psychological pressures to marry within the group. The cultural reproduction of the *famiglia* was at stake in the process of spouse selection, and marriage joined not just two families and two individuals but, ideally, two similar sets of values. What would have happened to their children's children—immigrants reasoned—if intermarriage took them away from their influence? "Whatever you do, marry an [Italian] girl," was the mother's pressing advice to her son. "They cook. They clean. They take good care of you. For your own good."[74] One of Covello's students was terrorized by the prospect of informing his family of his affair with a Scottish American girl. His parents "spoke nasty things about girls born in America" and had been long arranging to send him to Italy to find a good wife. "I was born in America where people marry for love and regardless whether the girl can cook," the young man said, relieving his feelings to his teacher.[75] Once again, food and cooking were vital to the superiority of "Italian family" and the Italian way of upbringing. "Italian children should marry people of their own kind," an elderly immigrant from the province of Bari argued. "No good comes from marrying American boys and girls. . . . The Italian girl is specially educated. She knows how to obey the husband; she knows how to shut her mouth; she can always save a penny; she is absolutely faithful to the husband; she is never nervous; she can cook."[76]

In fact, the marriage patterns of second-generation Italian Americans may well be the best evidence of the degree to which they had internalized the ideology of the "Italian family." By the 1930s, the family-arranged marriage had almost vanished, and young people "freely chose" their spouses. Nevertheless, they married other Italian Americans at a rate only slightly less than that of their parents. A second-generation Italian American man remarked, "You married your friend's sister or somebody in the neighborhood who you knew all your life. And you married and where did you live? A block away from where your parents lived, two blocks away."[77] In New York, between 1908 and 1912, no other racial and national group, except for Jews and African Americans, had a higher endogamy rate than first- and second-generation Italian Americans, whose rate of intermarriage remained below 6 percent at least until the early 1920s.[78] This pattern persisted even during the profound social change of the interwar years. Before World War II, marriages with non-Italian spouses remained rare.[79] A study conducted in the 1960s among elderly second-generation Italian Americans in East Harlem showed that fully 85 percent had married a spouse of Italian ancestry.[80]

What happened, then, to the second generation's longing for autonomy, for integration into the larger society, and for a real emancipation from parental culture? Had the American-born of Italian Harlem accepted the moral world that their parents so assiduously tried to pass on in symbolic lessons during years of family food ceremonies? Had their parents in fact succeeded in convincing their children to accept the ideology of the "Italian family" as their own?

In the early 1940s, Tony, a twenty-eight-year-old son of Neapolitan immigrants, told Covello how years earlier the hostility of his parents toward the German American girl he was in love with had wrecked his plans for marriage. Now Tony saw things differently. "How it came about I don't know, but somehow today I share my mother's viewpoint. I have nothing against American girls, but just the same I feel they carry things a little too far," he confessed. The ideal of romantic love was no longer important for him; the ideal of the good Italian girl was.

> My mother's sister is still in Italy, and has a large family of 12 daughters—from 14 to 32 years old—and no sons. They are, I understand, rather poor, but, as my mother tells me, they are very well brought up. They can cook, sew, work, help the husband to earn a living, and they are quite free from modern crazy ideas. . . . My mother works on me for several years, suggesting that I should marry anyone of the girls. They don't look to me like great beauties, but I gave up long ago to be attracted by good looks. . . . As my mother says, any of the girls would make a good wife; besides my marriage would greatly help the family.[81]

The new strategies of socialization granted immigrant children some autonomy and the freedom to organize their own lives; rarely were parents in the position to force them to comply with the *famiglia*'s expectations. But many children of immigrants had made the ideology of the family their own and internalized its symbolic code. A son who had once dismissed his mother's claim that a girl who accumulated kitchen utensils and other domestic objects demonstrated a serious disposition toward marriage now thought twice about it. "These words sound funny to me for I was born in America," he explained to Covello. "Yet somehow they make sense. At least, I feel that when a girl cares for her dowry, and spends many an hour in sewing and knitting for future use, there is no reason to ridicule it. I even would say that it is a good custom."[82] A young woman similarly demonstrated that she had interiorized the notion of the "good Italian woman" when she argued that she was pleased to be seen while doing housework and cooking. In that way, her boyfriend would consider her "a good worker who thinks of the family. A man is sure of this kind of girl."[83]

The persistence of family traditions was also affected by social and structural forces. Many second-generation Italian Americans still had few opportunities to meet potential partners from other groups. The realities of social class could also easily persuade younger Italian Americans, confronting the harsh reality of life after school, that family and kin remained crucial for survival and welfare. The importance of the working-class *famiglia* emerged with renewed force during the Depression. If the relative upward mobility of the 1920s had weakened the role of family networks in economic and social life, the Depression managed to turn back the clock. Immigrant children realized that the future described in school bore no relation to their actual lives. They also felt their limited access to scarce jobs was threatened by the new immigrants to the area. Even for the unprecedented number of Italian Americans who attended high school in the 1930s, much of the value of school as a window on America was gone. With the end of mass migration and the redefinition of race in New York as a black and white issue, the critical role of the school in the domestic world of Italian children—the most problematic "new immigrant" group—had faded. Young American-born Italians had come to feel that disparaging their parents' culture was the price for full access to the mainstream of American life. But over time they learned that abandoning their immigrant background did not mean emancipation from class and cultural divides. Many young Italian Americans began to rethink the family as a source of emotional and material support: "As a kid, I was ashamed of everything Italian," one of them recalled.

> I would deny my own mother. I would hate to come home after school. But after several years at elementary school I learned that home means something solid, a source of comfort, rich with the warmth of family friendship. It ceased to be a place to which I reluctantly returned to eat and sleep. I saw I was not born to be a president of the United States. And when my parents spoke of my approaching age—I was fourteen at the time—and recommended my going into the trucking business with a cousin, I counted the days till school would be over.[84]

Italian immigrants in Harlem apparently succeeded in making the ideology of the "Italian family" into a strong, flexible narrative that could respond to some of the social and economic changes in American urban life, and one they could use to control the effects of autonomy and subjectivity on their children.

As a result, younger generations eventually adopted and endorsed their own negotiated version of the food patterns they inherited from their parents. The food culture that represented the strategic symbolic code in the building of the "Italian family, and its norms and values" became in large measure their own. In the Tiano family, American-born young men openly poked fun at their parents' customs but at the same time shared their beliefs in highly differentiated gender roles and in the supremacy of husbands over wives. Marco, the son who "almost broke his Mother's heart" by marrying a Protestant Scottish American g determined, he said, "to bring up his children as Catholics, and to teach them the Italian language." Marco admitted "that as a child he resented Italian cooking, but now ha[d] come to like it and insist[ed] that his wife learn how to cook Italian dishes."[85]

The food culture of East Harlem Italian Americans was not the inert legacy of a distant rural past. Nor was it a tradition preserved whole cloth within the boundaries of the family threatened by external forces. It was, in effect, a tradition created as part of a symbolic strategy of socialization and discipline and mobilized frequently in response to crises and changes occurring inside and outside the immigrant family. The relative persistence of immigrant foodways across generations was neither uniform nor automatic but rather the result of conflict and negotiation in a changing context of power. Food, no less than language, was a contested cultural ground on which Italian Harlem immigrants and their children had to walk as they reimagined their identity as Italian Americans.[86] In their families, food produced many meanings. It gave Italian Americans an enduring sense of themselves as a group with its own history and an identity articulated often in the narratives about Italy that immigrants shared with their children during food-centered gatherings. Food was endowed with ritual significance, and food culture was a vital component for a new Italian American domesticity. In the immigrant home, second-generation Italian Americans learned that the family, albeit poor, always nurtured its members; that the people deserving of trust were those with whom food was shared; that familiar food enjoyed with familiar company was the legitimate reward for a working life. The "Italian family" ideology "was not taught" but "simply absorbed" around the table. It assisted in the creation of a collective identity that, although often conflicted and insecure, helped immigrants and their children locate themselves in American society and in the Italian diaspora as Italian Americans.

Originally developed in contrast to "white" America, with its racialization of Italian immigrants and its perceived influence in pitting immigrant children against their parents, by the 1930s the ideology of *the family that eats together* needed a new nemesis in order to remain a source of collective identification. As the ethnic composition of East Harlem changed, the ideological connection between food and cultural identity was put to work to define the distance between Italians and the different, darker-skinned newcomers. As we will see in the next chapter, many in the Italian community used food culture to reclaim their own whiteness and full American citizenship in a context of racial confrontation. The idea that food was a symbolic code with which a collective Italian American identity could be fully expressed was further reinforced in the process.

3

An American Foodscape

Food, Place, and Race in Italian Harlem

Food and Place(s) in Italian Harlem

The 1930s were difficult years for Italian Harlem. In New York, the Depression hit Italian Americans—the most proletarianized of the European ethnic groups in the city—especially hard. Italians were disproportionately represented among the recipients of city and federal subsidies, particularly in Harlem, where the poorest among them lived. Covello estimates that "more than 75 percent of the people in the community [were] being sustained, at present [1938], through Home Relief Bureaus and other organizations assisting in the amelioration of conditions due to unemployment."[1] Joblessness, a deteriorating housing stock, crime, and disease (the annual tuberculosis mortality rate in East Harlem was almost double that of New York City) kept conditions of life in the neighborhood extremely grim.[2]

However, in those same years, Italian immigrants and their children managed to make East Harlem their home in America through a careful deployment of social, material, and emotional responses. Inside the cold-water "railroad flats" of bleak pre-twentieth-century tenements, Italian Harlem was born from the shared ethnic working-class culture that revolved around the private bastion of the family and the public arena of the community. To be sure, the system of mores and values that bound the people of Italian Harlem together should not be romanticized; the costs of complying with the unwritten rules of the "culture" were huge and often painful. Yet out of the shared poverty that marked life in a strange environment, there arose a common system of meaning, a community spirit, and a sense of solidarity that turned a distressed urban settlement setting into a relatively dependable sanctuary. Defying what the rest of the world may have thought about Italian Harlem, its inhabitants shared a considerable pride in their neighborhood.[3] As a lifelong resident attempted to convey about the essence of life in the community, "the neighborhood was one big family. Doors were kept open, everybody socialized with each other, everybody borrowed from each other, and everybody paid back what [they] had borrowed."[4]

The most significant way that Italians articulated their love for Italian Harlem was investing in it—emotionally and materially. Love requires devotion, sacrifice, and time, and Italian lovers of the neighborhood went to great lengths to show that they were ready to pay its price. As early as the 1880s, the construction workers who predominated among early Italian immigrants freely put their labor and skills at the service of the construction in the neighborhood of a new "Italian" church.[5] By building the Church of the Madonna of Mount Carmel, they planted deep roots in the swampland along the East River, roots watered with their own sweat. The church was meant to last, as it has, long after they were gone.

While the building of churches was important, Italians in Harlem invested in their neighborhood most heavily by acts of consumption, using their hard-earned money not only to express how they saw themselves, what they cared about, and what they wanted to become, but also to make sense of the place in which they lived. They did so notably with regard to food. Italian immigrants spent extravagantly on food for communal events such as baptisms, first communions, wedding parties, and funerals, all to be held in *local* churches, restaurants, apartments, and funeral homes. The consumption of food, on which New York Italians spent vastly more than any other ethnic group, was at base a strategy for the production of place, as an investment in, and an expression of love for, the local community.[6] In Italian Harlem, the production, commerce, preparation, and consumption of food created a distinct urban ethnic foodscape and smellscape that shaped social identities. Italian Americans created around them a sensually familiar world, surrounded every hour by the tastes, aromas, and colors of Italian food. Routine and festive food events alike not only cemented family and community relationships but also helped Italians to call their gridded zone of Upper Manhattan *home*, turning otherwise anonymous streets and buildings into familiar objects of affection and helping Italians draw mental, cultural, and political boundaries between themselves and other groups. Ironically, Italian Harlem was home to some sixty-four other ethnic groups, from Jews and Hungarians to West Indians, Chinese, and Finns, all of whom mingled with one another and with Italians. This large corner of Manhattan was constructed, understood, and represented as Italian Harlem not only because of the large numbers of Italians but also because of Italians' hegemonic impact on the nature of public space. Food, in all its declinations, was arguably the most important factor in the production of a space-bound community framed, narrated, and experienced as an Italian neighborhood.

Crucial to these geographies of consumption and taste were the many Italian food stores and markets that dotted the neighborhood. Italian immigrants surrounded themselves with ethnic food stores and supported them well. ("Ethnic" was signified by the kind of foodstuffs for sale, the Italian shop signs, and the language and the ethnicity shared by owners and customers.) Despite the competition from large numbers of stores fighting for shares of an impoverished customer base, until the 1940s these small independent businesses successfully resisted the new chain stores and supermarkets. The loyalty of Italian immigrants to ethnic businesses can be explained partly by the social and cultural capital created by ethnic entrepreneurs, who, deeply embedded in networks of family and community relations, were uniquely able to understand the special needs of fellow Italians.[7] But immigrant loyalty was also a consequence of the fact that Italian groceries, bakeries, and cheese, meat, and fruit shops marked the landscape with specific signifiers of identity and provided the raw materials that enabled the community to nurture a self-sufficient cultural identity. At the neighborhood level, consumer institutions and practices consistently *made* the Italian immigrant community.

The production of local identity that took place in Italian grocery stores and pushcart markets was shaped by complex emotions toward another, distant place. Most immigrants in Italian Harlem had been an agricultural people tied to rural villages. They remembered with great fondness the food of the Italian past, a product of the land and lives they had left behind. Now, as American consumers nostalgic for Italy, they looked to the colors, tastes, smells, names, packages, and popular brands of imported foods for the comforts of authenticity. These foods permitted immigrants who could not, or would not, return to Italy to at least return to an imaginary home by consuming products that mirrored Italian places and were handed to them by Italian hands.[8] For women especially, consuming Italian food was a socially approved way to inhabit the hierarchical male public spaces of streets, open markets, and grocery stores; enjoy sociability and exchange information; and reaffirm—through gendered consumer practices—their commitment to "Italian culture." Ethnic food retailers, drawing almost all their profit from the enclave economy, were active in the community, sponsoring leisure activities and nationalist commemorations and helping to make the neighborhood safe for the Italian majority by policing the streets against intruders. But they also maintained strong connections with Italy and as specialized importers met the demands of a regionally heterogeneous clientele, while at the same time providing the products and practices that would eventually create a new kind of Italian-style cooking for a diasporic consumer subculture.

This complex diasporic architecture of taste, place, and emotions would not survive forever. Its eventual demise demanded a cause, and one was found in the "invasion" of "darker" newcomers: black and Puerto Rican migrants. Here, then, were the scapegoats in a story that began in the 1920s, when Italians had been leaving Harlem as soon as they could afford to, or, just as often, as they saw their children leave them behind. Many of the Italians who stayed until World War II and afterward strengthened their identities as white people against blacks and Puerto Ricans in a struggle to disassociate themselves from the groups disparaged by white America. Against these neighbors, Italians deployed another emotional geography, this one of hatred and resentment, but one also created by the codes of food. This process of assertion and resistance ended in the 1950s and 1960s, when massive urban renewal destroyed the texture of Italian Harlem—notably its food shops and open markets—and made sentiments of loss and animosity a permanent part of the collective memory.

One of the most significant and painful tensions underlying Italian Harlem history was the chasm between the "American" urge to leave and the "Italian" expectation that families should stay together as adults and young people both grew older. Leaving Italian Harlem was never easy, despite the great efforts made at reconstituting the community elsewhere (in the Bronx, for example) and at returning regularly, either to shop for Italian food or to celebrate the annual Feast of the Madonna of Mount Carmel.[9] The community was unambiguous in expressing its feelings toward those who left. A young woman in this group recalled the guilt she felt when told by a local priest, "You people who might have contributed much to the life of this community moved as soon as you acquired your education and position in life. We needed you right here to guide and lead our younger groups and to inspire the older groups with your courage and sympathy."[10]

To the many who left Italian Harlem, any act of love for the neighborhood would soothe the pain of separation. In a community built so solidly on its social networks and distinctive streetscapes, those who left for a better place to live would always have a place to return to, if only for an hour or a day. When, in the 1950s, Italian Harlem finally started to age and shrink and finally vanish, the few remaining Italian bakeries, grocery stores, and restaurants stood as heroic landmarks of a bygone era in a landscape now home to poor non-Italian minorities. As returning suburbanite shoppers visited the neighborhood and devotees of the Madonna of Mount Carmel joined the annual procession and feast, food again became a powerful medium in creating yet another place. This new place was Cara Harlem, as it was called in the letters that ex-parishioners sent to the weekly church bulletin, remembered with feelings of nostalgia, loss, and anger. Like its lost physical counterpart, the remembered world of Cara Harlem would also occupy a central place in the historical imagination of the Italian migrant experience in America.

Italian Harlem, Italy, Cara Harlem: Italian immigrants crafted multiple geographies of belonging through food. Through food, they untangled their sense of self from a fixed, inherited notion of identity and refashioned it into new, translocal forms, linking a place that immigrants lived, shaped, and eventually lost and reinvented in memory—the neighborhood—to a place they remembered and thought about, Italy.[11] Food filled these spaces and gave them sensual meaning; it functioned as a language through which immigrants made sense of themselves and their place in the world; it shaped historical spaces that shifted and reconfigured themselves in immigrants' imagination, as they remembered the past, coped with the present, and imagined the future.

Food, Race, and Power: Blacks, Puerto Ricans, and the Italian Descent into Whiteness

The collective Italian American identity that drew so widely on the ideology of the family was also strengthened by a narrative of the otherness of the nonwhites increasingly encountered in the streets, at school, at work, and even in the homes of East Harlem in the 1930s and 1940s. In these decades, racial tensions arose as Italian Americans started to perceive their neighborhood as threatened by Puerto Rican and African American newcomers. As Italian Americans felt the need to distinguish themselves privately and publicly from the "nonwhite" people with whom they now shared the same urban space, their sense of identity and difference was again articulated in the language of family and food.

The great irony of Italian Harlem is that, just as the community was at the peak of its numerical, political, and cultural power, the forces that would bring about its downfall were unfolding. Italians who could afford to leave the dangerous streets and cramped tenements of Harlem and realize their dream of homeownership did so in large numbers in the 1920s and even in the troubled 1930s.[12] Commenting on the 1930 U.S. census, *Il Progresso Italo-Americano* noted, "The Italians who remain on the East Side are with few exceptions of the poorest element. . . . Many apartment houses are vacant, while in 1920 one could not find a room here for an arm and a leg."[13] By 1934, 90 percent of East Harlem's population was squeezed into 60 percent of the area's blocks, and 21.5 percent of the housing stock was vacant.[14] Soon, however, explanations for the fragile state of Italian Harlem shifted from internal causes—the flow of upwardly mobile residents out of the community—to the arrival of dangerous outsiders. While the black population of East Harlem in 1920 was a mere 3,735, by 1930 it had grown to 29,422, and because of segregation, high rents, and overcrowding in West Harlem continued growing throughout the 1930s.[15] In 1920, about 6,000 Puerto Ricans lived on the western edge of the neighborhood, but in one decade they had grown to 14,000 and became the majority population between Fifth and Park Avenues. As a result, the elevated tracks of the New York Central Railroad along Park Avenue came to be known as the "Chinese Wall" dividing Italian Harlem linguistically, culturally, and mentally from its Latino counterpart.[16]

Many Puerto Rican migrants had dark skin; by the mid-1930s, Spanish Harlem's streets were seething with "fair-skinned Creoles with dark eyes, lean-faced copper-complexion Spanish Indians, sensitive-looking West Indian Negroes."[17] It was due to the color line that Italians experienced the Puerto Rican arrival as a collective trauma, an "invasion" that provoked fear, hatred, and fatalism. Italians seemed to foresee the end of a world where "the doors were kept open." "In the last three years [the colored people, Puerto Ricans, Cubans, West Indians] have penetrated in such large numbers that they are pushing the Italians away," a shop owner who had come to East Harlem in 1898 told his interviewer. "Eventually the whole East Harlem will be a section of colored people."[18] Salvatore Cimmiluca, a New York University student who completed his thesis on the history of East Harlem in 1930, reflected the common Italian sentiment in the following statement: "At present [East Harlem] is being invaded by Puerto Ricans; these people speak their native language which is Spanish, and they are commonly called 'spicks.'"[19]

The Italian American preoccupation with color was born out of insecurity and feelings of inadequacy; it was a specific product of the racialization of southern Italians in both Italy and America; in East Harlem, Italians constructed the otherness of their "nonwhite" neighbors out of fear of *identification* with them. Since the 1920s, newspapers had presented all of Harlem as a ghetto, and its infamous reputation grew with the arrival of more migrants from Puerto Rico and the American South. The filth, the stench, and the danger of East Harlem streets came to reflect the threat to the community of an unnatural mixing of races. To this was to be added the morbid interest of the press in any instance of racial conflict. "The core of Manhattan's sprawling 18th Congressional District is a verminous, crime-ridden slum called East Harlem," wrote *Time*. "Its hordes of Italians, Puerto Ricans, Jews and Negroes have traditionally voted Republican. But in the last decade a new force came into power: the patchwork patronage machine of shrill, stooped, angry-eyed, pro-Communist Representative Vito Marcantonio. . . . To its gunmen, madams, policy and dope peddlers, he is 'The Hon. *Fritto Misto*' [Mixed Fry]."[20] Against these cynical tales of racial hierarchies and racial privilege, one lifelong resident explained,

> When they say East Harlem, Harlem was never East Harlem, Harlem was Harlem, this was called Harlem. When the blacks started to come towards this area, in order for us to explain where we lived (when you said Harlem, they said black)

> we said we live in East Harlem, that's where the name East came into being, to separate the white and the black. The people who were in East Harlem were the Italians, and the other Harlem, they didn't say West Harlem, then Harlem itself, that's where the blacks were. So, when they said where are you going, if you are white you had to say East Harlem, if you say Harlem they would look at you . . . "Do you live in the black area?"[21]

It was largely in a desperate effort to distance themselves from their "darker-skinned" Puerto Rican, West Indian, and African American neighbors that Italian Americans in Harlem reclaimed a white American identity.[22]

Southern Italian immigrants were, of course, familiar with racist prejudices long before they came to America. Despite the integrative goals of liberal Italy's nation-building project, the romantic ideal of a single Italian people began to break up immediately after the unification of the country in 1861, when the notion of southern Italian racial inferiority started to spread among northern Italians. By the end of the Risorgimento, the people of the South and Sicily had already been widely depicted as "savages," "barbarians," and "Africans" by northern Italian travelers, writers, and public officials: "But, my friend, what lands are these, Molise and the south!" wrote General Luigi Carlo Farini to Prime Minister Camillo Benso Count of Cavour on October 27, 1860. "What barbarism! This is not Italy! This is Africa: compared to these peasants the Bedouins are the pinnacle of civilization."[23] By the end of the nineteenth century, in the wake of the bloody war waged by the new republic against brigandage in the south, popular discourses about southern inferiority had found a "scientific" foundation. Following Cesare Lombroso's work on phenotypical features in criminology, the anthropologists Giuseppe Sergi and Alfredo Niceforo explained regional Italian differences as the result of two distinct Italian races; the superior Alpine-Celt, and the "degenerate" Mediterranean scarred by Levantine and African influences.[24]

At the turn of the twentieth century, American commentators and lawmakers appropriated these popular racist prejudices and the "findings" of Lombrosian scholars in the effort to make sense of the racial identity of the masses of migrants from southern Italy, especially in the heat of the public debate on immigration restriction.[25] Jacob Riis wrote that the Italian immigrant's "universal vice was his dirtiness; he was dirtier than the Negro, and the [Mulberry] Bend was scarce dirtier then the Little Italy of Harlem."[26] In the American South, Italians were lynched—especially when they mingled with American blacks—and their whiteness was constantly questioned. In 1922 in Alabama, a black man was acquitted of the charge of miscegenation because the woman in question was Sicilian and therefore the court could find no proof that she was white.[27] Beliefs about the racial ambiguity of Italians were long-lived and widely shared; in an early 1960s speech, Malcolm X (himself a resident of Harlem in the 1940s) referred to the "Hannibal blood" running in Italian veins: "No Italian will ever jump up in my face and start putting bad mouth on me, because I know his history. I tell him 'when you talk about me, you're talking about your pappy.'"[28]

Notwithstanding these claims of racial proximity, many Italian immigrants encountered diasporic Africans for the first time in New York and in large numbers only after World War I. Before the large migration from the American South and the West Indies in the 1920s, contacts between the two groups had been sporadic and largely free of public conflict.[29] In the interwar years, the resentment of blacks toward relatively more upwardly mobile Italians grew, as blacks began to blame Italians for stealing traditionally "black" jobs in the service sector (in 1905, 11.2 percent of black males in the city worked as waiters, and another 5 percent as bartenders and cooks, all occupations that Italians took over in the following years).[30] In the mid-1930s, the fascist war against Ethiopia, with its imperialist and racist connotations, added a transnational element to local conflicts. But the gap between Italians and their black neighbors was increasingly due to the way Italians successfully internalized the dynamics of American racism in order to strengthen their position in the U.S. social order.[31] By the 1930s, Italian American students in East Harlem were no longer fearful of the "Americans" they once admired from the margins. Now they had mastered the terms of a racist discourse regulating social inclusion and exclusion: "My most miserable days were the first two years at public school," one of them told Covello.

> I was scared even to talk to the other boys, not to mention chumming with them. In the sixth and seventh grades I could hold my ground. They didn't scare me any more. I knew I was just good as they were. Just a bunch of kikes, spiks, no real American among them. In high school it was the same thing. Why should I feel inferior when I know I am a better American than this bunch of Negroes, Puerto Ricans, Poles and Germans? My father came here fifty years ago, and he is anyway more American than those. I think East Harlem is a good place to live in. Without Puerto Ricans and Negroes it would be swell.[32]

Immigrants and their children had also learned that even the discourses on food and eating had racist implications. For both generations, food security was linked to racial status, even if under different conditions. In the newly unified Italy, the poor nutrition of southerners was used to explain their "moral" and "biological" weakness. Niceforo, for example, insisted that undernourishment, malnutrition, and in particular the minimal intake of animal proteins in the diet of southern Italians had contributed to their physical, intellectual, and psychological inferiority and to "the degeneration of an entire civilization."[33] More popularly, middle-class Italians described southern Italian food as "low," associated with toil, and degraded. In one of the earliest written accounts of pizza (1886), popular Tuscan writer Collodi (the author of *Pinocchio*) thus described the food he encountered in streets of Naples: "The blackened aspect of the toasted crust, the whitish sheen of garlic and anchovy, the greenish-yellow tint of the oil and fried herbs, and those red bits of tomato here and there give pizza the appearance of complicated filth that matches the dirt of the vendor."[34]

In the early days of the Harlem "colony," middle-class criticism of Italian immigrant foodways had clearly racist overtones and often insisted on the similarities between Italians and blacks.[35] By the early twentieth century, nutrition experts argued that the Italian immigrant diet was indigestible, overstimulated the nervous system, and encouraged alcohol consumption. Teachers blamed immigrants' ignorance for the high rates of malnutrition, rickets, and tuberculosis among Italian schoolchildren. Young generations in Italian Harlem grew up with the awareness that racism against southern Italians found a powerful expression in the language of food.

The debate on ethnic food habits that developed in New York in the 1930s convinced Italians of a direct relation between food, race, and power. At a time when one in six New Yorkers was first- or second-generation Italian American and an Italian American mayor ruled from City Hall, Italian American food culture began to be reevaluated. Italian specialties became popular outside ethnic markets, and Italian restaurants attracted an unprecedented number of non-Italian patrons. Nutritionists now praised the Italian American diet as "balanced" and economical and made it a part of programs developed in response to the food crisis of the Depression. The Home Relief Bureau, for example, recommended spaghetti as a nutritious and cost-effective food in the Spanish-language flyers aimed at its Puerto Rican clients.[36]

As satisfying as the new appreciation of their cuisine must have been, Italian immigrants were more pleased that their American victory over hunger and access to a richer material life had healed the social, cultural, and physiological wounds caused by the discrimination they had suffered in Italy and New York. This sense of group victory through food helped them claim a higher place in the ethnic and racial order, separate themselves from blacks, and connect whiteness to the rewards of citizenship. Once again, immigrants could measure the change in their lives by looking at their children's. In 1937, a correspondent for the Italian newspaper *La Stampa*, Amerigo Ruggiero, argued that dietary improvements made possible by the American marketplace had paved the way for a full anthropological transformation of Italian American bodies.[37] Ruggiero was quick to point to skin color:

> Our immigrants and their children, especially those from southern Italy, suffered from dietary defects different from those that afflicted Americans. While

> the latter ate too much meat and little or no vegetables, fruits, and legumes, for our people it was the opposite. They ate abundant fruit and vegetables, but only every now and then meat, milk, and butter. Over here as well, [as in Italy,] vitamin deficiency frequently produced rickets. One had to feel the mortification of seeing in American scientific texts Italians ranking along with Negroes in rates of rickets. In immigrants' hometowns, dietary deficiencies influenced profoundly the skeletal development producing the low height of those populations, and the miserable appearance which disturbed Americans so much that they came to consider us a degenerate race, . . . but it was right here in America that the fact that height deficiency is not a fixed character of our race was brilliantly proved. . . . From rickety, dwarf-like, and simian-paced parents, a spawn of giants is born. When you enter some Italian homes, and mother and father introduce you to their children, you are immediately prompted to ask: 'Are they really your children?' . . . Another feature that tends to fade away in America is the dark complexion of southern Italians. It is apparent that this, too, is not a fixed character and distinctive of race, but a consequence of climatic conditions. The children born in America are far more light-skinned than their ancestors.[38]

Not coincidentally, by the 1930s public discourse on ethnic foodways reflected the shifting position of racial groups of New York on the socioeconomic ladder. Just as the Italian immigrant diet was being reappraised, the food habits of recent migrants from Puerto Rico and below the Mason-Dixon Line were becoming objects of expert and official criticism. The critique had a familiar accent. Nutritionists attacked the Puerto Rican diet for providing too few calories, minerals, and vitamins. According to these studies, Puerto Ricans of the poorer classes sustained themselves on little more than rice and beans and did not eat meat more than a few times a year. Poverty, however, was not the only cause of their malnutrition; unsuccessful acculturation was also complicit. "The average Puerto Rican woman knows very little about the cooking of American food," noted an observer. "Some of the vegetables found in Puerto Rico are unknown in New York [and] the Puerto Rican cook uses too much grease or lard to suit the American taste. Their diet in New York . . . remains much the same as in their native land: a roll and coffee for breakfast; for the other meals canned tomatoes, white rice, dried fish, and meat about twice a month."[39]

As had happened to earlier groups of immigrants, social workers as well as sensationalizing journalists blamed flaws in diet, hygiene, and domestic skills for many of the problems that afflicted the Puerto Rican community and posed a threat to public health.[40] Biological differences and the senses were discursively brought in to link Puerto Ricans and food to the risk of contamination, with overtones unheard of even in the Jim Crow South, where white masters regularly ate the food cooked by their black servants. In 1940, the *World-Telegram* warned readers, "The problem is that [Puerto Ricans] have a high frequency of tuberculosis. The most serious thing about their poor health is that the large majority of them work in the city's restaurants, hotels, and clubs, where they handle food, plates, and other kitchen utensils."[41]

Widespread malnutrition was thought to be the main cause of Puerto Ricans' physical underdevelopment and resulting unsuitability for urban life and industrial work. High rates of mortality from tuberculosis in Puerto Rican Harlem, four to ten times higher than the city average, and the city's highest infant mortality rate were also linked to diet and living conditions.[42] As the number of poorer Puerto Rican migrants increased, conservative newspapers and magazines decried the burden that their ill health placed on taxpayers. "In an average home on 112th Street I found nearly 80 persons using a single outdoor privy," a reporter for *Scribner's Commentator* wrote in 1940: "Negroes, whites, and every intermediate shade of human being were living not only under the same roof but by the dozen in the same rooms. Few have running water, but most are not even conscious of that lack; for it is unknown in Porto Rico."[43] Newspapers and official reports alike targeted Puerto Ricans as carriers of tropical diseases.[44] Even the travel guide *New York Confidential* worried that "Puerto Ricans were not born to be New Yorkers. They are mostly crude farmers subject to congenital tropical diseases, physically unfitted for the northern climate, unskilled, uneducated, non English-speaking, and almost impossible to assimilate and condition for healthful and useful existence in an active city of stone and steel."[45]

During the Depression, the widespread malnutrition of black children and adults in Central Harlem was also regularly cited as a major source of the spread of tuberculosis, the most common cause of death of Harlemites in the 1930s. The New York Tuberculosis and Health Association insisted that "a better diet" and the consumption of "wholesome food" were the most urgent reform needed by the black poor in Harlem.[46] But the low value placed on typical African American fare (what since the 1960s became known as "soul food") derived from its status as the food of poor migrants. Between 1920 and 1930, the black population of New York City more than doubled, so that by 1930 only one-quarter of the city's blacks had been born in New York State; blacks from the Caribbean and Africa alone numbered 54,754 out of a total population of 327,706.[47] The migrants' greasy, substantial southern-style food and tradition of commensality identified the rural foodways of newcomers from rural Virginia and the Carolinas in the eyes of New York–born blacks, who had painstakingly shaped their own sense of respectability through their urban foodways. "The prejudice against food practices that smacked of Southerness—heavy meats, excessive carbohydrates, and especially hot sauces and condiments, . . . deleterious to the liver and . . . the digestive system" mounted in Central Harlem as "food became a symbolic battleground for the public image of the race."[48]

As they were consolidating the view that foodways were representative of racial and national family culture, Italian Americans used the same ideas of domesticity that they had mobilized on their own behalf to define their new neighbors as unwelcome and threatening. By taking the model of the *family that eats together* as an ideological prism through which to understand the Puerto Rican and African American presence in East Harlem, they condemned Puerto Rican and African American family life as dishonorable and inferior. The fear that the perceived immorality of black and Puerto Rican families would corrupt their own beloved *famiglia* was especially powerful in broadening the chasm between the communities. An Italian mother, for example, affirmed that she was most worried by

> the peril which faces her Italian neighborhood, namely the increase of Negroes in the Italian community and in the surrounding district. She expressed a horror that there are so many colored children in Peter's class this year. She believes that the Italian children will come in contact with Negro children who have entirely different ideas about everything, and that would certainly be bad company for her own children. . . . It will be difficult for her to bring up her children in the right way if they learn things from Negro children. American parents, she said, cannot educate their children, although their ideas about it are good. Negro parents, on the other hand, neither can nor want to educate their children in the Christian way.[49]

Italian Americans in the southern blocks of Italian Harlem, where the influx of Puerto Ricans was most intense, articulated a similar view: Puerto Ricans lived an amoral family life and were sabotaging the order of community life. "The Porto Ricans are all Negroes, lazy and never working," an immigrant said. "The men spend all their time drinking and smoking and gambling." "Do you see my side of the street a few families moved away because they did not like the Porto Ricans, and their floors were rented to Porto Ricans," another immigrant woman explained. "From what I can hear all the people are complaining and I think will move away. And I am afraid by the end of the year everybody will be out as I too am thinking of moving away. Oh, [Puerto Ricans] are awful dirty people, the women are all bad."[50]

To Italians, the large number of single mothers, desertions, neglected children, and unstable households, which were mostly the result of poverty and migration, were felt to be cultural traits that revealed an innate tendency of Puerto Ricans and African Americans toward a lack of morality and families that failed. In Central Harlem, by the mid-1930s 25 percent of black families were headed by women.[51] Because women's wages were needed to counter the effects of high male unemployment, 60 percent of black married women worked, twice as many as native white women. Especially in the early years of the Depression, discrimination by employers and unions excluded African Americans from many occupations.

Discriminatory practices in the welfare system also swelled the ranks of "lazy" black men who loitered in the streets of the neighborhood. Many black women worked as domestic workers, often under brutal conditions, frequently for less than half the minimum wage.[52] Many Harlem children lived in poverty: between 1931 and 1935, the Juvenile Court deliberated cases of neglect for more than three thousand black children. Poor housing conditions completed the picture; it was common for two families to share a small and unhealthy apartment.[53] Finally, in Harlem alcoholism and prostitution were common.[54]

The Puerto Rican community suffered from similar problems. A late 1930s study claimed that 60 percent of Puerto Ricans who had arrived in New York during the decade had never found a job.[55] The suspicion that Puerto Ricans were coming to the city to live on welfare, continuously revived by the press, was widespread.[56] For both groups, labor market conditions heavily influenced family life and structure. Just like blacks, Puerto Rican women had many more employment opportunities than men. Many Puerto Rican men moved seasonally between the island and the mainland, as dictated by changing economic conditions. As it was for other immigrant groups (including Italians), Puerto Rican migrants tended to live in mixed households where boarding was a common practice. Socioeconomic conditions in the migrant community encouraged desertions, common-law unions, and illegitimate births.[57] Moreover, the living conditions of poor newcomers did not allow them to conceal from strangers many behaviors, including bodily functions that Italian Americans had come to regard as private. As Bernardo Vega remembered about the role of food in creating the political ecology and economy of El Barrio, "There were many Hispanic *bodegas*, barbershops, and butchers. Branches of green plantains hung in the store windows, and the sidewalks were lined with food and vegetable stands. In the stores and in the streets, all you heard was Spanish. But the other nationality groups living in the area resented the constantly growing Puerto Rican population. For them the way of life of the *boricuas* was scandalous, and the relations between the national groups were fraught with tension. Women would often clash while shopping, and at times the fights in the neighborhood bars would become serious."[58] In East Harlem, food was a source of political creativity for the making of racialized identities.

In this case, too, Italian Americans criticized behaviors for which they had been criticized only a few years earlier. However, by now Italian American notions of "privacy," "decency," and "shame" had been reshaped by the new material conditions that enabled the construction of the "Italian family" in America: a home in which to hold convivial events; at the same time, a domestic space for privacy; and a clear boundary between what was to be shown in public and what was to remain hidden.[59] For mostly black Central Harlem, the early years of the

Depression meant that the "lack of sufficient food was a common experience." In 1930, 16 percent of all students were malnourished, an increase of 20 percent over the previous year. Social workers noted that hunger was causing "a lowered vitality among the people they [saw] and more sickness than usual."[60] Black men, women, and children could be seen searching through garbage bins for food in competition with dogs and cats.[61] In Spanish Harlem, ill-clad and emaciated children wandered along East 110th Street nibbling scanty leftovers.[62] Here, a reporter noted, "The steps in front of tenements, the doors, windows, and even fire escapes, are always occupied in hot-weather by half-naked men, women, and children, and many people put chairs and tables on the sidewalks in front of their homes. They eat, drink, make love, and suckle their babes on the streets because there is no space for them to do so indoors."[63] Things were different in Italian Harlem, as a lifelong resident second-generation Italian American was anxious to tell an interviewer: "One thing about those days, we never said we were poor. We always had something to eat."[64] For the community that "ate as a family" and symbolically expressed respectability, status, affection, inclusion, and exclusion in terms of food, it was natural to use food habits to distinguish itself morally from the hungry newcomers who didn't "eat as a family."

In East Harlem, the smells and tastes of food had always been carriers of personal dislike and disgust. Intolerance of the food of other groups was common in such a diverse, densely populated community. Early in the century, an Irish immigrant woman told a sociologist that she had no prejudices against her new Italian neighbors, but the smell of the garlic in their food made cohabitation intolerable.[65] An Italian immigrant woman convinced her husband to move away from their Jewish neighbors because she could not stand the stench of herrings in brine that rose from the grocery store below.[66] But by the 1930s, Italian Americans narrated their frame of difference by making careful use of the same racist discourse linking food habits to social hierarchies and citizenship that had so recently victimized them. In 1938, after violent clashes between Italian American and Puerto Rican youth gangs, Covello walked the streets trying to understand the reasons for the fight. A group of young Italian Americans explained to him: "[Puerto Ricans] are not like us. We're American. We eat meat at least three times a week. What do they eat? Beans! So they work for beans. That's why we have trouble here."[67]

The children of Italian Harlem were taught in school that one could not be an American without eating the food an American is supposed to eat. While accepting this notion, which they had even used against their own families, young Italian Americans acknowledged that becoming American meant struggling to fit into a racial and class hierarchy. Fitting in meant defining oneself in opposition to others, and this process of identifying who was in and who was out operated on the uncertain terrain of culture, race, and consumption. Along with the ideology of the "Italian family" that they had interiorized around the family table, the ability to connect their own position as ethnic consumers to discourses of race and citizenship earned them a public, collective identity that allowed them to fit into the U.S. social order as Italian Americans.

The Taste of the Slum: Making Place(s) across the Boundaries of Race and Taste

Throughout the neighborhood's complicated ethnic history, its public spaces were always segmented and its boundaries attentively, and often violently, guarded. The competition for jobs, housing, and social entitlements produced in some adults a racial hatred that young people brought to the street in the form of a permanent gang war for the defense of turf.[68] Racial, ethnic, and class differences were effectively reproduced in space, heavily influencing the behaviors and identities of the area's inhabitants. "The neighborhood had its boundaries," Puerto Rican poet and community activist Jack Agueros recalled.

> Third Avenue and east, Italian. Fifth Avenue and west, black. South, there was a hill on 103rd Street known locally as Cooney's Hill. When you got to the top of the hill, something strange happened: America began, because from the hill south was where the "Americans" lived. When, as a group of Puerto Rican kids, we decided to go swimming to Jefferson Park pool, we knew we risked a fight and a beating from the Italians. And when we went to La Milagrosa Church in Harlem, we knew we risked a fight and a beating from the blacks. But when we went over Cooney's Hill, we risked dirty looks, disapproving looks, and questions from the police like, "What are you doing in this neighborhood?" and "Why don't you kids go back to where you belong?"[69]

The work of defending one's own territory—symbolically or physically—against others perceived as hostile helped consolidate fragmented communities. The "Puerto Ricans" that Italians saw as a homogeneous group were divided socially and racially; and many Harlem "blacks" had been born in places as diverse as Jamaica, Virginia, and Georgia.[70] Similarly, the residential topography of Italian Harlem reproduced a localism that only its residents knew well. "Every section was so demarcated," a second-generation Italian American remembered. "They knew you, you knew them. From 103rd to about 106th Street it was all *Alta Italia* [northern Italians], mostly Piacentini. 106th to 108th was all Napoletani; 108th to 115th Basilicata. On 107th Street only Sicilians. On 108th Street mostly Calabrese. On 109th Street, where I came from, and 110th Neapolitans and Salernitani. On 112th Baresi. Going along to 116th, 117th, there was a mixture, mostly were Campanians."[71] In such a finely segmented society, different foodways, while imperceptible to outsiders, conveyed to insiders the cultural differences inscribed in places. Food habits and rituals (and the stereotypes linked to them) helped create a symbolic geography of different places, relationships, and identities that for immigrants was summed up in the notion of Italy. As a malleable element in almost every important relationship, food embodied for immigrants the different concentric geographic scales of "Italy"—hometown, region, and nation. "I could enter the neighborhood at one end and sample the air quality of the gravy," a son of immigrants remembered, "and the odds were that it would be about the same at the other end of the neighborhood, with the exception of the Sicilians, who were strange in just about every other department, too. They were much more violent than the Neapolitans and as far as their dialect went, we couldn't understand a word they were saying. They ate weird things; at least we Neapolitans thought so. They ate macaroni with pumpkin, and who the hell would do something like that?"[72]

For the most part, East Harlem residents considered spatial, cultural, and food boundaries as overlapping. The local geography of food replicated ethnocultural divisions, created an apparent group coherence and unity, and reinforced the sense of belonging to the community. Encounters with the other also typically started (and sometimes ended) with food. Orlando Guadalupe, the student of Covello, framed the differences that he encountered in the foods of the other: "The other day while I lost myself around the Italian neighborhood, I was attracted by the 'pizza' stands on almost every corner of the Italian market," Guadalupe noted.

> These stands offer a certain kind of big round, and flat pie made of wheat-flour and spread with cheese or meat and tomato sauce. People gather around to buy and eat them. These I compared with the similar stands in the Puerto Rican neighborhood; the difference being the sale of eatables. Puerto Ricans eat pork entrails while drinking liquors. The entrails—heart, kidneys, liver, etc.—are fried in grease. Weekends we find the Puerto Ricans drinking and consuming this type of food known as *cuchifrito*. . . . Entering a particular [Italian] restaurant, by which older folk frequent, I noticed that on every table where food was displayed large glasses of wine were also served. This wine drinking with food is a trait brought directly from Italy. Wine is a part of the Italian menu. Black coffee served in small cups—demitasse—is also served on their tables. The Puerto Ricans, the Irish, and the Negroes drink their coffee with milk, usually served in regular standard sized cups. Wine is not important in their menus. Puerto Ricans, so far as I have observed, eat their dessert before they drink their coffee, whereas, the Italians drink their black coffee first and then dessert. Usually the Italian dessert is composed of dried fruit such as oranges, apples and nuts. The Puerto Ricans have either canned fruit or cooked dessert."[73]

As Guadalupe noted, in just a few years Puerto Rican migrants created place and territory west of Park Avenue, transforming the urban landscape with previously unknown voices, sounds, colors, and tastes. They turned the streets of a once predominantly residential area into a busy center for food trade and consumption, opening *bodegas* (grocery stores) and *carnicerias* (butcher shops).[74] Home kitchens, restaurants, and street vendors filled the air with the smell of *arroz con gandules* (rice, pigeon peas, and pork), *arroz con pollo* (rice and chicken), *pasteles* (mashed green banana and meat wrapped in banana leaves), *tostones* (deep-fried sliced platanos), and *carne guisada* (meat stew). The unpublished research of the WPA Federal Writers' Project, "America Eats," reported that by the 1930s there were numerous community restaurants in El Barrio "patronized by a heterogeneous clientele of Latin-Americans, Spaniards, British West Indians, and African Americans": Pascual Quintana's El Carribe at 235 West 116th Street, where you could get *mofongo con chicharrones*, mashed green plantains mixed with mashed fried pig skin and covered with garlic, onion, and hot pepper sauce; or "El Favorito, . . . a well-known Puerto Rican eatery open twenty-four hours a day that sold rice and beans along with bread and butter for thirty-five cents."[75] In the market on Park Avenue between 110th and 116th Streets—later rechristened La Marqueta—avocados, mangos, papayas, guavas, garbanzos, platanos, and the other fruits and vegetables loved by Spanish-speaking migrants were for sale.[76] West Indian vendors cried loudly: "Yo tengo guineos! Yo tengo cocoas! Yo tengo piñas, tambien!" (I've got green bananas! I've got coconuts! I've got pineapples, too!)[77] Puerto Rican shoppers "came to the Marqueta not only to buy those items that could not be found in North American supermarkets but to indulge in a form of exchange that they or their forebears had known back on the island. One was assaulted by the pungent, exotic fragrances and earthy smells of fruit and other produce. A cacophony of noise and images."[78] As Italian immigrants had earlier done farther east and black migrants were trying to do north in Central Harlem, Puerto Rican newcomers surrounded themselves with distinctive and familiar foods, redefining the cultural map of the neighborhood and appropriating the streets for themselves in a successful narration of identity.[79]

Along these food boundaries there developed prejudices, aversions, and disgusts as well as curiosities, attractions, and desires to taste the exotic. The narratives about others that communities elaborated in their code of food were as much narratives of themselves, of their own needs, aspirations, and fears. Food narratives added elements to the flexible identities of ethnic groups in the great American city, which were shaped by relations with multiple, opposing others. Of all those relations, it was in group conflict that the connections between food, place, and cultural identity emerged most strongly. "Sometimes you don't fit in," Piri Thomas writes in his autobiography *Down These Mean Streets*. "Like if you're a Puerto Rican on an Italian block." Because of his dark skin and Spanish accent, young Thomas was often beaten up by Italian boys. One day, he recalls,

> Momma sent me off the stoop to the Italian Market on 115th Street and First Avenue, deep in Italian country. Man, that was stompin' territory, but I went. Ten minutes later I was on my way back with Momma's stuff. I got to the corner on First Avenue and 114th Street and crushed myself into Rocky and his fellas. "Well, fellas," Rocky said, "lookee who's here." "Say *paisan*," one guy said, "you even buying from us *paisans*, eh? You must wantta be Italian." Before I could bite that dopey tongue of mine, I said, "I wouldn't be a guinea on a motherfucking bet." . . . "Ya little sonavabitch, we'll kick the shit outta ya," said one guy, Tony, who had made a habit of asking me if I had any *sen-your-ritas* for sisters. . . . I heard the home cheers of "Yea, yea, bust that spic wide open!"[80]

Back home, trying to hide his bruises, Thomas was overwhelmed by great emotion and pride: "Momma was cooking, and the smell of rice and beans was beating the smell of Parmesan cheese from the other apartment."[81] Thomas's Proustian memory of food and self suggests its importance in his search for identity and resistance to the cages of urban racism. Certainly, it suggests that for him—as well as for Rocky, his friends, and the many others of East Harlem—it was *instinctive* to use food to articulate emotions, race, power, and place.

As cultural landmarks in the neighborhood, open food markets, grocery stores, *bodegas*, pizzerias, and restaurants were especially representative of different identities and, as such, easy objects of hostility from rival groups. The first notorious disturbance in a series of widely publicized Harlem riots occurred on July 28, 1926, and involved the destruction of most Puerto Rican *bodegas* in what was then Spanish Harlem, allegedly the work of local mobsters hired to do so by Jewish storeowners enraged with the competition from the newly arrived migrant businessmen. As a witness recalled, "Several stores owned by Puerto Ricans [were] attacked. The sidewalks in front of the bodegas were covered with shattered glass, rice, beans, plantains, and tropical vegetables. A *piragua* [shaved ice covered with fruit flavored syrup] cart was broken to bits on the corner, the gutter littered with broken bottles. Terror gripped El Barrio. The attack had left more than fifty people wounded, some critically."[82]

In 1935–36, the "Don't Buy Where You Can't Work" campaign in Harlem aimed at boycotting white-owned stores that refused to hire black workers or segregated them in menial occupations grew from a grassroots action to an organized movement. When the Italo-Ethiopian War sparked tensions between black and Italian communities, groups like the Consolidated Tenants League and the Harlem Labor Union led demonstrations against Italian-owned pushcarts, food shops, and restaurants located around 125th Street—the main shopping thoroughfare of Harlem.[83] After a pro-Ethiopian rally on the night of May 18, 1936, about four hundred protesters looted and devastated Patsy's Fish Market at 466 Lenox Avenue. After being dispersed by police, the mob attacked the fruit and vegetable shop of Joseph De Lucca at 368 Lenox Avenue.[84] On July 12, members of the Ethiopian Progressive Association destroyed the restaurant of Angelo Ruffalo.[85] The Harlem riots against Italian-owned stores and restaurants drove nearly all Italian food businesses from Central Harlem. The few restaurant and café owners who decided to remain changed the name and look of their businesses, removing from them any trace of *Italianità*.[86]

Even as they retreated behind the boundary of color, however, small Italian businesses continued to shape the unique foodscape and identity of Italian Harlem, fashioning the choreography of its streets with smells, sounds, colors, and signs as they had done since the beginning of the twentieth century.

Food, Place, Emotions, and the Making of Italian Harlem

An astonishing number of food retail businesses dotted the Italian Harlem landscape. In 1935, the block bounded by First Avenue, East 109th Street, East 110th Street, and Second Avenue hosted a macaroni shop, a pastry shop, an Italian deli, two grocery stores, a butcher shop, and a bread bakery, all Italian owned. There was a Jewish-owned restaurant on First Avenue; a butcher shop, two fruit and vegetable stores, and a restaurant, all Italian owned, on 109th Street; an Italian deli, a candy store, a butcher shop, and a grocery store, all Italian owned, on Second Avenue; and an Italian butcher shop and a Jewish live-poultry market on 110th Street.[87] Almost every block in the Italian section had its bakery, butcher shop, deli, grocery store, fruit and vegetable store, and candy store. In this mostly residential neighborhood, food retailing was one of the principal sources of jobs for residents.[88] Just as noteworthy were the social functions filled by food shops, markets, cafés, and restaurants, which nurtured a variety of interpersonal relations and infused streets and spaces with meaning. In her classic *The Death and Life of Great American Cities*, Jane Jacobs often used the case of East Harlem—before and after the massive public housing programs of the 1950s and 1960s that wiped most of them away—to illustrate the fundamental role that small independent businesses played in the neighborhood by monitoring street activities to improve safety and by fostering responsibility and loyalty toward the community.[89]

Since survival largely depended on the quality of the relations that their owners were able to maintain with their nearest customers, food stores and other small businesses were deeply involved in the everyday life of street, block, and community. Because of residential segmentation by immigrant regional and national origins, a shared ethnic background and the ability to develop comfortably familiar relations with the local clientele were essential resources for food entrepreneurs in Italian Harlem. The fact that some Jewish and Greek grocers learned to speak Neapolitan or Sicilian dialects illustrates the level of intimacy that food retailers and their immediate neighbors could achieve.[90] Also, being forced to sell food on credit to a mostly poor clientele meant that storeowners had to know enough about them to determine who could be trusted.[91] Another required skill of shopkeepers was the ability to deal with local mobsters who demanded payment to "protect" their stores, restaurants, and pushcarts and who would damage and then destroy the shops of those who failed to pay.[92] Despite the informal neighborhood watchdog service that organized crime provided (often a fond memory of life in the "old neighborhood"), the streets of East Harlem were still always a dangerous place for storeowners, who were among the few known to carry money. Storeowners looked for the solidarity of neighbors, often returning home accompanied by a customer they knew.[93] In turn, food shops provided social services for their neighbors. For example, grocery store and candy store telephones often served the entire population of the block.[94] The face-to-face relations established between small businessmen and the community are further illustrated by the fact that Italian regional mutual benefit associations and especially family networks supported the businesses of their *paesani* and family members most loyally. Italian Harlem boys complained about being forced by their parents to walk for blocks and blocks to shop for food in the store of one of their relatives.[95] For all these reasons, a sweeping change of population in a single block meant the sudden failure of many food stores: these microcommunities and the food institutions that helped create for them a sense of place and self-sufficiency flourished or fell together.[96]

The public markets and grocery stores where Italian food was sold were especially important as gendered experiences. In a community that imposed layers of restrictions on women's use of public space, shopping for food—along with preparing and sharing it—was an accepted sphere of women's visibility and sociability. In the oral histories of Italian immigrant women to New York collected in the project "World of Our Mothers," their daily shopping expeditions for food were the only routine activities to take place outside the home.[97] Shopping helped immigrant women not only to develop social relations but also to grasp the uses and meaning of urban space. This was especially true for newly arrived women. One who came to East Harlem from Sicily in 1924, for example, had suffered intensely from displacement and hostility: "Mrs. X cried a great deal at having to leave her familiar surroundings. . . . Mrs. X was obliged to do her own marketing whereas in the old country the vendors brought the foods that she wanted to the very kitchen. Also, she was truly amazed at the price of foods and other articles, because she could not help but figure out the amount of Italian 'lire' that she paid.

In the streets she was constantly afraid because there were too many automobiles that whizzed by very fast." However,

> after about a year, a family moved into the apartment next door to that of the Italian family, and it was soon discovered that the new tenants had come from Italy too, but they had been in New York a long time. These people were very friendly, and soon there developed the first real friendship that Mrs. X had known in the new land. She thought less and less of the old country. She and the new friend would go out together during school hours, and do their shopping together, and this duty had become a very pleasant one. Little by little she learned the names of the food articles, and patronized the shops where other Italian women went. She was getting to like more and more the small apartment, and began to realize that hot and cold running water were indeed very useful, just like the peculiar black gas stove, which at first had put fear into her.[98]

Geographer Kevin Lynch first theorized that urban dwellers like Mrs. X experienced the city's space by moving daily along certain *paths*. Along these paths, Lynch argued, they recognize strongly visible *nodes*, "strategic spots," or "points," which might be junctions at the crossing of paths, or "thematic concentrations" that help urban dwellers organize large areas around them, including spatial landmarks upon which they increasingly rely. The familiarity with nodes and landmarks allows people to take hold of urban space and shape a subjective *image of the city*.[99]

In Italian Harlem, the large number and variety of food places served as landmarks along the daily paths traveled by Italian Harlem residents, and helped them learn and organize the bustling urban space around them. The main "node" of the area—"the core, focus, and symbol of a region"—was the open-air pushcart market on First Avenue, the neighborhood's principal north–south thoroughfare, between 110th Street and 116th Street.[100] The market was formed in 1898, when Italian peddlers who pushed their fruit and vegetable carts across Harlem began to take the corners of First Avenue and 110th Street.[101] At the time, all over the East Side of Manhattan, pushcart markets were becoming the institutions that defined every Jewish and Italian immigrant neighborhood. Their popularity came from the convergence of high demand for inexpensive food by immigrants in densely populated areas and the overrepresentation of newcomers in a demanding, scarcely profitable, and often illegal occupation—peddling—that required minimal startup capital. One of the most important of the institutions of immigrant New York, the First Avenue pushcart market was well into the 1930s the vital commercial and spatial center of Italian Harlem. Colorful, noisy, and exotic, the market made the six-block tract of First Avenue and its side streets the busiest in the neighborhood: even brick-and-mortar food shops benefited from the flood of people shopping the market.[102] Before dawn, peddlers stocked at the wholesale Harlem Market, on First Avenue between 100th and 106th Streets. In front of their wooden carts, they proclaimed the quality of their goods in a "half dozen Italian dialects: Sicilian, Calabrese, Neapolitan, Apulian, and so forth" and sold fruits and vegetables that were unknown elsewhere in the city, such as broccoli, cauliflower, zucchini, eggplants, artichokes, prickly pears, and many types of table olives. Other vendors sold inexpensive clothes, plates, kitchenware, and toys.[103] The pushcart market gave the neighborhood identity and spirit, and local shoppers quickly learned its complex topography and semantics. "Every morning my mother would take the shoppin' bag from 116th Street and walk all the way down to 111th to see what the story is," a second-generation Italian American man explained.

> After 111th, she comes back and starts buyin', because she might have figured that at 116th it was more expensive than 114th or 111th. All the aristocrats would go at 115th and 116th. My mother had to go at 113th and 114th. Everything was cheaper there. Ya hadda know how to shop. It was a show—the Jewish merchant and Italian, it's a riot. . . . Some of the Jews, they never wanted to lose their first customer. . . . They would lose money, but if they lost their first customer, that day was gone. So everybody would go early to be the first customer. "Wait till he opens. No, me first."[104]

The complex experience of the open market was not just a visual one. Odors, flavors, surfaces, and sounds influence the perception of the environment, the emotional relations that city dwellers establish with places, whether feelings of belonging or estrangement. These *multisensual* encounters are, of course, heavily subjective and culturally specific: they convey meanings through a variety of signs understood differently by outsiders and community insiders. In fact, to most middle-class observers of the time, Italian Harlem was a dense, overbuilt area of monotonous ugliness, in an unvarying landscape of poverty, decaying tenements and vacant lots, and piles of garbage abandoned everywhere on curbs. Even human activities seemed to outside observers to have no direction or meaning. But area residents lived a different reality. Individuals pictured different "mental maps" of their neighborhood. There was a topography of social class: 116th Street from Third to Pleasant Avenues, where local professionals lived, was considered the most attractive section, while streets to the south were known to be the least desirable.[105] There was a topography of race and ethnicity, block by block, which was essential to roving youth gangs.[106] There was a secret topography of courtship and sexuality that took lovers to certain corners of Central Park and Jefferson Park.[107] A topography of leisure located bocce courts for the elderly, the best walls for stickball for boys, and the safest spots for swimming in the East River for children.[108] A topography of survival and theft named places to steal wood and coal from the railroad and pilfer the crates to resell for a few nickels or to hide the fruits stolen from pushcarts.[109] A sacred topography marked the shrines and churches of different confessions, whether the path of the procession of the Madonna of Mount Carmel or the place on 106th Street where the Giglio of Saint Paulinus was "danced."[110] Alongside, topography of popular beliefs and superstition mapped the surroundings of the Consolidated Gas Company's tank on 110th Street, where the air was supposed to treat whooping cough in children, or the "damned house" on the corner of 108th Street and First Avenue, which many thought inhabited by the ghosts of the fifty-five victims of killings that had been perpetrated there.[111]

Italian Harlem was also mapped by class-based olfactory geographies. To middle-class visitors, Italian Harlem meant the "stench of the poor."[112] In the early 1890s, newspapers reported on the reeking air that disgusted middle-class residents of Harlem when they passed through the quarters where the newly arrived Italians lived. The lowlands along the East River were covered with the stench of open latrines in the back of shanties and the omnipresent sweet-and-sour stink of deep-fried garlic.[113] In the 1930s, the smellscape of Italian Harlem was still said to evoke the mysterious stink that resulted from the "urine-draft of air that move[d] up the stairs" from "unforgettable toilets" and the soaked "garbage [that] litter[ed] the gutters." The open market on First Avenue was noted above all for the rot that it left behind every night.[114]

Describing the aromas that also characterized his Lower East Side, the actor and singer Eddie Cantor questioned the ultimate value of the deodorized streets prevalent in middle-class urban reform projects. "There had long been a movement on the East Side for fresh air," Cantor writes.

> But the East Siders were not clear on the subject of air and could never quite distinguish it from food vapors. Each street had its own favorite flavor which it cherished with a certain local and civic pride. If, for instance, the tang of the herring was missing from Hester Street, the Hester Streeters thought they were walking in a vacuum. Similarly, the Italian quarter had its air pockets filled with garlic; under Williamsburg Bridge blew strong fish breezes, and no rich supply of ozone was complete without the ingredients of a dozen stables and the thousand and one fumes arising from vegetable pushcarts, poultry and meat markets, pickle works, and refuse cans. . . . Under such circumstances the uninitiated uptowners who knew nothing about air and described it as a tasteless, odorless, colorless, meaningless substance . . . were a crowd of visionary reformers who were trying to tamper with the fundamental laws of nature. Their insidious propaganda that windows should be opened and air allowed into homes was an obvious plot to destroy the home. For each little flat manufactured a thick, tasty atmosphere of its own gravy, which must never be allowed to escape or mingle with the aromas of street.[115]

Italian Harlem residents also managed a much more elaborate olfactory palette of their neighborhood than outsiders possibly could. Their ability to catch the many sweet, sour, pungent, and spiced odors of their streets was important in imbuing space with meaning, conferring identity to space, and making it familiar. "There was the reassuring fragrance of warm bread," one of them recalled about the street where he lived, "the heady aroma of roasting coffee, the musty smell of wooden barrels filled with wine, the pungent odors of ripe olives and anchovies in brine, of gorgonzola and provolone cheese and hanging salami."[116]

Immigrants had to cope with the transition to the strange and often depressing streets and apartments of Italian Harlem, where they experienced hard work, unemployment, family crises, violence, disease, and death. Tastes, flavors, smells, and other food signs helped them manage their estranged environment through a system of meaningful symbols and places. Indeed, the connections between food and place worked most intensely at the level of emotions. The stronger the individual's emotional involvement with people, spaces, and familiar tastes and smells, the more inseparable these three dimensions became. In the common narrative of Italian Harlem, people celebrated the uniqueness of their own family food cultures. Women in the family, in particular, were thought to be the keepers and the embodiment of a specific, irreproducible tradition. Most importantly, the elements of this narrative of food—people, family, and community—were set in emotionally charged places. "My mother was the greatest cook in the world," a second-generation Italian American man recalled.

> Everybody thought their mother was the best. I don't know why they think that, but my mother was the best. It was a fact. Her bread was the best-smelling bread in the whole world. When she made bread, the whole house smelled—three floors. Everybody knew that Antoinette was making bread. My sister lived on the first floor of our building. My grandmother was on the second floor, and we were on the third. Years ago when I came home from church, my sister would make meatballs, and I would steal a couple. My grandmother would make meatballs, and I would take from her, and by the time I got to my mother's I was full. My mother made good meatballs, but my grandmother had something different in hers. I think it was more garlic. . . . There was a woman next door named Jenny. She was Neapolitan. Her meatballs were different. They were good, but they weren't as good as my mother's or my sister's or my grandmother's.[117]

The symbolic significance of home food rituals also depended on the integration of food sharing and family gathering in the home. The ritual Sunday dinner, celebrated in one of the households of the extended family—*la famiglia*—consolidated a seamless network of familiar faces, voices, places, tastes, and smells. As another man remembered, "We didn't go out to eat. We ate either at our house, or Cousin Ronnie's, or Uncle Dom's, or wherever. My grandmother would start making her meat sauce at seven in the morning on Sunday and within five or six hours that smell would be all through the house, covering everything—clothing, furniture, appliances—and then it would go out the front door and into the streets, to mix with the aroma of neighboring meat sauces."[118]

The relationship of residents to the ethnic space they inhabited was grounded in the sensual experiences of food, so much that its code of tastes and smells became a powerful, portable toolkit for understanding the world outside the enclave. Covello experienced this himself during a visit to an Italian section of Greenwich Village. Walking to meet the violent father of one of his students, his nervousness was relieved by a familiar smell: "As I entered the downstairs hall and caught the odor of garlic and tomato sauce, I felt right at home." The sensorium of food in Harlem also helped immigrants articulate their own transnational narratives. "When I'm in Italy I want to be in America," a man complained to Covello. "When I'm there I always dream of home. I remember these dirty, ugly streets; these squalid houses, the smell of *baccalà* (dried cod fish). I thought of the time I slept in my native vineyard, how the larks or the crowing roosters woke me up. I saw the sea and the clouds. Oh, I tell you it is a difficult thing to forget this country (Italy)."[119]

Food, finally, played an essential role in the immigrants' domestication of space during the most important diasporic cultural event in Italian Harlem: the annual Feast of Our Lady of Mount Carmel, an annual event also widely celebrated throughout southern Italy. In New York, the annual procession of the statue of the Madonna through the streets of Italian Harlem was the heart of a collective performance of the strong symbolic connection between food, place(s), and identity.[120] In the 1930s, tens of thousands swelled the streets decorated with Italian and U.S. flags. Bands played Italian religious and patriotic songs. The procession of the statue of the Madonna, protector of Harlem's Italians, wound through streets from Pleasant to Second Avenues and from 111th to 116th Streets, where sidewalks were lined with sellers of watermelon, sausages and peppers, nougat, and ice cream; vendors wormed their way into the crowd with pizzas, *zeppole* (deep-fried dough dusted with sugar), roasted chickpeas and fava beans, and cotton candy. As the Madonna was carried through the streets, these foods reminded immigrants of their home overseas and reclaimed the place as *their* place. For Italian participants, the feast was a ritualized experience that forged a close relation between food consumption, a sense of place, and collective identity.

Through food, immigrants in Italian Harlem tried and to a large extent succeeded in humanizing a place that at first seemed hostile and disturbing, making it meet their needs and fit their diasporic view of the world. They used the tastes, flavors, sights, and odors of food to re-create a nonplace (Italy) that was for them the repository of both unsustainable poverty and authentic humanity. Food was a narrative that reconnected them to that imagined place as it also created a place (Harlem) that they could legitimately call home.

Many Happy Returns: Food, Memory, and the Creation of Cara Harlem

This successful construction of a working-class consumer culture, however, would not survive the urban changes of the 1940s and afterward. The eventual demise of the Italian Harlem foodscape signaled more effectively than anything else the end of what the neighborhood had meant for the community as a sense of social space.

The community and its own aspirations were often the source of those changes. Many immigrants, and more so their children, looked forward to the day they could leave Harlem. Many had already left the neighborhood in the 1920s and 1930s. After World War II, the outflow of migrants became a swollen river.[121] The urge to better themselves once again by moving was enabled by such incentives as the GI Bill and new urban policies aimed at routing the white middle-class (including white ethnics) toward the suburbs and turning neighborhoods like East Harlem into subsidized low-income public housing zones for people of color.[122] Departing Italians blamed urban renewal and racial change for their decision to leave—and for the loss of their neighborhood and its painstakingly constructed foodscape. By leaving family and community behind, they also abandoned the ideology that had protected them from the middle-class American values they were now ready to embrace: *the family that eats together.*

Urban renewal had already begun to damage the Italian Harlem foodscape before the effects of racial and ethnic succession could be fully felt in the area. The first significant blow was struck against the neighborhood's open markets in the mid-1930s, when the La Guardia administration, reflecting New Deal reform politics, made the elimination of pushcarts a top priority in the modernization of the city. In Harlem, as elsewhere in the city, peddlers were accused of causing traffic jams, being a threat to public health (because of both the garbage they produced and the food they sold), and lowering the value of real estate.[123] As early as 1891, Harlem's merchants and street cleaners mobilized against the opening of the new wholesale Harlem Market near the East River.[124] In the 1920s, the Harlem Board of Commerce repeatedly—if unsuccessfully—fought to eliminate street peddling in the area.[125] In 1935, however, the opening of the Bronx Terminal Market, which replaced Harlem Market as the wholesale fruit and vegetable source for Upper Manhattan, stripped East Harlem of one of its few significant economic activities and condemned the site between the river, First Avenue, and 100th and 106th Streets to clearance.[126] To La Guardia, the presence of pushcarts in the streets was incompatible with a modern economy based on the rapid movement of commodities and consumers and the creation of regulated shopping centers.[127] The mayor proposed the construction of indoor markets to house pushcart vendors at a minimal monthly rent as the best solution to clearing the streets of the East Side of Manhattan. The first indoor market was in East Harlem: the Park Avenue Market, a glass and steel structure built underneath the New York Central Railroad between East 111th and East 116th Streets, was inaugurated in 1936. The new, two-hundred-thousand-dollar enclosed marketplace could accommodate only 141 of the 200 vendors who used to work in the Park Avenue open market alone. On opening day, La Guardia was booed in disapproval. Some in the crowd, though, applauded when the mayor argued, "The market was my idea and I had to fight to put it through. Today you have graduated from pushcart peddlers into merchants."[128] Efforts to close the other open markets in the area continued. The First Avenue market, so important in giving the area its Italian flavor and identity, was subjected to a restrictive policy on licenses and more active policing. Already suffering from competition and neighborhood change, the market died out in the 1940s, making room for the growing rush of cars and trucks up the avenue.

The wider Italian community reacted ambiguously to the end of the pushcart era. While many residents were frustrated by the loss of the open market, others had protested against it. A group of local mothers asked Covello to help them close the First Avenue open market, making the same arguments once offered by middle-class outsiders:

> Not only are these pushcarts causing accidents, they are also very unsanitary. The streets are full of flies and at night when they leave, there are about thirty ash-cans on the sidewalks full of garbage. Now that school is over, we dread having the children around in such a filthy street and most of us cannot afford sending them away. We have signed petitions to have them eliminated but up to the present time nothing has been done. We therefore ask you to try to do something to have these pushcarts taken away from our streets and make it a better and safer place to live in.[129]

Cleaning food and its odors from the streets seemed to many Italians a necessary step in their path toward respectability, which, together with material progress, the creation of a unique disaporic domesticity, and their increasing differentiation from "nonwhite" groups, was bringing them closer to the cultural values of the urban middle class.

Also controversial was Italian support for the construction of low-rent public housing projects in East Harlem. After Congress passed the United States Housing Act in 1937 providing federal money for massive urban redevelopment, the La Guardia administration pushed for the construction of public housing in densely populated areas identified as slums, which were seen as the source of disease, crime, and demoralization among the poor. Slum clearance and the construction of low-rent housing for "respectable" working-class families were thought to solve most of the problems of the city's poor. Once again, because of Marcantonio's and Covello's lobbying, East Harlem was chosen as the site of some of the earliest projects of the New York City Housing Authority (NYCHA), the agency in charge of public housing. The area between First Avenue, East 102nd Street, East 105th Street, and the East River Drive, once occupied by the Harlem Market, was totally demolished, and in 1941 East Harlem had the new 1,170-unit, racially integrated East River Houses, the first high-rise public housing project to be built in New York City. However, these successful beginnings were undone by World War II and its social and political aftermath and by the deaths of La Guardia (1947) and Marcantonio (1954). In the 1950s, the powerful urban planner Robert Moses—formerly La Guardia's parks commissioner—designated East Harlem a condemned area to be razed to the ground and rebuilt with low-income public housing for dispossessed minorities, while upper-working-class and middle-income families were encouraged to disperse to the suburbs. Thirteen more "megablocks" had been built in East Harlem by 1961. As poor blacks and Puerto Ricans from other areas moved to East Harlem as tenants of the new "tower in the city" projects, the remaining Italians, whose income often made them ineligible to apply, fled. "In came the bulldozers," one resident recalled in 1966, "and out went the Italians."[130]

Slum clearance not only demolished tenement blocks; it also destroyed a foodscape. Some fifteen hundred independent shops were destroyed and never replaced, as NYCHA decided in 1944 to abandon its original plan for including stores on the first floors of projects, claiming that it did not want to compete with free enterprise.[131] The building of the Benjamin Franklin Houses alone required the removal of fourteen grocery stores, fourteen candy stores, eleven bakeries, seven fruit and vegetable stores, seven restaurants, five butchers, three cheese shops, and two egg shops in a six-block area. At night, the surrounding streets, once illuminated by store signs, were now gloomy and empty. Storeowners, including many who lived outside the neighborhood, formed committees against slum clearance, but their protest was ignored.[132]

Along with love, fear, hatred, and nostalgia, the emotional geography and history of Italians in East Harlem also included another important sentiment: guilt. Guilt was the paramount emotion associated with the idea of leaving for better and safer areas and by default turning the place into yet another nonplace, devoid of Italians and charged only with feelings of loss. To deal with this feeling, the many who left rationalized the loss of Cara Harlem as something beyond their control. Like a betrayed lover, Italian Harlemites blamed the men they had long worshipped, La Guardia, Marcantonio, and Covello, for "bringing the Puerto Ricans in," in a desperate attempt to deny their own willingness to go.[133] But the mourning for a lost home so painstakingly constructed was again articulated in memories of food and geography. Food was a forceful narrative of the "history" of Italian Harlem, its tastes and smells connecting emotional relationships with sentiments for place. To the interviewer who asked her if she returned to the old neighborhood, an immigrant woman explained: "I've got a house over there, but I don't wanna live over there." She went on to suggest who was to blame for the disappearance of her community. "There are Spanish people there now. Before there were all Italian people, all *Paisano* in the house. I miss them, because I used to go over there, and smell the Italian cookin' in the hall. Now no more. I don't have nothing to do there."[134] Another old-timer "reminisced about running through the unlocked apartments, where pots of pasta sauce bubbled on every stove and the oppressive heat forced them to sleep on the fire escapes. 'Everybody had nothing,' he said. 'Yet we had everything.'"[135]

Besides scapegoating and blame, another strategy for countering guilt was the pilgrimage. Weekly returns to what remained of Italian Harlem to buy Italian products and the yearly expedition to the Feast of the Madonna of Mount Carmel were always punctuated by food, as the most immediate, sensual reconnection with a lost past, place, and identity. In the late 1960s, the few remaining Italian grocers admitted that, as "one by one, the old families [were] going," any of their shops "now [did] 60 percent of its business with former residents who stop[ped] on their way to their new homes in the Bronx, Queens, or Westchester. They [came] back for the fruits and vegetables they [could not] get elsewhere."[136] "We come together to express loyalty to the past," echoed Rev. Terzo Vinci, opening the 1986 Mount Carmel festival. "It is a past that may not be here physically, but it is in our hearts. Some memories are very joyful, and some are so sad. But the idea of remembering is important. For when we remember, we start to live again." The celebrants, from all over the New York region as well as places like Florida and California, greeted the annual feast of the Madonna as the occasion "to recall days of stickball and checkers and savor again the prosciutto bread and the lemon ices that never taste[d] so good anywhere else."[137]

In this geography of remembering and losing the remaining landmarks—which by the closing of the century could be counted on the fingers of one hand: Rao's restaurant, Patsy's pizzeria, Morrone's bakery, Claudio's barber shop, and Farenga's funeral home—functioned as outposts in enemy territory, shrines to be visited in the sweet-and-sour mood of nostalgia. The few Italians who still lived there were accordingly revered as defenders of the neighborhood—mythical figures who reignited place with meaning, guaranteeing that Italian was still spoken, the annual feast held, and Italian food prepared for the returnees. These modern pilgrims had left like everybody else, except for a few "heroes" or "saints." They might have lost a little of their humanity in the leaving, but they could return to recover some of what they had lost, disguised in the sound of crackling Italian bread right out of the oven or in the greasy smoke of sizzling sausage. Cara Harlem was the last of the multiple and intertwining geographies of belonging that Italian Harlem immigrants crafted through food. Like Italian Harlem and "Italy," Cara Harlem was a place constructed in experience, memory, and emotion, at the intersection of the local and the global, in the language of food and taste.

The distinctive food patterns that developed in the family and the community depended in fact on a global system of food importing, production, and distribution. The food choices of Italians in the diaspora were conditioned by such factors as the availability of foodstuffs in the marketplace, by competing narratives of the quality of imported and domestic food products, and the role of a large and important Italian American food trade. The market conditions that influenced the formation, survival, and success of Italian American foodways are the subject matter of the next three chapters. The first of them will deal with the production of Italian-style food in New York and the rest of the United States.

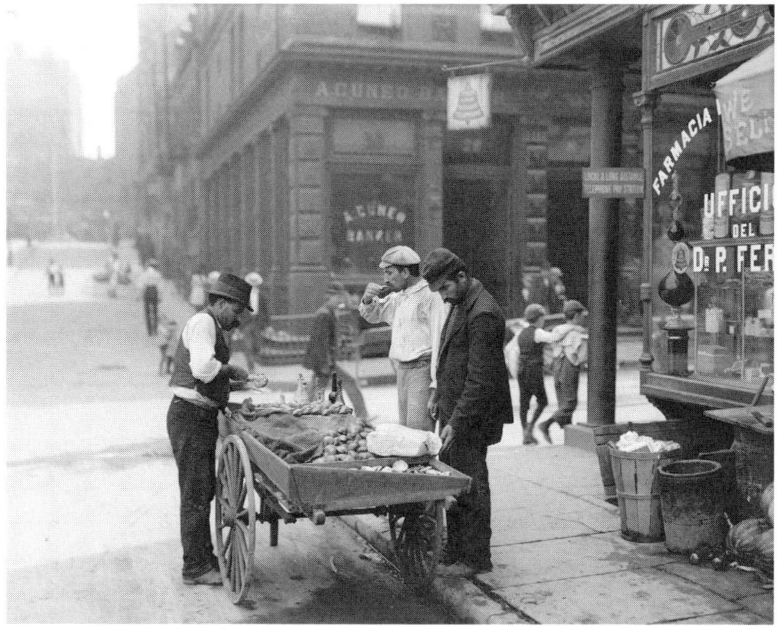

1. An Italian clam seller on Mulberry Street, ca. 1905. At the turn of the twentieth century, thousands of otherwise unskilled Italian immigrants peddled foods of all kinds in the streets of New York. In later years, the Italian dominance in the food business helped the community maintain culinary self-sufficiency and familiar food habits at the same time that it created a strong link between food and Italian identity. Library of Congress, Prints & Photographs Division, Detroit Publishing Company Collection, LC-D401-13642.

2. Italian bread peddlers, Mulberry Street, New York, ca. 1905. Often condemned by reformers as unhealthy and uneconomical, the practice of selling and eating food on the street helped transform bleak tenement-house areas into neighborhoods clearly known by residents and nonresidents alike as Italian (Little Italies). Library of Congress, Prints & Photographs Division, Detroit Publishing Company Collection, LC-DIG-ppmsca-4a09005.

3. The pushcart market of Mulberry Street, ca. 1905. The open markets of New York's Italian neighborhoods were both commercial and cultural centers of immigrant life. This image reveals the mixed feelings of danger and excitement that the view of the crowd flooding Little Italy's thoroughfare (supposedly typical of a European city) aroused among middle-class Americans. Library of Congress, Prints & Photographs Division, Detroit Publishing Company Collection, LC-D401-12683.

4. The pushcart market on First Avenue between East 110th and East 116th, looking south from East 116th, ca. 1905. First developed spontaneously at the end of the nineteenth century, this street market was the busiest spot in Italian Harlem until the early 1940s, when it finally fell victim to Mayor Fiorello La Guardia's campaign to modernize the city by forcing street vendors into new, enclosed, "sanitary" public markets. Library of Congress, Prints & Photographs Division, LC-DIG-ggbain-03087.

5. Lewis Hine, *An Italian Family Has Supper, East Side, New York City, 1915.* Hine's photograph vividly represents the generational drama staged every night around the immigrant family table in Italian Harlem between 1910 and 1930—a ritual that would evolve into a distinctive Italian ethnic domesticity and conviviality.

Photography Collection, Miriam and Ira D. Wallach Division of Art, Prints, and Photographs, New York Public Library, Astor, Lenox and Tilden Foundations.

6. Italian women and child at the corner of First Avenue and East 108th Street, May 23, 1934. Food provided women in Italian Harlem opportunities to take their place in the public sphere, from shopping to such solidarity-building activities as cooking for family, friends, and even fellow political militants. Many women were also peddlers of fruit and vegetables in the streets of Italian Harlem.

Photo by Percy Loomis Sperr © Milstein Division, New York Public Library.

7. Italian fruit and vegetable vendor, East Harlem, ca. 1935.

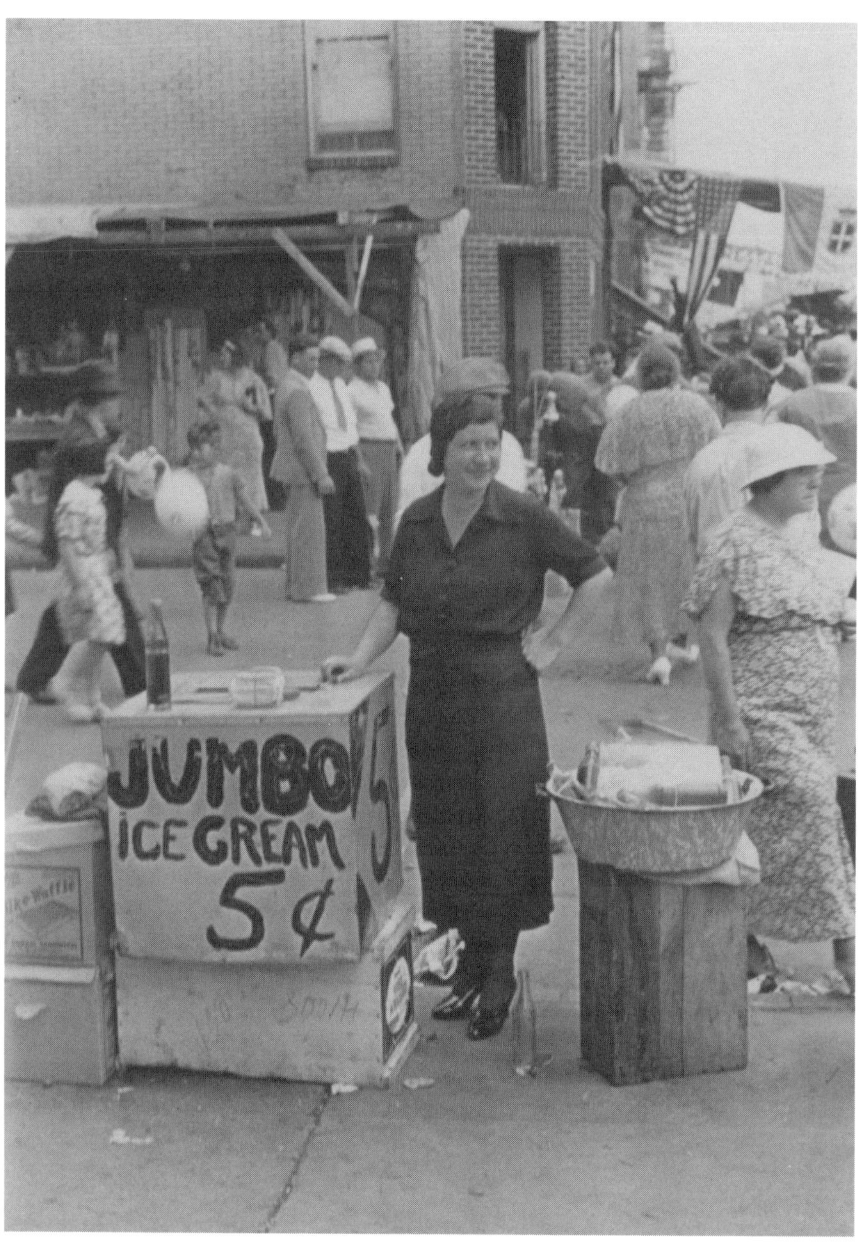

8. "Feast of Our Lady of Mt. Carmel: A siren with the euphonious name of Theresa Cararabella stands with her ice cream and waffles on the S.W. corner of Pleasant Avenue and 115th Street," July 16, 1935. The annual Feast of Our Lady of Mt. Carmel, held in mid-July, was by the 1930s the largest Italian religious celebration in the United States, attended by tens of thousands of Italians from all over the city and region. The feast was an occasion for consuming large amounts of food, whether in extended family banquets at home, at street stalls, or in local restaurants. Eating familiar food during the feast was an important communal reconnection with migration and settlement. Amid the celebrations, the smells and tastes of Italian food helped reclaim the neighborhood as the immigrants' place in America.

Photo by Percy Loomis Sperr © Milstein Division, New York Public Library.

9. “Man in front of pasta store—spaghetti hanging in window ‘Macaroni 8¢.’ Mothers with small children,” 1937. In turn-of-the-twentieth-century Italy, pasta was the food of the lower classes of Naples and other cities. In New York, pasta became the staple of the Italian American diet thanks to importers and domestic manufacturers who supplied this cheap, filling, and easy to prepare product. In this shop, fresh spaghetti dries above stacks of canned tomatoes, another basic ingredient of Italian American cooking that most immigrants became familiar with only in America. WPA Federal Writers’ Project Photographs Collection. Courtesy NYC Municipal Archives.

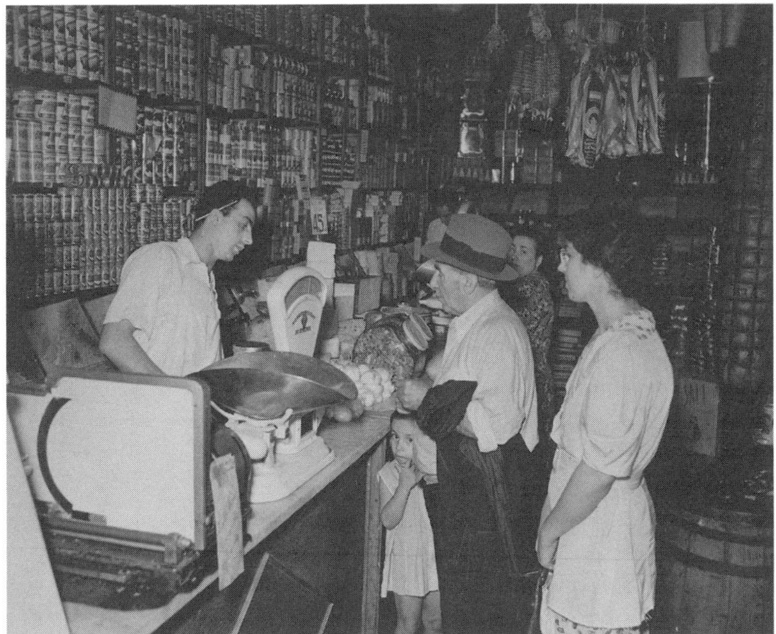

10. “Italians in New York buying groceries. Clerk waiting on Italian customers, very true to type,” 1937. Italian immigrants used food to construct an ideology of the Italian family in their new home. The salami, olive oil, and cheese displayed here were the staples of a Italian cuisine that took shape during the interwar period. WPA Federal Writers’ Project Photographs Collection. Courtesy NYC Municipal Archives.

11. “Italian grocer in the First Avenue market at Tenth Street,” January 1943. This image vividly conveys the great variety of foods that Italians in New York could use to create and maintain their diasporic food habits. Some of these foods were produced by Italian immigrants in the United States, while others were imported from Italy and other countries in a globalized network of Italian food production and consumption. Library of Congress, Prints & Photographs Division, FSA/OWI Collection, LC-USW3-014502-D.

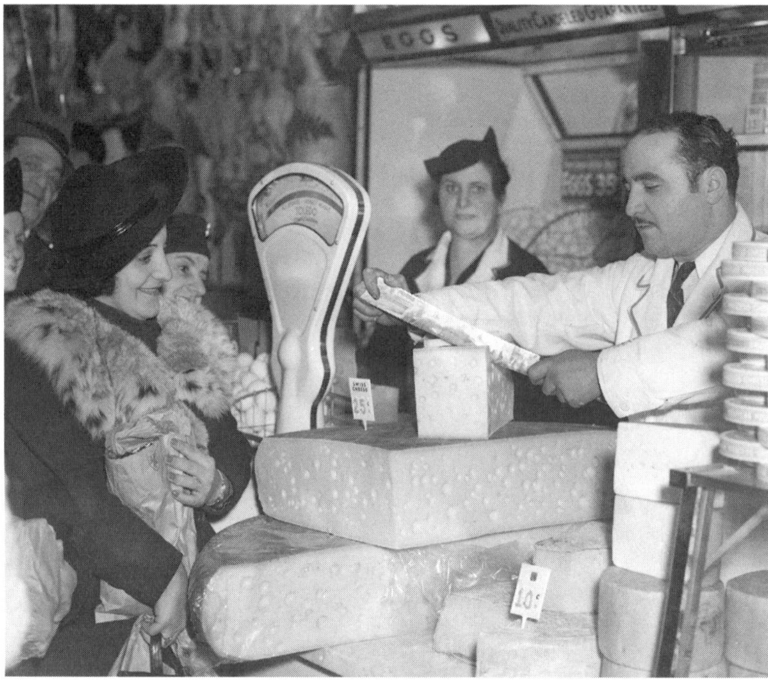

12. “Italian vendor at the First Avenue Market slicing cheese for a customer,” 1938. Library of Congress, Prints & Photographs Division, NYWT&S Collection, LC-DIG-ppmsca-12693.

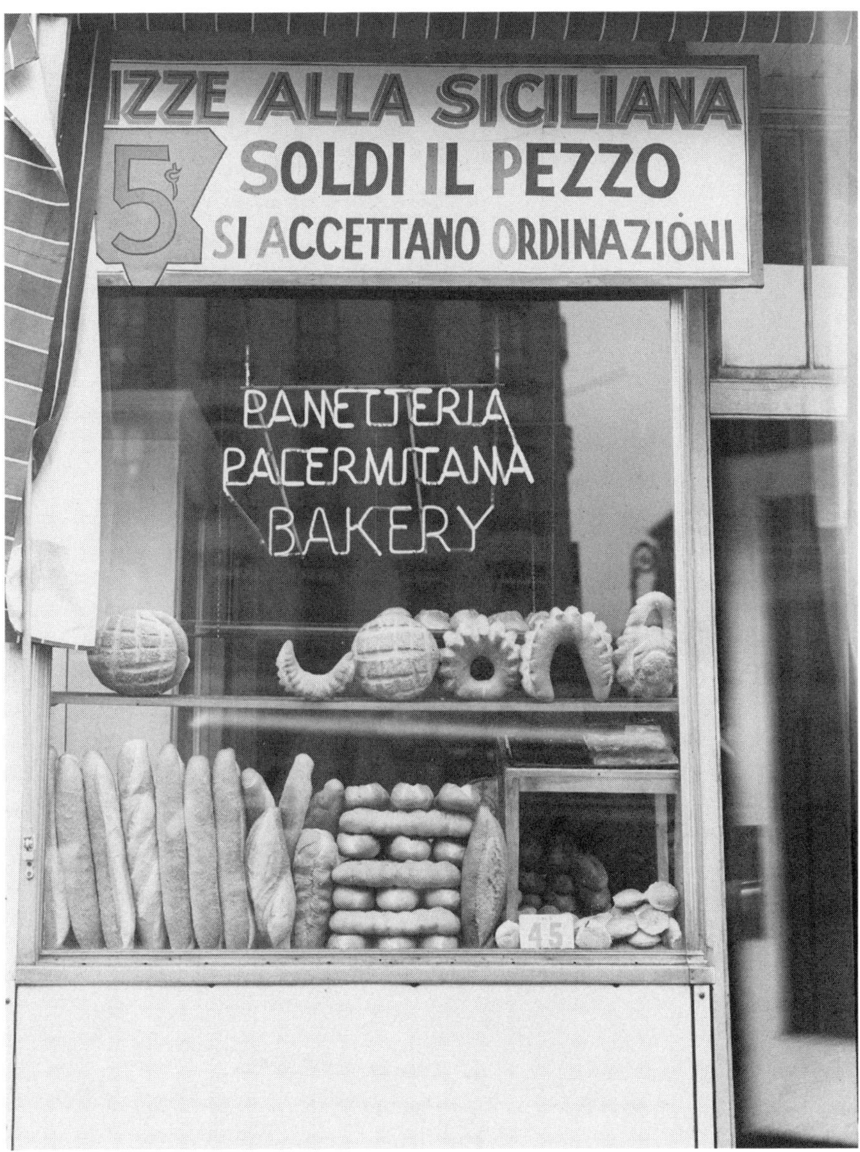

13. "Italian bakery of First Avenue between Tenth and Fourteenth Streets," February 1943. The storefront of this Sicilian bakery in the East Village displays the many shapes of the Italian "staff of life." The different regional and seasonal varieties of bread helped create a distinctive material culture. Library of Congress, Prints & Photographs Division, FSA/OWI Collection, LC-USW3-015096-D.

GENTE MAGRA E DI POCA SALUTE

Se volete ingrassare e stare bene non state a pigliare medicine

MANGIATE I MACCHERONI CARUSO BRAND

Una Settimana di prova vi convincerà.

I MACCHERONI CARUSO BRAND

sono manifatturati dalla parte più nutritiva dei migliori grani duri e lo speciale metodo seguito nell'estrarre la parte nutritiva dal grano e manifatturarne Maccheroni fa dei **MACCHERONI CARUSO BRAND**

L'ALIMENTO PIU' NUTRITIVO.

I MACCHERONI CARUSO BRAND

Non possono naturalmente essere venduti allo stesso prezzo degli altri, ma sebbene apparentemente più cari,

CONSIDERANDO IL NUTRIMENTO CHE SE NE RICAVA ESSI SONO L'ALIMENTO PIU' A BUON MERCATO.

I veri Maccheroni Caruso Brand sono in pacchi da una Libbra e ogni pacco è sigillato coll'etichetta che ha la firma ed il ritratto del Comm. Enrico Caruso.

GUARDATEVI DALLE CONTRAFFAZIONI

I MACCHERONI CARUSO BRAND SONO IN VENDITA PRESSO I SEGUENTI:

NEW YORK CITY

C. BASILEA & CO.	507 West Broadway
L. BERGONZI & CO.	134 Bleecker St.
CAFIERO BROS	3519 Broadway
CAMPANIA IMPORTING CO.	64 Gansewoort St.
CELLAS' INC.	427 West Broadway
L. DE BELLIS	2472 Arthur Ave.
FAIR, LENNON & CO.	32 Gansewoort St.
FORMIGLI BROS. & CO.	33 Downing St.
GENOVA IMPORTING CO.	34 Carmine St.
ITALIAN IMPORTING CO.	426 Washington St.
LATORRACA BROS	206 Spring St.
R. MARTORELLI	44 Mulberry St.
V. ORLANDO	102 Bayard St.
P. PANTANO	40 Mulberry St.
PARODI, ERMINIO & CO.	53½ West Broadway
P. PASTENE & CO.	152 Franklin St.
L. RAIMONDI	314 West 43rd St.
H. RESSLER	71½ Mulberry St.
R. ROMEO & CO.	374 Washington St.
SCARSI BROS.	109 Mcdougal St.
A. J. TRASSO & CO.	35 - 6th Ave.

BROOKLYN, N. Y.

M. AJELLO CO.	74 Sedgwick St.
ANGIOLILLO BROS.	60 Sackett St.
B. BENDIN, INC.	1020 Wallabout Market
J. BRUCK	1018 Wallabout Market
LEO FEDER	1013 Wallabout Market
JACOBS & COHEN	13 Wallabout Market
MAROTTA & CELLA	4 Wallabout Market
FRANK MOSCA, INC.	265 Flushing Ave.
S. MONTAPERTO	186 Sackett St.
G. SASSO & SONS	1003 Wallabout Market
SCHIAFFINO GROCERY CO.	1010 Wallabout Market
SCKOLNIK & LANGER	3 Washington Ave.

JERSEY CITY, N. J.

G. CRESCI	601 Palisade Avenue

HOBOKEN, N. J.

L. GARIBALDI & SON	516 Jefferson Street
C. D'ONOFRIO	4th & Madison Sts.

HARTFORD, CONN.

C. CALIO	83 Temple Street

BOSTON, MASS.

ALBERTI IMP. & EXP. CO.	57 Fulton St.
SCARAMELLI & CO.	145 Fulton St.
J. R. DAGNINO & CO.	61 Fulton St.
L. AVANZINO BROS.	154 Commercial St.
ORIENT COFFEE IMP. CO.	134 Commercial St.
P. PASTENE CO.	69 Fulton St.
SAMUEL ABRAMSON	191 North St.
RE BROS.	173 Fulton St.
G. SAVARESE & SONS	Battery Street.
ROMA IMPORTING CO.	161 Fulton St.

THE ATLANTIC MACARONI CO., Inc.

295-303 Vernon Avenue, Long Island City, N. Y.

14. The availability of abundant, nutritious food was still a somewhat new experience for Italian immigrants when this ad appeared in the city's most popular Italian-language newspaper. "How could you become so fat in just a few weeks?" the character on the left enviously asks his healthy-looking friend. The Atlantic Macaroni Company promised that its spaghetti would help immigrant consumers put on weight; in Italian peasant culture, a fat body was a sign of worth and well-being. *Il Progresso Italo-Americano*, April 24, 1921.

15. "Don't waste the pleasure of a good meal!" This ad is for Effervescente Galeffi, one of the lemon-flavored powders that immigrant eaters mixed with water to create a digestive drink after each meal. In the interwar years, *Il Progresso* was filled with ads for tonics that promised digestive relief from the unprecedented problem of abundance. *Il Progresso Italo-Americano*, November 23, 1930.

RICORSE AL LATTE

Per Migliorare la Sua Carnagione

QUANDO tutti gli altri rimedi falliscono, il latte è l'unico rimedio al quale ricorrere per chiarire la vostra carnagione. Come sapete, il latte è la più ricca fonte di *calcio* conosciuta. Persino i migliori specialisti della pelle raccomandano il *calcio* come l'ingrediente più necessario alla bellezza della pelle. Con ogni bicchiere di latte che bevete, voi date alla vostra pelle un *trattamento a base di calcio!*

Sembra piuttosto facile, nevvero?... Latte fresco! Per soli pochi soldi! Eppure è così! Voi dovreste bere un bicchiere di latte al giorno, preferibilmente con uno dei vostri pasti.

Non dimenticate che il latte è non solamente il più *ricco dei cibi, ma anche il più economico.*

Chiarite la vostra pelle col latte

COME RIDURRE DI PESO COL LATTE: *Se volete dimagrire in modo scientifico, mandate a chiedere l'opuscoletto di cui parla tutta Hollywood: "La Via Lattea". Esso contiene tutte le diete seguite dalle stelle cinematografiche. Inviate una cartolina postale con il vostro nome ed indirizzo. Scrivete al Bureau of Milk Publicity, Albany.*

THE STATE OF NEW YORK

16. "She drinks milk to improve her complexion." Consuming "American" food—like milk—was a popular way for first- and second-generation Italian Americans to break with immigrant culture and be accepted into modern, urban, "white" society. This clearly racialized ad, funded by the State of New York, urged Italian women to drink more milk in order to achieve whiter skin. *Il Progresso Italo-Americano*, November 6, 1935.

PER LE
FAMIGLIE
La Pasta Bologna — marca EMANUELE RONZONI, ha un aspetto tanto appetitoso,
che fa piacere solo a guardarla. E' molto più saporita delle paste comuni.
Manifatturata con i migliori materiali.
La Pasta Genova — marca EMANUELE RONZONI, possiede un gusto squisito, che
impartisce anche al brodo ed alla minestra. Per la composizione di cui è formata,
è raccomandata come cibo necessario per la vera nutrizione.
Manifatturata con la migliore SEMOLINA, garantita senza colore artificiale.
La Pasta Gragnano — marca LE MIETITRICI. Una volta che l'avete gustata, non
esiterete a raccomandarla ai vostri migliori clienti od amici.
Manifatturata con la migliore SEMOLINA, garantita senza colore artificiale.
RONZONI MACARONI CO., Inc.
Long Island City New York
RONZONI
RONZONI

17. Both Italian importers of Italian food and Italian American food manufacturers sought to dominate the ethnic market through narratives linking their products to an Italian identity in America. Here the Queens-based Ronzoni Macaroni Company constructs an imagined heritage rooted in Italian cities known for their food: Bologna, Genoa, and Gragnano (Naples). The family around the table was a powerful symbol of Italian transnational identity. *Il Progresso Italo-Americano*, May 15, 1921.

18. Commercial packaged pasta was a novelty when this advertisement was published in 1930. At the time, pasta was sold mostly in bulk from wooden bins in neighborhood shops. With its packaged spaghetti the La Rosa and Sons Macaroni Company promised the growing second generation of Italian Americans a modern version of traditional ethnic food with "superior quality; exquisite taste; nutritional value; and cleanliness." *Il Progresso Italo-Americano*, November 23, 1930.

I Prodotti che godono il favore del pubblico in tutta l'America del Nord

CAMPANIA
BRAND
SALSA DI POMIDORO
CONCENTRATA NEL VUOTO
QUALITA FINISSIMA
CONCENTRATED
TOMATO PASTE
PACKED BY
ITALIAN FOOD PRODUCTS CO. INC.
LONG BEACH, CALIFORNIA

SQUISITISSIMI

TOMATO PASTE
MARIUCCIA
SALSA DI POMIDORO
QUALITA' FINISSIMA

Preparati con Pomidoro fresco e scelto di giusta maturazione e la rigorosa osservanza dei METODI SANITARI MODERNI PIU' EFFICACI PER LA CONCENTRAZIONE NEL VUOTO.

DOPPIO
CONCENTRATO
DI POMIDORO
In Scatole
Cromo-Litografate
di misura diversa
CONCENTRATO DI POMIDORO
La Parmense
BRAND
CONCENTRATED
TOMATO PASTE
PACKED AND GUARANTEED BY
ITALIAN FOOD PRODUCTS CO.
LOS ANGELES, CAL., U.S.A.

In vendita presso i migliori Negozii di Generi alimentari

Prodotti dalla

ITALIAN FOOD PRODUCTS CO., INC.

LONG BEACH, CALIFORNIA

Agente generale pel Nord America

H. D. CAPRIATA

100 Hudson Street, New York, N. Y.

19. Italian American food manufacturers sought to create an Italian American consumer by combining—as the Long Beach, California, Italian Food Products Company did with this advertisement—the guarantee of advanced technology with the reassuring appeal of traditionalism. The cans of these tomato products evoke the natural Italian origins ("Campania" and "Parma" and the romanticized smiling peasant woman), while the text boasts that the products are "prepared in compliance with the most modern and effective methods of vacuum packing." *Il Progresso Italo-Americano*, September 7, 1930.

PLANTERS EDIBLE OIL CO.
PRESENTA
AI CONSUMATORI ITALIANI

ALI D'ITALIA OLIO

Prezzo unico $ 1 00
PER GALLONE
Chiedetelo al vostro Grossiere

Puro di Arachide - Per Cucinare, per Insalata e per qualsiasi altro uso comune dell'Olio di Olive

Da non confondersi con Olii vegetali di cotone o di corn; QUEST'OLIO E' GARANTITO 85% UGUALE ALL'OLIO DI OLIVE IN SOSTANZA; migliore per dolcezza, odore e sapore, più economico perchè resistente ad alta temperatura senza bruciare o produrre fumi. (Dichiarato dal Dipartimento di Agricoltura degli Stati Uniti, più digestivo di qualsiasi altro olio, Bollettino No. 505).

Provatelo e convincetevi dei meriti eccezionali di questo prodotto che non ha rivali neanche nel più fine olio di olive o burro.

PLANTERS EDIBLE OIL CO. — 5 Union Square, New York, N. Y.
Telephone: Algonquin 4-7257

20. Even entirely new products were marketed to Italian American consumers by using names, images, and ideas conveying *Italianità*. In this advertisement from the Planters Edible Oil Company, Ali d'Italia peanut oil is claimed to be an equal of olive oil; this "Wings of Italy" brand celebrated the 1933 flight from Rome to Chicago of fascist leader Italo Balbo, which brought nationalist pride to many Italian Americans. *Il Progresso Italo-Americano*, January 4, 1935.

Il Signor

RAFFAELE RAINONE

Presidente della

GEM PACKING CORPORATION

Impaccatrice dell'OLIO GEMMA

PRESENTA PER IL VOSTRO GODIMENTO

L'Olio Preferito dagli Italiani d'America

IL NUOVO PROGRAMMA RADIOFONICO

Alla WOV New York

e WPEN Philadelphia, Pa.

OGNI GIORNO, ECCETTO LA DOMENICA, ALLE ORE 12.15 P. M. CON GLI ARTISTI

RIA ROSA, GIUSEPPE MASIELLO e PORZIO (O' DON NICOLA)

21. Italian American food manufacturers pioneered the use of Italian-language radio to promote their products. This advertisement from the Gem Packing Corporation, maker of Gemma brand olive oil, announces its sponsorship of a popular Italian music show broadcast weekdays on stations WOV New York and WPEN Philadelphia. *Il Progresso Italo-Americano*, August 6, 1939.

ALL'ABISSINIA

dove i Soldati d'Italia avanzano e combattono per la nostra Grande Madre comune sono oggi rivolte le menti ed i cuori di tutti gli Italo-Americani

•

La Ditta MATTIA LOCATELLI ritiene di fare cosa utile e gradita ai suoi numerosi ed affezionati amici offrendo loro in dono una bellissima carta geografica italiana, a colori, rappresentante l'Italia, i suoi Possedimenti Coloniali e l'attuale zona d'operazioni in Abissinia.

La Carta verrà inviata a chi ne farà richiesta mediante l'unico tagliando. Non vi sarà nulla da pagare—nemmeno la spesa di affrancazione postale.

In compenso la Ditta MATTIA LOCATELLI vi chiede — oggi più che mai — di

Usare, difendere e diffondere i Prodotti Italiani

Sarà la vostra risposta a quelle sanzioni, a quel boicottaggio che certi biechi interessi vorrebbero applicare contro la nostra Madre Patria.

MATTIA LOCATELLI, N. Y. BRANCH, Inc. (?)
24 Varick Street, New York, N. Y.

Vogliate spedirmi gratuitamente una copia della Carta Geografica dell'Italia e Possedimenti Coloniali. Grazie e saluti.

A

NOME..

STRADA..

CITTA'...............................**STATO**............

22. In their losing campaign against Italian American domestic manufacturers of Italian food, importers increasingly played the nationalist card during the 1930s. Fascist Italy's war against Ethiopia in 1935–36 and the consequent world boycott of Italian products gave importers an opportunity to play upon the nationalist sentiments of Italian American consumers. Here cheese importer Mattia Locatelli asks Italians in New York to "buy and defend" Italian-imported foods as a way to "respond to the vile boycott that evil interests declared against the Motherland." *Il Progresso Italo-Americano*, November 3, 1935.

HOLIDAY GREETINGS

to the

COMMANDER IN CHIEF

and to all members of our Armed Forces fighting on all fronts

OUR PLEDGE

We pledge our undivided loyalty and unconditional allegiance to the Flag of the United States and to the Republic for which it stands.

We pledge to fight all enemies of the United States, to co-operate with our Government in the observance of all wartime regulations and to make every sacrifice required of us until final and complete victory is achieved.

ATLANTIC MACARONI COMPANY, Inc.

LONG ISLAND CITY, N. Y.

23. On Columbus Day, 1942, the day the classification of six hundred thousand nonnaturalized Italian American as "enemy aliens" was repealed, food manufacturers publicly professed their patriotism, as shown by this advertisement from the Atlantic Macaroni Company of Long Island City, makers of Caruso Spaghetti. *Il Progresso Italo-Americano*, October 12, 1942.

E' assai spesso un problema il trovare un ristorante ove si sia certi di essere serviti cibi sani all'Italiana e vini domestici od importati di prima qualità. I ritrovi che elenchiamo per comodità del lettore sono fra quelli che godono la reputazione più lusinghiera nella Greater New York.

GUFFANTI
CASA DOMINICK, INC.
274 - 7th Ave., N.Y.C. alle 26 St. Chl. 4-9628
Pietanze nuove ogni Giorno. Alla Carta e Table D'ote. Accomodazioni per Banchetti e Parties per ogni occasione. — Facilità di spazio per automobili.

RICCOBONO
225 LAFAYETTE ST. CAn. 6-8937
East River Sav. Bank Bldg. 12. piano
LUNCH — — 60c
E SERVIZIO ALLA CARTA
CUCINA ITALO - AMERICANA
APERTO FINO ALLA 10 DI SERA.

ZUCCA'S
118 WEST 49TH STREET
TELEFONO: BRYANT 9 — 5511
PER 20 ANNI ALLO STESSO POSTO
UNA LARGA SCELTA DI VINI
— LE MIGLIORI VIVANDE —
Lunch $1.00 — Pranzo $1.50
Il Bar del Restaurant aperto fino all'1 a. m.
MODERNISSIMO IMPIANTO PER ARIA CONDIZIONATA

VESUVIO
163 WEST 48th ST., N. Y. C.
Telefono: MEdallion 3-8916
Moderno Impianto ad Aria Fresca
Cucina Italiana
A LA CARTE
Si servono i migliori vini e liquori

CLARIDGE
HOTEL RESTAURANT
182 WEST 44th ST. (2o PIANO)
Giovanni Selvaggio *Cuoco e Manager*
CUCINA ITALIANA
A LA CARTA E TABLE D'HOTE
VINI E LIQUORI
Sale per banchetti, sposalizi e altre partite

John's Italian Rest.
612 - 8th AVE. (39 e 40 St.)
TEL. MED. 3-9195
FAMOSA CUCINA NAPOLETANA
TABLE D'HOTE & A LA CARTE
VINI E LIQUORI SCELTI
PREZZI MODICI

RICCIARDI — CUCINA NAPOLETANA
RESTAURANT
TABLE D'HOTE — A LA CARTE
VENETIAN GARDEN
132 WEST 43rd ST., East of Broadway
Per Banchetti e Sposalizi accomodazione per 500 persone

CONEY ISLAND, N. Y.

GARGIULO'S RESTAURANT INC.
2913 WEST 15th STREET
Coney Island MAyflower 9-8785
DOVE SI GUSTANO I CIBI PIU' FINI ALL'ITALIANA — Alla Carta
VINI E LIQUORI SCELTI
Sale per Banchetti e Sposalizi
— APERTO TUTTO L'ANNO —

ELDORADO
RESTAURANT
FORTUNA BAMBARDELLA. (Prop.)
PRANZI SULLA SPIAGGIA
ANCHE
SERVIZIO ALLA CARTA
CUCINA NAPOLETANA
MUSICA — BALLO
3000 EMMONS AVE., SHEEPSHEAD BAY — *Sotto nuova gestione*

24. By the end of the 1930s, leading Italian restaurants in New York used the ethnic press to reach the many Italian American customers who had deserted them, promising to once again serve genuine Italian food and wine. *Il Progresso Italo-Americano*, June 4, 1938.

25. "The Di Costanzo family, owners of Marconi's restaurant on Mulberry Street, hold their annual family dinner in the restaurant on New Year's Eve. There are few customers on that night. Gypsy friend who comes to eat, dances to entertain them," December 31, 1942. The decor of Marconi's and other New York Italian restaurants in the interwar years creatively combined images of a primitive, sensual, "black Italy" with those of Rome, the Renaissance, and the romantic Grand Tour of "white Italy." Library of Congress, Prints & Photographs Division, FSA/OWI Collection, LC-USW3-013445-D.

26. Moneta's restaurant at 32 Mulberry Street, 1937. By the end of the 1930s there was a wide variety of Italian restaurants in New York. Some, like Moneta's, attracted an upscale clientele with a classy atmosphere and an elaborate version of Italian cuisine. WPA Federal Writers' Project Photographs Collection. Courtesy NYC Municipal Archives.

27. "Italian-American café espresso shop on MacDougal Street where coffee and soft drinks are sold. The coffee machine cost one thousand dollars," August 1942. Espresso coffee did not originate in the Italian South but rather in the middle-class cafés of northern Italian cities; the first espresso machine was produced in 1905 in Milan by Pavoni. By the 1920s coffee shops like this one in the Italian heart of Greenwich Village started to import these expensive machines to reinforce their exotic European atmosphere. Library of Congress, Prints & Photographs Division, FSA/OWI Collection, LC-USW3-006923-E.

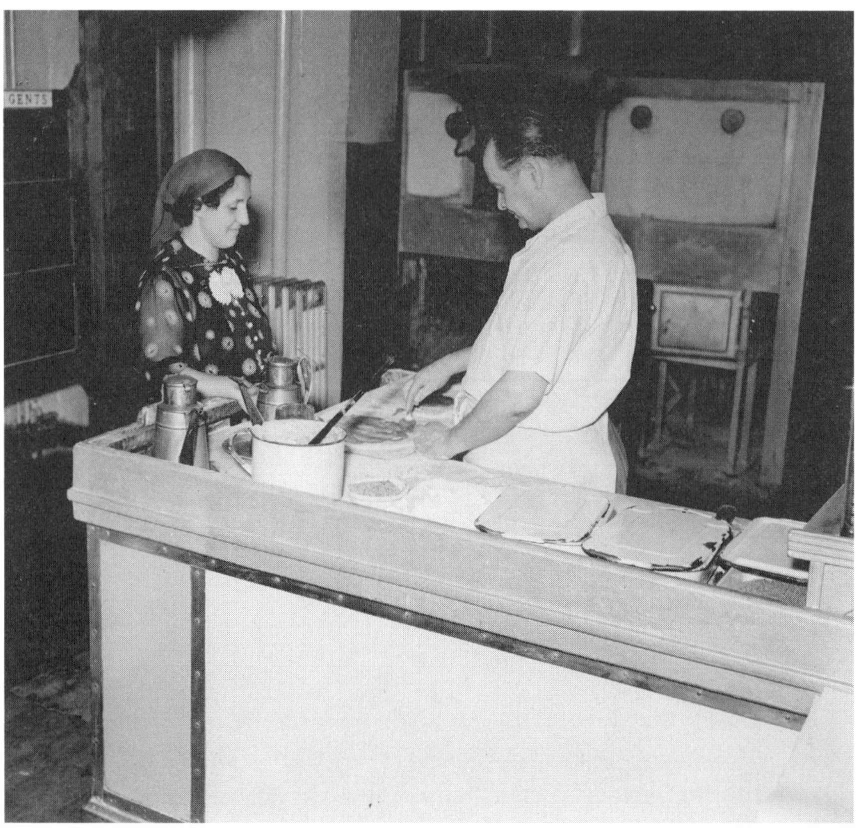

28. “Interior Italian Pizzeria. Man spreading sauce on pizza for customer,” 1937. Pizza was almost completely unknown to non-Italian New Yorkers before World War II. The irresistible appeal of the Italian culinary triangle of dough, tomato, and melted cheese, however, paved the way for the extraordinary success of pizza since the late 1940s. WPA Federal Writers’ Project Photographs Collection. Courtesy NYC Municipal Archives.

PART II

Producing and Consuming Italian American Identities

The Ethnic Food Trade

4

The American Business of Italian Food

Producers, Consumers, and the Making of Ethnic Identities

The Modern Taste of Italian Food in America

From the beginning of the Italian experience in America, the importing, production, and sale of food has played an important part in the growth of the Italian American business community, and understanding the central role of food in the making of Italian American identity means understanding what the business of food represents in the economic life of the community. In New York, the largest immigrant market in the country, the relationship between economic interests and the promotion of an Italian diasporic identity was particularly strong and enduring. Immigrant entrepreneurs in every line of the food business sought to link food with ethnic identity. Italian food importers, producers, wholesalers, store owners, and restaurateurs emphasized the ethnic content of their products and invoked ethnic solidarity by asking fellow Italians to keep their money in the community by buying their products and services. Since the Italian immigrant community was by far their most important market, food entrepreneurs were always active in fostering the centrality of food in a developing diasporic *Italianità* as well as supporting Italian American nationalism. This chapter discusses the history of American-made Italian food in the 1920s and 1930s, focusing on the strategies with which its Italian American producers responded to economic and social change both in the immigrant community and in U.S. society at large. In those years, Italian American producers of Italian food did not limit their enterprises to the formation of an exclusive "Italian American community of taste" but rather created innovative communication strategies to exploit the connection between American modernity and progressive capitalism and the production of "traditional" foodstuffs. In the process, many entrepreneurs took advantage of the new opportunities offered by mass media to shape the mentality and lifestyle of a new ethnic consumer.

Indeed, the marketing strategies of Italian food producers and the response of Italian American consumers in the interwar years can illuminate the relationship between ethnicity and modernity. In the 1920s, as industrial expansion, urbanization, bureaucratization, and mass culture redefined the terms of modern living, "Americanism" became almost synonymous with modernity, as a secular, urban, and industrial society and civilization, marked by a relative profusion of goods and services.[1] To the many Italian immigrants to New York, modernity and American civilization also tended to overlap and to signify a "culture" different from their own. For the Italians of Harlem, their ethnicity came to be defined by their attachment to the notions of home, family, and community, each a place of production, reproduction, consumption, and socialization, as opposed to the specialized spaces and institutions and the values of autonomy and personal initiative that defined urban American culture. In dialogue with "American" scientific rationality, economic efficiency, and the belief in progress, immigrants insisted on group solidarity based on race, blood, and traditional wisdom as the defining characteristics of their identity. At the same time, Italian American ethnicity and modernity were not, as immigrants believed, binary opposites; rather, the making of an Italian ethnicity was itself a reaction to modernity in a process that drew on many aspects of modern life, from the interaction with many ethnic others in the spheres of everyday life—work, religion, school—to the shedding of established identities, values, and meanings in the transition to an urban, industrial society. Foods produced in distant places with advanced technologies traveled through complex networks of distribution to Italian immigrant tables, where they were enjoyed (as *Italian* food) in family and community gatherings that reinforced group identity. This ethnic use of industrial food witnesses that technological innovations and impersonal systems of supply often enact creative productions of authentic forms of ethnic identity.[2]

As the narratives of Italian immigrants in Harlem have demonstrated, Italian American foodways retained special symbolic value in the making of Italian American identity because of the assumption that they arrived intact from an Old World preindustrial, premodern past. This ideology barely hid the fact that modern transportation, industrialization, urbanization, mass production, and marketing helped *shape* an original Italian American eating pattern and provide a source for cultural difference, rather than threaten an imagined authenticity. The fact that some foods introduced to America by immigrants managed to become mass-produced commodities that retained their ethnic character was due mostly to the Italian American food entrepreneurs who skillfully applied mass-production systems in the manufacturing of "ethnic" food while exploiting their own ethnic identity to make it credible to an ethnic marketplace. The agency of ethnic food entrepreneurs also created Italian American consumers, on the one hand, by showing immigrants how to express their ethnic affiliation through consumption, on the other hand, by modernizing immigrants through regular encounters with advertising, branding, and the other features of mass consumerism. The integration of an enclave market economy into the national industrial system redefined Italian American identities. The history of Italian American food entrepreneurs, products, and consumers in the interwar years is one of the making and remaking of identities in which industrial modernity played a decisive part.

The Production of Italian Food in the United States in the Age of Mass Migration, 1890–1920

The production of Italian-style food in New York began with the earliest Italian settlements in the city, in the 1870s. The development of local alternatives to imports from Italy anticipated the great wave of more than three million Italians between 1900 and 1914.[3] In fact, these immigrants found a system for the production, import, and retailing of Italian food already established. Since the food business offered immigrants one of the few opportunities for an independent occupation, Italians soon created economic niches in a trade where both employers and workers were Italian. A small business like a grocery store could be opened with little starting capital and became a popular alternative to unskilled wage labor. "Many general laborers, miners, and others are tempted to enter '*bisinisse*,'" Robert Foerster noted early in the century, "and (. . .) they can do so by learning fifty words of English and buying a fruit stand. In New York many men have begun with a pushcart, then got the privilege of a stand, then a concession to sell garden produce in connection with a grocery store, and finally have set up a shop on their own."[4]

For these small entrepreneurs, cultural capital (an exclusive knowledge of ethnic food and familiarity with purveyors and consumers) and social capital (an "embeddedness" in exclusive ethnic and family networks) were as important as financial capital. Often the source of the start-up money was credit from family, *paesani*, or Italian bankers.[5] Ethnicity was also an asset for immigrant entrepreneurs seeking to secure cheap labor or limit labor conflict. Family and ethnic bonds encouraged paternalism and often convinced immigrant employees to work long shifts for minimal wages. In particular, these family networks were vital for the survival and success of ethnic food businesses, which depended on women's and children's unpaid labor. On the other hand, easy access to the food trade generated a large number of small food businesses, which struggled against sharp competition and a poor and transient consumer base. Until World War I, the number of large-scale immigrant businesses specializing in the production of Italian food was very limited.

The labor conditions in immigrant-run food businesses were often poor and the target of middle-class reformers. At the turn of the twentieth century, as the industrialization of food production widened the distance between producer and consumer, growing concerns about fraud and adulteration created national debates about the way food was manufactured. In 1906, Upton Sinclair's muckraking novel *The Jungle* brought national attention to the horrific conditions of Chicago slaughterhouses. That same year, the Pure Food and Drug Act was approved, targeting the manufacture and sale of adulterated food and providing for federal inspection of food processing plants. Reformers, betraying an anti-urban, anti-immigrant bias, were quick to point to the unsanitary conditions in which food was produced in ethnic city neighborhoods.

In New York City, many immigrant food shops and factories were indeed dirty and located in the most densely populated, disease-prone neighborhoods. In these small businesses, hours and labor conditions were exacting and the exploitation of the workforce widespread. This was the case, for example, in pasta manufacturing, which Italians monopolized as both employers and workers as early as 1880 in small, family-run businesses.[6] "The small pasta shops, employing three to five workers, where everything [was] primitive," multiplied with the growth of the Italian community in the city, and there were hundreds of them by 1900.[7] "Macaroni is made in every block of the Italian neighborhoods of New York," the consumer activist Mary Sherman noted in 1906. "In many streets you will find three or four little shops in one block of houses, with the macaroni drying in the doorways and windows. The front room is the shop, the family living in the middle and rear rooms."[8] In these shops, family members and one or two employees worked long hours for low wages. In 1906, Italian workers in pasta factories earned on average eleven dollars a week for a ten-hour workday, but those in small pasta shops "where the owner [was] himself a worker" worked twelve hours a day for a six-to-eight-dollar weekly salary. The competition created by the continuing arrival of new immigrants made these jobs insecure and undercut the bargaining power of laborers.[9]

Non-Italian observers often found the conditions of pasta making offensive. Joseph Adams, a reformer with the Congregational Home Missionary Society, said of his visit to Little Italy around Mulberry Street: "Throughout the district one will see the spaghetti shop, outside of which the 'green' article fresh from the macaroni press, is hanging on long poles and moving in the breeze as a field of ripe wheat is swayed by the wind. Inside the shop are also rows of poles loaded with spaghetti, and with the often filthy conditions prevailing in these shops and the dirt blown on the macaroni hanging outside, one can imagine the great amount of filth, disease germs, and other impurities the Italians take unto their systems through this one medium alone."[10] Reporting the case of "a child [lying] sick of diphtheria in the back room [while] the father manufactured macaroni in the front adjoining room, and [he] would go directly from holding the child in his arms to the macaroni machine, pulling the macaroni with his hands and hanging it over racks to dry," Mary Sherman cautioned, "However willing we might be to overlook the fact that the Italians in the cities are obliged to buy food made in dirty rooms, we certainly are not willing that contagious diseases be carried in this manner."[11]

Bakeries were just as numerous as pasta shops in Manhattan's Italian neighborhoods. On almost any block in Little Italy and Italian Harlem, there was an oven for baking many local varieties of Italian bread. Independent bakeries were also as a rule family businesses; the husband baked bread overnight, and the wife sold it in the shop during the day.[12] Customers were often from the same region as the baker, who typically lived in the neighborhood or even on the same block. The crusty regional Italian bread was very different from the soft, uniform "American" bread and made in a great variety of traditional shapes.[13] Reformers and city officials also targeted Italian immigrant bakers for the poor hygienic conditions of their shops. In 1906, the New York Factory Investigating Commission found that the bakeries in the basement of tenement houses were generally dirty, badly lit, and unventilated. An amazing 32 percent of bakers showed symptoms of tuberculosis and asthma. Following these investigations, a new city law required annual medical examinations for bakers and compliance to strict cleanliness standards for the new bakery licenses.[14] In 1906, the fifteen hundred Italian bakers of New York earned a meager five dollars per week plus board and lodging. Again, the treatment of workers in small neighborhood bakeries was worse than that of the more organized workers in industrial bakeries.[15] The unions' efforts to organize Italian bakers were frustrated by organized crime; racketeers took control of the trade, dictating the price of bread and imposing long hours and low wages on workers. During Prohibition, gangsters grabbed even more control of the Italian bread industry; Joe Catania, the brother-in-law of the famous "artichoke king" Ciro Terranova, reportedly took two cents on any loaf of bread sold in the Bronx.[16]

Many Italian immigrants found jobs making pastries, ice cream, and candy. At the beginning of the twentieth century, some twenty Italian-owned candy factories in the city employed "several hundred workers, nearly all Italian."[17] For the mostly women workers, conditions were especially grim. In a candy factory that Mary Sherman visited, Italian women workers cracked and shelled nuts for twelve hours a day. The pay was six cents a pound, and it took six hours of work to clean fifteen pounds of nuts. At busy times, women brought work home.[18] In her study of Italian women in New York industries, Louise Odencrantz noted that the absence of unions made the candy industry perhaps the worst in terms of hours of work: 41 percent of women employees worked for more than ten hours a day. Although a job in a candy factory was known to be demanding and underpaid, it was often the only opportunity for immigrant women who were very young, old, or did not speak English, as in the example Odencrantz offers: "Biagia, who had come four months before from Sicily, was peeling almonds in a large West Side candy factory for $4.50 a week. As she could speak no English, she could not get anything better than this work which she had secured through the aunt with whom she lived."[19]

The food trade that early Italian immigrants to New York dominated was the fruit and vegetable wholesale and retail business. According to the Italian consul general, as early as 1870 three-fifths of the apple, peach, pear, and chestnut vendors in the city were Italian (mostly Genoese and Sicilian). Twenty years later, the same source reported that more than ten thousand Italians worked in the fruit and vegetable trade, and some were fairly successful.[20] By 1880, 12 percent of New York Italian workers were peddlers of fruits, vegetables, and fish, making them the largest independent occupational group.[21] The "independence" of Italian pushcart peddlers was, in fact, nominal. The Mayor's Pushcart Commission, established in 1906 to investigate the conditions of open markets, discovered the presence of a "*padrone* or 'boss' system among the Italians . . . by which one man own[ed] or control[led] many licenses and push-carts, hire[d] men to operate them for him and [paid] them a small daily or weekly compensation, acting as middleman or capitalist and reaping in such cases large profits from this industry. . . . In Manhattan it was found that one man controlled as many as 170 different push-carts."[22] It was also common wisdom that organized crime controlled the Italian markets of the city. Early on, gangs in Italian Harlem extorted money each week from local Italian merchants.[23] By the 1930s, organized crime controlled open markets not just through extortion but also by price fixing. Racketeer Ciro Terranova earned himself the title of "artichoke king" by forcing New York peddlers to buy from purveyors he selected. Joseph Castaldo, a former Terranova associate, used the same strategies to control the local pepper trade. Serious efforts at fighting these criminal activities were not enforced until the mid-1930s.[24]

Its growth in the first three decades of the century explains the interest of organized crime in the Italian fruit and vegetable business. The large Italian presence in produce trade spurred the creation of a system that linked Italians in the city's wholesale markets to the many small Italian garden farms around the city as well as to the larger industrial farms that Italians were establishing in New York State, New Jersey, and California. As a result, pushcart peddlers could be supplied the produce that Italians preferred. Zucchini, asparagus, eggplants, celery, fennel, peppers, chicory, and broccoli were some of the vegetables introduced to New York markets through distribution channels that Italians created and managed.[25] Fruit and vegetable shops were more numerous in Little Italies than in any other sections of the city. "These stores have a surprising variety of fresh vegetables and fruits all the year," a study observed. "The variety of salad greens is remarkable. More Swiss chard, mustard, dandelion leaves, endive, squash blossoms, and escarole are to be seen in one little Italian store than in a half dozen American markets."[26]

Some immigrants cultivated truck gardens in undeveloped areas of the city. "A few thousand Italians . . . have taken up farming—or as they call it 'market gardening'—right in the city of New York," a Federal Writers' Project's report notes.[27] More often, the produce, once it reached Washington and Gansevoort Markets in downtown Manhattan, Harlem Market uptown, or Wallabout Market in Brooklyn, was purchased by wholesale merchants and sold to retailers. Truck gardening, although not always profitable and often risky, was a good opportunity for many immigrant farmers to put their skills to use. In fact, Italian truck gardening in the outer boroughs and on Long Island was revived during the Depression and lasted into the 1940s.[28] Local Italians also raised goats and pigs and produced Italian-style cheeses, dairy products, and sausages.[29]

The presence of so many Italians in all areas of the food business was vital in preserving the distinctive foodways of immigrant communities. In the early twentieth century, the expansion of relatively homogenous Italian enclaves across the city (table 2) supported the emergence of an unparalleled number of businesses to meet their culinary needs: independent fruit and vegetable vendors, grocers, bakers, butchers, and fishmongers; Italian food importers; and domestic Italian food manufacturers.

This did not mean, though, that Italians in New York ate the way they had done in Italy. On the contrary, their ethnic food production and distribution network allowed immigrants to have much wider access to more varied food than they

Table 2. Population of Italian neighborhoods in New York City, 1910

Section	Types	Population
Mulberry Bend Park (Worth, Lafayette, Houston, Bowery Sts.)	Genoese, Calabrian, Neapolitan, Sicilian	110,000
Lower West Side (Canal, West Broadway, North River)	Calabrian, Piedmontese, Tuscan, Neapolitan	70,000
Middle East Side (E. 9th St., East River, 2nd Ave., E. 33th St.)	Sicilian, Calabrian	18,000
West Side (34th St., 59th St., North River, 9th Ave.)	Neapolitan, Genoese, Turinese, Milanese	15,000
East Harlem (104th St., 125th St., 2nd Ave., East River)	Neapolitan, Calabrian, Sicilian, Salernitano	75,000
White Plains Avenue	Neapolitan	3,500
Van Cortlandt	Sicilian	2,000
Gun Hill Road	Calabrian	1,500
Miscellaneous	Miscellaneous	15,000
	Total	310,000*

* In 1910 the total Italian-born immigrant population in New York was 340,770.

Source: John Horace Mariano, *The Italian Contribution to American Democracy* (Boston: Christopher Publishing House, 1921).

had in rural Italy. The industry that brought "Italian" foods to Italian enclaves was just one part of a complex, global trade system that early on represented one of the most significant factors of *change* in the immigrants' diet. In 1900, progressive reformer Joseph Adams had noted the striking abundance and variety of food for sale in Little Italy: "Tubs of pickles that can be smelled a block away, dried fish, baskets full of dandelion plants fresh from the country, barrels of vegetables, tubs of dried beans and peas, coconuts, bananas, strings of red peppers and garlic, bladders full of imported lard, bundles of kindling wood, dried beans, and links of sausages, are but a few items of the miscellaneous assortment that one sees in traveling but a few steps."[30] Besides the wine grapes that Sicilian farmers grew upstate and shipped to New York; the greens that Italian truck farmers grew on Long Island; the bread and mozzarella made in the neighborhood; and the olive oil, cheeses, and tomato paste imported from Italy, in the Italian quarters shoppers could also find an extraordinary array of foods.[31] A researcher for *Feeding the City*—a study by the Federal Writers' Project of New York's food system—was amazed by the range of products in a First Avenue grocery store catering to local Italian immigrants:

> North Italian Pignoli seeds; Cape Cod stock-fish, Dalmatian sour cherries for making red wine; Oregano from Northern Italy and Greece, used for seasoning; California garlic; Newfoundland cod-fish; Spanish and Italian olive oil in 6 gallons tins; bags of Mexican fave bean, Chile lentils for soups and macaroni, and domestic split peas for soups; two pans of Greek and Italian black olives; can of Brazilian raw green coffee for roasting; two cans of Abyssinian coffee, roasted, ready for demitasse; two silver-wrapped balls of Albanian Mizritha cheese for eating and grating; Provoloni cheese, used for eating, from Northern Italy; Gorgonzola cheese, imported from Rome, the aristocrat of Italian cheese; four varieties of Caciocavallo (Sicilian style) cheese, used for grating and eating, and imported from Ragusa, Italy; imported Roman cheese used for grating; imported Parmesan cheese from Italy, used for grating, canned Italian *caponata*, a mixture of eggplant and vegetable, American-made Brioschi Effervescenti, California tuna fish in olive oil and Italian peeled tomatoes, two cans of Italian olive oil; Locatelli brand of *provolonina* cheese imported from Naples, Chicago-made Salami, Sicilian style; Provoloncini cheese made in Wisconsin; Genoa-style Salami made in Chicago and used with *antipasta* [*sic*], which is a mixture of peppers, olives and anchovies.[32]

The Development of the U.S. Food Industry at the Turn of the Twentieth Century

As a globalizing marketplace transformed the Italian food universe, Italian immigrants were catapulted into a world where the powerful forces of mass production and mass consumption were fully under way. Immigrants from rural Italy, along with others from rural southern and eastern Europe, Asia, Central America, and the American South, made up the inexpensive labor force that fueled the historic expansion of the U.S. economy at the turn of the twentieth century. The transformation of food production and the diet of millions of Americans was equally the result of industrialization, immigration, urbanization, and technological change. From 1880 to World War I, the industrialization of food, enabled by new systems of production, preservation, transportation, distribution, and marketing, led to a revolutionary transition from the processing of local resources into products for local consumption to mass production aimed at national and international markets.

In the 1860s, U.S. food production was still mostly localized and dependent on independent farmers. But the westward expansion of the railroad after the Civil War opened the Great Plains of Minnesota and the Dakotas to grain cultivation. In the Midwest, open lands were converted to raise corn, wheat, and dairy cattle. By the end of the 1880s, the railroads provided major cities with daily supplies of milk, fruit and vegetables. The introduction of the refrigerated railroad car in the early 1870s opened the large urban markets of the east to produce from California and Florida and pork and beef from the Midwest. Up to that point, livestock raised on the ranges of Texas and the Midwest had to be shipped alive to the large cities of the east. Refrigeration made it possible to ship butchered beef from Chicago and other Midwest cities cheaply across the country. The new vertical organization of the beef industry and management innovations such as the "disassembly lines" in slaughterhouses allowed the price of beef to decline as the quality of the product rose.[33] By the 1880s, the food industry was one of the most advanced sectors of the U.S. economy. Fruit and vegetable canning, beer brewing, flour milling, and meatpacking were by then all largely mechanized operations.[34] Beginning in the 1880s, meat, peas, soup, corn, and condensed milk came ever more often in cans, as the productivity of the canning industry continued to increase exponentially.[35] The production of butter and cheese also moved from kitchens and farms into factories after the invention in 1879 of a mechanical centrifuge that could separate cream from milk. Bread baking and beer brewing also shifted from independent ovens and artisanal breweries into large industrial plants.[36]

Because of the mechanization of food processing, the availability of cheap labor, and progress in transportation, the price of food decreased sharply at the end of the nineteenth century. A dollar bought 15 pounds of flour in 1872 and 34 in 1897. In 1898, a dollar bought 43 percent more rice than it did in 1872, and 51 percent more coffee, 114 percent more sugar, and 25 percent more fresh pork. In 1900, food accounted for one-fifth of the total value of U.S. industrial output. As in other sectors, the expansion of the industry resulted in the concentration of firms and the formation of trusts. Since mechanization required large investments, the major food companies set out to control the market by creating oligopolies and acquiring or destroying independent competitors. Even the progressive fight against fraud and adulteration helped the consolidation of food companies into large corporations, since the new laws requiring the pasteurization of milk, for example, hurt small distributors who could not meet the costs of modernization. After World War I, a few national corporations like Borden's and National Dairy Products controlled most of the milk industry.[37]

The rapid transformation of food processing into mass production involved a similar change in distribution and marketing and resulted in the emergence of mass-advertised brand products. Food corporations used the latest promotional methods to create a new national market for their products. In stores, packaged brand products, made familiar through national advertising, gradually replaced food sold in bulk. The first modern advertising agency, N. W. Ayer and Son, Inc., was founded in Philadelphia in 1869. By the end of the century, sophisticated promotional campaigns were able to create desires and needs and could build a market where none existed.[38] In turn, the wide-ranging impact of advertising was made possible by the spread of mass media and the mass audience it created. The national chain newspapers increased their circulation and influence on the profits earned by the sale of advertising space. Between 1918 and 1929, the profits from advertising in national magazines such as *Collier's* and *Good Housekeeping* tripled to more than $200 million. By the end of the 1920s, radio became not only a popular mass medium but also a powerful means of product marketing.[39] On the retail front, chain stores began to compete successfully with independent grocery stores for the urban food market. The first national chain food store, the Great Atlantic & Pacific Tea Company (A&P), was founded in 1859, but it was not until the interwar years that it became an important market force. A&P and other chain stores purchased wholesale quantities of food directly from manufacturers, allowing their franchised stores to sell national-brand packaged foods at discount prices. The diffusion of chain stores, along with mass advertising, helped brand-name foods dominate the market. The new standardized brands guaranteed the quality and safety of products already made familiar by advertising.

Many Americans had become modern food consumers by the early decades of the twentieth century. The effects of supply and demand on a mass scale made an unprecedented quantity and variety of foodstuffs available even to working-class families. Those families, like others across social classes, became customers of the same national brands and mass-produced foods: Nabisco's Uneeda crackers, General Mills' Gold Medal flour, Borden's condensed milk, Kellogg's Corn Flakes, Campbell's canned soups, Heinz's sauces, and Del Monte's canned fruit. The emergence of commodities produced by national corporations and sold to a mass consumer base through advertising consolidated a nation still significantly divided by cultural and regional differences. The national marketplace of standardized foods also disseminated a single dietary discourse, reflecting urban middle-class values, into diverse communities defined by place, race, class, and culture. However, as the example of Italian immigrant consumers would demonstrate, the homogenizing forces of capitalism, science, and middle-class culture encountered resistance in their efforts at conquering the markets and shaping the tastes of America.[40]

Food Consumption among Italian Migrants in the Age of Mass Migration, 1890–1920

The revolution in food supply, in fact, had contrasting effects on the diet of the Italians who arrived in New York in the peak years of immigration. Even as the U.S. marketplace allowed migrants to enrich their daily fare with foods (such as white bread, pasta, meat, coffee, and sugar) that had long been out of reach in Italy, their isolation and poverty shielded them from most of the lures of mass culture, mass consumption, and mass advertising. Living frugally in ethnically bounded enclaves, they maintained highly distinctive foodways. In their homes, Italian immigrant women, barely exposed to mass marketing and advertising, continued to prepare foods purchased in local, independent stores in the neighborhood. This closed circle of consumption meant that until World War II, chain stores selling mass-produced foodstuffs made relatively few inroads into the city's Little Italies. Italian immigrants were resisting the lures of mass consumerism.

Two-thirds of the Italian immigrants to New York were peasants and farmers from southern Italy whose diet had long been characterized by scarcity and monotony. According to an 1899 study, southern Italian peasants ate only "bread in the day and a vegetable soup at night." When an agrarian crisis struck southern Italy in the late nineteenth century, their diet was reduced to black bread and small amounts of vegetables, legumes, cheese, salted fish, and lard.[41] Against this scarcity, America was idealized as the land of abundance. "The desire to leave the 'land of hunger' and the dream of a world where food was plentiful were decisive factors in creating a mass exodus," Calabrian anthropologist Vito Teti writes. "The myth of America was the myth of a marvelous and fertile world, of endless plains rich in wheat and animals that provided abundant meat."[42]

Myth or not, the American marketplace allowed migrants to improve their diet substantially.[43] The most dramatic change was in the regular consumption of beef, once unthinkable for poorer Italians. In the late nineteenth century, each year northern Italians consumed on average thirty-nine pounds of beef per person; the amount was eleven pounds in Sicily and seven pounds in Basilicata and Puglia.[44] Eating beef had symbolic relevance in many immigrant memories. Rocco Corresca, an immigrant shoe shiner in Brooklyn, recalled: "[We had] very little money and our clothes were some of those that were found on the street. Still we had enough to eat and we had meat quite often, which we never had in Italy."[45] Low prices and the chance to buy inexpensive cuts of meat meant that even unskilled workers could afford to eat meat once or twice a week. An immigrant to East Harlem noted that, even in his family of eleven children, "We had meat three or four times a week in my family. In Italy if you had a chicken once a month you're lucky, I mean you're lucky, over here chicken was nothing, it was a cheap item, very cheap."[46] Although the moderate use of frequently inexpensive cuts of meat was a distinctive trait of early Italian migrant foodways, the place of meat in the immigrant diet increased steadily. A study of the Lower East Side during the wartime winter of 1917–18 revealed that Italian families spent 23 percent of their food budget on meat as compared to 35 percent by other groups (of all groups, Italians spent the most on food, more than 60 percent of total family income).[47] Five years later, another study in the same area showed that Italian expenditures for meat had increased to 27 percent of the family food budget, and unlike other groups, poorer Italian families still spent the same proportion of their budgets on meat as did higher-income families, so valued was meat as a sign of status.[48]

Another significant addition to the immigrant diet was sugar, which, because of the nineteenth-century food revolution, provided the working classes of North America and western Europe with an inexpensive source of calories.[49] In Italy, however, as late as 1900 the annual per capita consumption of sugar was one of the lowest in Europe, barely reaching five pounds; in the U.S. it was the highest in the world, sixty-five pounds.[50] Easy access to sugar became, for Italians, one of the most prized rewards of their migration experience. Covello had literally sweet memories of his first day of school in New York:

> Before entering the school, my father led us into a little store close at hand and in it all manner and kinds of sweets such as we had never seen before. "*Candì*!" my father told us, grinning. "This is what is called *candì* in America." We were even allowed to select the kind we wanted. I remember how I selected some little round cream-filled chocolates which tasted like nothing I had ever eaten before. The only candy I knew was *confetti*, the sugar-coated almond confection which we had only on feast days or from the pocket of my uncle the priest on some very special occasion, and for which we kissed his hand in return.[51]

The American-born generation developed such a taste for candies, donuts, and cakes that social workers blamed the overconsumption of sweets for the widespread malnutrition among Italian schoolchildren.[52] Immigrants rarely discouraged their children's habit because in southern Italian culture sugar, like meat, was a rich, festive food, and access to it symbolized the achievement of a superior social status.

The consumption of coffee, another commodity that the American marketplace made available to most Italian migrants for the first time, reflected similar dynamics. In Italy, peasants watched as the local rich drank coffee in the village cafés but could hardly afford it themselves. Like sugar, coffee was a luxury because it needed to be purchased, and most rural Italians had to resort to an ersatz brew made of such ingredients as chicory, barley, wheat, chestnuts, and lentils that were roasted, ground, and mixed with hot water.[53] But in New York drinking coffee became a daily habit. Breakfast in immigrant homes typically included coffee and bread for both adults and children, sometimes with sweets but rarely with milk. A worker of the New York Association for Improving the Conditions of the Poor noted, "The Italian baby eats bread soaked in coffee as soon as he can chew solid food."[54] Phyllis Williams also reported a three-year-old child who "sat in a high-chair holding a cup of strong, black sweet Italian coffee with a trace of whiskey in it and dipping doughnuts in powdered sugar before eating them."[55] Nutritionists, teachers, and social workers tried frequently, but unsuccessfully, to change this habit. To Italian immigrant workers, coffee was the perfect drink to begin a demanding day of work and, with wine and beer, the drink that fueled male sociability. It was also the drink that Italian families offered to visitors. In immigrant families, a social worker noted, "The coffee pot is constantly at hand, and if anyone should drop in between meals it is expected that he or she will accept a cup of coffee."[56]

Finally, the American marketplace gave two other foods a central place in Italian immigrant foodways: bread and pasta. In late nineteenth-century southern Italy, bread was the staple food of the *contadino*, eaten in the morning with "coffee," water, and a chunk of cheese; at noon, in the fields, with cooked vegetables, olives, cheese, or fruit; and at night soaked in soup. Bread was baked at home or in the village's public oven once or twice a week. In southern Italian rural society, bread articulated a precise social hierarchy. Among the poorer classes, almost anything could be mixed in the dough: corn, oat, barley, rye, chestnuts, lupini and fava beans, chickpeas, or potatoes. White wheat bread, by contrast, was reserved for the tables of the rich. In the early nineteenth century, a survey of the French-ruled Kingdom of Naples, the *Statistica Murattiana del Regno di Napoli*, observed, "The urban poor generally eat whole wheat bread. The populations who live on the infertile mountains, though, use to mix chestnuts into the flour. Often they made bread with chestnuts alone or plain oat. The bread of the artisan class is made of whole wheat and rye; that of the landowners of wheat alone." One century later, little had changed.[57]

Access to inexpensive white flour was yet another significant outcome of immigrants' encounter with the American marketplace. Immigrants used it to prepare traditional breads that were popular in Italy, as Little Italy's bakers could proudly tell their Italian customers. "The bread [my father] made was the same bread that had been made in Gravina for generations," an Italian American man remembered. "The secret of the bread had been brought by my grandfather all the way from the Mediterranean to Manhattan, down into the tenement basement where he had installed wooden vats and tables. The bakers were two dark wiry men, *paisani da Gravina*, who rhythmically and endlessly pounded their powdery white hands into the dough, molding the bread with finesse and strength."[58] In New York, bread was valued as food, as a symbolic source of material life, and as an object of popular devotion. The making and consuming of bread had its own beliefs, practices, and taboos; "good like bread" was a universal saying. Among Sicilians, it was a deadly sin to waste bread or throw it away; some kissed the blade of the knife before cutting it. A loaf of bread was never to be set upside down, and particular shapes were thought to bring good luck and were prepared for special feasts.[59] As they did with meat, immigrant bakers began to take advantage of inexpensive wheat flour and use it to make traditional breads more affordable, so that the spongy bread baked in the city's industrial ovens rarely entered immigrant homes. Leonard Covello remembered that, when he was in the first grade, "at noontime a bowl of soup was served to [the children] with some white, soft bread that made better spitballs than eating in comparison with the substantial and solid homemade bread to which [he] was accustomed."[60] Immigrant children could not avoid the implications of cultural identity embodied in the worlds of "Italian" and "American" bread.

The modernization of the food production and market in the United States dramatically influenced the taste for pasta among Italian immigrants, helping to make it the Italian American signature food. Contrary to popular belief, pasta was neither common throughout Italy at the time of the "great migration" nor an everyday dish for poor families. Only in Naples had pasta become an important part of the popular diet, and then only since the eighteenth century. As historian Emilio Sereni artfully explains, the introduction of dried pasta in Naples was a clever way to replace the meats and green vegetables on which Neapolitans had relied for centuries but which had experienced severe shortages following the city's population boom.[61] In Naples and its surroundings—the main markets for the excellent durum wheat produced in Puglia and Campania—the macaroni industry had developed as early as the sixteenth century with the invention of the mechanical press and kneading machine (*gramola*). It was in the eighteenth century, though, with the introduction of steam power, that productivity rose, costs fell, and larger markets were created. Not until the 1830s, however, did pasta in Naples began to be topped with tomato sauce instead of cheese (even though it was introduced in Italy in the 1500s, the tomato, thought to be poisonous, had been used mostly as an ornamental plant).[62] By the late nineteenth century, the centers of Italian pasta manufacturing were located in three areas: the province of Naples, in Torre Annunziata, Torre del Greco, Gragnano, and Portici; Genoa; and Palermo. Industrial "dry" pasta, long-lived and easily shipped—unlike fresh pasta, which was handmade at home almost everywhere in Italy—quickly became a commodity sold throughout the country. Outside Naples, Genoa, and Palermo, though, pasta was considered a luxury food, much superior to the homemade product, and remained so—"an exceptional and festive food for the poor, an ordinary and everyday one for the rich"—well into the twentieth century.[63]

It was only with transatlantic migration that pasta (or macaroni, as it was called at the time) became the daily food of Italians of moderate means. Pasta became the most representative food of *cucina italiana* in America and the staple of the Italian American diet, materially and symbolically, for three reasons. First, unlike other foods that were popular in some Italian regions but unknown or disliked in others, pasta was universally liked in Italy and among all groups of Italian immigrants. The diffusion of pasta in the Italian communities of New York also resulted from the fact that the Italian food trade in the city was controlled by a mercantile class first largely made up of Genoese and, later, of Neapolitans and Sicilians.[64] Immigrant merchants from these regions had not only access to Italian sources for importing pasta but also pasta machines and the technical knowledge necessary to start a domestic pasta industry; they played a crucial role in making macaroni one of the essential commodities of the diasporic food market. Finally, despite suspicion of immigrant food in general and urban pasta production in particular, spaghetti was the first Italian food to become popular among non-Italian New Yorkers, and pasta dishes were the most popular items on the menus of Italian restaurants in New York. The widespread approval of middle-class Americans eventually legitimized pasta as the signature dish of Italian American cuisine and, at the same time, established the role of cuisine in the ethnic identity of Italian immigrants.

Even though many considered their stay in New York temporary and continued to live transnational lives, Italian migrants took full advantage of the high-status foods (pasta, white bread, meat, sugar, and coffee) made available by the revolution in food production. Albeit constrained by poverty, this migrant cuisine came to represent a new social and cultural pattern: in immigrant kitchens, traditional recipes were enriched, modified, and adapted to the new availability of ingredients. The New York marketplace offered immigrants not only a greater quantity but also a wider variety of foods. Exchanges between different regional foodways were common, since foods from different Italian regions were more widely available in New York than in rural Italy. By and large, the Americanization of immigrant food habits meant greater access to traditional Italian foods and the ability to emulate Italian food practices that had been prerogatives of the ruling classes, thus helping to overcome social distance. Immigrants could now be persuaded that the marketplace, consumption, and money would deliver on the American promise of freedom from want and the liberation from the oppressive class barriers of Italian society. By becoming free consumers in a free marketplace—however constrained by limited resources—immigrants found they could overcome material privation and social restrictions. And food was the arena in which this freedom could most profitably be exercised: Italian immigrant families were "more generous in providing food for themselves than for any other need of life."[65]

To Italian newcomers in New York between 1900 and 1920, Italians who had arrived before them seemed, indeed, to be *americani*, Americans. Their apartments, the clothes they wore, and the extraordinary quantity and quality of the food for sale in their stores spoke of a complete anthropological transfiguration.[66] These earlier migrants were themselves derided as *'mericani* (returnees from America) when they went back to their native villages, especially because of what they now ate and drank. Eating better was a sign of material success that could challenge social distinctions literally by making over the returning migrant body. The new consumer behavior of these *'mericani* not only caused jealousy but also carried a potential for subversion. "Some returnees buy meat, fish, etc.," noted a study of Calabria in 1900. "Against all this the class of small and big landowners lashes out, with outcries of deviance and viciousness. I still remember the indignation of a rich man of Nicastro [Lamezia Terme]: 'Once,' he told me, 'the *contadino* used to eat bread made of corn and hay. Today, he doesn't hesitate to buy luxuries, fish and meat! . . . He used to eat a meal a day, now he wants to have three meals like the decent people!'"[67]

In New York, immigrant food habits were modernized in many ways, but Italian immigrant foodways seemed notably resistant to national food corporations, mass advertising, chain store marketing, and the urgings of nutrition and home economics experts. The forces of mass consumer culture, at work erasing the differences in regional and ethnic foodways, largely failed to transform Italian immigrants into undifferentiated working-class consumers. First-generation Italian Americans were cautious about adding new foods to their diet, resisting what they perceived to be "American" eating patterns. The ways in which Italian immigrants spent their limited budget on food, clothing, and other necessities functioned as a distinctive sign of difference and an investment in family and community ties—statements not only of who they were but what they wanted to become.[68] To the extent that Italian immigrant consumer culture articulated a resistance to cultural assimilation, nowhere was that resistance as strong as in the arena of food.

Until the 1920s, progressive reformers worked diligently at assimilating Italian immigrants by changing their food habits. Reformers believed that many of the problems caused by rapid industrialization and urbanization could be addressed by educating the urban poor about hygiene and home economics. Philanthropists, scientists, and social workers believed that immigrants in particular would be better off by abandoning their heavy, spicy dishes and alcoholic beverages for wholesome, nutritious, and cost-effective meals. Not only would these dietary changes improve immigrants' health; they would also reduce the sense of marginalization that made immigrants prey to the lures of radicals and labor organizers. To reformers, the widespread malnutrition of immigrants was caused not by poverty but by bad habits, irrational beliefs, and inefficient foodways; educating immigrant women and children about nutrition and domestic science would become an essential task. The New York Association for Improving the Conditions of the Poor was especially active among Italian immigrants. In 1913 NYAICP organized an exhibit in the Mulberry District's Little Italy under the supervision of Teachers College nutritionist Winifred Gibbs. Gibbs prepared large Italian-language posters of recommended menus for changing immigrant diets. The campaign urged immigrants to introduce milk and cereals for breakfast, substitute coffee with cocoa, reduce the use of oil and frying, and, to improve digestion, stop mixing different foods in one-pot dishes. NYACP activists tried, finally, to discourage immigrants from patronizing street vendors and grocery stores, which they described as carriers of deadly germs and bacteria.[69]

To the often aggressively ethnocentric approach of social workers—who considered Italian women's ways of cooking, childcare, and housework not simply "different" but "wrong"—immigrant women responded with mistrust and skepticism. "The Italian argument against social work [is] that it is done in a patronizing spirit by Americans who come down among them to civilize them as if they were barbarians," Italian Protestant pastor Enrico Sartorio argued in 1906. "Social workers burst into their homes and upset the usual routine of their lives, opening windows, undressing children, giving orders not to eat this and eat that. . . . The mother of five or six children may, with some reason, be inclined to think that she knows a little more about how to bring up children than the young-looking damsel who insists upon trying to teach her how to do it." Sartorio also noted that at the bottom of their report on a group of Italian families some social workers had written, "Not yet Americanized; still eating Italian food."[70]

The encounter of immigrants with food reformers provides a vivid example of the circular relationship among scientific discoveries, the interests of the corporate food industry, and reformers' propaganda. Historian Harvey Levenstein has suggested that early food reformers focused on the economics of food consumption and tried to introduce working families to an economical diet that optimized the relationship between cost and nutrition. This early generation of food experts was most concerned about the way that the basic components of food—carbohydrates, fats, and proteins—worked to supply calories and demonstrated how the same nutrients could be gotten less expensively from different foods. The discovery of vitamins—vitamin A was isolated in 1912 and B complex, C, and D soon followed—shifted attention more specifically to the relationship of food to health, and over the next decade scientists would demonstrate the link between vitamin deficiency and disease. The discovery of so many vitamins by the early 1920s had the effect of increasing the consumption of specific foods: under the rubric of "protective foods" were milk, some fruits, and some vegetables. Food corporations and advertising agencies, eager to find new ways to differentiate their products in a saturated market, soon discovered in vitamins a new marketing frontier. Products like Fleischmann's yeast and Sunkist oranges became popular across the country thanks to advertising campaigns based on their supposed miraculous properties.[71] The reformers who worked among immigrants were influenced by the same nutrition scientists whose discoveries drove the food industry and its advertising. Advertising championed modern home economics as the liberator of women from household drudgery and trumpeted the science of childcare and the dietary rules of the "new nutrition"; everything good could be achieved through the consumption of mass-produced goods. Although these messages were meant primarily for a middle-class audience, they were also targeted at Italian immigrants.

The case of milk is an example of the close relationship among science, the interests of the corporate food industry, and the reform campaign among immigrants. In late nineteenth-century southern Italy, adults rarely drank milk, which was considered an occasional drink for children, the elderly, and the sick. It was thought that combining milk with wine, fish, or tomatoes was harmful, and only the transformation of milk into cheese eliminated its impurities.[72] Even in the United States, before World War I milk was mostly a drink for children, but the discoveries of milk's vitamin-based benefits were used by food and dairy corporations to transform milk into a drink essential for everyone's health. Leaders in the dairy industry like Borden's and National Dairy Products, both of which controlled the distribution of milk in New York, used promotional campaigns in newspapers and in schools to encourage milk consumption as an essential source of vitamin D and calcium. As a result, after a long declining trend milk consumption increased after 1917 to reach a record of more than eight hundred pounds of milk per capita by 1925.[73]

The new popularity of milk forced nutritionists to investigate its proper share of a family's food budget, and they paid special attention to immigrant families. Not surprisingly, Italian immigrants were found to consume insufficient amounts of the drink. Lucy Gillett, the director of social service of the American Dietetic Association, was an enthusiastic advocate of the idea of protective foods and the importance of vitamins for health, stature, and longevity. From her studies of

Italians, Gillett concluded that the most serious weakness of the Italian American diet was indeed the absence of milk: "When they have to economize, they frequently economize in the wrong direction. . . . The price of milk in this country seems excessive and, not knowing its food value, a spirit of economy prompts them to use coffee instead." Gillett was afraid that "because of the scarcity of milk, calcium [was] probably deficient." She surmised, "Unless milk and butter are used freely, and in all probability they will not be if economy has caused a scarcity of vegetables, the fat soluble vitamins may be deficient also."[74] For many low-income Italian families the daily purchase of an unpopular food like milk was simply not a priority, a choice whose wisdom was indirectly confirmed by other studies showing that, because their low consumption of milk corresponded to high consumption of cheese, deficiency of calcium was not especially relevant among Italian families.[75]

Practical reasons also limited the use of milk among poorer Italian immigrants. Milk was difficult to preserve, and bottled milk, safer than the milk sold in bulk in neighborhood shops, was expensive. A resident of Italian Harlem remembered that "the grocer dispensed milk from the large cans by means of a one-quart ladle. The milk was placed into the customer's milk can, which held two or three quarts. The grocer would remove the cover from the milk can, fill the ladle, and pour its contents into the customer's can. He would invariably spill some of the milk. If the grocer was busy and forgot to put the cover back on the can, chances were that flies would find their way into the can. When a fly got into the milk can, the grocer would remove it, by cupping the first and second fingers on his right hand to remove the fly."[76] The many deaths of children from contaminated milk contributed to fears of cheap milk sold in bulk.[77] As a result, the initiatives of social work organizations to promote milk consumption among Italian immigrants had very limited success. The NYAICP conceded that economic issues were involved, for consumption varied predictably with the price of milk. Public milk stations that distributed price-controlled bottled milk were established in immigrant neighborhoods.[78] But most effective was propaganda in schools: it was the new generation that promoted the necessity of daily consumption of milk in immigrant homes.[79] Still, Italian immigrants continued to consume less milk than the recommended standard of one quart a day for each schoolchild.[80]

The case of milk illustrates how socioeconomic and cultural factors helped maintain the relative insularity of Italian immigrant foodways. Illiteracy and a limited knowledge of English, in the first place, frustrated the efforts of corporate food marketers and social workers alike in reaching out to Italian New Yorkers. "These people are illiterate, and the material telling them how to do things, material that would stimulate them to a sense of responsibility, is not within reach," Lucy Gillett lamented in 1921. "They have few books or magazines. They have so few contacts with the outside world that they do not know what is going on."[81] Illiteracy was in fact widespread among Italian immigrants. Between 1899 and 1910, 54 percent of those coming from the south of Italy were registered as illiterate.[82] As late as 1930, 18.1 percent of the Italian-born population of New York was unable to speak any English, compared to 7.6 percent of all the foreign-born.[83] The large number of non-English-speaking Italians was the consequence of particular labor conditions (Italian immigrants often worked in all-Italian gangs), the existence of segregated, "self-sufficient" communities (every Italian enclave had merchants, doctors, lawyers, and bankers who spoke Italian and its dialects), and the presence of many Italian-language community institutions—churches, union locals, mutual benefit societies, newspapers, publishing houses, and theaters. Linguistic and cultural barriers, coupled with discrimination, isolated the first generation of immigrants.[84] "My grandparents—all four of them—never did learn the language of their reluctantly adopted country," Jerry Della Femina remembered. "My grandmother did pull herself together and learn two words of English: 'no home.' It didn't matter who was at the door; 'no home' was good enough for any busybody. Life revolved around family, the children, sickness, and death. . . . Not one of my grandparents ever knew who the President of the United States was, and this was during the four terms of Franklin D. Roosevelt."[85] Since they often served as cultural mediators between the family and modern consumer culture, the second generation was targeted by educators, reformers, and advertisers who needed to reach out to immigrant families. A health official anxious to inform Italian immigrants about tuberculosis was advised by the Italian physician Antonio Stella, "The majority of adult Italians do not read any language, either Italian or English. On the other hand, most of the children read English, but few read Italian. If you want your plan to be successful, print your poster in English. The children will then read it and translate it for their parents."[86]

Italian immigrants at the turn of the twentieth century also resisted dietary changes because of poverty, the passion for saving money, and transience. The majority of Italian immigrants arrived with very little money and found work in the lowest-paid unskilled jobs available.[87] The U.S. Immigrant Commission found that in 1909 76 percent of the families in Italian neighborhoods earned less than six hundred dollars a year, among the lowest of all immigrant groups and well below the minimum required for a decent living in New York.[88] Furthermore, Italian immigrants were inclined to save much of their income by severely limiting consumption, replicating older practices that drew on the *contadino*'s fear of an uncertain future. In America, the traditional measure of social standing—land ownership—was replaced by new metrics: homeownership and cash. As early as 1904, Italians had more than $15 million on deposit in New York banks and owned properties worth $20 million.[89] Remittances to Italy were especially important, and in a peak immigration year of the 1900s, immigrants sent $85 million back to Italy.[90] The large scale of remittance reflected the transitory, short-term character of pre–World War I Italian migration to New York. Before 1914, nearly two-thirds of Italian migrants to New York were young single males, many of whom planned to stay in America only long enough to accumulate enough money to return and buy property in their home villages. Others worked seasonal jobs and returned to Italy for the winter.[91] From 1907 to 1911, seventy-three out of one hundred migrants to New York returned to Italy.[92]

The transnational mobility of Italian migrants had consequences for their foodways. First, the need to save money meant that little was spent on food. "One comes to America to work, not to eat," two Sicilian women told a doctor who, having diagnosed their anemia, was asking them about their daily diet.[93] A 1906 Bureau of Labor study found that "salaries being equal, Italian workers save[d] more than workers of any other nationality." In the bureau's sample of five hundred construction workers, most of them Sicilians, nearly all "ate only bread, onions, and two or three sardine cans a week."[94] Secondly, transnational migrants who contemplated an eventual future in Italy were scarcely interested in embracing American customs, including food. "The Italian in America eats well, when he has achieved—most of the time by eating bad—a relative prosperity," noted a 1906 report. "But his diet is immune from Americanizing influences. He is wholly Italian in his eating ways. . . . All that arrives on his table must be imported from Italy, or, when he cannot afford it, made in the Italian style by producers in our colony here."[95]

The mercantile institutions of the Italian community contributed not only to the formation of distinctive ethnic foodways but also to their long-term persistence, especially as viable local alternatives to the expanding national chain stores. In the early twentieth century, Italian food shops and open markets were, as we have seen, preferred targets of reformers, who criticized them as unclean and poorly organized. "The retail trade, being unstandardized, gives no help to the immigrant woman in the matter of efficient buying," according to social worker Sophonisba Breckinridge. "There is great waste in the number of stores, in the number of persons engaged in conducting them, in the needless duplication of even such meager equipment as is found in them. This waste will reflect itself in needlessly high prices which, while they mulct the buyer, bring the seller little gain."[96] This analysis typically overlooked the important functions that independent food shops and markets fulfilled, first of all in meeting immigrants' desire for specialized foods. Even Breckinridge notes, "The number of food stores in a block is about the same as in other districts, but the stock carried differs greatly. There are four or five greengrocery shops to one meat market, and these stores have a surprising variety of fresh vegetable and fruits all the year. . . . Every store has a large case of different varieties of Italian cheese, and the variety of macaroni, spaghetti, and noodles is amazing to an American."[97]

A common language and culture were vital in fostering relations of trust between Italian consumers and vendors. Merchants painstakingly nurtured that trust by sponsoring community events, religious feasts, and sports teams, providing jobs for young Italian Americans, and acting as channels to the larger society. Most important, the strong connections of food vendors to the community and the face-to-face relations they established with customers made it possible for them to give customers credit, which was essential for immigrant families trying to survive the ups and downs of the labor market. Among the Italian families studied by Odencrantz, "some paid cash for all purchases, while a number ran weekly or monthly bills for food. In times of dearth they were all glad 'to take out trust with the grocery man.'"[98] Credit secured the loyalty of immigrant consumers to Italian food vendors, even when the vendors' prices were higher than elsewhere. The immigrants' loyalty that was created by the various services offered by independent "ethnic" grocers explains in large measure why chain stores entered Manhattan's immigrant communities much more slowly than they did middle-class neighborhoods. Table 3 shows the marketplace penetration for city areas in 1933.

Chain stores—the most popular were A&P markets—offered rational, standardized shopping experiences. The stores looked the same, were "tidier" than local stores, and their uniformed clerks (who to immigrant eyes seemed "American" or "Irish") sold the branded, packaged foods that big corporations advertised on a national scale.[99] The policy of A&P was based on fast turnover and low inventory. Purchasing a large volume of commodities allowed A&P to offer competitive retail prices on easily marketable items; high volume meant high profits.[100] An integral part of this policy was the absence of customer service, including home delivery but most notably the availability of credit. A cash-and-carry policy denied immigrant consumers the possibility, in times of need, to buy food now and pay for it later. As a result, Italian Harlem families shopped at local A&P stores only occasionally, and during the late 1930s, families in the Italian neighborhoods of New York continued to buy most of their food from other Italians in independent grocery stores and public markets.

For all these reasons, and as a form of cultural resistance, Italian immigrants were only marginally exposed to the workings of the modern food industry. They were also characteristically suspicious of processed, packaged, and canned foods. Their predilection for fresh food, which they never seemed tired of declaring, may well have been the result of not having much of it in Italy, where, contrary to popular notions, southern peasants rarely ate "fresh" and "in season," relying mostly on cereals (bread, soups, pastas, or pulses) and poorly preserved cheese, fish, and sausages. These were the cheap, durable foods that could alleviate the ever-present fear of famine and hunger, while fresh fruits, vegetables, meat, and fish were highly perishable and often unavailable. The American marketplace, with its abundant supply of fresh produce, managed to fulfill ideals and desires

Table 3. Manhattan grocery stores and sales, 1933

			Total		Chain		Independent	
District	Spending Power	Families	Stores	Sales	Stores	Sales	Stores	Sales
1. Battery Park	$1,437	1,763	29	$1,220,371	9	$384,179	20	$836,192
2. Greenwich Village	2,657	23,990	232	5,097,226	58	2,600,110	174	2,497,116
3. Lower East Side	1,358	69,119	722	8,472,888	23	941,611	699	7,531,277
4. Hell's Kitchen	1,376	1,938	14	112,207		(combined with district 8)		
5. Chelsea	2,086	15,116	191	4,854,198	48	2,134,234	143	2,719,964
6. Madison Square	4,202	3,239	20	623,658	10	395,429	10	228,229
7. Stuyvesant Square	1,718	18,075	167	2,857,915	36	1,499,700	131	1,358,215
8. DeWitt Clinton	1,504	9,542	90	1,386,674	27	917,861	77	581,020
9. Columbus Circle	2,392	13,019	121	2,509,979	36	1,437,265	85	1,072,714
10. Times Square	6,804	8,001	67	3,496,534	37	2,464,539	30	1,031,995
11. Plaza	8,961	6,761	42	2,663,217	26	2,090,808	16	572,409
12. Queensboro	2,236	16,456	142	3,345,891	54	2,291,763	88	1,054,128
13. Central Park West	8,702	32,695	196	9,254,881	120	6,550,230	76	2,704,651
14. Fifth Avenue	10,511	17,934	152	8,163,810	88	5,316,083	64	2,847,727
15. Yorkville	1,863	29,712	252	4,539,491	58	2,024,820	194	2,514,671
16 Columbia University	6,238	18,629	82	3,169,458	38	1,747,135	44	1,422,323
17. Manhattanville	2,954	21,490	158	3,833,814	71	2,425,078	87	1,408,736
18. Mt. Morris Park	3,515	14,330	128	3,958,663	26	754,585	102	3,204,078
19. Jefferson Park	1,760	38,607	429	5,293,108	39	1,456,462	390	3,836,646
20. Harlem Bridge	1,720	8,635	76	1,106,413	10	466,254	66	640,159
21. City College	4,041	23,429	149	4,088,988	67	2,597,039	82	1,491,949
22. Harlem	3,097	26,869	223	4,480,475	64	1,967,464	159	2,513,011
23. Washington Heights	4,031	28,268	150	4,003,214	60	2,422,280	90	1,580,934
24. Inwood	3,715	21,133	84	2,468,233	43	1,809,890	41	658,343
TOTAL		468,750	3,916	91,001,306	1,048	46,694,819	2.868	44,306,487

Note: Districts containing the largest Italian enclaves (Mulberry Street's Little Italy and Italian Harlem) were 3 (Lower East Side) and 19 (Jefferson Park).

Sources: "District Sales Figures" specially compiled by U.S. Census Bureau. "Spending Power" is median annual family expenditure from "New York City Market Analysis." "Families" are from the 1930 Federal Census. Classification includes grocery stores with and without meats. reel 132, FTC.

that—despite romantic notions of the Old Country—were more often than not unfulfilled in southern Italy. In America, ironically, the easy availability of fresh produce spurred immigrants' opposition to mass-produced processed foods, which they saw as symbols of a threatening American modernity: immigrants rejected "mysterious" packaged and canned foods as either tasteless or bad tasting, harmful, and—not unreasonably—even poisonous.[101] "Canned food was not eaten at all," an East Harlem Italian American proudly remembered. "My mother went out shopping each and every day, for fresh fruit, fresh vegetables, fresh meat, and all the rest."[102] Except for familiar canned tomato paste, tuna, and sardines, canned food (soups, fruits, vegetables, meats, and sauces) rarely appeared on Italian immigrant tables.[103] There were even reports of Italian immigrants who, having received canned meat and other foods, sold them, exchanged them with neighbors, or just threw them away.[104]

The time-saving properties of packaged and canned foods had a certain appeal for middle-class women, literate in the language of modern consumer culture. But immigrant mothers were often hostile to easy-to-prepare or ready-to-eat foods that seemed to undermine their traditional role as persons in charge of meals and food rituals in the home. For many first-generation Italian American women, cooking was not only a duty but also a way to show off their specialist skills and earn the gratitude, respect, and affection of family and community. "There were no pre-packaged foods—they were against our religion," a third-generation Italian American recalled.

> One summer night my mother committed a sacrilege by bringing home a Betty Crocker apple pie mix. My grandmother, seeing Betty Crocker as a threat to both her sovereignty and her ability to run the house, started a tremendous fight. She predicted death and destruction if anyone ate the alien apple pie, and her prediction was made with the fervor of a gypsy. . . . With grandmother absolutely enraged, my mother went ahead and cooked the pie and served it after dinner. My grandmother sat there predicting that the children would die. Whether it was voodoo or botulism, the entire family got deathly ill from the pie. . . . It was the last alien food to enter the house for a good ten years.[105]

The widespread suspicion that early-twentieth-century consumers held about industrial processed foods was, of course, well known to marketers and advertisers. But to "traditional" consumers like southern Italian immigrants—used to producing their own food—mass-produced food was especially problematic: it was food reduced to an alien but edible thing, deprived of an origin, history, and identity.[106] Italians also mistrusted the advertising campaigns that, after the scientific discoveries of the 1910s and 1920s, claimed that certain foods were rich in vitamins, minerals, and proteins. In the course of a study that revealed the negligible consumption of vitamin-enriched bread and flour by New York Italians, interviewees would respond by noting, "On the other side they don't go in for all that business, and they're all healthier, much healthier than here."[107] An Italian bakery on First Avenue and 111th Street displayed a "No Pills Used in Our Bread" sign in its window. "The appearance of this sign coincided with the spread of the vitamin-vogue into East Harlem," Covello commented. "Contrary to the advertisements of American bakers which announced a new vitamin-enriched bread, this Italian bakery made it known to his Italian customers that he continues the old policy of supplying old-fashioned bread. This Italian baker was well aware of the popular suspicion against innovations in food habits, and capitalized on it."[108]

To many first-generation Italian Americans, "natural" food was whatever they had consumed in Italy or, more generally, what was a part of the normative dietary system that they had learned early in life. The insistence on this form of traditionalism and the great importance given to the freshness of food shaped the consumer behavior of Italian immigrants, many of whom still produced much of their food at home, even in crowded neighborhoods. First-generation Italian women wanted everything "fresh," whether fruit, vegetables, meat, fish, bread, or eggs. Poultry was bought alive and butchered on the spot. In Italian Harlem there were several "chicken markets" that also sold live rabbits, geese, and turkeys.[109] The pushcart peddler, aware of this obsession for freshness, yelled, "Roba della mia farma" (Stuff from my farm), even though his or her fruits or vegetables might have been bought at the wholesale market nearby. Shoppers often took such claims of provenance with a grain of salt, because Italian vendors always allowed them to smell, touch, and carefully examine their produce before they bought it off the cart.[110] In the city, fruits, vegetables, and herbs were grown in any available plot, in backyards, on rooftops, and on tenement fire escapes. Joe Vergara recalled that, in his house in Queens,

> The back yard was all Pop's—his little patch of Italy on Long Island. He spent every spare minute working in his tiny plot. . . . Rows of tomato and pepper plant in the center, tied neatly to individual stakes; beans along the fence, trained on strings; sometimes a few eggplants. . . . In the north corner of the yard, Pop built a grape arbor and under it he placed two benches. This was his retreat. Sitting under his maturing grapes—wine-to-be—he could forget the growing pile of bills in his shop, the overdue payment on the furniture, and his fading prospects of returning to Calabria with a trunkful of gold.[111]

Even chickens, rabbits, and goats were raised in backyards, basements, and attics. This practice, a violation of city law, fulfilled the desire of immigrants to maintain a high level of control and (emotional) participation in the food they produced. An immigrant couple confessed to Covello that what they missed the most about their native village was living with their animals.[112]

Sometimes, the act of processing domestic foods turned into collective rituals filled with symbolic meanings. One of these was wine making, an activity widespread in all of New York's Little Italies, where every fall, crates of California grapes were piled up in front of tenements and brownstones. Many families had their own presses, barrels, and bottling equipment in their basements.[113] Another common seasonal event was the making of tomato paste. In August and September, bushels of tomatoes were peeled, seeded, and boiled and the pulp left to dry under the sun on tenement rooftops. The dark, thick paste was then put up in jars under olive oil.[114] Making food at home was not only a strategy for saving money; its rituals also imbued simple foods with an identity that spoke of the whole experience of migration, and of the remaking of home in an American city.

The industrialization of food production and the dynamics of the food marketplace in turn-of-the-twentieth-century New York profoundly changed immigrant diets and was perhaps the most significant feature of their migration experience. However, their distinctive subculture was not receptive to the rhetoric and institutions of mass consumer culture. Although this resistance contributed to the longevity of distinctive patterns of Italian American food consumption and supported a large ethnic food market, it hindered the development in the United States of a modern Italian food industry before World War I. With few exceptions, it was only after the war that Italian-style food manufacturing shed its proto-industrial character to take its place beside other mid- to large-scale food companies. This happened alongside major demographic and social transformations in the Italian community as a whole.

A New Generation of Consumers, a New Generation of Food Businesses, 1920–1940

Between World War I and the mid-1920s, the Italian community of New York underwent major changes. First, with the outbreak of war in 1914, migration from Italy came to an almost complete stop. Migration rebounded strongly in 1919–20, but the racist Immigration Acts of 1921 and 1924 soon reduced immigration from Italy and southern Europe to a trickle. After the passage of the immigration restriction laws, new immigrants were mostly relatives (many of them women) of previous immigrants who had come to make the United States their permanent residence (table 4); many who had arrived before World War I as temporary migrants decided to stay in New York permanently. The steady flow of migrants, which constantly renewed the bonds between communities in New York and those in Italy, began to shrink. From 1921 to 1930, the percentage of Italian-born New Yorkers who chose to be naturalized as U.S. citizens grew from less than 20 percent to 33 percent.[115]

Table 4. Immigration year of Italian-born population resident in the United States, 1930 (percent)

Immigration Year	1930 (to April 30)	1925–29	1920–24	1915–19	1911–14	1901–10	1900 and earlier	NA
Total	0.3	4.2	14.9	6.2	17.2	36.4	17.8	3.0
Men	0.2	3.3	14.4	5.3	17.0	38.2	18.9	2.7
Women	0.4	5.6	15.5	7.3	17.4	34.0	16.4	3.4

Source: Adapted from Massimo Livi Bacci, *L'immigrazione e l'assimilazione degli italiani negli Stati Uniti secondo le statistiche demografiche americane* (Milan: Giuffrè, 1961), 20.

The practical end to Italian immigration after 1924 put greater pressure on Italian Americans to assimilate into American society as a requirement of permanent settlement, and immigrants began to think of themselves as new Americans. Another major demographic modification—the coming of age of the American-born generation—significantly helped the process. By 1920, New York City's second generation of Italians was larger than the first (table 5).

The slow but steady movement up from the lowest rungs of the social ladder was equally as important in the redefinition of Italian American consumer patterns. By the late 1920s, the Italian Americans of New York were more often employed in skilled and semiskilled occupations than they were before World War I (table 6).

In the 1920s, the Italian community of immigrants and their children began to experience upward mobility. Many families relocated from areas of first settlement in Manhattan to Brooklyn, Queens, the Bronx, and suburban areas now accessible by public transportation, much of which Italians had helped build. Many moved out in order to become homeowners; as a result, between 1920 and 1930

Table 5. First- and second-generation Italian Americans in New York City, 1890–1930

Year	Italian-Born	U.S.-Born	Total
1890	49,514	14,000*	65,000*
1900	145,433	73,471	218,904
1910	340,770	204,408	545,178
1920	390,832	416,216	807,048
1930	440,250	630,105	1,070,355

* Approximate estimation. 1890 figures are for Manhattan only. The Bronx, Brooklyn, Manhattan, Queens, and Staten Island (Richmond) were consolidated into a single city in 1898.

Source: U.S. Census, box 92, folder 20, FTC.

Table 6. Leading occupations of Italian fathers of children born in New York, 1916 and 1931

1916				1931			
Rank	Occupation	Number	Percent	Rank	Occupation	Number	Percent
1	Laborer	15,905	50.4	1	Laborer	5,321	31.4
2	Tailor	1,697	5.4	2	Barber	850	5.0
3	Barber	1,667	5.3	3	Tailor	713	4.2
4	Shoemaker	909	2.9	4	Shoemaker	633	3.7
5	Carpenter	651	2.1	5	Chauffeur	608	3.6
6	Longshoreman	596	1.9	6	Carpenter	429	2.5
7	Driver	546	1.7	7	Ice dealer	392	2.3
8	Coal man	325	1.0	8	Painter	379	2.2
9	Businessman	289	.9	9	Mechanic	363	2.1
10	Mechanic	278	.9	10	Plasterer	306	1.8
11	Cook	258	.8	11	Longshoreman	257	1.5
12	Baker	257	.8	12	Clerk	253	1.5
13	Painter	256	.8	13	Salesman	250	1.5
14	Bricklayer	237	.8	14	Baker	231	1.4
15	Printer	214	.7	15	Butcher	228	1.3
16	Fruit dealer	199	.6	16	Bricklayer	216	1.3
17	Plasterer	198	.6	17	Iceman	192	1.1
18	Presser	195	.6	18	Driver	180	1.1
19	Bootblack	192	.6	19	Presser	170	1.0
20	Butcher	191	.6	20	Fruit dealer	142	.8
21	Waiter	176	.6	21	Ice and coal	139	.8
22	Proprietor	167	.5	22	Cook	133	.8
23	Musician	155	.5	23	Businessman	130	.8
24	Merchant	151	.5	24	Peddler	116	.7
25	Salesman	147	.5	25	Printer	114	.7
26	Street cleaner	143	.5	26	Trucking	101	.6
27	Machinist	140	.4	27	Plumber	99	.6
28	Mason	137	.4	28	Electrician	93	.5
29	Piano maker	131	.4	29	Machinist	93	.5
30	Clerk	130	.4	30	Musician	89	.5
31	Operator	125	.4	31	Contractor	88	.5
32	Grocer	118	.4	32	Proprietor	88	.5
33	Bartender	112	.4	33	Waiter	87	.5
34	Porter	108	.3	34	Mason	76	.4
35	Iceman	106	.3	35	Foreman	73	.4
36	Chauffeur	103	.3	36	Cabinetmaker	69	.4
Total		31,556	100.0	Total		16,945	100.0
36 leading occupations		27,209	86.2	36 leading occupations		13,700	80.5
All other occupations		4,092	13.0	All other occupations		3,053	18.4
Unknown		255	.8	Unknown		117	.7
				Unemployed		75	.4

Source: Birth certificates on file at the Division of Vital Statistics, Department of Health, New York City. John J. D'Alesandre, *Occupational Trends of Italians in New York City* (New York: Casa Italiana Educational Bureau, Columbia University, 1934).

the Italian population of Brooklyn surpassed that of Manhattan (table 7). Only the Depression interrupted this second, internal migration, which would resume vigorously after World War II. Even though those who left went to great lengths to recreate their Little Italies elsewhere, their new communities were often more ethnically mixed than the old neighborhoods had been, and their own ethnic institutions began to weaken.

All these changes redefined the Italian American market. The consumer patterns that had characterized immigrants at the turn of the twentieth century—isolation from middle-class values and consumer styles, suspicion of advertising and branded products, resistance to nutritional reformers, and preference for food homemade or bought from Italian-run independent businesses—became more complex. Their tastes shaped in America, second-generation Italian Americans were less concerned about such traditional values as thrift and self-denial. Food imported from Italy was no longer essential to their diets. They were at ease with English, and although they generally liked to patronize neighborhood businesses, they were open to other options. They ate Italian pasta, cheeses, and sausages like their parents did but were more attentive to modern quality and packaging standards. Change alternated with persistence: many second-generation Italian Americans tended to incorporate the food habits, culinary practices, and consumer styles of American culture into a gastronomic system whose deep structures echoed that of their parents. Herbert Gans notes about the consumer behavior of Boston Italian Americans in the 1950s, "[Second-generation Italian Americans]—like their parents before them—place great value on fresh meat

Table 7. Distribution of Italian-born population in New York City's five boroughs, 1900–1930 (percent)

	1900	1910	1920	1930
Manhattan	71.4*	58.6	47.2	26.7
Brooklyn	25.6	29.5	35.3	43.9
Bronx	*	7.4	10.1	15.3
Queens	2.1	3.3	5.1	11.4
Richmond	1.0	1.3	2.2	2.5
Total Number	145,433	340,756	390,862	440, 250

* The figures for Manhattan and the Bronx in 1900 are combined because the Bronx became a separate county only in 1904.

Sources: U.S. Census, 1900, 1910, and 1920, adapted from Thomas Kessner, *The Golden Door: Italian and Jewish Immigrant Mobility in New York City, 1880–1915* (New York: Oxford University Press, 1977), 155; New York City Census, 1930, adapted from William B. Shedd, *Italian Population in New York* (New York: Casa Italiana Educational Bureau, 1934), 3.

and produce, and the refrigerator is useful for eliminating daily shopping trips. But this fact has not encouraged the use of more American dishes, or frozen and canned goods. Refrigerators can be used to store the foods of any culture, and require no changes in basic patterns of living."[116]

The Italian business community of New York, especially its entrepreneurs in the Italian food trade, was deeply affected by the social changes that marked the interwar years. In the 1920s and 1930s, many of the food businesses aimed at the Italian American market expanded to become important players in the local and national economy. After World War I, the community's wealth, much of which used to be sent back home in remittances, stayed more often in New York, providing Italian American businesses with unprecedented amounts of investment capital.[117] In the late 1920s, a study of the five largest banks in the city revealed that Italian American deposits accounted for 15 to 35 percent of the banks' total value, or more than $150 million. An equally large amount was on deposit in the city's three largest Italian banks.[118] This was an extraordinary pool of money, and it formed the bulk of the capital available for the development of ethnic entrepreneurship. The Italian American business community also experienced important changes in terms of human capital. A new generation of American-born entrepreneurs educated in public and Catholic high schools and sometimes in colleges, fluent in English and equipped with professional skills, was able to overcome the barriers that had often kept the previous generation within the relatively safe boundaries of the ethnic marketplace. These factors heralded a new Italian entrepreneurial class and a new, larger presence of Italian ethnic businesses in the national economy.

This development was helped significantly by World War I, the turning point in the growth of the domestic Italian food industry. The end of food imports from Italy during the war spurred the expansion of local Italian food manufacturing. Later, the Depression and a long list of tariffs that culminated in the Smoot-Hawley Tariff Act of 1930 dramatically reduced the consumption of Italian imports. The WPA Federal Writers' Project noted, "The manufacture of macaroni, in New York City as well in the entire U.S., prior to 1914 was more or less in the stage of a household industry and more than one-third of the quantity domestically consumed was imported principally from Italy. From 1914 to 1932 the production has increased about 100 percent, while imports declined 92 percent." By the mid-1930s, the local pasta industry was "one of the major Italian industries engaging thousands of workers and doing a tremendous volume of business per annum."[119]

It was from this changing marketplace of many small businesses serving immigrant enclaves that a few medium- to large-sized Italian food manufacturing businesses emerged, some of which gradually developed into large firms that attracted a nationwide Italian American consumer base. The new generation of Italian food entrepreneurs helped reshape the Italian American market by adding their ethnic social and cultural capital to modernized methods of production and marketing; they managed to create an aura of *Italianità* around their products by asserting the Italian identity of their products or inventing one where it did not exist, while at the same time meeting the standards required by modern consumer culture—low price, quality, purity, and ease of preparation.

These "new" Italian food businesses, typically located in outer boroughs or the suburbs, depended on modern public relations rather than the face-to-face relations and everyday transactions that characterized small neighborhood businesses. "New" Italian food entrepreneurs enthusiastically joined what they thought to be the "American system" of conducting business through mass production and scientific management. They were especially proud of the advanced technology, efficiency, and cleanliness of their production plants. An important early Italian American pasta manufacturer, for example, argued, "Italians of Italy have much to learn from us. The American methods and systems of division of labor, perfect equipment, and constant innovation aimed at increasing production—that is, achieving a greater output with the same or less effort—have been adopted by us with no hesitation, with benefits that in our homeland of origin are positively not appreciated enough. For this reason, despite a two or three times more expensive labor, we can produce at the same price as in Italy."[120] Italian American food entrepreneurs were staunch supporters of new business cultures, new marketing strategies, and new production methods. By the 1920s, they were operating successfully in the larger consumer marketplace and continually modernizing their companies in response to the competitive threats of non-Italian businessmen, who were increasingly entering the Italian food market. Technological changes and growing commercial acumen were not the only reasons that Italian foods moved from an ethnic niche to broad national acceptance; this transformation was also enabled by cultural and social changes, from the "whitening" and improved public image of Italian Americans to the growing appreciation of the healthfulness and economy of the Italian American diet. In the shift from semiartisanal production to carefully controlled industrial processing, packaging, and marketing, pasta, in particular, lost its exclusive immigrant character and became a popular staple whose *Italianità* demonstrated the surprising appeal of cultural difference.

Before World War I, when the domestic pasta industry was small and imports from Italy dominated the market, the Atlantic Macaroni Company was the most important large-scale pasta manufacturer in New York. Its story is paradigmatic of the development of the entire industry: its birth as a small family business serving only the immigrant market, its growth under the guidance of American-educated entrepreneurs with access to capital and credit, and its early introduction of technologically advanced production. Andrea Cuneo, the founder of the company, was the nephew of Antonio Cuneo, a Genoese immigrant who opened a grocery store on Baxter Street, the nucleus of what would become Little Italy. With the expansion of the Italian immigrant neighborhood, Cuneo's business grew to include an Italian food import warehouse on Mulberry Street, where he later created Banca Nazionale Italiana. The bank's deposits were almost all the savings of immigrants, to whom the bank offered other services, such as currency exchange and remittances to Italy. When Antonio Cuneo died childless in 1896, Andrea Cuneo succeeded him as director of the bank. Andrea, who had attended college in New York, rejuvenated and diversified the business and purchased the Atlantic Macaroni Company in 1902. At that time, the company consisted of a shop at the corner of Ninth Avenue and West Twenty-Third Street, had no offices, and was worth barely $12,000. The next year, Cuneo increased its venture capital to $120,000 and built a futuristic steel and glass factory in Long Island City, Queens. The four-story building, 47–33 Vernon Boulevard, was three hundred yards long. Inside manufacturing, packing, and shipping operations were all automated.[121] Offices, the storehouse, and the huge drying room—where electrically operated fans dried the pasta—were on the ground floor. The top floors were connected with elevators and crisscrossed by tracks on which shuttled freight cars loaded with pasta ran. On the second floor, a hatch opened on a loading platform to fill the freight trains of the Pennsylvania Railroad with pasta. Observers praised the clean, ventilated, and well-lit building—a world apart from the often crumbling conditions of small independent pasta shops. By 1906, two hundred workers, almost all Italian men and women, produced sixty-six thousand pounds of pasta every day.[122] Three decades later, the Atlantic Macaroni Company was still one of the leading pasta manufacturers in New York and inspired a number of local Italian American companies to expand and mostly replace the small pasta shops that had once outraged food reformers. By the mid-1930s, under the direction of the Genoese immigrant Francesco Zunino, the Atlantic Macaroni Company produced twelve million pounds of pasta annually.[123]

The move of the Atlantic Macaroni Company from Manhattan to Long Island City made sense for a firm that sought to sell its goods beyond local markets. The nearby East River made it easy to ship pasta to New Jersey, Pennsylvania, and elsewhere. The opening of the Queensboro Bridge in 1909 and the subway that connected Queens to Manhattan and Brooklyn in 1913 accelerated the strategic development of Long Island City and put the factory within easy reach of a large labor force.[124] By the 1920s, the emerging Italian American competitors of the Atlantic Macaroni Company all had plants in Brooklyn or Queens. The Ronzoni Macaroni Company, founded by a former Atlantic Macaroni employee, Emanuele Ronzoni, was also based in Long Island City. Ronzoni arrived in New York from Genoa in 1882 and entered the pasta business in 1892 by opening a small shop with his cousin Giovanni Di Martino. One year later, Di Martino and Ronzoni merged with Atlantic, but Ronzoni branched out on his own again in 1917 with the help of his three American-born children. By the late 1930s, Ronzoni employed 250 workers and sold its products across a nationwide market.[125]

The third leader in the city's Italian American pasta industry was the V. La Rosa and Sons. An olive oil merchant who immigrated to New York from Sicily in 1907, Vincenzo La Rosa founded his pasta business in 1914. When he died in 1927, he left a thriving business to his five children, who transformed it into one of the leading companies in the trade. Control of the firm was taken by Stefano La Rosa. In 1936, La Rosa was the largest pasta company in the Northeast: the factory at 473 Kent Avenue, in the Williamsburg section of Brooklyn, employed over three hundred workers, and its yearly sales were estimated between three and five million dollars.[126] The key to La Rosa's success was its pioneering role in introducing packaged pasta to a market still dominated by loose pasta sold in bulk. La Rosa succeeded in creating a steady demand for packaged pasta, largely through massive advertising in the Italian-language press and radio. A true believer in technological innovation and modern marketing, Stefano LaRosa felt strongly that Italian Americans consumers had to be "modernized." In 1936, La Rosa claimed,

> [I have] always done the best to be in step with the times, which change continuously and always prompt new needs. There were, five years ago, packaged beans and lentils on sale; oranges and walnuts were sold under a brand name; soap, olive oil, and sugar were not sold anymore, like they used to do in the small shop in Italy, by the slice from a case, or by the pound from a sack. The housewife, even if poor, had learned to ask for every item by brand name when she shopped . . . everything except macaroni. Without doubt, there must have been a way to educate her to look for her favorite brand of macaroni, so she could know what she was bringing home.[127]

The eagerness of La Rosa to be "in step with the times, which change continuously" was shared by most forward-looking ethnic leaders. The dramatic social and economic changes of the postwar years were an alarm bell for the Italian American professional and mercantile middle class, whose market was primarily first- and second-generation immigrants and whose success depended on the willingness of Italian Americans to buy goods and services from community members. Faced with the growing influence of mass culture on individual choices and lifestyles, the most dynamic of the ethnic elite elaborated new, more sophisticated strategies to maintain their influence on the life of the community. Ethnic entrepreneurs extolled the advantages of industrial rationality, presenting their personal success stories as examples of the opportunities provided by the "American system"; on the other hand, they encouraged the community to maintain a strong ethnic identity and preserve Italian cultural practices. The consumption of Italian food products proved to be an especially fertile terrain for the coexistence and convergence of these apparently divergent discourses. For the most part, the new ethnic middle class fervently supported the capitalist economic and industrial order. Yet it was also enthusiastic in publicly demonstrating solidarity with the Italian diaspora, as long as it did not conflict with the celebration of the American values of the free market and modernity.[128]

The decline of food imports from Italy after World War I, the growing non-Italian competition for the Italian food market, and a changing Italian American consumer base helped Americanize New York's Italian food industry.[129] Still, retaining the loyalty of the Italian American market and the immigrant community was crucial to the fortunes of food industrialists. In the interwar years, even second- and third-generation Italian food entrepreneurs continued to emphasize the *Italianità* of their products and themselves. They demonstrated their involvement in community life by participating in patriotic events, charity initiatives, and ethnic associations. They supported Italian American political candidates. And they were the largest advertisers in the Italian American press radio. As community leaders, they kept investing in their prime market by celebrating national solidarity and supporting the diasporic needs of immigrants. In the Italian community's *Who's Who*—biographies of prominent people in the community, often published at their own expenses—food entrepreneurs often chose to be represented as the proudest Italian nationalists. Emanuele Ronzoni "was second to no one for charity work and for the admiration and the affection he nurtured for his homeland."[130] Eager to express his patriotism was Pasquale Margarella, the first-generation owner of a large chocolate and candy factory on Broome Street. Margarella opened his first shop in 1904, and by 1935 the Margarella Candy Corporation had an annual turnover of more than one million dollars. Margarella was proud of the "American" features of his state-of-the-art business: the scrupulous cleanliness, the purity of ingredients, the advanced technology of its machines, and the excellent salaries he paid his two hundred employees. Even though Italians were not his major market, Margarella paid for the reconstruction of the bell tower of the church in his native village in Basilicata. He was honorary president of the Mulberry League, president of the Italian Child Welfare Association, and president of the Italian Hospital of New York.[131]

Other food entrepreneurs turned to politics for prominence. Alberto Addeo, a Neapolitan immigrant and the owner of a large wholesale fruit and vegetable business, was the president of several Democratic clubs in Brooklyn. A tireless supporter of Fiorello La Guardia's 1933 mayoral campaign, Addeo organized members of his clubs to "watch the ballots" on Election Day and ensure "the vote en masse for the Italian American candidate."[132] Some food industrialists were active presences in the everyday life of the Italian community. Salvatore Russo, an ex-actor who had become rich in the 1920s from his vermouth and tonic venture, American Vermouth Company, was "highly esteemed among the Italians in Harlem, where he [was] extremely popular for his affability and inexhaustible humor, which he every now and then instill[ed] . . . in performances in which he star[red] himself."[133] In Italian Harlem, food producers and merchants were active sponsors of the feast of the Madonna of Mount Carmel. Marching at the head of the procession with the other notables of the community, they earned visibility and social status.[134] In Italian American communities, food ventures were also especially esteemed for the job opportunities they provided. The major New York pasta companies, La Rosa, Ronzoni, and Atlantic Macaroni, employed hundreds of Italian workers. During the Depression, in working-class neighborhoods most harmed by unemployment, "a great many workers who previously were engaged in different types of industries [were] absorbed by these ever-growing food concerns."[135]

In the 1930s, large Italian food companies found in the most revolutionary mass media of the era—radio—a powerful means for entering the everyday life of Italian Americans. Radio offered Italian American food companies the tools to influence the tastes and habits of consumers. The use of radio to promote Italian American food is a telling example of the construction of "traditional" Italian American cuisine through the creative blending of modern practices and traditional narratives. Radio programs of all types were important in the shaping of Italian American identity. Local broadcasts of Italian-language or Italian-oriented programs—Italian dramas, musical shows, and news, many of which were influenced by fascist propaganda—helped reinforce the diasporic nationalism of Italians in America. Equally important, program sponsorship by Italian American businesses encouraged listeners to believe that belonging to this diasporic nation could be expressed through a distinctive (ethnic) consumer behavior. Radio allowed immigrant entrepreneurs to give value to their products as symbols of ethnic identity and thereby shape a loyal market of ethnic consumers.[136]

In New York, radio stations began to air Italian programs (or English programs aimed at an Italian American audience) in the late 1920s, but daily Italian programming started only in 1930 at station WOV, owned by its founder John Iraci, the only radio station in the country to broadcast only foreign-language programs.[137] From the beginning, the WOV programs sponsored by pasta brands were by far the most popular. Ronzoni and La Rosa pasta companies invested heavily in ethnic radio advertising to support the launch of their packaged pasta. Sponsoring an Italian-oriented radio program was often a more subtle way of advertising than the use of commercials, providing the opportunity for richer narratives of *Italianità*; on WOV, Ronzoni sponsored the Sunday program "In viaggio per l'Italia" (On a voyage to Italy), in which an elderly couple described famous cities, beautiful landscapes, and folkloric events in different parts of the country; La Rosa and Sons offered its own very popular daily show of Italian songs and opera arias.[138]

In newspapers, these same brands took a more direct approach in their advertising. Their advertisements, which ran frequently, explained that thousands of Italian Americans had already chosen their products, which were produced through time-tested methods, and used shared ethnicity to create feelings of trust and intimacy. La Rosa's ads in *Il Progresso Italo-Americano* invited consumers to visit their "spacious, most modern, and spotlessly clean" Brooklyn plant in person.[139] In this way, by associating progress and modernity with foods perceived as traditional, Italian American entrepreneurs could overcome the resistance of ethnic consumers to mass-produced foodstuffs. Thanks to the ethnic advertising strategies of Italian American entrepreneurs, branded ethnic foods—albeit produced industrially and on a mass scale—gradually became part of the everyday lives of Italian American families and earned the same trust accorded to "natural" and "traditional" nonprocessed foods. The expansion of advertising on ethnic radio and in the ethnic press rested in turn on the maturation of the Italian food market in New York. By the late 1930s, the market, once made up of many small businesses, was dominated by a few major companies. In 1938, La Rosa and Ronzoni accounted for, respectively, 33 percent and 24 percent of all packaged pasta sales in heavily Italian working-class neighborhoods.[140] Although the Italian food trade, and pasta in particular, had been experiencing concentration from the early 1920s, the process accelerated in the 1930s for a number of reasons: the Depression; the larger producers' efforts to drive smaller competitors out of business; and the legislation against food adulteration and frauds that greatly benefited larger companies.

The Depression was indeed a turning point for the pasta industry. The economic crisis interrupted the long period of growth since World War I, during which the trade had experienced a steady influx of capital, technological innovation, improvement in production and packaging, and an expansion in demand. By the end of the 1920s and the early Depression years, overproduction and falling prices hit the industry hard. By 1931, the sales of U.S. pasta had dropped by 23.4 percent in only two years (table 8).

Small businesses were especially hurt. Some small pasta manufacturers tried to respond to the crisis by increasing production and spending less on raw materials, selling low-quality pasta at low prices.[141] The gambit did not work. By the mid-1930s, however, packaged pasta claimed almost half of the market. According to *Il Progresso Italo-Americano*, which reported favorably on the large manufacturers investing in packaged pasta, many of whom were advertisers, only the production of

Table 8. Census of U.S. macaroni manufacture, 1929 and 1931

	1929	1931	Percent of decrease
No. of establishments	353	306	-13.3
Wage earners	5,072	4,764	-6.1
Wages	$5,384,353	$4,473,494	-16.9
Value of products	$46,243,164	$35,442,187	-23.4

Source: *Macaroni Journal* 14, no. 5 (September 15, 1932).

brand-name packaged pasta could solve "all the problems of the industry." "The fall of prices barely concerns the packaged macaroni whose name is established in the confidence of consumers," the newspaper claimed. "Quality becomes the decisive factor because recognizable; frauds and imitations are basically impracticable."[142] In fact, sales of packaged pasta steadily grew and, as soon as working families began to have more spending power, eclipsed the sales of pasta sold in bulk.

Smaller pasta shops also had to bear the highest cost of local and federal regulations. The Committee on Standardization of Packaged Foods of the Department of Markets of New York fought hard against frauds in processing, ingredients, and package weight. The committee prosecuted manufacturers of "egg" pasta without eggs and "meat" ravioli containing little or no meat but harmful ersatz ingredients.[143] The 1938 federal Food, Drug and Cosmetic Act, which embraced the recommendations of the committee and was strongly supported by La Guardia, regulated the standardization and traceability of pasta products. For the first time, the law required manufacturers to provide their name, production plant address, net weight, and ingredients on the package. The law also set product standards for each shape of pasta. It specified that "spaghetti is the macaroni product the units of which are tube-shaped or cord-shaped (not tubular) and more than 0.006 inch but not more than 0.009 inch in diameter" And that "egg alimentary pastes are alimentary pastes which contain, upon a moisture free basis, not less than 5.5 per cent by weight of the solids of egg or of egg yolk."[144] The new legislation was a boon to the major companies, which had the capital necessary to comply with new requirements. By the end of the 1930s, the annual consumption of pasta in New York topped fifty million pounds (Italian American families ate on average ten to fifteen pounds each week), and there were a dozen pasta companies in the city.[145] Overall, though, the presence of local companies was waning, the victim of industry concentration and the rapid expansion of national companies. The Denver-based American Beauty Macaroni Company of Louis Vagnino, for example, merged with the Macaroni and Import Company of Kansas City, and the new firm's reach extended from Saint Louis to Los Angeles.[146]

New York City, the Magnet of a National Ethnic Food Market

It was not just the Italian pasta industry that grew to reach a national market in the interwar years. By the late 1930s, Italian Americans, like other Americans, ate food produced in factories located in distant places. On Italian American tables, sausages, wine, cheese, and other Italian food made in a number of U.S. states had mostly replaced the Italian imports that had dominated the market two decades earlier. The domestic Italian food industry took advantage of two turning points—the Depression and the introduction of high prices due to steep import tariffs—to capture most of the market. Beyond these competitive advantages, however, American-made Italian food won favor with the "new" Italian American consumers by successfully combining American standards of quality with the familiarity of Italian-style food made by other Italians according to authentic standards. In her survey of Italian Harlem, Marie Concistré notes, "It is believed that the macaroni produced by these now famous firms [La Rosa, Ronzoni, Caruso, and La Perla] is superior to the imported product. Cheeses made by Italians in America are growing in popularity. Wines made by Italians on the West Coast and here in the City are used more commonly than imported wines. The same may be said of ham and sausages, Italian style. Most of the meat products come from Chicago."[147]

Because of its huge Italian American population, New York became the main market for production and distribution networks that extended from coast to coast. New York's Italian community, reaching its maximum size around 1930, was still concentrated in relatively homogeneous enclaves, each well served by a comprehensive food distribution system. By the mid-1930s, there were 10,000 Italian-owned grocery stores, 2,000 bakeries, 875 butcher shops, and 757 restaurants in the five boroughs.[148] There were 497 grocery stores, 204 butcher shops and 409 restaurants serving Manhattan's 260,000 Italians; while 747 grocery stores, 362 butcher shops and 204 restaurants catered to Brooklyn's 487,344.[149] Ethnicity, as an important form of social capital, connected Italian food entrepreneurs and their communities in a web of personal relationships that made possible the development of nationwide commercial networks. This cultural capital was also important because it helped entrepreneurs understand and satisfy the tastes and preferences of diasporic consumers.

However, other modernizing factors—rarely highlighted in discussions about ethnic economies and enclave markets—were just as important. The national scope of Italian food, which linked Italian American producers in California, Illinois, Virginia, and elsewhere with Italian merchants and consumers in New York, could only have developed because of regular innovations in production, preservation, and long-distance transportation. Italian American food producers also integrated their companies into the economic system by paying close attention to the dynamics of the mass market and the regulatory environment. They also reached out beyond the ethnic marketplace and competed vigorously with larger, non-Italian food companies to increase market share. In product research and development, marketing, and advertising, Italian American fruit and vegetable canners, winemakers, cheese makers, and other food producers were often equals of the most advanced American food processing companies.

Examining the developing market for three basic products in the Italian American diet—tomatoes, wine, and cheese—provides a comprehensive picture of the industrialization of Italian food production in the interwar years. The canned tomato industry aimed at Italian American consumers first developed in California and New Jersey during World War I, stimulated by the end of Italian imports. It was in fact Italian importers desperate for product who prompted domestic tomato paste and tomato sauce canners to supply them with canned, whole, "Italian-style" tomatoes. Some California producers successfully matched the imported products, but when imports from Italy resumed after the war, the only appeal domestic canned tomato products retained was a slightly better price. The California "Italian" tomato industry barely managed to survive until 1930, when Italian American producers lobbied for government protection, and won, through the Smoot-Hawley Tariff Act, a daunting tariff of 50 percent of the value on canned tomatoes imported from Italy. Tariff protection spurred fresh investment, expansion, quality improvement, and technical progress. As a result, imports of canned tomatoes declined from 1,299,553 cases in 1931 to 854,081 cases in 1937. The imports of tomato paste decreased from 228,051 cases in 1931 to 162,520 cases in 1937. At the same time, the twelve Italian American tomato paste canning firms in California produced 1,516,787 cases, and four Italian American firms produced 202,882 cases of canned tomatoes.[150]

Also in 1937, researchers for the Federal Writers' Project study *Feeding the City* visited one such firm, the River Bank Canning Company of River Bank, California. The first to produce Italian-style tomato paste on an industrial scale, the company was founded in 1923 by Lorenzo Zerillo, who had come to the United States carrying varieties of tomato seeds. The company had rapidly grown in the 1930s thanks to the availability of a vast cheap labor force. Small farmers grew the tomatoes between July and October and sold the entire crop to River Bank. A few hundred seasonal Mexican migrant workers, mostly women, then processed and canned the tomatoes, which were shipped from Stockton, California, to New York in less than four weeks. The New York branch office at 99 Hudson Street sold the output to wholesale contractors and major chain stores like A&P and Bohack. By 1937, the company was shipping each year to New York more than three hundred thousand cases of peeled tomatoes and tomato paste under the Madonna Tomato

Products label; River Bank controlled 60 percent of the city's market. From its lead position, the company worked with the director of the city's Department of Weights and Measures, Alex Pisciotta, to develop the standardized packaging of canned tomato products. The company had long embraced modern, scientific management; it was proud of the cleanliness and organization of its plants and the automation of its production processes, even though much of the work still involved manual labor. In a River Bank promotional brochure, special emphasis was devoted to the photos of its lab, where "each batch of Madonna Tomato Paste [was] tested for purity to comply with the U.S. Food, Drug and Cosmetic Laws."[151]

In California, other Italian immigrants developed grape-growing and winemaking businesses whose principal markets were the large Italian enclaves of New York and the other big cities of the industrial East. Italian grape growers and winemakers made California wine a quintessentially immigrant product and industry, joining already established German, French, and Scandinavian immigrant winemakers when they first entered the field in the 1880s. Soon afterward and since then, Italians played perhaps the major role in shaping the California wine industry, eventually transforming the American wine market from the reserve of immigrant groups and Europhile elites into the mass national market it remains today. While other early California winemakers emphasized white and sweet wines, Italians specialized in strong, dry, red wine stable enough to be shipped long distances to the crucial Italian markets across the United States. Italian winemaking in California was from the beginning a transcontinental ethnic enterprise, and many Italian American wineries overcame Prohibition, the Depression, and the relative disinterest of the non-Italian mass market because they could easily reach the vast market of Italian immigrant consumers in New York through a thick network of Italian brokers, distributors, retailers, and restaurants.[152]

The blend of personal relations based on common ethnicity combined with the faith of immigrant entrepreneurs in innovation, scientific management, and American capitalism defined the history of the first major Italian winemaking company in California, the Italian-Swiss Colony of Asti. The Italian-Swiss Colony was founded in 1881 as a grape-growing cooperative by the Genoese merchant and real estate developer Andrea Sbarboro (1839–1923) supported by the wealthiest northern Italian businessmen of San Francisco. This same elite produced other immigrant success stories, such as Mark J. Fontana, the founder of the California Packing Corporation, later known as Del Monte, chocolate tycoon Domenico "Domingo" Ghirardelli, and Amadeo P. Giannini, founder of the Bank of America. The Italian-Swiss Colony's and other Italian wineries' access to credit through preferential ethnic channels is clearly one of the factors that explain the prominence of Italians in the California winemaking industry.[153] Sbarboro decided to invest in grape growing because of the steady growth of grape prices on the San

Francisco market during the 1870s and the availability in San Francisco of many unemployed but skilled Piedmontese, Tuscan, and Genoese immigrant farmers. Using the modest capital provided by the Italian businessmen, Sbarboro acquired fifteen thousand acres of land in Sonoma County, which had just been reached by the Northwestern Pacific Railroad. He then brought in northern Italian immigrant laborers and renamed the site Asti in honor of the Italian town famous for its wines.

By Sbarboro's design, the colony should have been an ethnic utopia. While he demanded that colony workers be naturalized—thus affirming his Americanism as well as marking the distance between Italian and Asian immigrants, who were denied citizenship—he also insisted that the community maintain an Italian character, providing exclusive benefits to Italian immigrant workers (company housing, an Italian school, and an Italian church) while banning Asian labor, placing a premium on Italian immigrants' (still contested) whiteness. Sbarboro's racist paternalism was advertised as a successful experiment in creating "perhaps the happiest community on the face of the earth."[154]

Asti had difficult beginnings, though. Not only did grape prices plummet during the 1880s; it also took almost a decade to achieve a successful harvest, at which point the colony was on the edge of bankruptcy. The key to the colony's survival materialized in 1888, when Pietro Carlo Rossi (1855–1911), a pharmacology graduate of the University of Turin, took the reins. Rossi wisely decided to transform the company into a winery as a way to cope with the fluctuations of the grape market. He began to experiment with innovative winemaking techniques and made the fateful decision to produce bulk wine and ship it to the thirsty immigrant markets of New York, Chicago, and Philadelphia. By the end of the century, the Italian-Swiss Colony had become the largest winery in California in terms of acreage, production capacity, distribution network, and market reach. Asti had grown from a plot of empty land to a small town, where Rossi's colonial house and Sbarboro's neoclassical villa advertised the settlement's prosperity.[155] Both Rossi and Sbarboro were true believers in technical innovation and modern marketing and advertising. The colony's mechanized system of winemaking and giant wine-storage tanks were widely publicized, and its wines were soon winning awards. "Tipo Chianti"—a red table wine made from a blend of varietals and bottled in traditional wicker-covered flasks (imported from Italy)—was arguably the first mass-produced, widely advertised, brand-name wine marketed in the United States. The unprecedented popularity of Tipo Chianti went a long way in establishing the Italian-Swiss Colony's reputation as the best producer of authentic California wine.[156]

The thirteen years of Prohibition were a crossroads for the first generation of Italian winemakers in California. On the one hand, Prohibition frustrated the efforts of Italian wineries to break out of their secure but limited immigrant market and reach a truly national audience; on the other, it provided new opportunities by scaring away competitors and creating an informal market for wine grapes thanks to a provision that allowed the domestic annual production of two hundred gallons of wine per household. At the same time, a new generation of Italian American entrepreneurs entered the scene. Two years after the death of Rossi in 1911, Sbarboro retired and the direction of the colony passed to Robert and Edmund Rossi. Together with Asti head-winemaker Enrico Prati, the Rossis reorganized the company to produce grape juices and ship to New York tons of grapes for Italian American home winemakers. With its established name and the proven dependability of its network of ethnic distributors, Italian-Swiss Colony was one of the leading winemaking companies in California and the United States in 1933, the year Prohibition was repealed.[157]

The consumption of wine in the United States actually increased during Prohibition in part due to the increase in household winemaking, an activity in which New York Italian Americans excelled. The national production of homemade wine in 1934 was estimated to exceed 25 million gallons, with Greater New York accounting for 10 million gallons.[158] In the early Prohibition years, buyers from the East "would wander around the wine grape districts," paying twice or three times the pre-Prohibition market price for grapes.[159] Vines that sold for one hundred dollars an acre before Prohibition were worth five hundred dollars in 1921 and one thousand dollars in 1923. By the late 1920s, with grape prices falling due to overproduction, the California wine industry was in very difficult circumstances. The repeal of Prohibition in 1933, though, meant a few positive years (the consumption of California wine grew from 26 million gallons in 1934 to 41 million in 1935 and 60 million in 1936), and Italian-Swiss Colony and a few other Italian wineries that had prospered selling grapes emerged as market leaders.[160] The trend toward corporate concentration also affected the world of California wine.[161] In 1929, Fruit Industries, Ltd. was born as a giant winemaking corporation amalgamating the Italian Vineyard Company (a very large winery founded in 1900 by the Piedmontese immigrant Secondo Guasti in Cucamonga, a former Mexican rancho east of Los Angeles in the San Bernardino Valley), California Grape Products, the California Wine Association, the Di Giorgio Fruit Corporation, and other fruit growers and winemakers. The new giant also targeted the Italian American market of New York.[162]

While many California Italian wineries specialized in the nationwide sale of bulk wine or wine grapes, others succeeded by bottling their own wines. In the 1930s, the Cella brothers' Roma Winery competed with the Italian-Swiss Company for the leading position in this market. Giovanni Battista and Lorenzo Cella emigrated from the northern Italian province of Piacenza to New York at the turn of the century, where they founded a wholesale business distributing both Italian and California wines. In 1923, the Cellas bought the Roma Winery in Lodi, California, which had been started by another immigrant, Martin Scatena, in 1890. In 1924, John Battista Cella moved to Lodi, leaving Lorenzo in New York to supervise sales. During Prohibition, the Roma Winery survived by selling grapes and making fruit juices, tonics, and liturgical wine. By 1933, the Cellas had heavily invested in new land and an expansion of the Lodi winery, building the country's largest. The Cella brothers proudly announced that their winery represented state-of-the-art modern winemaking, pointing to "the new brandy distillery, the recently-installed French sparkling wine equipment, the high-capacity crushers, the big fermentation tanks of coated cement, the temperature controls, and the seven million gallons of cooperage."[163] Two years later, after the Cellas had acquired the Santa Lucia Winery in Fresno, they expanded to almost twenty million gallons. In a few years, the innovative products of the Roma Winery were by far the most widely distributed in New York, and in 1938 *American Business Survey* claimed that the Cella brothers' was the largest winery in the world.[164]

The meshing of ethnicity and modernity, the importance of community and family relations, and the use of technology and modern marketing were decisive factors in another Italian food industry: cheese making. As they were for canned tomato products and wine, the 1930s were a period of growth and transformation for the production of Italian-style cheese. In little more than a decade, the cheese trade grew from a collection of small businesses, each linked to a local market, to a large-volume industry based in the most important dairy states of the country, Wisconsin, New York, and Michigan. Far from the large urban ethnic markets that absorbed much of their production, Italian immigrant cheese makers often became the principal buyers of local milk. By the late 1930s, the total output of Italian cheeses (Asiago, Caciocavallo, Gorgonzola, Parmesan, provolone, ricotta, Romano, and others) was second only to that of cheddar cheese.[165] In the interwar years, national production of Italian cheeses increased from less than two million pounds in the early 1920s to more than twenty-five million pounds in 1940, and finally—after the end of imports from Italy in World War II—to forty-five million pounds in 1943 and seventy-five million pounds in 1946.

Until the late 1920s, Italian cheese had been a fraction of U.S. dairy production. First-generation Italian immigrants preferred Italian imports to domestic products, so much so that the United States was the final destination of half of all Italian cheese exports, or eighty to ninety million pounds each year. At that time, domestic production was controlled by immigrant cheese makers around New York City, the most important market. Since most immigrants could not afford to run dairy farms, they bought milk from local non-Italian farmers. By

1929, the industry was thriving: twenty-six Italian dairy farms, concentrated in the upper Delaware Valley and in the southern Hudson Valley, produced Italian cheeses that were brought to the large New York City market by Italian brokers and wholesale merchants. The Italian cheese industry grew even more rapidly in the 1930s because of an ever-larger ethnic market, declining imports from Italy, improvements in production technology, and a new preference for domestic products by second-generation Italian American consumers. At the same time, as competition for raw materials caused prices to rise and the industry's value to escalate, the Italian cheese industry expanded in less costly areas of production that were distant from main consumer markets, most notably in Wisconsin.

The history of Wisconsin's Stella Cheese Company highlights again the importance of such factors as the availability of start-up capital and credit, the application of scientific and technical knowledge to the production of "traditional" foods, and the development of nationwide, commercial networks for the success of a business aimed at an enclave market. The Stella Cheese Company was founded in the late 1920s by two wealthy immigrants: Count Giulio Bolognesi, who had been the Italian consul in Chicago in the preceding decade, and Attilio Castigliano, the Italian consul in Duluth, Minnesota. Bolognesi and Castigliano purchased seventeen hundred acres of pastureland in Lake Nebagamon, Wisconsin, and started a small cheese-making operation with the help of a skilled cheese maker from Italy. The Italian communities in the iron and copper mine regions of Minnesota, Wisconsin, and Michigan absorbed this first production. Bolognesi and Castigliano traveled to northern Italy to perfect their still basic cheese-making skills and returned to Wisconsin with ten expert Italian cheese makers. Its location at the very center of the largest dairy region of the country helped the company—renamed Stella after the original name, Nebagamon Cheese Company, failed to excite Italian American consumers—purchase milk at favorable prices from local farmers, themselves "German, Irish, and Yankee immigrants." The success of the Stella Cheese Company was due to easy access to quality raw materials, efficient commercial distribution, and technically advanced production.[166] Because of Stella's success, many areas of Wisconsin "entered Italian cheese manufacture as a result of the coming of the Stella Cheese Company to the regions, and building with them . . . large modern cheese factories, equipped to manufacture several Italian varieties."[167]

The expansion of the Italian cheese industry in the Midwest in the 1930s also meant that the industry had moved beyond its exclusively Italian identity. Gradually, as markets multiplied across ethnic boundaries and as workers and entrepreneurs of different ethnic backgrounds joined the trade, the original Italian character of the business and the Italian origin of both cheese makers and consumers faded. This was not to be an isolated instance.

Made by American Hands: Non-Italian Producers of Italian Food

The interest of big corporations in immigrant and ethnic food is a relatively recent phenomenon. Only after World War II, and most notably since the 1970s, did food corporations looking for new products and untapped consumer segments begin to invest in ethnic foods by acquiring established independent ethnic food businesses or developing their own "ethnic" food lines. It was the counterculture of the 1960s and the prize it placed on cultural diversity, along with the drive of third-generation immigrants to "rediscover their roots" and the attraction of the new cosmopolitan middle class to exotic cuisines, that created a large consumer market for ethnic foods.[168]

The case of pasta, however, presents an intriguing historical exception. In New York, the success of Italian restaurants made pasta, their signature dish and quintessential "Italian" food, immensely popular by the early 1920s. By the end of that decade, spaghetti was so well liked by non-Italians that a kind of proto-fast food restaurant—the spaghetti house—became popular for lunch with businessmen, office workers, and store clerks in Manhattan's financial and shopping districts. Everyone, it seemed, wanted to eat pasta cooked in a large cauldron and covered with tomato sauce and grated cheese.[169] The entry of non-Italian entrepreneurs into pasta manufacturing and the growing consumption of pasta by non-Italian consumers were consequences of this success and offer two examples of the ethnic food crossovers that prefigured by decades the mass appeal of ethnic cuisines in the United States.

Non-Italian entrepreneurs, decisive in making pasta more popular among non-Italian Americans in the interwar years, also accelerated the industrialization of the pasta industry. On April 19, 1904, in Pittsburgh, the major pasta manufacturers created a trade association called the National Macaroni Manufacturers Association (NMMA). For the next four decades, leadership of the association was often in the hands of industrialists with Anglo-Saxon-sounding names, although Italian members were in the majority. In the 1920s and 1930s, the NMMA was especially active establishing its presence in mass media, utilizing the advice of nutrition experts and insisting on the dietary, nutritional, and convenience qualities of their products, just as the other food associations were doing. By the late 1930s, NMMA-coordinated advertising campaigns would help pasta become the first food from a non–northern European immigrant group to be widely consumed in New York and most of the rest of the country.

Not surprisingly, given the popular association of pasta with seedy immigrant ghettoes, the first task of non-Italian pasta manufacturers was to rescue the image of the product from its origins. To make a foreign food like pasta acceptable, they banked on the use of "modern" automated production to clean up its image and mute its ethnicity. Foulds, the company that first started selling pasta in sanitized packages in 1890, advertised its product as "Cleanly Made by Americans."[170] Franco-American, the company founded in Jersey City in 1887 by French immigrant Alphonse Biardot that first marketed canned spaghetti and tomato sauce, specified on labels that its "Spaghetti à la Milanaise" was "prepared according to the recipe of A. Biardot of Paris."[171] It was not until the 1920s, though, with the arrival on the scene of more "American" manufacturers and an all-mechanized production process able to deliver a standardized product, that pasta finally found a positive reception in the national press—in women's magazines in particular—and on American tables. The NMMA's effort at coordinating pasta manufacturers' marketing strategies was vitally important to this success. Through its trade publication, the *Macaroni Journal*, the NMMA lobbied Congress to increase tariffs on pasta imports, encouraged states to pass more-effective laws against adulteration, asked associates to cooperate to control prices, and coordinated national advertising drives.[172] These activities were aimed at protecting the industry against the possible return of imports from Italy, preventing overproduction, and stopping small independent businesses (most of them Italian American) from undercutting prices with lower-quality products. These small producers were the ultimate targets of NMMA's massive antiadulteration and antidumping campaigns. Since everyone understood that the only growth market for pasta was among non-Italian consumers (by the early 1930s Italian Americans were eating twelve times more pasta than the national average), NMMA's campaigns exalted the nutritional properties of pasta—an approach successfully applied to other foods—and explained how mechanized, "scientific" production methods guaranteed the safety of a food still largely perceived as ethnic.[173]

The *Italianità* of pasta was rarely celebrated in NMMA-sponsored advertising, a move that often divided the association's Italian and non-Italian members. The ethnic dimension of pasta was still problematic well into the 1930s for non-Italian manufacturers who wanted to turn it into an all-American food of easy, universal appeal. Henry Mueller, director of the C. F. Mueller of Jersey City and NMMA's president from 1922 to 1927, asserted in 1932 that pasta had actually been invented in China. Mueller credited Italy with sustaining its use "during the Middle Ages" but said it took U.S. industry to deliver a clean, healthy, and nutritious product. "Macaroni and spaghetti were famous in Italy," Mueller claimed. "Like many other good things, they migrated to America. Today America makes better macaroni and spaghetti than Italy has ever seen. It is easy to see the reason why. We have better manufacturing facilities. Our sanitary requirements are higher than those in Italy. It is a far cry from the macaroni of Italy, made by hand and dried on great racks in the open air, to the modern package macaroni of America, made in the most scientific of sunlit factories, entirely by machinery, and packed in triple sealed moisture proof containers."[174] The NMMA vice president, Joseph Freschi, sent a resentful reply to the *Macaroni Journal* accusing Mueller of deliberate bad faith.[175] In the end, Mueller's attempt at marginalizing the Italian identity of pasta illustrates the challenging nature of an immigrant food and the critical role played by modern industry in its Americanization.

In its promotional campaigns, the NMMA insisted on two key selling points: the low cost and the high nutritional values of pasta. In this effort, the NMMA was able to take advantage of two beneficial trends: the dietary reevaluation of Italian immigrant cuisine and the food emergency caused by the Depression. By the early 1930s, nutritionists and social workers had largely changed their minds about Italian immigrant foodways and, supported by the new scientific findings recommending a "balanced" diet, praised the rich fruit, vegetable, and fiber intake of Italian Americans. The end of immigration brought with it a new approach to urban reform, one that celebrated cultural pluralism. Women's magazines and home economics journals now discussed Italian food in a more positive light, and many social workers looked at food as a way to build mutual understanding with Italian American families.[176] In an Italian-language booklet of the late 1920s, Cecil L. Griel of the Division on Work for Foreign Born Women of New York's YMCA addressed a typical immigrant mother. "Your dinner is delicious," Griel states. "Your *minestra* is a thick and rich soup of which we Americans know nothing. Yet, it is really nutritious and inexpensive. Cauliflower, beans, a few slices of onions, a little cheese, and here's the soup! A little money's worth of each of these ingredients make for your daily fare, and it is perfect food. It contains all the quality nutrients that we need. We American women have much to learn from you."[177]

In New York, the Depression significantly helped revise public opinion about Italian immigrant foodways. At a time of universal scarcity, the traditional gastronomic wisdom of immigrants was now thought to be useful in maximizing meager resources. Italian American foodways, with their emphasis on inexpensive foods like vegetables, pasta, and the sparing use of meat, were often praised for being both healthy and cost effective. Frances Foley Gannon, the director of the Bureau of Consumers' Service of the Department of Markets urged the one million listeners to her radio program to include in their shopping list the cheap vegetables that were once eaten almost only by Italian Americans: bell peppers, escarole, chicory, zucchini, broccoli, artichokes, and eggplant. "Try a bunch of broccoli rabe today," Gannon suggested. "If your own vegetable dealer does not handle it, you will undoubtedly find it for sale at a nearby Italian vegetable store."[178] Pasta invariably appeared in the list of "nutritious and economic" foods the city distributed to poor New Yorkers, while the Home Relief Bureau included spaghetti among the foods that could be purchased with the grocery stamps it gave to the needy.[179]

To the NMMA, the harsh early years of the Depression seemed the ideal time to promote pasta as an inexpensive food. In 1930–31, the association, supported by big flour producers, mounted a $1.3 million advertising campaign in newspapers, magazines, and on radio, complete with giveaway cookbooks and gadgets. The ads showcased the endorsement by nutrition experts of pasta as an easy-to-make, nutritious food. Dressed with tomato sauce and cheese, pasta was a complete, balanced meal providing a perfect contribution of vitamins and proteins.[180] Nutritionists reversed their earlier opinions, now arguing that pasta was easy to digest and suitable for all tastes. According to the *Macaroni Journal*, "[Macaroni] is a food . . . highly recommended by physicians and food experts as the ideal food for children and grown-ups; for the sick and the healthy; for people of leisure as well of those under heavy business or labor duties."[181] Big business also joined the campaign for pasta. Betty Crocker, the cultural icon invented by General Mills, was enlisted to praise the value of pasta in managing a frugal household and keeping families together in hard times. "Unpaid bills," Betty Crocker warned, "can do more to wreck married happiness than almost anything else. Macaroni products, considering their food value, are the cheapest food we have." On radio stations coast to coast, Betty Crocker provided instructions and recipes for spaghetti and other types of pasta to an audience of sixteen million consumers. Her recipes were heavily "Americanized" and scarcely resembled the Italian originals: they included pasta salads; pasta with butter and cream sauce; pasta with hamburger and mushrooms; and pasta with bananas, pineapple, and marshmallows.[182] Betty Crocker's recipes did reinforce the core NMMA message: pasta might have come from Europe, but the U.S. industry had reformed it, turning it into an inexpensive, clean, pure, nutritious, versatile, and safe product ideal for any consumer.

For many Americans, though, the spaghetti and tomato sauce that Italian restaurants of New York were making popular came in cans. Food giants such as Heinz, Kraft Foods, and Campbell's began to market canned spaghetti in the 1920s, doing more than anyone else to make Americans familiar with Italian food. It mattered little that most Italian Americans looked with disgust at such an "unnatural" combination of modernity (cans) and tradition (pasta)—the popularity of canned spaghetti was an unavoidable sign of the interest big business was now taking in a cultural product of an immigrant minority that not long before had been denigrated by reformers and nutritionists and ignored by most U.S. consumers. Heinz added spaghetti with tomato sauce and cheese to its "57 varieties" in 1921, and Campbell's—ahead of the times for including spaghetti as accompaniment for its tomato soup in its 1913 cookbook—purchased Franco-American, the pioneering canned spaghetti company. The Franco-American brand survived the acquisition precisely because of its strong links to that most popular product.[183]

The canned spaghetti industry provides a vivid example of the link between ethnicity and modernity that characterized Italian food in America. The label of the canned spaghetti bought by thousands of Americans in the 1930s carried the smiling face and chef's hat and neckerchief of Ettore Boiardi. A native of Piacenza,

Boiardi arrived in New York to join his brother Paul, who, apparently on Enrico Caruso's recommendation, had found work in some of the most famous hotels of the city. After having worked at the Plaza, Rector's, Claridge's, and the Ritz Carlton, in 1924 Ettore Boiardi moved to Cleveland to open his own restaurant, the Giardino d'Italia. His *spaghetti al pomodoro* was so popular that restaurant regulars began to ask for portions to take home, which gave Boiardi the idea to start a cannery. Initially, the Chef Boiardi Food Products Company produced canned spaghetti in a small shop near the restaurant, but Boiardi soon purchased an abandoned silk factory in Milton, Pennsylvania. He signed local farmers to supply the tomatoes for expanded production. He also decided to change the name of his canned spaghetti to Chef Boy-Ar-Dee, to facilitate pronunciation by non-Italian middlemen, grocers, and consumers. "Everyone is proud of his own family name," Boiardi said, "but sacrifices are necessary for progress." In the meantime, his brother, still working in New York at the Plaza, introduced Boiardi to the president of the Atlantic & Pacific Tea Company, John Hartford; soon afterward, the A&P chain agreed to stock Chef Boy-Ar-Dee canned spaghetti in thousands of its stores across the country. This was the turning point for Boiardi's company, which now counted its customers by the millions. Chef Boy-Ar-Dee spaghetti became even more popular at the end of the decade, when the U.S. Army chose the company as a source for its rations. When the army adopted the food of an enemy country, a circle seemed to have closed; industrialization had transformed spaghetti into an all-American food. In the war's aftermath, however, Hector Boiardi no longer ran his company. In 1946, it was acquired for a substantial sum by the American Foods Company, which expanded and renovated the plants in Milton, adding a research division and restructuring management. Boiardi continued to work for the company as a consultant.[184]

In the postwar years, the acquisition of Chef Boy-Ar-Dee by the American Foods Company would represent a common pattern: the appeal of ethnic food to large corporations lay not just in the profit that they hoped to reap from the sales of new products and the exploitation of new markets but also in the responsive markets, proven networks of purveyors, and skilled workforces that independent immigrant businesses had created. The national popularity of Italian American food owed much to the innovative work of ethnic entrepreneurs. By the late 1930s, a group of experienced and skillful businessmen and a large market of consumers trained in Italian American food had come together in the Italian food trade. The acquisition of the best family-run competitors gave giant corporations an attractive point of entry into the "new" business of Italian ethnic food.[185]

Eating Italian: The Food of Modernity and Tradition

The culinary traditions that immigrants brought to New York underwent a process of modernization and industrialization in the years between the world wars.

While the mass marketing of food was expanding in the United States, New York's Italian immigrants and their children were elaborating a distinctive eating pattern that selected elements from their own food cultures and preferences, from exchanges with other cultures, and especially from an urban marketplace that offered them an unprecedented variety of foods. The authenticity of Italian American foodways—that is, their value in maintaining group identity across generations—was not simply the result of efforts to preserve traditions. It was also very much the result of immigrants' capacity to create a diasporic taste from their own transnational cultures, often reworked and refashioned, and from the careful incorporation of foods from different culinary contexts.

Much of the "Italian" food that New York's Italian Americans ate in the 1930s was produced by ethnic firms as technologically advanced as any of their American counterparts. Italians, like their fellow New Yorkers, ate food grown in faraway places that reached the city in modern refrigerated cars or freighters. Any understanding of Italian American foodways based on the simple opposition of nature to industry or tradition to modernity would be incorrect. During the 1920s and 1930s, in the demographic and social transformation of Italian New York, Italian American consumers found in food the most effective means for reinforcing social and emotional bonds in the family and the community—not simply as nostalgic longing for a lost home but more importantly as a meaningful response to life in an urban, multiethnic, and industrial society. Italian food was the food that reflected the experiences of Italian New York, as it was reinterpreted, transformed, and perpetuated in different reincarnations of many different Italian cuisines.

In all this, the extraordinary prominence of food entrepreneurs in the Italian American business community is telling; that such an important share of the immigrant economy was based on food and that food played such an important role in Italian American ethnicity eloquently affirms the theory that the maintenance of modern, urban ethnicity always reproduces political and economic interests. While the Italian American producers of Italian food in America were mostly effective in combining ethnic cultural capital with all-American capitalism to create modern ethnic consumers out of Italian immigrants, other food entrepreneurs followed different paths. The importers of Italian food from Italy, more concerned about maintaining commercial and political relations with Italy, invested more in immigrants' diasporic nationalism and emotional bonds with the motherland. The next chapter explores their strategies, strengths, and shortcomings.

5

"Buy Italian!"

Imports, Diasporic Nationalism, and the Politics of Authenticity

Food Importers and Diasporic Italian Nationalism

Nearly every one of the many actors involved in the Italian food business in New York between the turn of the twentieth century and World War II tried to make consumers aware of the relationship between Italian food and Italian identities. No other group played a more important role in connecting food consumption with Italian nationalism than the city's importers of food from Italy. From the time New York Italians constituted in a large immigrant market at the end of the nineteenth century to the declaration of war on December 11, 1941, New York–based Italian food importers worked strenuously to convince Italian immigrants that Italian imported foods, from pasta and cheese to canned tomatoes and olive oil, were essential links with their distant homeland and consuming them was an act of patriotism. The fondness of Italian immigrants for imported foods—which were at the heart of attempts to articulate a diasporic nostalgia, identity, and taste through shopping—helped make the food import business crucial to the project of diasporic nationalism. It was a large, complex process encouraged by immigrant mercantile elites in New York and their many supporters in the Italian government overseas. In fact, while food importers were just one of the many community institutions active in creating Italian nationalists out of immigrants who "had never been Italians in Italy," the nature of their business made them obvious nationalist leaders in the developing "Italian colony" of New York.[1] The promotion of an Italian identity among immigrants so clearly reflected the economic interests of importers that most invested heavily in it. The importing business required close relations with Italy, motivating second- and third-generation immigrants to learn and use standard Italian. Finally, this transnational trade in food went beyond vague cultural notions of *Italianità* to a relationship grounded in the material realities of economic gain meant to benefit an Italian diasporic nation at home and abroad.[2]

Exporting food to the Americas was a major sector of the Italian national economy. For this reason, first the liberal, then the fascist Italian state supported food importers in New York in all possible ways, making them prominent ambassadors of the uniquely Italian colonialism that was built upon its global proletarian emigration. Much poorer than the other colonial nations of the time, Great Britain and France, Italy set out to reinforce its weak international position by utilizing the communities of Italian migrants abroad as beachheads for its exports, as sources of hard foreign currencies through migrant remittances, and as strongholds of Italian culture around the world. Knowing that this transnational project could succeed only if the millions of Italian immigrants continued to prefer Italian imported foods to the similar products of Italian American entrepreneurs, various Italian governments consistently supported importers against local ethnic producers in the competition for the immigrant market. The Italian state's most important strategy was to establish Italian Chambers of Commerce in the major cities home to mass Italian migration in order to represent Italian export interests and assist local importers. The Italian Chamber of Commerce of New York was among the first to be opened (in 1887) and continued to be subsidized heavily by the Italian government through the following decades. One of its key functions was to unify the many import businesses that had developed out of local Genoese, Neapolitan, or Sicilian migrations by creating a powerful national import trade aimed at an inclusively *Italian* market rather than one split across smaller and more vulnerable regional communities.[3]

In New York City, many of the Italian food importers were immigrants who had started their businesses by catering to small circles of migrants from their own village, hometown, or region. In order to provide "colonial" goods and services to their fellow immigrants, they had developed close commercial relationships with specific places and producers in Italy. These early import businesses were as much informal economies of memory and emotions as they were of money. An example can be found among immigrants from Cinisi, Sicily: "Someone takes his chances in the business world. He writes to his relatives in Cinisi, has olive oil, wine, and figs, lemons, nuts, etc., sent to him, and then he goes from house to house. He does not enter in a business way, but goes to visit some family, talks about Cinisi, then informs them that he has received some produce from the hometown. And sure enough, the people will say, 'You will let us get some, eh?' 'Of course. Tell your relatives. I can get all you want.' In this way the business man makes his sales."[4] The circulation of food between the villages in southern Italy and their villagers in New York helped create the perception of synchronicity between one place and its mirror across the ocean and expanded the transnational dynamics that linked these distant places.

The number and influence of food importers grew at the turn of the century, taking advantage of the expansion of New York's Little Italies and the social isolation and culinary preferences of Italian migrants in the great migration waves of 1890–1914. From the beginning, the food import trade was a leading sector of the immigrant economy. By 1890, a group of wholesale importers, many of them Sicilians, controlled most of the citrus fruit and wine importing business in the city and also became the nascent class of so-called *prominenti* (community leaders). The wealthiest immigrant merchants accumulated not only money but also power and status by offering Italians a range of essential services. Food importers were often agents who collected immigrant paychecks to be sent as remittances to Italy. They served as share brokers (*banchieri*), who lent migrants money; as middlemen (*padroni*) who contracted out the labor of immigrant gangs; and as travel agents for shipping lines. Impressed by the concentration of so many activities in the hands of single individuals, Robert Foerster observes, "Capitalizing the timidity which the Italian often shows about trusting many people with his affairs, a versatile fellow will be at once a barber, banker, undertaker, wholesale and retail dealer, perhaps also a real estate and employment agent."[5] Money so earned was reinvested in food importing, which became an increasingly profitable business as the Italian population of the city grew.

After the turn of the twentieth century, however, food importers became mobile, transnational entrepreneurs who were transferred by their Italian firms to New York temporarily and who conducted their business both in New York and in Italy. This transnational entrepreneurship brought the business to a new level, both in terms of its systematic cooperation with institutions like the Italian Chamber of Commerce in New York and the Ministry of Foreign Affairs in Rome and for the strategic access to markets and opportunities it enabled across borders.[6]

At the same time, food importers had begun to develop strategies and alliances with the Italian Chamber of Commerce, Italian-language newspapers, and other community institutions aimed at nationalizing an immigrant market still segmented along village lines. These localist identities encouraged immigrants to consume the olive oil, wine, cheese, hard sausages, dried figs, or ripe prickly pears from their home villages, as a cherished way to reconnect to the place where they were born. Discussions about the old *paese* held in cafés or kitchens often revolved around hometown food—food eaten at the annual patron saint's festival, or corresponding to a season or moment of the rural cycle. Small-scale importers could survive on the specialized commerce that served the affective ties between immigrant consumers and their local food specialties, but larger-scale importing operations needed a broader, standardized market that connected ideas of identity and taste with the grander images of region and nation.

The notion of a regional cuisine functioned as a buffer zone in the immigrants' symbolic geography of places, scales, and nested identities. The intensive circulation of food between Italy and New York gave immigrants for perhaps the first time a sense of belonging to a region, since much of Italian imported food in immigrant communities in New York was sold under a regional name and origin. Sicilian Marsala wine, Ligurian olive oil, and Campanian peeled tomatoes featured prominently in the aisles of Italian grocery stores in Manhattan, their regional provenance clearly identified by names, symbols, and evocative images. Italian regional cuisines had emerged as distinct culinary patterns as recently as the nineteenth century, when middle-class and urban professional cooks drew selectively on local cooking and reworked popular dishes to their own tastes. The importance of native American foods such as tomatoes, peppers, potatoes, and corn in Italian regional cuisines betrays the deeply hybrid nature of supposedly timeless culinary repertoires, which were constructed by an emerging Italian bourgeoisie as a gastronomic model comparable to that of France.[7] In New York, imported regional food products may have had a particular appeal for immigrants from that same region. But the emphasis importers put on the rich regional variety of Italian food imports in their advertisements in the Italian-language press illustrated a continuing dialectic between the local and the national that was aimed ultimately at fostering immigrants' nationalism as well as their cultural and consumer identities. Inspired by the Italian Chamber of Commerce in New York, food importers insisted that immigrant consumers recognize the greatness of regional identities, which all together made the perfect mosaic of the Italian nation. Since the 1920s, discourses about the regional origins of imported foodstuffs also reflected a more specific political rationale: the fascist regime's effort at incorporating regional identities in the project of nation-building, which, with Rome at its indisputable center, acknowledged and praised the distinct historical, cultural, and economic identities of regions as coherent parts of the nation. Italian fascism encouraged a "return to traditions" that included the "preservation" of peasant and artisanal cultures and the promotion of folklore, involving peasants in festivals and costume exhibitions. Such a nostalgic, antimodern, and conservative revisitation of history—which Antonio Gramsci attacked as the bourgeois mimicry of popular culture—aimed at providing rural masses with a readily accessible identity to use in the celebration of national pride, in a culture that emphasized order, hierarchy, and patriarchal authority.[8] Food was so important to the effort that "during the two decades of fascist rule, the exploration of [Italian culinary diversity] was completed by [mapping] food regions, sketching out inventories of typical products, and promoting the awareness of local cuisines with books, advertising campaigns, shows, and festivals." Taken together, these practices effectively *created* the world of modern Italian food based on an organic system of regional cuisines.[9]

The establishment of a sense of a broadly Italian nationalism among Italian immigrants in New York resulted from a number of factors, including intermarriage, workplace and community interactions across regional and local boundaries, the emergence of an American-born generation, and the widespread definition by non-Italians of Calabrian, Sicilians, and Neapolitan immigrants simply as "Italians." But the immigrant middle class that strove to promote Italian nationalism among immigrants as a way to consolidate a stable market for their products and services certainly played a decisive role in the process.[10] Signs like "Grande Grosseria Italiana" or "Alimentari Italiani" in the windows of stores selling imported food were designed to overcome immigrant provincialism or their tradition of *campanilismo* (local loyalty extending only as far as the village church bell could be heard) and create instead a community of consumers defining itself as *Italian*. As New York's Italian American leaders fostered nationalism among working-class immigrants by building monuments to prominent Italians (Columbus, Garibaldi, Dante), organizing parades to celebrate the Italian participation in World War I, and encouraging the nationalist rhetoric of the Italian-language press, immigrant merchants managed to make food an integral part of many of these organized public celebrations.[11] From the perspective of overwhelmingly conservative immigrant elites, the instrumental display of Italian food was a particularly convenient expression of immigrant cultural nationalism; along with other "inoffensive" cultural features selected from an idealized past—such as folkloric music, dances, and costumes—food was central to the ceremonies that while feasting Italy's greatness, at the same paid homage to America by stressing group patriotism and avoiding conflicts of class.[12] Immigrants from different parts of Italy soon came to associate the green, white, and red flag with specialty Italian foods on shelves, stands, and pushcarts during nationalist parades and commemorations. The daughter of the owner of an Italian restaurant in Greenwich Village, Maria Sermolino, described the place of food in one such demonstration, a parade organized in June 1917 by the Italian Red Cross and other charities to support the Allied war effort. Italian and American flags waved all along Macdougal Alley, which painted wooden facades had turned into a replica of a street of Naples: "Clotheslines were strung across the alley and rows of gay wash vied with hanging strands of spaghetti to give a genuine atmosphere to the place." The supporters of the parade were community leaders and neighborhood merchants: Sermolino's father contributed a supply of spaghetti. The mother, "who had never been farther south, in Italy, than Milan, dreamed up some costumes for [her daughters] which may not have been authentic but were flattering and picturesque." In their "ethnic" dresses, Maria and her sister sold the family's food up and down the street.[13]

Immigrant workers endorsed the diasporic nationalism promoted by ethnic leaders less out of ideological passion than in response to specific challenges of life in New York. They became Italian nationalists in order to gain some advantage in the racial competition for social status that pitted ethnic groups one against the other. By trumpeting a robust Italian nationalism, immigrants reclaimed more dignity, respect, and security in their sometimes-disparaged American lives. Fascism succeeded among Italian Americans by meeting many of the same needs. Until the late 1930s, the Italian-language press in New York was not alone in boasting about the achievements of Mussolini; many influential Americans also praised the Duce for having defeated Italian bolshevism, modernized Italy and brought it into the circle of the world's great powers. Many Italian Americans rejoiced in the accomplishments of fascism for what it represented in their everyday lives: a sense of personal redemption and revenge and the opportunity to express to others pride in their home country.[14] A second-generation Italian American man told his friends: "Whatever you fellows may think of Mussolini, you've got to admit one thing. He has done more to get respect for the Italian people than anybody else. The Italians get a lot more respect now than when I started going to school. And you can thank Mussolini for that."[15]

In accord with such sentiments, food importers heralded a politics of food that linked the consumption of Italian food to patriotic support for the nationalist messages that Italian fascists spread among Italians in America. Indeed, the language used by food importers in trade journals and Italian-language newspapers was indistinguishable from fascist rhetoric. In 1935–36, in particular, the Italo-Ethiopian War provided importers with an opportunity both to prove their loyalty to fascist authorities (on whom the fortunes of their businesses largely depended) and to encourage immigrants to buy made-in-Italy foods. The embargo against Italy by the League of Nations offered food importers an opportunity to promote the consumption of the foods they sold as the most effective means that immigrants had to help an Italy oppressed and starved by powerful and evil enemies. Importers launched a "Buy Italian!" campaign hosted by pro-fascist newspapers, including the most important Italian-language daily in New York, Generoso Pope's *Il Progresso Italo-Americano*, the voice of the immigrant mercantile elite as well as of blatant fascist nationalism and imperialism. In spite of the energies and funds expended, though, the campaign was largely unsuccessful.

Overall, the decisive weapon that food importers used to reach their goals was *authenticity*: the idea that imported food embodied the smells, flavors, and taste of Italy, as well as the history, love for beauty, and time-blessed rural wisdom of Italian peoples, in a repository of attributes and values (today it would be called *terroir*) which no made-in-America "imitation" food could possibly replicate. The special financial sacrifice that importers required from immigrant consumers—imported foods were usually more expensive than equivalent domestic products—embodied another kind of authenticity: by spending their money on imported food, immigrants showed solidarity with their distant homeland and reaffirmed their belonging to the Italian nation.[16]

By the late 1930s, it had become clear that these expensive efforts to secure a committed consumer base had largely failed. In the long run, the failed experiment in food-based nation building demonstrated that the special value food had in the definition of Italian American identities was a result neither of the provenance of Italian foods nor the persistence of premigration food habits in diasporic New York. Rather, it was the experience of life in New York that helped decide what authentic Italian cooking was—the foods and the eating rituals that were embedded in and articulated the meaning of that unique experience.

The Golden Age of Food Imports from Italy, 1890–1920

Major Italian food importers kept close ties with Italy and with their Italian purveyors. Often they had their own company in Italy. Backed by the Italian state, they had an interest in the maintenance of good political and commercial relations between Italy and the United States and depended on positive images of Italy in U.S. public opinion. They worked carefully with Italian authorities in New York, and with community institutions such as the Italian press, banks, and shipping lines. The Italian Chamber of Commerce of New York, which organized all major import businesses and Italian companies with a local branch, was headed through most of the 1930s by food importer Ercole Locatelli. Like that of other major food importers in New York, most of Locatelli's business was in Italy. The core of his importing business was the cheese produced by his family's company in Lecco (near Milan), which owned several industrial-sized dairies throughout northern and central Italy. Even the cheeses he imported (Gorgonzola, Bel Paese, provolone, etc.) belonged to various regional traditions. Scion of a family of industrialists, Locatelli was born in the province of Varese in 1881 and studied in prestigious schools in Italy and Switzerland. In 1904, his family sent him to New York to open a branch of Locatelli, Inc. In 1915, Locatelli went back to Italy to volunteer in the army and joined the Italian military mission in London before returning to New York in 1920. Besides his office at the Italian Chamber of Commerce, in New York Locatelli was the honorary president of the powerful Italian National Tiro a Segno association, general consul of the Republic of San Marino, and Grand Officer of the Italian Crown. In 1939, he was appointed to the executive committee of the New York World's Fair.[17]

Many other major food importers held positions in the Italian Chamber of Commerce. Florindo Del Gaizo, born in Naples in 1872 and living in New York since 1909, was counsel to the chamber for many years. A manufacturer and importer of tomato products, he owned a canning company near Naples that employed hundreds of workers. Despite a minimal education, Del Gaizo dominated the canned tomato paste market of New York for twenty years, in the process becoming a millionaire and a Commander of the Italian Crown.[18]

A third noted figure was "Garlic King" Giuseppe Vitelli, president of the chamber in 1922–23. While Locatelli and others became rich in America on the shoulders of consolidated companies in Italy, F. Vitelli and Sons was among the businesses that developed out of the immigrant colony of New York. The founder, Francesco Saverio Vitelli, was a coral dealer in Torre del Greco, Naples. Through contacts with Genoese merchants, Vitelli began to export Italian food to New York and eventually opened a branch in Brooklyn in 1880. In 1901, Vitelli was succeeded by his son Giuseppe as the head of a business that now imported garlic, canned tomatoes, wine, fish, cheese, olive oil, and table olives in such quantity that several farms in Naples, Sicily, and Abruzzo worked exclusively to supply the New York firm. In 1905, Giuseppe Vitelli married the daughter of one of the three Savarese brothers, owners of a large pasta factory in Brooklyn, and created a new joint family corporation.[19]

Family relationships were often valuable assets for importers. Family cooperation, the free labor of family members, and leadership succession along family lines are recurrent factors in the biographies of these entrepreneurs. Stefano Crisafulli, a Sicilian-born counselor to the Italian Chamber of Commerce, ran his olive oil importing business (Crisafulli Brothers) with his siblings.[20] Raffaele Romano, born in Sulmona, founded the company bearing his name with his son Giuseppe. Under the Romano brand, they imported and sold such popular staples as Pomodori Sole d'Italia, Pasta Fara San Martino, and Olio Maiella.[21]

Successful importers liked to boast of their past patriotic endeavors (Francesco Saverio Vitelli, for example, would recall his participation in the Third Italian War of Independence at Prince Amedeo of Savoy's side) and often displayed both a fervent nationalism and an enthusiasm for fascism. The Tuscan immigrant Enrico Fucini, wine importer and licensee of Italian vermouth and bitters, was known to be a fascist from the very beginning. Antonio Piccini, the owner of an importing company of Brooklyn, had ten thousand copies of Mussolini's speech ordering the invasion of Ethiopia printed on parchment and distributed free of charge among the Italians of Brooklyn and Manhattan "to immortalize its memory." Piccini then sent Mussolini a bronze bust made by an Italian American sculptor.[22] The reasons for the importers' support of fascism were economic as much as they were ideological. Fascist Italy, with the active cooperation of the Italian consuls in major U.S. cities, refused to grant export licenses to Italian American importers who were not politically aligned. Even the currency conversion rates for commercial transactions with Italy varied according to the attitude of Italian authorities toward the U.S. importer involved. Often the political loyalty of importers was measured by the amount of advertising space they purchased in the pro-fascist Italian-language press.[23]

The wealth and influence of importers was built almost entirely on an Italian immigrant market that was in continuous expansion from the 1880s onward. From 1900 through World War I, especially, the enormous size of Italian immigration gave the Italian food importing business its golden age. The number of new immigrants to New York—the fundamental reason for the growing consumption of Italian imported food—climbed from 100,000 in 1900 to 286,000 in 1907; more than half a million Italians lived in New York in 1910 and more than 800,000 in 1920. Such a large market guaranteed a rather spectacular advance of the trade, even managing to counter the effects of mounting customs duties. In 1898, 550,000 gallons of wine and vermouth were imported from Italy; by 1910, nearly 4 million gallons were. Pasta imports grew from 5,016 tons in 1898 to 55,903 tons in 1910; olive oil from 3,324 tons to 10,586; cheese from 1,784 tons to 9,270; tomato products from 361 to 12,471 tons.[24]

The Italian population of New York bought food imports from Italy with extraordinary loyalty. Immigrants preferred imported foodstuffs such as pasta, canned tomatoes, olive oil, cheese, and cured meats over domestic replicas even when the latter were significantly cheaper. Although many pasta shops and factories were active in New York's Little Italies, until the second decade of the twentieth century imported pasta was widely considered of superior quality and dominated the market regardless of its significantly higher price.[25] This "profligate" consumer behavior frustrated social workers and nutritionists working with Italian immigrants. Not even the scarce supply and the resulting escalating prices during the Great War discouraged Italian families from devoting a large share of their food budgets to imported olive oil or cheese. Researchers at Teachers College studying immigrant diets during the winter of 1917–18 found that families that could not afford to buy enough food and heating oil still regularly purchased Italian olive oil for $4 a gallon and Romano cheese for $1.25 a pound (the average household in the study included seven members and had a $19.45 weekly income).[26] A later study by the New York Association for Improving the Condition of the Poor produced similar findings: "During the last few years, when Italian cheese was $1.50 a pound, [Italians] preferred to use less rather than to substitute American cheese at 50 cents. They could not see that $1.50 spent for American cheese would buy three times as much nourishment."[27]

As the Italian Chamber of Commerce recognized, immigrants not only were the heart of the Italian food importing trade but also were instrumental in popularizing those foods among non-Italian consumers, something Italian commercial institutions were unable to do. In a 1937 book celebrating the fiftieth anniversary of the founding of the chamber, Italian transnational entrepreneurs looked back with nostalgia at the "golden age" of food imports, while regretting their failure to create an American market that could supplement the large enclave markets on which so much of their profits depended. This ethnic market, in fact, had already started dwindling in the 1920s.[28]

The Food Import Crisis and the "Buy Italian" Campaign, 1920–1940

To be sure, even in the mass-migration years not everything was so "golden." The main obstacle to food importing had been the periodic revisions of tariffs to protect domestic foods and the domestic market from imports. In 1897, a tariff law increased customs duties on foods and other articles of wide consumption imported from Italy. Another protectionist raise followed in 1909, targeting especially food products, which by that time accounted for about 75 percent of total imports from Italy. The duty on canned tomatoes, tomato sauce, and tomato paste, for example, was set at 40 percent of the value. In 1906–9, claiming that there was a danger of blight, the U.S. banned imports of most fresh fruit from the Mediterranean; Italian lemons were among the few exceptions.[29] Italian food imports were also hurt by legislation. The Pure Food and Drug Act of 1906, a time when the domestic Italian food industry was still far from producing good-quality products, fought fraud and adulteration only in the course of interstate or international commerce (such as importing from Italy) but did not control intrastate trade, creating a large loophole for dishonest local manufacturers.

World War had an enormous impact on the importers' fortunes and on Italian food products as a whole. War needs compelled the Italian government to suspend exports almost completely. Frustrating the potentially beneficial effects of a liberal U.S. tariff law (1913), the outbreak of the war reduced exports from Italy to near zero. The predictable result was the rapid growth of domestic competition, with mostly Italian American entrepreneurs in the lead. Before the war, the production in the United States of such "Italian" crops as citrus, grapes, and tomatoes had already been growing; during the war, the absence of Italian produce imports allowed American growers to capture most of the Italian enclave market. California's Italian producers of wine grapes and canned tomatoes soon took over the New York Italian market. Emerging Italian American producers of wine, tomato products, pasta, and cheese were quick to seize the chance to lobby Congress not only for protective tariffs but also for favorable regulatory legislation, an opportunity mostly denied to importers of food from Italy. By the end of the war, many domestic Italian food companies were finally able to produce foods comparable to imports in quality, while significantly lower in price.

The most striking example of this change was pasta. During the war years, local manufacturing of pasta developed into a mass production industry engaging thousands of workers and producing 550 million pounds annually. Thanks to a better quality of durum wheat from the Dakotas, Montana, and Minnesota; cheaper fuel; and better-organized distribution and sales, the domestic pasta industry (a third of which was concentrated in New York State) offered a good product at competitive prices.[30] Almost overnight, Italian imports were virtually driven out of business; imports declined from an annual average of 113 million pounds in the five-year period 1909–14 to 2,567,933 pounds in 1927. The growing consumption of domestic pasta helped other related products, such as olive oil, cheese, and processed tomatoes, become increasingly popular. And the U.S. pasta industry even started exporting, conquering important shares of the market in Latin America and Great Britain (9,979,375 pounds exported, for a $900,000 value, in 1928) and becoming a serious global competitor for Italian exports.[31]

As discussed in chapter 4, similar processes were at play for other fundamental foodstuffs of the Italian diet, such as canned tomato products and cheese. Immigrant entrepreneurs established well-organized production systems and adopted marketing strategies aimed at the enclave Italian market that combined an emphasis on the modernity and quality of their products with a presentation that squarely conveyed the enduring *Italianità* of the foods. For example, the Italian Food Products Company of Long Beach, California, could advertise its canned tomato paste in *Il Progresso Italo-Americano* as "products popular with Italian consumers all over North America—Made with perfectly ripe, choice fresh tomatoes [and] following rigorously the most modern techniques of vacuum concentration and standards of purity and cleanliness." The brand names on its colorful tin cans were "Salsa di Pomidoro Campania Brand," "Tomato Paste Mariuccia," and "Concentrato La Parmense." Labels featured vibrant images of smiling peasant women, handkerchiefs on heads and wicker baskets under arms, that reassured the Italian consumer about the "natural" contents within.[32] The dairy industry in New York State, Wisconsin, and Michigan captured significant shares of the Italian markets from previously dominant imported cheeses because of—in the words of the Italian Chamber of Commerce—"an advertising campaign aimed at the Italian immigrant masses based on all-Italian names, nomenclature, and geographical indications."[33]

In the face of these marketing strategies, importers felt themselves defrauded of their principal customers by illegal or at least unfair means. Their frustration derived from the lack of effective means to oppose the dynamism of Italian American producers, who seemed to be better skilled and equipped to compete in the new consumer culture of brands and modern advertising. Imported Italian food was for the most part sold loose, leaving product promotion to the retailer, who personally guaranteed the quality of the product. With the emergence of branded packaged food, products were increasingly sold through advertising before they even hit stores, the guarantee of quality being provided by the brand; communication between producer and consumer thus took on paramount importance.[34] Importers fell behind their fellow Italian immigrants in the Italian food production business also because the latter, having lower production costs, could devote more resources to marketing.

By the mid-1920s, the end of mass migration, coupled with the emergence of second-generation Italian American consumers and even the Americanizing taste of earlier immigrants, made things worse for importers. The deficient appearance and quality of imported food packaging did not help overcome the preference of second-generation Italian American shoppers for foods that met American standards of presentation. Seemingly, foods imported from Sicily went from having a predominant position in Italian imports to a marginal one because of the low quality of their packing and packaging. "Sicilian cheese is packed in large barrels, and this package is absolutely not popular with the trade here," the *Italian-American Review* wrote. "Genoa and Naples have been continually improving their cans to such an extent that they are shipping now really beautifully decorated packages. Sicily not only has not improved in the cans (still using the old-fashioned ones), but the exporters have not even been careful enough to ship clean cans. . . . The olive oil cans are really primitive."[35] Finally, with the outbreak of the Depression, imported Italian foods, which had always been expensive in relation to the purchasing power of immigrant workers, were now perhaps simply inaccessible: in 1934, 200,000 Italian New Yorkers received some form of unemployment compensation.[36] Previously reluctant immigrants felt forced to resort to cheaper American substitutes. Even olive oil—an Italian import that, until then, had suffered hardly any competition—begun to struggle. In such a weak economy, the advertising strategies of domestic producers could better penetrate the market. Planters Nuts (the large corporation founded by the Venetian immigrant Amedeo Obici) canned its peanut oil in a special package targeting the Italian American market. The brand of the oil was "Ali d'Italia" (Wings of Italy) and on the can were reproduced the seaplanes made famous at the time by the transoceanic flight of fascist war hero Italo Balbo. The "Ali d'Italia" peanut oil cost $1 a gallon against the $2.50 average price of imported olive oil.[37]

If all these factors are added to particularly punishing U.S. tariff laws (1930), it is clear why most Italian food imports, after an overall good performance in the late 1920s, dropped significantly between 1930 and 1933. Sales of imported cheese grew from $8,582,000 in 1925 to $9,164,000 in 1930, but declined to $4,537,000 in 1933; a similar pattern for olive oil sales, which grew from $6,259,000 in 1925 to $7,353,000 in 1930, only to crash to $1,500,000 in 1933.

Table 9. Major food imports from Italy into the United States, 1925–1933 (figures in thousand dollars)

	1925	1926	1927	1928	1929	1930	1931	1932	1933
Cheese	8,582	9,321	11,187	12,898	9,745	9,164	7,255	6,666	4,537
Canned tomatoes	5,327	5,503	5,950	4,712	8,960	3,102	3,992	3,572	3,230
Olive oil	6,259	3,780	6,432	1,988	6,158	7,353	5,137	2,875	1,500
Citrus and essential oils	3,154	3,505	3,490	4,636	3,990	3,449	1,127	578	623
Dried fruit	5,921	5,730	4,955	4,587	4,446	2,558	2,926	1,147	678

Source: U.S. Department of Commerce, *Commerce Year Book*, vol. 2, Special Circular N. 294, Division of Regional Information, Italian Foreign Trade in 1933.

The passage of the Hawley-Smoot Tariff Act in 1930 was an outcome of the 1928 economic platform of the Republican Party, which focused on protectionist duties as a way to improve the dire position of American agriculture. It was no surprise, therefore, that, despite the vigorous lobbying efforts of the Italian Chamber of Commerce, tariffs once again raised serious barriers to imports of Italian foods, this time to an unprecedented degree.[38] Predictably, the sectors hardest hit were those in which a domestic industry was developing; the duty on cheese, for instance, increased from a minimum 25 percent of the product's market value to 35 percent; the duty on tomato paste increased from 40 percent to 50 percent.[39] The Hawley-Smoot Tariff Act made the next decade a difficult one for Italian imported food.

Until 1929, the importers' trade journals were self-critical in their analysis of their problems. Accepting the fact that mass immigration was over, importers agreed that they needed to organize and capture the non-Italian market: "An objective examination of the situation brings to the conclusion that our food trade in this country has just followed the easiest path; that imports had just focused on the tastes of the Italian consumer; and that very little has been done to attract on them the attention of potential American consumers," an article in the *Rivista Commerciale Italo-Americana* noted. The journal encouraged importers to improve distribution and marketing of their products, stressing the importance of modern packaging. Why, it asked, were Italian foods unavailable in delicatessens and groceries that served working-class housewives, laborers, and children by the thousands? An Italian antipasti importing company, for example, could promote the product by calling it "assorted lunch," sending its sales agents to visit food shops, and enticing their owners with advertising. Why not study what non-Italian consumers want—or don't want? Why not change the traditional oval shape of provolone cheese to fit mechanical slicers and make it possible to offer provolone as an interesting tasty alternative to "tasteless" sliced Swiss or American store cheese on luncheon sandwiches?[40]

Unfortunately, these strategies to broaden the market went unrealized. The Depression made competing with domestic products even more challenging, forcing importers to rethink their plans. The new priority reflected an old challenge: retaining or rebuilding market share in Italian immigrant communities that could still be a significant source of profits. The *Rivista Commerciale Italo-Americana* urged importers "to realize that unfortunately market conditions ha[d] changed and be prepared not to expand operations anymore, but to defend the positions previously achieved. Because [there was] no need to think about the American consumer, but to preserve the market of Italian products among their natural consumers; that is, the Italians of America." Modernization was still key. Importers needed to copy what the domestic producers of Italian food had done in "making a rush at" the Italian American market, and that meant using radio, the most effective form of advertising. According to the *Rivista* article, 80 percent of the advertising on Italian-language radio stations was by "domestic manufacturers," who were generally highly satisfied with the effect of radio advertising on sales.[41]

The Italian Chamber of Commerce finally took the plunge in the fall of 1935 when it funded a collective radio and newspaper advertising campaign. Prompting importers into action was the international political situation, which offered them the opportunity to use their most effective narrative: an appeal to the nationalist sentiments of the Italian immigrant community. The Second Italo-Ethiopian War had just begun, and the League of Nations had declared an embargo on commercial relations with Italy in response to its colonial aggression against the only independent African state. Britain, France, Canada, and forty-nine other nations joined the embargo. Timing could not have been better, importers thought, to launch a campaign to promote Italian imported food that would also be a call to defend diasporic national interests. Similar programs aimed at helping the homeland "strangled" by the League of Nations and world powers "envious" of Italy's successes multiplied in the city and across the United States. The major Italian-language papers, *Il Progresso Italo-Americano* and *Il Corriere d'America*, which had already begun fund-raising for the Italian Red Cross (to help Italy's war effort) eagerly participated in the importers' initiative.

The first appeal for "the defense, the diffusion, and the consumption" of Italian products in the United States was aired on radio station WOV Sunday morning, November 10, 1935. Ercole Locatelli, the New York chamber's president, addressed "the great mass of Italians, that more than any other factor, ha[d] contributed first to create, and then to expand the flux of commercial exchange between the two homelands; to the fellow Italians who ha[d] been the most important means of penetration of Italian products in the United States," asking them to "defend and promote Italian products in this country, setting a good practical example [themselves] in the first place by consuming them." He stressed, "This exhortation is not at all dictated by the selfish spirit for the benefit of a single class, but rather by the duty which all of us feel bound to help our native land." Since "nature ha[d] generously given Italy the gift of beauty" but not the resources necessary for survival, it was the obligation of Italians on this side of the Atlantic to buy Italian products and to provide an isolated Italy much-needed hard currency. On November 12, the consul general of Italy in New York, Gaetano Vecchiotti, similarly appealed to the "Italic feeling of the immigrant masses" that "represent[ed] a rock-like block in defense of the supreme interests of the fatherland," asking them to answer "Present!" to the call to buy Italian products.[42] The campaign also attracted local Italian intellectuals and cultural figures of all political orientations. Giuseppe Prezzolini, the pro-fascist director of Casa Italiana at Columbia University, claimed that the cuisine immigrants brought from Italy was a valuable contribution to American life, and Americans appreciated it as an expression of the conviviality and sociability of Italian life. Foods and wines were seen as an integral part of Italian culture, enriching it and, most importantly, transforming it into an valuable economic asset.[43] Leonard Covello, who at the time was fighting to introduce the teaching of Italian into the public schools of New York, also fought to prevent the disappearance of "customs like foods, drinks, and delicious local specialties," arguing, "If we allowed them to disappear we would just make the enjoyment of our existence poorer."[44]

For all its clamor, the importers' campaign produced disappointing results. In 1936, the volume of food imports from Italy declined below even the poor levels of 1934 and 1935 (table 10).

The economic impact on Italy of its war with Ethiopia negated any new growth in sales of Italian imports among Italian consumers in America. The international political situation caused the planned treaty on commerce between Italy and the United States to be postponed. Witnessing the downbeat political climate, on November 9, 1935, Locatelli wrote to the editor of the *New York Times* to protest the paper's "persistent attitude of manifest resentful antagonism against Italy" in its treatment of the Italo-Ethiopian War.[45] (The *New York Times* had called for the Italian arms embargo decreed by President Roosevelt on October 2 to be extended to include any trade between the United States and Italy.)

Table 10. Major food imports from Italy into the United States, 1935 and 1936 (figures in thousand lbs.)

	1935	1936
Cheese	28,173	26,400
Olive oil	28,573	22,317
Canned tomatoes	82,602	68,000

Source: Alberto Cupelli, "Foreign Trade of Italy," May 17, 1937, Reel 25, NYCG.

The general response of leading importers and their backers to the negative results of their "Buy Italian!" campaign was to blame "disloyal" Italian Americans. On May 3, 1936, the general manager of Isotta Fraschini Motors in New York, Elmo De Paoli, burst into an attack against the five million Italian Americans, calling them traitors to the race: "Even though these people became American citizens and pitched their tents under the flag of stars, that doesn't absolutely mean that they lost their right and duty to the feelings of friendliness, sympathy, brotherhood, and devotion toward the people of their own race who live in Italy. Their imperative, compulsory, peremptory, binding duty is to help Italy, already boycotted by many enemies, by purchasing its products."[46]

Italian Food versus Italian Food: Frauds, Imitations, and Canned Symbols

Indeed, the failed campaign for the patriotic support of Italian imported food was one of a number of flashpoints in the development of a diasporic and transnational food system. Three other volatile issues also took center stage: the fight against food adulterations; against "imitations," that is, the use of Italian names and images on foods that were not made in Italy; and against the acceptance, if not the complicity, of Italian grocers—in Italglish, the *grossieri*—in both areas. These three issues sparked a continuous, if mostly masked, conflict between Italian food importers, on the one side, and domestic Italian food producers and *grossieri*, on the other.

The long-standing practice of adulterating olive oil, for example, had become an especially profitable one in 1930s New York. Thanks to the social and cultural changes that had transformed the Italian enclave market, Italian American consumers were less and less interested in the authenticity of food from Italy. At the same time, modern advertising was *constructing* an effective Italian image of food products regardless of the actual place of origin. In this new marketplace, price rather than provenance began directing consumer choice. The consumption of olive oil in the United States rose in the 1920s (by 56 percent from 1920 to 1927). It became one of the leading imports from Italy, because of the expanding purchasing power of Italian immigrants as well as the discovery of its beneficial effects on health. Until that point, most Americans bought small bottles of olive oil in pharmacies as a digestive, cleanser, or cosmetic. The emergence of olive oil as a food and its new place in American kitchens were especially important for the Italian export economy because olive oil was the sole commodity without significant domestic competition. Attempts at developing an olive oil industry in California, a natural location, had been disappointing early in the century. The scale of production in California was far too small, local cultivars were suited more for table use than for oil, quality was inferior, and California oil, even if it could be found in eastern cities, cost just as much as Italian oil.[47] As an essential commodity in Italian American kitchens, olive oil was an important item in the Italian importing portfolio. In the first eight months of 1929, the consumption of Italian olive oil grew by almost a third—for the last time until after World War II—from 38,160,626 pounds in the same period of 1928 to 50,238,982 pounds.[48]

Frauds, however, were a notable feature of this flourishing trade. Cases of adulterated "Italian" olive oil, in fact, were reported back in the early days of the Pure Food and Drug Act. On August 2, 1907, an inspector for the U.S. Department of Agriculture caught an Italian grocer in Newark, New Jersey, with a shipment of oil labeled in Italian as "Olio per Insalata Sopraffino, Qualità Extra" (Superfine salad oil, superior quality). The package was judged to be fraudulent because it led consumers to think that the oil was manufactured in Italy from olives, when it was 100 percent New Jersey cottonseed oil. The court fined the grocer one hundred dollars. This was the first in a series of convictions under the Pure Food and Drug Act, which by 1936 topped one thousand cases a year.[49] Violations of the laws on adulteration had become so widespread in the mid-1930s that W. G. Campbell, chief of the Food and Drug Administration, strongly cautioned all olive oil packers and wholesalers and threatened them with severe penalties. In the Greater New York area, where both olive oil consumption and adulteration were most common, federal, state, and city officers joined in inspecting production plants and markets. The campaign led to charges against more than one hundred companies and their owners.[50]

The adulteration issue became even more complicated by the mid-1930s because manufacturers of inferior oils had by then learned how to market blends of different oils using language on their labels that technically kept their fraudulent products within the letter of the law.[51] Another cause of proliferating frauds was the easy availability of counterfeit or misleading packaging. Any small producer could readily obtain cleverly designed tin cans and fill them with anything from a mixture of Italian and other, cheaper, olive oils to blends of seed and vegetable oils. The deceptive labeling usually convinced consumers that the oil inside was all from olives, and all from Italy, when, often enough, it was neither. Given the lion's share of the market held by Italian consumers, it was clear to importers why Italian grocers agreed to participate in these practices. "Many of our Italian grocers are honest people," *Il Commerciante Italiano* argued.

> They purchase from big, serious, and responsible importing businesses; however, they often rise to the bait of the salesman trying to sell them "foods that are excellent substitutes, indistinguishable from the genuine product." Their greed for

> a few more dollars of profit and the salesman's pitch work wonders. Our "honest *grossiere*" became the accomplice in a crime which in the long run does not benefit him, but devalues the products that had made his store appreciated and damage his commerce in imported foods. If all the olive oil that is sold in American as "pure Italian olive oil" really came from Italy, the miracle of the transformation of the Tyrrhenian Sea into olive oil would be needed.[52]

Much to the chagrin of importers, the damage these frauds inflicted on the image of Italian olive oil was a boon to domestic manufacturers of corn, peanut, and sunflower oil. Already advantaged by the tariffs that burdened olive oil, they could now win over the large consumer market of disaffected "Italian masses," whose loyalty to Italian goods importers naturally had begun to doubt.[53] The damages of fraudulent olive oil and the effects of the Depression on Italian American food budgets combined to reduce Italy to the worst performing country among major exporters to the United States in the first five years of the 1930s.

Despite earlier efforts, the first significant successes in the repression of olive oil adulteration came only at the end of the decade and were the work of three Italian Americans. At the end of 1938, upon a request of the president of the Olive Oil Association, Henry Andreini, Mayor La Guardia ordered Alex Pisciotta, the director of the Bureau of Weights and Measures of the Department of Markets, to launch a massive campaign against adulteration and fraud in the olive oil trade. In two months, Pisciotta had 379 plants and warehouses inspected and seventy samples of suspect oil collected. Some of the samples, taken from cans labeled as "Olive Oil Imported from Italy," contained cottonseed, peanut, corn, or sesame oil and artificial coloring. These oils were sold at three or four times their normal value. At a single warehouse, nine different brands of fraudulent "olive oil" were discovered.[54] Following these seizures, Pisciotta used radio programs to alert consumers against all the possible scams they were exposed to and invite them to step forward and cooperate. In a March 4, 1939, broadcast, Pisciotta boasted that he had finally succeeded, giving special thanks to the work of the courts. In a Queens court, judges punished a storeowner with thirty days in jail and a $250 fine for selling artificially colored tea-seed oil as olive oil. The can in question was found to be especially deceitful because it featured an Italian flag, an olive

Table 11. Edible olive oil imports into the United States, 1930–1934 (lbs.)

Country	1930	1931	1932	1933	1934
Italy	63,172,081	45,950,078	44,605,850	43,789,211	29,691,280
Spain	24,546,034	24,016,100	26,052,384	22,006,321	23,399,353
France	3,157,197	2,707,436	1,698,074	2,412,712	2,414,295

Source: *La Rivista Commerciale Italo-Americana*, March 1, 1935.

tree, and an indication in Italian of its origin in an Italian region famous for the quality of its olive oil. The city's campaign concluded with the mayor presiding over a spectacular public destruction of huge quantities of fraudulent "olive oil."[55]

Frauds have been part of the food trade forever, but adulteration became widespread in the nineteenth century as a result of the growing separation between the spheres of food production and consumption. In the twentieth-century, ever more complex laws were passed to regulate the quality, contents, weight, and origin of the packaged, branded foods that came to replace foods sold in bulk.[56] In the interwar years, American ethnic food was still in the middle of the transition: much of it (as in the case of Italian imports) was still sold loose and was of marginal interest to brand-name food corporations.[57] In the case of Italian food, most frauds were perpetrated by Italian manufacturers or vendors at the expense of their Italian consumers.

Food frauds, in fact, overlapped with the second issue that disturbed Italian food importers: the use of Italian names and symbols to "fake" a nonexistent *Italianità* or to take advantage of the popularity of certain Italian foods in order to sell American-made foods under a slightly different name. Italian food importers in New York prefigured late twentieth-century concerns about authenticity (such as the European Union's systems of labeling to protect the names and geographical origins of specialty foods) in suggesting that genuine Italian food and methods of processing and manufacturing should be treated as patented trademarks against copies, imitations, and misleading names.

Authenticity, though, is a difficult project in the age of mechanical reproduction.[58] Alex Pisciotta failed to replicate his success in the fight against olive oil adulteration when he confronted the use of Italian nomenclature for domestically produced food, such as American cheese sold as "Italian-style" or "Italian-type" cheese. Those who sold a cheese made in America as "Parmesan style," Pisciotta argued, upheld a lie and should be prosecuted; parmigiano was an Italian cheese that had to be made in defined areas of the region of Emilia-Romagna. This time, however, the courts disagreed. A New York court ruled that the products were legal because the presence of the words "Parmesan style" and "Parmesan type" on labels indicated clearly enough that the cheeses were of domestic origin and made with the same recipe as the Italian parmigiano.[59] Since no U.S. law explicitly protected imported food from similar appropriations of original names and reference to places of production, imitations of Italian cheeses continued to be made and marketed by domestic dairies, many of which had Italian Americans at their head and Italian Americans among their principal consumers.

A third decisive issue that troubled importers was, indeed, the growing distance of Italian immigrant food producers and vendors from the bonds of Italian American diasporic nationalism, accompanied by a broader identity shift of New York Italians from identities as transnational Italians to those of ethnic Americans. Frustrated by the lack of legislation to protect the designation of the origin of imported foods, the Italian Chamber of Commerce began accusing Italian American food manufacturers and retailers of dishonesty and disloyalty. The "unfair competition" from the domestic Italian food industry, "to which grocers [lent] themselves willingly as well as opportunistically," infuriated importers. Tomatoes grown and canned in California could not be called *pomodoro d'Italia* (tomatoes of Italy) but the designation *pomodoro italiano* (Italian tomatoes) could be lawfully used for Italian tomato varieties grown in America. Importers knew well enough that the difference was too subtle for the everyday consumer. The possibility of using the adjective "Italian," the colors of the Italian flag, or Italian names, images, and characters for products manufactured in the United States set local producers free to devise marketing narratives and brand strategies that appealed to Italian American consumers.[60] "It is very easy, walking in any *grosseria*, to become acquainted with the names of the most illustrious Italians: kings and queens, princes and generals, poets and artists," observed *Il Commerciante Italiano* in 1934. "Try to ask for an anchovies can and they will offer you the Garibaldi brand; while you turn, you will probably hit your nose against a Dante Alighieri turned into a salami."[61]

The proliferation of national historic figures on packaged Italian food aimed at Italian consumers was a symbolic and aesthetic effort to set apart standardized products in modern consumer culture. While the value of every good is socially and culturally determined, mass-produced goods in particular demand an appropriate strategy of signification; to gain a competitive advantage, one company's standardized products or commodities must be distinguished from every other—individualized and enriched with symbols meaningful to consumers swimming in a sea of meanings. In this perspective, brands, logos, names, and images on the packages of commodities are widely understood signs that create a code of interaction through which consumers navigate the "world of goods" in reference to their own taste, distinction, and identity.[62] Roland Barthes, writing on the semantics of food, insists that the role of packaging and advertising is to invest a system of values in products otherwise barely distinguishable from one another. To the consumer, a brand-name food not only promises pleasure or the satisfaction of a physiological need but also offers a sign that "subsumes and conveys a situation, communicates an information [that] it is significant." The discourses of food communication identified by Barthes in 1960s France were the same as those utilized by Italian American food producers in 1930s New York, most notably, the representation of a particular food as the repository of a tradition inscribed in a national past. This was (and is) accomplished by mobilizing two different kinds of "heritages." The first heritage is popular and populist, reconnecting a food to an idealized rural past and its artisanal traditions. The second is "high-brow," representing a food's aristocratic tradition through icons of kings, queens, and highly representative historical figures, as well as dynasties of producers.[63]

These discourses are helpful in understanding the construction of *Italianità* in the branding and advertising of foods aimed at meeting immigrants' symbolic needs. In an age when food adulteration was a widespread preoccupation, the use of "noble" symbols in brand-name foods functioned as a guarantee of product quality. More importantly, the brand names and advertising images depicting a glorious Italian past could touch the heart of immigrant consumers. "No matter how illiterate he may be, [the Italian immigrant] is conscious of belonging to an old civilization," a social worker noted. "He may not be able to read a word or to speak anything but a dialect, yet he thrills when he hears the name of Dante, of Michelangelo, of Garibaldi."[64] The reworking of these nationalist icons on the packages of Italian food made in America hinted at a nascent Italian American culture and a distinctively diasporic consumer style. In the hands of immigrant consumers, Dante, Michelangelo, and Garibaldi were detached from their historical context and meaning to become commodified signs used by Italians to confront their place in America and their position in America's racial hierarchy. The Italian national iconography that adorned cans, bottles, and pasta packages was used by immigrants to root themselves in whiteness by connecting their everyday lives to the distant sources of Western civilization.

In such a narrative, the actual Italian origin of the food products on which nationalist signs were inscribed was relatively unimportant; the immigrant-consumer purchased a symbol supplied to them by other Italian Americans who could speak the same textual and visual language. In turn, the matching of names, symbols, and images with Italian food—wherever it was produced—created a diasporic culture and code of consumption that in effect became *authentic*, that is, meaningful to the experiences of first- and second-generation immigrants. Italian American food as a whole was consistently shaped out of this production of commodified *Italianità*, and for immigrants who in Italy had never tasted the food of other regions, the *Italianità* represented by Italian food made in America was real and living. For these immigrants as well, the way that marketers of Italian food produced in America blended the modern language of science and industrialization with "Italian" rural culture and tradition paralleled the strategies they used in their own migration experience.

All in all, the success of "imitation foods" in the Italian American market were reflective of the development of new Italian American identities out of transnational immigrant identities. At the same time, the conflicts between importers and domestic manufacturers and grocers over "imitations" reflected important tensions between two different kinds of *diasporic authenticities*, these in the world of commerce. The harshness of the clash was increasingly evident in the trade journals of Italian food importers, domestic manufacturers, and retailers in the second half of the 1930s. Although *Il Commerciante Italiano* was the journal of the Amerita Grocers' Association—the *grossieri* trade association—it also championed the interests of importers and wholesale merchants of imported Italian food. "A tiny caption 'Packed in California' beneath a huge caption '*Tonno marca Italia*' [Tuna Italy Brand] and the shining coat of arms of the Italian royal house are not enough to avoid any misunderstanding between the real Italian product and the Californian one," the journal noted in criticizing an American packing company.[65] After a few weeks of such continuing criticism of "copies," a letter from a *grossiere* highlighted how divisive the question of authenticity had become in the Italian food business—and in discussions of Italian American identity writ large. "I have the impression that the only reason for [*Il Commerciante Italiano*] to exist is to extol to the hyperbolic the incomparable quality of the products imported from Italy and place them above all others," the grocer contended.

> I believe that pasta and tomatoes and other foodstuffs produced by Italian American companies are much better than any other product anywhere made and from anywhere imported. It is about time that the individual efforts, hard work, and determination of the Italians of America are honored and supported more effectively than it had been done in the past. It is time for everyone to open their eyes and acknowledge the encouraging reality that America's Italians individually succeeded on the market with many foods, making then nationally popular. And the Italian Americans who succeeded did so only because of their individual talent and willpower, because until now, in our own collective blindness, we have always thought of and promoted Italian imported foods as if they were superior to any other. It is time that the Italians of America are given the recognition and credit they positively deserve.[66]

On the opposite front, olive oil importer and prominent member of the Italian Chamber of Commerce Carlo Bertolaia disparaged Italian American food as an invention of the American marketplace, which took advantage of the confused nostalgia of immigrant consumers to create a pale copy of the original it strove to supplant. It was in fact something different and new, as different and new as Italian Americans themselves. "'Italian American food' [is] the brand-new euphemism coined by some . . . to define wholly American, nothing but American products, which imitate, copy, or try to surrogate genuine Italian foods, with the overused expedient of green-white-and-red labels and names that recall Italian history, geography, or culture."[67]

Diasporic Nationalism and the Politics of Authenticity

Overall, the 1930s were disastrous for imports from Italy. When the decade came to an end, the prospects of a new war, with Italy on the wrong side, made entrepreneurs in the Italian food business, either Italian Americans or transnational Italians, ever more cautious about proclaiming their own or their products' *Italianità*. Insecurity and embarrassment began to spread in the community. Some of the importers, to be sure, still found reasons for optimism, trusting the United States to keep out of the conflict. In June 1940, the importers' trade journal *Il Prodotto Italiano* invited readers to enjoy a good plate of spaghetti at the Italian pavilion of the New York World's Fair and to forget about the war, assuring them that a new "golden age" for Italian food imports was at hand. "A year from now affluence will return to the United States, like in the blessed age after the Great War, because one year from now in Europe they will have exhausted their supplies and will again turn to the help of the American capitalist. Unemployment will be over, salaries will rise: in essence, prosperity! A year from now, facts will say we were right, and imports and exports from Italy will be those that will take greatest advantage."[68] For the time being, though, the scarcity and the consequent price increases of Italian imported food further damaged an already exhausted industry. The price of imported olive oil climbed from $2.50 a gallon to a record $4.50, while the price of parmigiano doubled from 80 cents to $1.60 per pound. As it had been during World War I, the void left in the market by disappearing or expensive imported food was filled by domestic products. This shift in consumer culture contributed to the disaffection of Italian immigrants for Mussolini as much as his military defeats in Greece and Africa had done. A reporter for the *New York Times* noted the disappointment of elderly residents of the Mulberry Street district in the food shortage, as well as the disinterest of Italian American youngsters in either Il Duce or Italian food imports. Many of those same young Italian Americans were about to go to war against Italy.[69]

When Italy finally declared war on the United States on December 11, 1941, and all things Italian became suspect in the eyes of Americans, most Italian Americans did not hesitate to stand by their country of adoption. The six hundred thousand Italians who were not U.S. citizens at the beginning of the war saw their civil liberties restricted as "enemy aliens," but the measure was repealed by Columbus Day of 1942. Many immigrants were naturalized in the following months. Even if the forces of Italian American assimilation were already under way in the preceding decade—as the different patterns of consumption of Italians on the two sides of Atlantic could not have made more visible—World War II was a tremendous turning point in the reconfiguring of Italian immigrant identities.

Italian American businessmen in the Italian food trade—always prepared to encourage community sentiments that served their interests—led the Italians of New York in public demonstrations of Americanism. Importers as well as domestic manufacturers limited their expressions of support for Italy and its culture. They may have sold Italian food to Italian consumers, but many of their companies and most of their interests were American. The Italian-language newspapers controlled by the pro-fascist *prominenti* quickly and completely changed their politics. The advertisers of *Il Progresso Italo-Americano*, where Italian food companies were traditionally overrepresented, joined together to sponsor the buying of U.S. war bonds.[70] Antonio Piccini, the food importer who had earlier distributed thousands of portraits of Mussolini in the Italian neighborhoods of New York, purchased a full page of the paper to urge Italian readers to buy war bonds to stop Hitler.[71]

The support of the U.S. war effort and a conspicuous patriotism during World War II allowed Italian American businessmen and community leaders to remain safely in their positions through the end of the war. However, only in the 1970s did the import of food from Italy rebound to prewar levels—and on completely new terms. The most important market for these imports was no longer immigrant neighborhoods but cosmopolitan middle-class consumers ("foodies") bent on accumulating cultural capital by consuming what was by then understood as authentic Italian food (regional Italian foods, far from the red-sauce favorites of immigrants) and economically secure third-generation Italian Americans exploring and reinventing their diasporic identity by mastering the culinary patrimony of their grandparents' homeland. The new catchwords for imported Italian food in America were not diasporic nationalism, but taste, pleasure, distinction, and lifestyle.

The histories of New York's Italian food importers in the 1930s suggest a final reflection. The economic and political defeat of leading importers in the battle for authenticity and for market share came at a time when, thanks in large measure to Mussolini's empire building, Italian diasporic nationalism was at its pinnacle. By all rights, the "Buy Italian Food" campaign should have won the favor of immigrants. That it did not suggests that by the 1930s Italian American food patterns had attained a significant degree of autonomy and distinctiveness as vehicles of collective identification. The story of the contests over Italian American food loyalties is a vivid example of the fact that the symbolic and material "stuff" from which ethnicity is created need not be rooted in an immemorial past to be authentic, but does need to be meaningful in the lived experiences of people in a group and useful in articulating the relations of power in which they are involved. The contents of an authentic culture, especially its ethnic symbols and materials, are always changeable—and open to regular reinterpretation.

Other immigrant food entrepreneurs profited from this lesson to cater not just to immigrant families but also to an ethnically diversified and predominantly middle-class clientele. Italian restaurateurs who also connected food and ethnic identity and emphasized the traditional character of their "Italian cuisine," mostly served Italian food to non-Italian patrons during the interwar years. The emphasis placed on *Italianità* in these Italian restaurants was as functional to their success among middle-class diners as it was for the companies in the Italian food trade that supplied the immigrant market. Even the narratives of ethnicity elaborated by Italian restaurants drew selectively from such different repertories as ruralism, familism, the mythology of classical Italy, and the other imaginaries of *Italianità* created by American popular culture. The history of Italian restaurants in New York, the topic of the following chapter, is both a story of the crossing of racial boundaries by consumers and another example of the way narratives of identity are shaped by socioeconomic realities.

6

Serving Ethnicity

Italian Restaurants, American Eaters, and the Making of an Ethnic Popular Culture

Remaking Ethnicity at the Red-Checkered Table: Restaurants and Italian American Identity

One hot July evening in 1940, two men dined at Moneta's, at 32 Mulberry Street in the heart of what was by then known as Little Italy.[1] The men were Federal Writers' Project researchers working on a food guide to New York titled *Feeding the City*, and they had a lovely experience. The food was excellent, and the simple but fascinating atmosphere attracted a cheerful clientele. As they later wrote about the dinner, Moneta's was "an effective stage for the rendezvous of brilliant judges, lawyers, writers, celebrities and beautiful women."[2]

The popularity of Moneta's was not a passing fad. Ten years earlier, the columnist and screenwriter Rian James had similarly described Moneta's as "a haven for gourmets and epicures, for ladies and gentlemen who dine with leisure," its tables hosting the famous and the powerful.[3] Moneta's was just one of hundreds of Italian restaurants spread all over New York. In 1938, there were 600 self-described Italian eateries in Manhattan, 300 in Brooklyn, and 250 in the Bronx.[4] By that time, Italian restaurants had become a ubiquitous presence—public places where non-Italian New Yorkers, travelers, and tourists could feel like they were experiencing Italian culture. Decades before the ethnic food boom, going to Italian restaurants was an exciting adventure that appealed across the lines of gender, class, and ethnicity.

Did the popularity of Italian restaurants reflect a broader attraction among non-Italians to Italian Americans and Italian American life? It did not. In 1930, the same year in which James extolled the refinement of New York's Italian restaurants, President Herbert Hoover responded to a criticism from Manhattan congressman Fiorello La Guardia by telling him, "You should go back to where you belong and advise Mussolini on how to make good honest citizens in Italy. The Italians are predominantly our murderers and bootleggers. . . . Like a lot of other foreign spawn, you do not appreciate the country which supports and tolerates you."[5]

In the interwar years, the position of Italian Americans in the larger life of the city was still far from secure and subject to a complicated range of attitudes. Some of these attitudes, such as the one represented in Hoover's public attack, linked the group to social and cultural backwardness and a natural inclination to crime. The exclusionary Immigration Act of 1924 was filled with fearful allusions to the racial inadequacy of Italian immigrants and their inability to make good American citizens. At the same time, however, Italian immigrant restaurateurs and restaurant workers were beginning to transform cultural differences into highly marketable products for mass consumption.

In the dynamic urban popular culture of the 1920s and 1930s, Italian restaurateurs played an important role in shaping Italian American identities. In designing and presenting their restaurants, they drew selectively on southern Italian rural immigrant culture, aspects of Italian national culture (from opera to landscape painting), and even American popular culture, notably film. Skillfully juxtaposing elements from different cultural contexts, restaurateurs were able to articulate an original and ultimately appealing ethnic narrative. In the theatrical spaces of New York's Italian restaurants, Italian Americans were seen no longer as undercivilized immigrants or dangerous criminals but as a family-centered, artistically inclined, and emotionally exuberant people. The cuisine, often codified in easily recognizable preparations and menus, embodied these cultural values and helped create a new Italian imaginary—one that signified not crime or poverty but abundance, artistry, and tradition.

The success of Italian restaurants also depended on their ability to provide a safe, comfortable space where non-Italian middle-class Americans could enjoy Italian customs and culture, to share in the experience of "being Italian," or *Italianità*. In staging a kind of distorted mirror play, crafty Italian Americans in the restaurant business capitalized on Anglo-Protestant middle-class fantasies about Italians as a racially "in-between" people. These ethnic entrepreneurs managed to overturn stereotypes about themselves using equally racialized stereotypes of their Anglo-Protestant clientele. Through cuisine and conviviality, they served their customers the ideal of Italy as a pleasurable escape from another ideal: the Victorian model of middle-class respectability and restraint.

Italian restaurants responded to and fulfilled middle-class expectations for pleasure and "safe danger." In the process, these restaurants provided the Italian American community with a highly profitable economic niche, dotted the streets

of New York with Italian signs, and helped make the city the emblem of American multiculturalism that it still is. Although this "tasty" representation of cultural difference could not completely challenge existing relations of power, it did complicate the question of the racial identity and social position of Italian Americans. Italian restaurants defied the boundaries of high and low culture in the formation of a diasporic Italian American identity by producing an array of "positive" images that set the terms for the inclusion of Italians in the American nation.

From Boardinghouses to Roman Gardens: The Economy of Italian Restaurants, 1900–1940

At the turn of the century, most Italian restaurants were very different from Moneta's and the other large, often elaborate public spaces to be found almost everywhere in midtown and downtown Manhattan in the 1930s. Many started as humble taverns in Italian neighborhoods, serving cheap, familiar food to waves of single male immigrants.

Unlike Jewish immigration from eastern Europe but like that of the Chinese, before the beginning of World War I in 1914, many Italian migrants to New York were men who intended to return to their home village after a temporary stay in the United States. In the peak years between 1880 and 1910, males accounted for about 80 percent of the total Italian immigrant population.[6] For many of these labor migrants, New York was the first stop on a longer American journey or a place to wait for seasonal work. For migrants working in order to send money home, boarding was a cheaper alternative to renting. Boardinghouses were usually managed by immigrant families or widowed or single women who had converted their homes to profitable use and who offered boarders a familiar environment, often sharing the same regional dialects, customs, memories, and foods. Crowded five or six to a single room, migrants paid three to five dollars per month to sleep and have their laundry done. Communal meals, prepared by the owner, were charged separately. As the *Saturday Evening Post* noted, in the Mulberry Street neighborhood immigrants "instruct the housewife, the *padrona*, to buy their food. She cooks it and enters their individual expenses in a weekly account."[7] In these makeshift inns, overcrowding and the economic, cultural, and psychological stress on migrants could sometimes make mealtimes loud, riotous, and even dangerous adventures. An immigrant to Utica, New York, described a Sunday dinner in the fall of 1907:

> I am boarding in the Oronzo household and occasionally eat with the Liuzzi family. Liuzzi has a number of brothers and assorted relatives. Yesterday (Sunday) there were about twelve of us at the table. I can barely stand their company. They are a

> bunch of ignorant *cafoni* [bumpkins]. They slurp their soup, they shovel the pasta down their gullets like a bunch of pigs while smacking their lips and making the noodles whistle, they talk with their mouths full so that bits of food take flight across the table, and they belch when the occasion demands. Liuzzi's uncle is the worst offender. His shirts are always spotted with tomato sauce. One of the girls put a large towel around his neck in place of a napkin to the hilarity of everyone. There is constant bickering and jostling at the table. I must bear the insults of two of the kids who are always grabbing something that belongs to me and throwing it out the window. They do not converse; they shout. By evening everyone was drunk. Oronzo and Liuzzi's uncle got into a rough and tumble fistfight.[8]

The boarding system, condemned by American reformers and Italian government officials for promoting "promiscuity" that threatened immigrant women's and girls' sexuality, did not survive the era of mass migration. It faded after World War I, with the drastic reduction in the number of temporary migrants and the reconstitution of the families of those who had been boarders. Many boardinghouses were turned into family-owned restaurants, particularly in the Italian section of Greenwich Village, where many of the Italians who lived in the streets west of Broadway and south of Washington Square had migrated as families from the northern regions of Liguria, Lombardy, and Tuscany before the arrival of the substantial wave from southern Italy.[9] The entire family worked in the kitchen and dining room and lived in the back of their restaurant. Catering mainly to other Italians, these simple places thrived because of the limited working costs and free labor of family members.[10]

On the East Side, too, where nearly all immigrants came from southern Italy, tenement storefronts were converted into modest restaurants, with sawdust on the floor and grease on the windows. In basements below, immigrant cooks baked pizza and other Neapolitan and Sicilian delicacies to be sold along Mott, Elizabeth, and Mulberry Streets, and served frugal meals to immigrant workers.[11] Early restaurants in Italian Harlem were even humbler: simple, dark, and unadorned rooms on the ground floor of houses or tenements. On the upper floor, there would be apartments for boarders. The dining room itself held one or two rectangular tables, with no tablecloth or napkins, and two long benches. In a corner, the two or three dishes of the day were cooked on a wood or coal stove. Wine and beer were served.[12]

These taverns were popular meeting places and important sources of sociability for immigrants, who came for news from their Italian hometowns and to learn about job opportunities, labor actions, and when necessary, how to get relief money. Restaurants also attracted the mutual aid and other benevolent societies organized around the members' village of origin. Members made a point of holding their banquets at the restaurants of fellow *paesani*. For all these reasons, early restaurants in Italian neighborhoods offered a wide range of regional specialties. As George Pozzetta notes, "Such was the variety that existed in the [Mulberry] district, that one could do a tour of the principal Italian provinces and cities by visiting the restaurants."[13] In Italian Harlem, similarly, "each street had its own restaurant, cooking its own specialty. Thus, among the Sicilians on 107th Street you find the 'Vastella' and 'Capozzelle al Forno' restaurants. In other parts of the district, above all among the Neapolitans, you will find the 'Spaghetteria' and the 'Pizzeria' restaurants. The same goes for the other restaurants among Genovesi, Piemontesi, Romani etc., where they have specialties such as ravioli, polenta, and abbacchio al forno [roasted lamb]."[14]

Until World War I, middle-class New Yorkers mostly ignored these restaurants, shunning their immigrant clientele, heavy meals, and alcoholic beverages. Like other working-class saloons, they were not places that respectable women were supposed to patronize, even in the company of men. Indeed, before the turn of the twentieth century, eating out as a leisure activity was a practice restricted to a small elite. Bankers, rich merchants, and affluent industrialists dined at fancy restaurants like the famous Delmonico's or in such luxury hotels as the Waldorf-Astoria or the Knickerbocker in the routine displays of wealth and distinction that Thorstein Veblen described as conspicuous consumption. Even with their skilled northern Italian chefs, these select eating places served the glossy French cuisine that defined the taste of the international ruling classes from Moscow to Mexico City. Eating out at restaurants was a critical part of social life for privileged New Yorkers, but only for them.[15]

However, by 1900 restaurants were at the center of the commercial leisure industry that developed as New York became the financial capital of an informal economic empire and the city's affluent elite began to welcome an expanding middle class of businessmen and professionals. The emerging middle classes were constantly challenged to reaffirm their newly achieved and still uncertain social status by building cultural capital, following fashions and publicly displaying their tastes as consumers. Restaurants quickly became popular public spaces for middle-class consumer culture, and eating out joined a growing list of commercialized leisure activities. At the same time, being successful consumers required that the middle class abandon the Victorian values of sobriety for the pursuit of personal gratification and self-indulgence.[16]

The segment of the middle class that most consciously rejected Victorian norms—the artists, intellectuals, and radicals who congregated in Greenwich Village—were the first sizable contingent of non-Italian customers of Italian restaurants. Around 1910, a new class of bohemians began to flow into the Village, attracted by its cheap rents and quaint streets, turning this Italian and Irish working-class neighborhood into New York's Latin Quarter. To bohemians and radicals, patronizing Italian restaurants meant celebrating rebellion and nonconformity. They consciously confronted the racialization of southern and eastern European immigrants that encouraged immigrant residential segregation and fueled the campaign for immigration restriction. Living in a predominantly Italian neighborhood, "they became frequent patrons at many of the district's Italian resorts, fraternizing with the very immigrants who drew nativist ire" and expressing an appreciation of their cultural difference.[17] "A lot of artists lived in MacDougal Alley and they never tried to make us feel ashamed of our Italian descent but rather gave us reason to glory in it," Maria Sermolino, daughter of the co-owner of Gonfarone's restaurant, recalled. "We did not know why they thought it was wonderful to be 'Italian' but since they said so we believed it."[18] The small and smoky Italian restaurants of the Village, like Bertolotti's and Mori's on Bleecker Street or Del Prato's and Gonfarone's on MacDougal, became hangouts for writers and intellectuals such as Henry Roth, the *Partisan Review* group, e.e. cummings, and John Reed.[19] Some restaurants also served as meeting places for the growing gay and lesbian communities.[20]

These eccentric early patrons were crucial in opening the way for a larger, more mainstream clientele. Although the bohemian regulars might have seemed odd, they came predominantly from well-to-do Anglo-Saxon families, and their presence helped to change the face of an otherwise unremarkable ethnic neighborhood. By World War I, another new class, this one of male and female white-collar commuting workers, began to patronize the Village's Italian restaurants.[21] These were table d'hôte restaurants whose inexpensive fixed menus welcomed customers seeking neither rough working-class saloons nor expensive luxury dining rooms. The changing economic geography of the city made the Village a perfect location. Gonfarone's, for example, once a snug basement patronized mostly by Italian Americans, expanded to an entire block at the corner of West Eighth Street and MacDougal Alley to serve "businessmen, big and little, white collar workers and clerks from the big department stores which, in those days, were south of 23rd Street on Sixth and Fifth Avenues, and doctors and lawyers and professors and college students." White-collar patrons "came from all the boroughs, and the Eighth Street cross town trolley cars, which connected with the Hudson River ferries at Christopher Street, made [Gonfarone's] accessible to people from New Jersey."[22]

The Italian table d'hôte restaurants at first attracted mainly middle-class visitors because of their dollar value. At Enrico & Paglieri's, the meal that included antipasto (salami, stuffed eggs, and pickled celery and peppers); minestrone; spaghetti with tomato sauce, meat, and mushrooms; roasted chicken; salad; biscuit tortoni; and espresso coffee sold for only forty cents.[23] For ten cents more,

Gonfarone's offered an even richer menu.[24] This was much less than the checks of à la carte restaurants. Second, Italian restaurant cuisine was an exotic novelty. To most Americans, both the foods and their preparation were something new. And eating some dishes, like spaghetti, the signature dish of Italian restaurants, could pose technical challenges as well. Few could manage the correct technique, but the effort was fun anyway, until a waiter showed how it was done. "Then came the spaghetti . . . , which I had no idea how to begin to eat," a reporter for *Better Homes and Gardens* recalled. "My more sophisticated friends tried to show me the Italian method of eating it with the help of a fork against a spoon so that it could be wound into a portion which could be eaten at one mouthful. I was very much relieved when they were not too successful and turned back to American style and cut it into pieces with a fork."[25]

Italian restaurant owners capitalized on the new market opportunities. Turn-of-the-century revolutions in production, transport, and retailing kept basic costs generally low and greatly improved margins. At Gonfarone's, "the customer got a great deal for his fifty or sixty cents, but even at that price there was a margin of profit, because wholesale prices of foodstuffs were so low. Tenderloin of beef cost six and a half cents a pound; veal, seven cents a pound, chicken, nine cents, lamb, eight cents. A barrel of onions cost one dollar and fifty cents, and a bushel of tomatoes were forty cents. Potatoes were a dollar seventy-five a barrel and eggs, by the crate, cost fifteen cents a dozen."[26] Popular dishes like spaghetti and meatballs, chicken cacciatore, or veal scaloppini made economic use of meat, and pasta was cheap and quick to prepare. "From the standpoint of the restaurateur spaghetti had many advantages. A portion looked like, and was, a lot of food and yet it costs less than two cents a portion—including enough sauce and grated cheese to gratify a glutton. Furthermore, after gorging himself on a mound of spaghetti, a customer's appetite would have lost its edge and small portions of the remaining courses on the menu would abundantly satisfy him."[27]

However, the decisive factors for the success of the ethnic restaurant were human capital and cheap immigrant labor. Like other small ethnic retail or service businesses, Italian restaurants survived because they were able to convert the loyalties of fellow Italians into a key economic asset: low-cost, low-conflict labor. In family-run Italian restaurants, everyone in the family worked. The owners of Gonfarone's did not have a life outside their restaurant: "Papa would be in the dining-room from noon until midnight, with a few hours' respite in the afternoon, and Madama [Gonfarone] would be in the pantry, and mama at her cashier's desk, without taking time out for meals until the rush was over. Since they were young (at least papa and mama were) and working for themselves, the busier they were the better they liked it. On marketing days, Madama and papa would get up at five in the morning and go to Washington Market where they bought a week's supply of food at one time."[28]

A more important factor in the restaurant economy was the availability of inexpensive paid labor. Family ties provided access to a large pool of cheap, reliable workers, with women typically carrying the heaviest burdens. A student told Leonard Covello:

> My uncle and his wife saved sufficient money to go into the restaurant business. But before opening a business of his own he brought from Italy his parents, two brothers and a sister. This he did in the interest of himself for his relatives could be relied upon as trustworthy and industrious helpers. But he did this also in the interest of his family, for, as he said, he provided jobs for his relatives at good wages and, what's more important, a chance to work within the family. His wife and their two children were required to work hard. Josephine, the girl, helped a great deal though she was only eight years old. As a matter of fact, she did more work than her brother Nick who was fourteen years old. When Josephine was ten years old, the father forbade her to go to school. In his estimation, she could read and write, and that was enough for any Italian girl. The father insisted that she was big enough to give real help to her parents. Josephine had a difficult child-hood. She was helping to wait on the customers, and was also confined to kitchen duty. When caught on the street or daydreaming while washing dirty dishes, Josephine was frequently whipped by her father. . . . That was around 1910. Josephine is forty-two years old today, married, a mother of five children, and almost illiterate.[29]

Several studies have highlighted how other immigrant restaurants (in particular the Chinese) have succeeded by relying on the "free" and gendered labor of family members, much as Italian restaurants did.[30]

Italian restaurants employed recent immigrants as cooks, waiters, busboys, and dishwashers, even those with few skills and no command of English. For these recent immigrants, restaurant work may thus have offered advantages that partly balanced the exploitative salaries, hours, and working conditions. The ethnic channels of recruitment provided them with a job right off the boat and gave them a collective edge over other disadvantaged ethnic groups; Italians soon displaced African Americans from dominant positions in the catering business. Restaurants also could offer lodging, deducting rent from pay.[31] The at least superficially egalitarian relationship between employer and employee, the close contact between workers and customers, and even the aura of artistry could make restaurant jobs seem comparatively appealing.[32]

"Labor costs were practically nonexistent," recalled Maria Sermolino.

> Amedeo [the cook] was probably paid about forty dollars a month, the dishwashers about twenty dollars, and, in the early days, the waiters worked only for their food and tips or, at most, were paid about ten dollars a month. In some of the fancy uptown restaurants the waiters paid for the privilege of working, because on tips alone they could make up to two hundred dollars a month. The minimum

> tip at Gonfarone's was a dime a head and since one waiter could serve about fifty customers a day, counting luncheon and dinner, he could make about five dollars a day. Over a busy weekend he might double his take. Furthermore, since controls were lax, even a waiter who tried to be honest might find his pockets unaccountably bulging with dinner money that, somehow, got confused with his tip money. There was so much of it pouring in, that everybody shared.[33]

Restaurant work could also offer immigrant workers comparatively greater opportunity for economic mobility. At Gonfarone's, according to Sermolino, "most of them left after four or five prosperous years to open rival places of their own."[34]

Despite this Algeresque picture, though, exploitative conditions prevailed in most Italian restaurants. Jobs were insecure, salaries low, and unionization almost nonexistent. According to a 1906 survey, the average monthly pay of cooks in Italian restaurants was between twenty-five and fifty dollars for a fourteen- to sixteen-hour workday. Unorganized and threatened by new competitors who arrived regularly from Italy, these workers were nearly powerless.[35] The rapid growth of the Italian restaurant world was largely made possible by the exploitation of immigrants willing to accept almost any kind of work. Emanuel Carnevali found a job in an Italian restaurant thanks to the intercession of a fellow countryman.

> It was a table d'hote on West Eighth Street and there I worked seventeen hours a day and came back to my room at night to dream of plates, plates, plates. I ran about like a madman from one floor to another. I was busboy to the waiters and my work consisted of setting tables and clearing the dishes away. There were six or seven waiters and I had to help them all. My job was love and terror to me; thoughts of it kept me awake at night. For four days I had almost starved in that room in West Twelfth Street and to think of losing my job was disaster and despair.[36]

Carnevali's recollections echoed those of another immigrant, the tragically famous Italian radical Bartolomeo Vanzetti. On arrival at Ellis Island in 1908, Vanzetti (trained as a confectioner in Italy) met a man who brought him to an Italian restaurant that hired him as a dishwasher. Vanzetti worked a fourteen-hour a day, seven days a week, except for Sunday morning. "The vapor of the boiling water where the plates, pans and silver were washed formed great drops of water on the ceiling, took up all the dust and grime there, then fell slowly one by one upon my head, as I worked below," he wrote. "The heat was terrific. The table leavings amassed in barrels near the pantry gave out nauseating exhalations. The sinks had no direct sewage connection. Instead, the water was permitted to overrun to the floor. In the center of the room was a drain. Every night the pipe was clogged and the greasy water rose higher and higher and we trudged in the slime."[37] Vanzetti later worked in two other restaurants, only to be fired from both for no apparent reason. Later he learned that employment agents paid restaurant owners for every worker they hired. To get the commission, some owners laid off workers after a short while.[38]

Working conditions in Italian restaurants were far worse than those encountered by the professional immigrant cooks and waiters who landed jobs in the city's classy restaurants and hotels. Nearly all coming from northern Italy and Tuscany, they were by the 1920s a significant presence in the best-paying establishments.[39] Profiting from the rising popularity of Italian cuisine, some opened their own places and often offered a more sophisticated version of the fare served in places like Gonfarone's and Enrico and Paglieri's. Successful skilled chefs and waiters typically spent years working in many countries, in the process building professional relationships inside and outside the immigrant community. Ernest Cerutti was born in Savona, Liguria, where his father owned a restaurant. Cerutti met Gene (Osvaldo) Cavallero, the son of a farming family in Mantua, Lombardy, at the Savoy Hotel in London, where both worked as waiters. In 1913, Cavallero arrived in Boston to work at the Copley Plaza Hotel, while Cerutti went to the Knickerbocker Hotel in New York. In Boston, Cerutti met Joe Pani, a hotel owner who had been asked to consider opening a restaurant in a luxury Madison Avenue building. In 1920, Pani asked Cerutti and Cavallero to become headwaiters and associates at his new Colony restaurant. In the first year alone, the Colony earned profits of $75,000.[40] Restaurateurs' biographies are often parables of immigrant professional mobility. After immigrating from the Piedmont region as a child, Armando Golzio started work as a busboy in Louisville, Kentucky, in 1904. The following year, he worked at the German pavilion at the World's Fair in St. Louis and later in hotels and restaurants in London, Paris, Monte Carlo, and San Francisco. In 1930, Golzio and his brother finally opened the successful Louis and Armand on Fifty-Second Street in New York and attracted a high-society clientele.[41]

While Cerutti, Cavallero, and the Golzios excelled in French cuisine, another Piemontese immigrant, Costantino Zucca, succeeded in opening an Italian restaurant in the heart of Midtown Manhattan. Born in 1884, Zucca was raised in the hotel business. After arriving in New York in 1907, he worked as a waiter at the Van Rensselaer Hotel, the Plaza Hotel, and the Peck restaurant, where some influential customers lent him start-up capital. In 1911, he opened his first restaurant on Fulton Street, and in 1915 he opened Zucca's on West Forty-Ninth Street, which until the 1930s remained one of the city's most famous Italian restaurants.

The Volstead Act of 1920, which initiated the era of Prohibition, dramatically affected the Italian restaurant industry, just as it did almost all other segments of American society. For many Italian restaurants, Prohibition was a boon; it managed to usher in a period of new opportunities by remapping the competitive landscape in favor of Italian entrepreneurs. First, Prohibition drove out of business many competitors, such as Irish- and German-run saloons. Simultaneously, it provided a new market for the wine and liquors produced by the Italian community. In the early twentieth century, the sale of alcoholic beverages was the most important source of profit for chic restaurants and hotels such as Delmonico's, Churchill's, and Sherry's. Everything changed after Prohibition became law on January 16, 1920, not only for these bastions of New York high life, but also at the other end of the industry. Before Prohibition, saloons offered free lunches to a mostly male, beer- and whiskey-drinking clientele, and meant serious competition for table d'hôte restaurants. The disappearance of saloons and their free lunches stimulated the demand for restaurants serving the lower middle classes of both sexes. In the 1920s, the number of restaurants in the country tripled, not only to fill the gap left by now-closed saloons but also in response to a growing number of women customers, who no longer faced the stigma of being seen in places where alcohol was served. White-collar women workers and housewives alike were an important new clientele for "dry" restaurants, which frequently opened in locations formerly occupied by saloons and cafés.[42]

How Prohibition helped the Italian restaurant industry take off is one of the paradoxes of urban life, since the Volstead Act embodied distinctly nativist sentiments. By the turn of the twentieth century, the temperance movement had already singled out new European immigrants, especially Italians and other Catholics, as the main producers and consumers of wine and liquor. The struggle against alcohol was linked to the struggle against all anti-American elements: to temperance and prohibitionist leaders, the dangers of "Demon Rum" were also the dangers of immigration. Saloons were centers of political and social corruption where ethnic party bosses bought votes and immigrant workers wasted their meager wages, putting their families in jeopardy, ruining their chances for social mobility, and making themselves easy prey for radicals and labor agitators.

Still, few places were so resistant to temperance as was New York City, with its large immigrant population and its established culture of social drinking.[43] Italians in particular found Prohibition nonsensical, since it outlawed even wine, a beverage deeply rooted in Italian customs, religion, and civilization. Northern and southern Italian immigrants depended on wine as a vital source of calories as well as a traditional source of sociability, recreation, and, infrequently, intoxication. During the "dry decade," Italians skirted or violated the law by making, trading, and consuming alcoholic beverages—most notably wine—more than other Americans. Even before Prohibition, winemaking in Italian American neighborhoods achieved the status of a collective ritual. Taking advantage of the provision in the Volstead Act that allowed each household to make up to two hundred gallons of wine, Italians turned a domestic routine into a commercial livelihood. After 1920, sales of grapes skyrocketed in every Italian market in New

York City.[44] *Il Progresso Italo-Americano*, which staunchly opposed Prohibition, featured ads for California grapes sold by the crate, grape juice concentrates, presses, vats, and additives for making wine.

Even if it had been possible to end the manufacturing and sale of alcoholic beverages, the unpopularity of the law in the city made any serious effort unlikely. Congressman Fiorello La Guardia estimated that 250,000 policemen would have been needed to enforce Prohibition in New York—and another 200,000 to patrol the enforcers.[45] In 1923, New York State repealed local laws for enforcing the Volstead Act, leaving prosecution of Prohibition-related crimes to federal agencies. In the city, smuggling and illegal manufacturing swelled, all to the profit of organized crime and speakeasies, two sectors of the informal economy in which recent immigrants were overrepresented. In Greenwich Village, as Irish saloons were forced to close, local Italians nearly monopolized the sale of wine and liquors. "The liquor business in one form or another was the chief new source of employment or income for residents of the area—especially the Italians—during the second half of the decade," notes Caroline Ware.[46] In the Village, she found, bootleg wine was sold by "every Italian barber, bootblack, cigar store, and grocer."[47] Every fall, carloads of grapes would be unloaded in front of neighborhood houses and stores.[48]

Everyone knew that wine and grappa were available in Italian restaurants. At first, patrons needed a password to enter a secret room where wine was served in soda bottles, but over time even such simple precautions were abandoned. During the thirteen years of Prohibition, many Uptowners started going to Greenwich Village's Italian restaurants in search of "booze." "The area south of Fourth Street to Houston Street, between MacDougal and Irving Place was . . . peppered with small Italian restaurants," remembered former flapper Katherine Young. "They were generally spotlessly clean with marble-topped tables or red and white cloth-covered tables and sawdust on the floor. With excellent Italian food, wine [was] served in teacups, with waiters doing a sinuous dance between the tables, laden with hot platters of spaghetti, veal parmigiani and steaming minestrone soup slopping in flat soup-plates. The wine was raw and strong and everyone loosened up quickly and got drunk easily."[49]

During Prohibition, Italian restaurants became more popular than ever. Now serving a larger and more diverse clientele than the small avant-garde of local bohemians and white-collar commuters of the pre-Prohibition era, the nature of Italian restaurants changed in what had become a highly competitive market. Because their economy was based on the sale of alcoholic beverages, restaurant-speakeasies lured customers from their competitors by offering generous servings of food and drink for just a few cents. Diners also got more food for the same money in restaurants where liquors were served, and waiters would often ask patrons who did not order wine to leave, so essential were drinks to the bottom line.

Furthermore, every restaurant faced the burden of paying for protection—under the table cash or free drinks and meals to gangsters, federal agents, police, and politicians alike had to be added to overhead costs. In the Village, federal agents would be slipped fifty dollars, while police officers and political bosses and their guests were entertained with free dinners. Bribery was so widespread that gangsters disguised as law enforcement agents often had restaurant owners handing them money, before the real agents showed up to warn against the imposters.[50] Other illicit activities were added to the sale of alcohol. Some Italian restaurants allowed prostitution to be practiced on their premises. A study of East Harlem in the 1920s noted, "There is a fair degree of prostitution in the district. Usually a fellow will get a tip from his restaurant waiter who will furnish him with a card of introduction to the prostitute. In some cases, however, reserved rooms may be had on the second floor of Italian restaurants."[51] In the Village, Paul and Joe's was a notorious haunt for prostitutes, one of several places where "sailors and 'hardened neighborhood girls' congregated."[52]

As they matured, Italian restaurants helped make Greenwich Village the epicenter of New York's nightlife in the 1920s. For white middle-class thrill-seekers, the Village was a place as exciting but more reputable than Harlem, where liquor ran freely, and the possibilities for sexual and artistic experimentation were everywhere. Promoted by the new tourism industry as America's capital of nonconformity, the Village welcomed visitors in droves, the journey downtown made even easier by the expansion of West Side subway lines. The large crowds that filled its "black and tan" (integrated) nightclubs, tearooms, cabarets, speakeasies, and Italian restaurants helped transform Greenwich Village into a destination for slumming. It was a post-Victorian urban theme park luring tourists, celebrities, and ordinary white middle-class New Yorkers with the promise of escape from restraint. In the freedom and fantasy of the Village, women and men could relish moments of transgression and sensuality without compromising the respectability of their everyday lives.[53]

Italian restaurants were among the most popular places in the neighborhood, capitalizing on both their exuberant ethnic appeal and their legacy as bohemian hangouts. "There is almost no block in the Greenwich Village without an Italian restaurant," noted an observer.[54] This location was crucial to the success of the early Italian restaurant industry. Waves of visitors and residents were attracted to the Village, a busy place open almost around the clock, where they could stroll nighttime streets safer than those in the infamous immigrant neighborhoods of East Harlem or Little Italy. The large Italian community of the Village provided a picturesque Latin touch rather than a perceived danger. "The Italians along MacDougal Street below Fourth Street stayed up late," Katherine Young remembered. "The boys hanging around an outdoor sweets stand drinking soft drinks from the bottle would stop drinking as I passed and whistle, ogling naturally, blowing a kiss in their Italian fashion but never [made] a remark or a move. I was absolutely safe and I knew it."[55]

By the end of the 1920s, Village Italian restaurants had made their name among a large middle-class clientele of both sexes, and among artistic, theatrical, political, and big-business celebrities. They survived the repeal of Prohibition in 1933 and the influx of middle-class families and professionals who gentrified the neighborhood and displaced many of the remaining bohemians, radicals, and ethnic workers, including some Italians.[56] During the Depression, the popularity of Italian restaurants spread to other areas of Manhattan. Even as the number of Italian American patrons across the city reached its lowest point and many Italian restaurants went out of business in ethnic neighborhoods, many others opened in the Village and uptown in the theater district near Times Square to meet the growing demand of middle-class "American" customers. By the mid-thirties, *Good Housekeeping* reported that "everybody seem[ed] to know a Tony's or Joe's where one [could] get 'the best spaghetti in town.'"[57]

Popular Culture, Race, and Performance at Italian Restaurants

What attracted so many Americans to Italian restaurants? Although the food, the unintended effects of Prohibition, and new leisure patterns each played an essential role, the strongest draw was the experience of stepping inside a comfortably exotic space, where customers knew they would enjoy not only delicious Mediterranean flavors but also exciting cultural differences, all of it artfully orchestrated. As Sermolino noted about Gonfarone's, "Whatever 'atmosphere' existed sprang from the fact that papa, and Madama Gonfarone, his partner, and the waiters and bus boys and cooks, and the bartender and the dishwashers, and musicians, spoke and thought and acted 'Italian.' This little Italian world was friendly, pleasant and gay."[58]

The seductiveness of so many Italian restaurants in New York lay largely in the capacity to offer a complete cultural package; an encounter with the other that fulfilled the desires and fantasies of non-Italian customers. For middle-class Americans, "eating the other" at an Italian restaurant in New York in the 1920s and 1930s meant consuming the representations of Italy, the Italians, and the Italian diaspora that American novelists, journalists, illustrators, social photographers, social workers, and filmmakers had been creating since the high tide of Italian migration. Going to an Italian restaurant became a kind of ethnographic adventure, a journey to discover a culturally complex and racially puzzling population on the frontier of the largest American metropolis. In the restaurant's structured, mediating space of leisure and consumption, white middle-class American customers and the Italian staff together created a theater of racial and ethnic self-definitions, each side playing carefully to and for the other. The narratives of *Italianità* that flourished in restaurants—based on such positive features as family-centeredness, artistic skills, and an occasionally ambiguous link to a culture recognized as the cradle of Western civilization—enabled the incorporation of Italians as a group into the American nation in the interwar years and beyond.

As Sermolino's memories suggest, the role of cooks and waiters was crucial in creating a comforting version of "being Italian" that would meet the expectations of American customers. Looking into the social world of Italian restaurant kitchens and dining rooms, therefore, means to appreciate particular processes of racialization and agency that shaped the social standing of Italian Americans. Italian restaurant staffs, in fact, used stereotypical markers and racial narratives about themselves not only to draw economic profit from their white middle-class customers but also to challenge and redefine interethnic relations of power. In New York's Italian restaurants in the 1920s and 1930s, immigrants could reclaim an identity that combined the ruralism, primitivism, and spontaneity of "dark" southern Italy with the classic tradition of beauty and finesse, rooted in ancient Rome and the Renaissance, of "white man's Italy." While melting their very different culinary traditions into a new Italian cuisine and creating an improbable new visual syntax of gondolas, the Coliseum, and Vesuvius for their American clients, Italian immigrants found in their restaurants an opportunity to transcend the divides between northern and southern, Italian high and low cultures, and between proletarian and bourgeois. In the process, they were able to assemble a meaningful and empowering idea of nation.

The middle-class Americans who first patronized Italian restaurants typically did so equipped with a dual perception of Italian American identity. On the one hand were images of short-tempered, vindictive, and treacherous masculinity and prolific, cunning, and superstitious femininity; on the other, the pleasurable character of a sentimental, gregarious people naturally inclined to the family, beauty, and the arts.

This conflicted picture of southern Italians, who were by far the largest segment of the Italian immigrant community in New York, had taken hold in northern European culture as early as the seventeenth century.[59] At the turn of the twentieth century, American mass media modernized earlier narratives to make sense of the largely poor, Catholic, dark-haired offspring of an ancient Mediterranean civilization who swelled the most dangerous quarters of the industrial New World. A twofold image of southern Italian and Sicilian Americans matched the ambiguity of their "Mediterranean" racial identity. The popular press titillated readers with accounts of the gruesome enterprises of the Black Hand, the all-Italian crime organization that plagued Italian neighborhoods. Italian immigrants were regularly depicted not only as natural born gangsters but also as anarchists and terrorists, particularly during the Red scare of 1919–20 and Prohibition. Illustrators and photographers selectively portrayed the "swarthy" complexions of Italian immigrants, creating a set of racial types that would help Americans navigate the menacing racial map of immigrant difference without ever having to meet actual immigrants. Such popularizers of scientific racism as Edward Alsworth Ross and Madison Grant spurred the movement for immigration restriction by purporting to demonstrate the biological basis of southern Italians' propensity for crime.[60]

Other representations were more complex, though. At the turn of the century, the work of pioneering social photographer Jacob Riis blamed the abysmal lives of Mulberry Bend's Italian immigrants on the overcrowded and unsanitary neighborhood in which they were forced to live. Riis's photographs celebrated the vivacity of Little Italy's community and expressed hope that the strong Italian family would help immigrants make their way into U.S. society.[61] Early American cinema also provided multifaceted representations of Italian immigrant identity. Films like *The Black Hand* (1906) and *The Italian* (1915) showed evil Italian criminals alongside happy-go-lucky, sentimental, hardworking, and family-oriented immigrants trying to survive in Little Italy (Greenwich Village and the Mulberry District, respectively). These movies also frequently featured picturesque images of the Italian landscape, catering both to the American romance with Italy and to the memory and nostalgia of immigrant spectators.[62]

In New York's Italian restaurants of the 1920s and 1930s, food largely came to embody this latter set of Italian American identities. Food scholars have maintained that ethnic restaurants can easily be perceived as an alien, threatening presence in communities where interethnic relations are marked by suspicion and discrimination against newcomers. "The formula operating appears to be 'strange people equals strange food.'" At the same time, restaurants are places where cultural boundaries can be comfortably crossed and the diversity of the other gratifyingly explored. "The formula here seems to be: 'not-so-strange food equals not-so-strange people,' or perhaps, 'strange people but they sure can cook.'"[63] In the interwar years, New York's southern Italian immigrants, whose racial identity had been heavily disputed, underwent a significant process of whitening. This shift in status and perspective was one effect of the passage of the racist 1921–24 immigration laws, which reduced new immigration from Italy and other southern and eastern European countries to a trickle. As a result, immigration from southern Italy and Sicily ceased to be perceived as a threat, while at the same time the large-scale migration of African Americans north to New York became the real racial emergency. Recent European immigrants, even those as racially problematic as southern Italians, began to be thought of, and dealt with, as white.[64] No longer racialized as a danger for the American biological and political body, Italian Americans could be safely transformed into the quintessentially exotic Euro-American ethnic group, their identities commodified in the burgeoning spheres of mass entertainment and ethnic tourism. In this transition, mass media were especially important in creating and commodifying an Italian American ethnic identity, defining the kind of *Italianità* that New Yorkers liked and looked for in Italian restaurants by connecting positive traits of *Italianità* to Italian cuisine. As a result, Italian food and Italian restaurants eventually became powerful repositories of a desirable and marketable Italian cultural experience.

The controlling stereotypes of Italian Americans were characterized by two complementary associations: one, the idealized connection between Italian American food, family, and the larger community; two, the equally idealized connection between Italian American food and a native inclination for the arts, notably music.

The positive connection of Italian food and family to the larger society was also rooted in the nature of Italian community life in the city. As we have seen in previous chapters, even by the 1930s, the family set the boundaries of the moral and cultural worlds of immigrants and their children in the urban enclaves created by waves of southern Italian immigrants. Italian family values were so widely shared in the community that they reverberated in the public sphere; in the Little Italies of the city, the workings of the family were everywhere visible.[65] Unlike the protocols of middle-class domesticity, much of Italian social life took place in the streets of the neighborhood. As early as 1890, Jacob Riis noted this feature of Italian American culture: "When the sun shines the entire population seeks the street, carrying on its household work, its bargaining, its love-making on street or sidewalk, or idling there when it was nothing better to do, with the reverse of the impulse that makes the Polish Jew coop himself up in his den with the thermometer at stewing heat."[66] Riis and many other observers after him were in fact captivated by the "picturesque filth and poverty" of the Mulberry District streets, where women haggled with peddlers over the strange food in dialect, while a throng of children swarmed around them.[67] Other women unembarassingly breast-fed their babies.[68] Men also lived their lives outdoors. "Italian men are noticeably less domestic than Jews and Germans, and they avail themselves of the alternatives to tenements—street corners, clubs, and cafés," a social worker noted in 1900. "The cafés differ from American saloons in that very often they do not have doors to hide those inside from the street."[69]

In the streets of the Lower East Side, East Harlem, and the South Village, anyone seeking a picturesque Mediterranean scene could find it easily, from the colorful religious feasts and processions to the street foods that were a sensual, worldly, and vital part of the sacred celebration. Newspapers regularly provided detailed accounts of these feasts.[70] In the popular realist paintings of Ash Can

School artists, "the ever present children, the women with handkerchiefs on their heads, the organ grinders compose a humanity that seems to retain the past in the present, . . . the *paesello* under the imposing but faraway skyscrapers."[71]

By the interwar years, these Little Italies became "Little Italy." A distinct social world was commodified into a spectacle of cultural and racial difference, "a site of cultural disorder, . . . source of fascination, longing, and nostalgia for those people, especially in the middle class, who were developing bodily and emotional controls as part of the civilizing process."[72] Writers rarely failed to mention how poverty and overcrowding were balanced by a vibrant social life and a unique family ethos, all of it on display in the streets. Few forgot to delight in the smells, colors, and shapes of the food on peddlers' carts, in store windows, and in restaurants. "What strikes one first is the beauty and the variety of the vegetables and fruits sold there in what is supposed to be one of the poorest quarters," reported Konrad Bercovici.

> Peaches with blooms on, and the softest and the most luscious plums, the largest apples and most beautiful pears, the cleanest salads, are sorted and handled in the most expert and delicate way, lying near and between each other as to form a color-scheme—the most unusual vegetable leaves and roots. . . . You are in Little Italy, Elizabeth Street, with fruit push-carts on the sidewalks, groaning heavily with all the colors; with deep cellar stores and cellar restaurants, and the odor of fried fish and oil; the cries of the venders in that open-mouthed Latin of the Southern Italians are hurled at you.[73]

In the early 1930s, the symbolic Italian American relationship between food, family values, and tradition also emerged as a keynote in classic gangster films. In Mervyn LeRoy's *Little Caesar* (1930) and Howard Hawks's *Scarface* (1932), food is a pivotal feature of the private, "humane" sphere of the gangsters and particularly of the relationship with their mothers. The two movies are archetypes not only of the gangster genre but of the Hollywood image of Italian Americans as a group. Once again, this archetype has two sides: the Italian gangster has two families, the gang and his own proper family, and the impossibility of remaining loyal to both lead him to eventual disaster. Italian gangsters won the sympathy of contemporary audiences not only because they were in their own way trying to become Americans—that is, achieve the American Dream—during the most difficult years of the Depression. They also won a large public through their deep, sometimes even pathological, involvement with their families, a relationship powerfully articulated in the language of food.[74]

The white-haired immigrant mammas of *Little Caesar* and *Scarface* always wear completely black or flowered aprons, speak broken English, and never leave the kitchen. Their chief concern is nourishing their sons; their maternal joy is in the appreciation for the food they prepare, an ethnic antidote to the disorder of the outside "American" world. "I have some spaghetti for you on the stove. . . . You feel better . . . eat somethin' . . . do you good," says the mother to Tony Passa, the repentant bandit fleeing the revenge of Rico, the "Little Caesar." As a Neapolitan song is playing in the background, the tearful mother caresses and kisses her son, advising him to seek the priest's help. It is on the steps of the church that Tony Passa gets killed by Rico, a man without religion and without a family, an Italian without a *mamma*.[75] Tony Camonte, "Scarface," does have a mother and a sister. In the dinner scene, set in the rustic kitchen of their immigrant home, Tony is avidly eating the pasta his mother has lovingly prepared. He stops to ask where his sister Cesca is, since "traditionally" dinner is a ritual for the entire family. Opening the door, Tony finds Cesca hugging a strange man, who flees Tony's threats. Tony wants his sister to conform to the standards of Italian domesticity and gender roles while he pursues his personal American Dream. His very real struggle to reconcile devotion to both "business" and family intimacy struck a chord with immigrant as well as middle-class audiences.

In *Little Caesar* and *Scarface*, food is a central medium of family communication, where emotions are emphatically expressed. In these movies, food *constructs* the Italian home as a private space of domesticity, an ethnic haven in a cosmopolitan public world. Tony Camonte belongs to this world: he pursues the American symbols of power and success—beautiful women, trendy clothes, fancy cars, and a luxury home with the passion of an accomplished conspicuous consumer. His racial identity still marks his style of consumption, however, never more so than when food is involved. After killing a rival, he is welcomed at his restaurant headquarters by a waiter carrying a steaming plate of his favorite spaghetti. "Mmmhh, lots of garlic! Gimme some!" the gangster says. Rushing out to yet another job, he orders the waiter, "Keep them hot. I'll be back soon!" Camonte's love of Italian food and his devotion to family define his character in racial, as well as melodramatic, terms. And his racial heritage shapes his destiny: his primitive sense of honor and the overwhelming jealousy over Cesca prompt him to kill his friend Rinaldo and meet his own deadly fate.

In addition to linking Italian food to family, mass media regularly found in Italian food other attractive qualities, most vivid among them, Mediterranean cheerfulness, spontaneity, and musicality. Describing the Neapolitan pushcart peddlers of Mulberry Street, Konrad Bercovici notes, "There is something gay and easy about them, something of the blue sea of their homes. Even as they call out their wares, whether fish or peaches, apples or oranges, dates or figs, they interpolate little phrases from the Italian canzonettas, 'O Sole Mio' or 'Santa Lucia.'"[76] In early twentieth-century New York, Italian musical circles and Italian restaurants framed in fact a common ground for two alluring ethnic images.

Opera and Neapolitan song (itself a middle-class product) were popular among Italian immigrants.[77] The ethnic theater, radio, and press promoted music as national art, which appealed to working-class immigrants who might not have understood the meaning of the lyrics, but who could sing them by heart.[78] The power of music to build a diasporic national identity was reinforced by pride in the American appreciation of Italian operas, composers, singers, and orchestra conductors. Besides such national figures as Giulio Gatti-Casazza (head of the Metropolitan Opera), the conductor Arturo Toscanini, and the tenor Enrico Caruso, many of the most esteemed musicians in New York were Italian. Between 1899 and 1910, musicians represented the largest segment by far of the "skilled and professional" category of Italian immigrants in New York.[79] Being an Italian musician was in fact a significant professional asset, and the Italian restaurants in which they gathered attracted many music-minded New Yorkers.[80] By the early 1930s, the opera audience and the clientele of the Italian restaurants near Times Square overlapped. Romano's, Café de Capri, Barbetta's, and Casino Venezia were heavily patronized by the area's theatergoers, who enjoyed dining in the company of famed singers and instrumentalists.[81]

The ideal connection between Italian music and food was best embodied by Enrico Caruso. To New Yorkers, he was perhaps the celebrity most representative of the Italian character. His Italian exuberance was as renowned as his talent, wealth, and intimacy with the city's artistic, economic, and political elites. And Caruso loved spaghetti and Neapolitan cuisine. He boasted of his skill as a cook and enjoyed showing it off whenever he had a chance, in restaurants and in the homes of famous hosts, His passion for cooking was matched by a legendary appetite.[82] "In New York we had dinner together almost every night," the pianist Arthur Rubinstein remembered in an interview. "When we entered an Italian restaurant, everyone recognized him and would stop to see how he was going to manage with the spaghetti. One evening he became infuriated, threw down his fork, took a fistful of macaroni *alla pommarola* with his hands, held it up high over his face then let it drop into his open mouth, staining his face, tie and jacket with the sauce."[83] During the first decades of the century, Caruso arguably contributed more than anyone else to the popularity of Italian restaurants in New York. The Neapolitan singer was said to have invested in Mori's restaurant and dined there to attract customers.[84] For years, Del Pezzo's reserved a table for him and his guests every night he was in town.[85] Advertisers and marketers heavily capitalized on Caruso's association with Italian food and restaurants. One of the most popular brands of pasta and the first spaghetti house chain in New York carried his name, and countless other Italian restaurants claimed him as a customer.

As Italian restaurants began to find favor with Americans, journalists looked for the roots of this popularity in the same stereotypes that they themselves had created, busily circulating and recirculating images and meanings. "What makes Italian cooking so good?" asked *Good Housekeeping* as early as 1918. "Because of the true artist blood in every Italian's veins. Good cooking requires vision, imagination, a sensitiveness to fine shades of flavor, to beauty of color and form and composition. That is where the Latins have the advantage over us."[86] In women's magazines, Italian recipes were often enriched with accounts of the centrality of family, conviviality, and music in Italian life. Alongside its recipe for veal scaloppini, *Woman's Home Companion* described what the real "Italian dinner" atmosphere was supposed to be: "Dinner is always served outdoors, perhaps on a long table under the grape arbor. . . . The moment the guests arrive, everyone repairs to the back yard for *Le Boccie*. . . . The game goes on until dinner, begins again as soon as dinner is finished and continues after dark. Then mandolins and guitars appear and everyone sings Italian songs. Nothing could be more genuinely Italian in atmosphere than the sound of a tinkling guitar and merry young voices singing 'O Sole Mio' or 'Funiculi, Funicula.'"[87]

Italian restaurant staffs strengthened the appeal of their restaurants to a growing American clientele by responding quickly to the values of tradition, family, and artistry that were ascribed to Italian food. They translated the appealing stereotypes constructed by the popular press, photography, and cinema into a kind of staged authenticity in order to continue to attract more customers. Proprietors insisted on a homelike atmosphere for their restaurants to exploit the image of the "one-family *trattoria*, where mama cooked, papa served, one always found homemade red wine served in coffee cups and homely advice on how to bear life's burden."[88] The names of most Italian restaurants often suggested that they were family businesses: Guffanti's, Mori's, Roversi's, Solari's, Poggi's, Marabeni's, just to cite a few. Sometimes the images of nurturing food and family were explicitly gendered. By the mid-1930s, Mamma Leone's near Times Square and Mamma Bertolotti's in the Village were no longer the small places that resourceful widows had opened in the early years of the century. The former was popular among the theater crowd, the latter among the affluent clientele of the Village, but both traded successfully on the promise of warm, informal, homelike food and service.[89] The kitchen of the little Amalfi off Times Square was run by a woman chef. The service was slow—"but worth waiting for"—because she personally prepared the food to order.[90] At Maria Del Prato's in the Village, "guests competed for the honor of mixing the salad, which was then judged for quality by Maria, a benevolent despot who set the dinner hour at 7:00 p.m. and thereafter kept the front door locked against stragglers."[91] Placido Mori, the Tuscan immigrant who opened Mori's in 1893, insisted that his success was due mainly to his wife: "She has been very active through the years here and she shares all the responsibilities and burdens incident to the business, besides having the aptitude of making our guests feel welcome and at home."[92] The presence of so many women in the kitchens and lounges of Italian restaurants was most likely an attempt to offer a surrogate of the maternal figure central to the idealized matriarchal Italian family and a more accessible, unpretentious, but comforting kind of cuisine. Skillful restaurateurs also emphasized the aura of artistic sensibility surrounding the notion of Italian cuisine. Questioned by Federal Writers' Project researchers about the secrets of his cooking, Tony "Papa" Moneta explained, "It takes imagination and taste. What this world needs is more imagination in many things, but particularly in cooking . . . ; imagination, and I might say, heart."[93]

The craving of customers for a certain image of Italy and Italians began to define the business. Many restaurateurs used a village-style decor, views of Rome or Venice, and Neapolitan music to appeal to customers, many of whom were unable or uninterested in evaluating the quality of the food or the authenticity of the experience. At the end of the 1920s, some owners invested heavily in interior decoration, importing tiles and other materials from Italy to furnish places with such evocative names as Grotta Azzurra and Venetian Garden.[94] Even the old, smoky hangouts for immigrants and bohemians were expanded and renovated for a classy "Italian" look. Mori's was rebuilt for $200,000 in a classical Roman style by architect Raymond Hood. The interior of the modest Mori's, "the hideaway of the poet and the dreamer, the last resort of that selected little group of natural born epicures who were more literary than affluent," now included arches, palms, and frescoes.[95] Espresso coffee machines, albeit expensive, began to be imported from Italy. The $1,500 price tag was "not too big a price for any café or restaurant keeper to pay for true Italian atmosphere."[96] "We ate our dinner in the garden!" wrote a journalist from *Better Homes and Gardens* who visited Enrico and Paglieri's in the Village. "Of course, it was not exactly a garden because it had two-story walls with a canopy and a balcony, but it had a stone floor and there were a few trees and vines, and it amply fulfilled my conception of an Italian garden. Very odd, but very thrilling, too."[97]

The other useful stereotype, that of "Italian musicality," was widely in play in the 1920s and 1930s. Ethnic musicians and singers were ubiquitous in Italian restaurants, even if in many cases ethnicity, rather than musical talent, was more of an asset: non-Italian patrons were usually happy with a limited repertory to match the often clichéd ambiance. The proprietors of Gonfarone's never spent more than fifteen dollars a week for their musical trio, because "the American clientele, which was by far in the majority, was apathetic and uncritical. It liked the different-sounding, lively noises made by the Italian musicians and applauded indiscriminately."[98] Many places hired their own professional musicians and singers, but employees themselves often entertained, further strengthening the stereotype of an Italian inclination for music. The owner of Asti in the Village, a former opera singer, performed every night in his lounge "for the enjoyment of his clientele."[99] A researcher from the Federal Writers' Project described La Sportiva as a "favorite haunt of Italian residents who frequently organize[d] a home-talent entertainment of their own. Lively and interesting."[100] In modest Lower East Side restaurants, waiters sang all the time, while cleaning tables, taking orders, and serving food.

> The art of a singing waiter . . . consists of carrying a song over a multitude of busy doings. During the heartrending moments of the piece you may have to make change for a two-dollar bill and reckon up the amount due, put down the change, receive your tip, move to the next table, mop its surface dry, remove empty glasses on a tray, call at the little door for your ordered drinks, pass out the right brass tags to the checker, show people to the tables, smile to known frequenters, laugh at a friendly gibe and stoop to pick up a coin thrown as a compliment to your vocal efforts.[101]

The success of New York Italian restaurants in the interwar years is an example of the ways in which the ethnic identities of the 1920s and 1930s were regularly redefined to accommodate social and cultural change. Prodded by the emergence of mass culture, this process of redefinition challenges the notion of the inevitably homogenizing effects of modern mass society. Instead, it illuminates the need for mass popular and consumer culture to *produce* and *distribute*, in commodified forms, racial and cultural difference. That same history also illustrates the way ethnic images and symbols in multiethnic societies must be standardized and stereotyped in order to create a stable platform for group interaction and economic power. Many Italian American restaurateurs succeeded in consciously exploiting racial stereotypes, in the process stabilizing, reinforcing, and perpetuating them.

The ways in which diasporic national identities were used in Italian restaurants must be seen as part of the system of marketing and consumption of ethnicity that was multicultural New York in the 1920s and 1930s. Scholars insist that consumer culture is a coherent, if ever-changing, system in which consumers first assess the value and meaning of individual goods or experiences within a structure of relationships with all other goods.[102] In the context of an urban consumer culture in which racial and national identities were increasingly stereotyped, commodified, and marketed, consumers developed tools to decode many narratives of ethnic and racial difference by juxtaposing, comparing, and evaluating them.[103]

Italian restaurants were not, of course, the only institutions where race and nation were processed into objects for cross-cultural consumption. Other ethnic institutions in New York played similar roles; among these, the Chinese restaurant and the Harlem nightclub were particularly visible. In all these places, the process of ethnic commodification and crossing of racial boundaries was transnational in scope; imagined Italy, China, and Africa were the sources of the primal, authentic immigrant identities that fed consumer culture.[104] Under the white gaze, these racialized immigrants and the urban villages (streets, houses, shops, markets, churches) they inhabited were transformed into desirable destinations with evocative place names; the Village, Chinatown, Little Italy, Harlem formed a cosmopolitan geography of consumption.

In many ways, the Chinese restaurant followed a trajectory similar to that of the Italian.[105] Early Chinese joints fed the immigrant "bachelor society" of men and were seen by middle-class New Yorkers as unsafe places, even possibly as opium dens. Only the adventurous tried Chinese food before World War I. From the early 1920s onward, Chinese restaurants benefited from the proximity of Chinatown to the nearby Jewish ghetto and Little Italy, forming a large, contiguous zone for urban tourism. Chinese restaurants had their own signature dishes for ethnic tourists. Chop suey was a hybrid American invention and played the same role as spaghetti did in Italian restaurants: it helped immigrant food break through to become not only accepted but also popular in the larger society. By the end of the decade, everyone patronized Chinese restaurants, including Italians. As a detective from the Chinatown police station explained to one visitor in 1924, "Lots of Italians come in here to eat. Tired of spaghetti, I guess. The Italian quarter—Guinealand we call it—is right around the next block or so. The Italians run here pretty often."[106] Chinese restaurants were convenient, interesting, and inexpensive, and given the history of discrimination and the almost total segregation of Chinese New Yorkers, they were places where even Italians could exercise the power of color. The alchemies of racial privilege, in fact, made the most significant differences between the experience of Chinese and Italian restaurants in interwar New York.

Jazz, a cultural product of the city's African American minority, excited a large segment of white society in some of the same ways as did Italian cuisine. In the 1920s, as middle-class New Yorkers were patronizing the Italian restaurants of Bleecker and Thompson Streets in the Village, uptown in Harlem, at the Cotton Club, Connie's Inn, and other clubs and dancehalls mostly white crowds danced to all-black bands. The immense popularity of jazz and blues meant that for the first time whites were publicly expressing their admiration for African American culture. Many white youths were fascinated by the vitality and immediacy of black music, their praise sounding like an act of defiance of the lifestyle and values of their fathers' generation.[107] The similarly strong popularity of Italian food and restaurants also brought the Italian American community a new, positive visibility that partly overturned stigma and prejudice. Both black music and Italian food profited from the openness toward cultural difference and the search for alternative values that ran through New York in the post–World War

I years: "Back then, to eat a loaf of garlic bread was an act of bravado and to eat a garlic-laden spaghetti sauce was an act of liberation."[108] Both black music and Italian food offered the experience of authenticity, or primitivism, that white middle-class patrons were seeking as a respite from modern commercial urban life. Black music and Italian cuisine could both be consumed easily, without any need to understand their larger cultural contexts and without the need to carry on meaningful personal relations with actual African Americans or Italians. At night, Greenwich Village, like Harlem, was a world of escape, where restaurants and nightclubs alike made it safe to encounter ethnic and racial others, if only for the evening. Black dancers and musicians could also express their Africanness, and Italian waiters and chefs their *Italianità*, to white customers within the careful limits of clubs and restaurants. As an ethnic and racial culture was being commodified to meet the racialized expectations of white customers, local Italian and black customers rapidly became minorities in their Village restaurants and Harlem nightclubs.[109]

At the same time, race and color intervened again to make a significant difference in the trajectories of black and Italian American communities. Italian restaurant owners could open or move their places almost anywhere they wanted, an option largely unavailable to black entrepreneurs. The elements of "high" Italian culture that flavored southern Italian "primitivism" in Italian restaurants were also a powerful claim of whiteness that would resonate loudly among the mostly non-Italian diners.

"They Number Scarcely an Italian Patron": Customer-Worker Relations in Italian Restaurants

In his 1930 guide to the New York food scene, Rian James included much information on ethnic restaurants, which he believed helped make the American metropolis unique. James, who considered himself a gourmet who treasured culinary authenticity, was nonetheless frustrated by one characteristic of Italian restaurants: the near total absence of Italian diners. "Most of the Italian restaurants in New York are inclined to be paradoxical," James wrote disappointingly. "They are run by Italians, serve alleged Italian delicacies, and yet, with the exception of an occasional straggler who couldn't tell you how he came to be there himself, they number scarcely a single Italian among their patrons."[110]

The "paradox" that James highlighted was related to significant changes in immigrant society. Restaurants were no longer gathering places for single men who wanted to eat cheaply and mingle with fellow *paesani*. By the 1930s, the backbone of Italian communities was families who enjoyed sharing food at home, in the most cohesive ritual of their domestic life. The Depression also discouraged larger and poorer families from eating out more than occasionally. Many Italian Americans went to restaurants only for special family occasions like weddings or for the annual banquets of political, local, and mutual aid associations. An entire page of *Il Progresso Italo-Americano*, titled "Associazioni e Vita Coloniale" (Associations and community life), was still filled every day with notices about such social occasions. But these were, indeed, exceptions; as a student of Covello noted, "In New York and maybe all over the U.S.A. there are many Italian restaurants. However, it is strange to note that very few among our immigrant countrymen habitually patronize restaurants. Our immigrants prefer to eat at home and cook their own meals. They go to the restaurant to talk business or to attend a banquet."[111]

Still, the most important reason why many Italians avoided Italian restaurants lay in the kind of place that these restaurants had become by the 1930s. Evolving to meet the needs of their largely non-Italian clientele, most Italian restaurants offered a hybrid concoction of different regional dishes designed to satisfy the "American palate." Since "Americans" were presumed to be uninterested and perhaps even confused by the amazing variety of Italian cooking, chefs tended to serve a limited number of popular dishes prepared to the taste of the non-Italian majority. For this gradual gastronomic makeover, chefs borrowed the most popular dishes from different regional cuisines. They exploited some elements, most notably from the red sauce, melted cheese, and garlic template of Neapolitan cooking that came to identify Italian American food, and discarded others. By 1939, the New York City guide compiled by the Federal Writers' Project included sixteen Italian restaurants, compared to five Chinese, five French, four Jewish, three Mexican, and one Greek. But the fare served in these restaurants was limited to a small number of familiar dishes, such as "spaghetti in various styles, ravioli (small meat-filled dumplings), minestrone (thick vegetable soup), veal scaloppini (veal cooked with wine)." Even though the guide noted that at Amalfi "Neapolitan specialties" were served, and that at Balilla one could taste "Northern Italian cuisine," by the end of the 1930s the menus of the most popular restaurants, with very few exceptions, were almost entirely interchangeable.[112]

In fact, gastronomic massification was so widespread that it even began to bother some of the most discriminating "American" regulars. With a certain haughtiness, Rian James complained that Zucca's was "exactly what visitors from the middle west expect to find in an Italian table d'hotery." While conceding that many Italian restaurants sometimes offered excellent food, Harry Zahm of the Federal Writers' Project admitted that he, as a non-Italian, found it impossible to get courses cooked in the traditional way with authentic ingredients.

> Gastronomic differences have been largely smoothed over for those Americans who think they like Italian cooking. Both sets of restaurants, Northern and Southern, have realized that insofar as American customers are concerned, discretion is the better part of local patriotism which is retained as a private matter. Hence it is that the Epicurean will tell you the disillusioning news that if you want a real Italian dish there are two conditions which must obtain. First, one must have been in Italy where these dishes can be procured, and secondly, one must order these dishes in the Italian tongue, mentioning the ingredients you want in these dishes with pedantic precision. Otherwise you won't know what an Italian dish really tastes like. For practically all Italian dishes served in New York restaurants are doctored to accord with what is thought to be the American taste.[113]

Growing up in Queens in the 1930s, Joe Vergara recalled how his mother's passion and gift for cooking went hand in hand with her repulsion for Italian restaurants. "She rarely consented to eat out, but when it was necessary, she tried to avoid Italian restaurants. She especially disliked the pizzerias that featured mass-produced spaghetti and meatballs; this she considered fit only for pigs. She once accused the owner of such a place of doing more damage to Italian honor than all combined membership of the Mafia."[114] Italian travelers to the United States were even more trenchant in their criticism. Even as early as 1913, Italian diplomat Amy Bernardy observed, "One can have a decent Italian meal, avoiding dreadful Americanization, only if she takes care to be recognized as an Italian and order every course, particularly spaghetti, to be free from the most indecent concessions to the American culinary taste. Since it has become fashionable among Americans to go down to North Square 'for an Italian dinner,' everywhere in Little Italy there is the danger of eating spaghetti with a double citizenship. . . . And they eat spaghetti as if it were boiled potatoes or string beans, as an accompaniment to meat."[115] In the late 1930s, another Italian traveler to New York, Pier Antonio Quarantotti Gambini, recorded the same unenthusiastic impressions in his diary.

> Gone with Tass. to an Italian restaurant. Pasta. Chianti wine. I await my pasta anxiously, after having had for days just American food, replete with hot sauces, mustard, and God only knows what other spices that burn your tongue and palate. Pasta makes you happy just to look at it, but it is a sham. After the first forkful, it is hard to go on. It is seasoned with a sauce that tastes more of pepper than tomato. I look at Tass., but he keeps on eating avidly. Local Italians have adjusted their taste to strong flavors, even hot and violent, and cannot enjoy pasta the Italian way anymore. But they just don't realize it.[116]

The dislike of both Italian travelers and Italian Americans for Italian restaurants, if on different terms and for different reasons, reflected a sense of superiority that they felt about their foods. As if to mirror the persistent stereotype of the creative and warm-blooded Italian, Italians and Italian Americans had their own prejudices about middle-class, Anglo-Protestant Americans.[117] "American" was an adjective that Italian immigrants used to characterize, and usually disparage, anything that was not "Italian," from food to other areas of American life. "To my people," the Italian American novelist Pietro Di Donato wrote, "the Americans were colorless, unsalted, baloney munchers and 'gasoline' drinkers without culture, who . . . listened to caterwauling, imbecilic music, and all looked more or less alike."[118] In many Italian restaurants, this attitude sometimes translated into an arrogant habit of considering the average patron a culinary ignoramus. In Gonfarone's, for example, "when [the bartender] had drawn a full demijohn of wine, he would pour a demijohn of water into the barrel. This was the daily 'christening' of the wine, which, Madama Gonfarone said, was too heady for the American customers, and, anyway, they wouldn't know the difference."[119]

The attitude of Italian restaurateurs toward their "American" patrons reflected the dynamics of racialized and stereotyped interactions that characterized interactions at New York's Italian restaurants. Italian restaurant workers and their non-Italian middle-class customers performed for each other and for the benefit of each other. The role that such performances and exchanges play in ethnicity was first theorized by Fredrik Barth. Barth argues that in a multiethnic society the most important aspects of ethnicity lie on the borders, in zones where groups meet and interact. It is the system of stereotypes that groups create about each other, Barth maintains, that permit ethnic interactions to develop. In Barth's "ecological perspective," ethnic groups can adapt successfully to each other when there are significant and complementary cultural differences between them, when those differences can be standardized (that is, when every member of a group is "highly stereotyped"), and when these stable cultural traits "persist in the face of close inter-ethnic contact."[120]

In fact, the Italian restaurant of New York appears much more a place where mutual stereotypes were consolidated, rather than one where difference was melted by contact. By the 1930s, Italian restaurateurs had mastered the techniques of winning American customers. Cleverly instrumentalizing Italian identities, they created popular, successful businesses that shaped the ways in which Americans and Italians viewed, and acted toward, each other. They went to great lengths to align themselves and their restaurants to the most valuable images of Italy and Italians prevalent in American popular culture, because the identity created had to be—in Barth's terms—standardized, stereotyped, and stable to be profitable. The restaurant provided a safe arena for interaction (that is, one free from conflict) that helped Barth's "interethnic relation system" stabilize.[121]

Greenwich Village provides a particular rich example of the larger effects of this process. The Village both had the largest number of Italian restaurants in the city and was the only area where a large Italian immigrant community lived alongside many white middle-class Americans. Personal relations between the Villagers—students, artists, writers, professionals, and their families—and the local Italian American population were few and superficial. Even though they lived in close proximity and met daily in the streets, they largely ignored each other. "There was no evidence that years of living in an Italian community had any effect on the Villagers' attitude toward 'foreigners' in general or Italians in particular," notes Caroline Ware. "The fact that the Villagers almost all entered the area as adults meant that their point of view was originally shaped elsewhere, while the social gulf between them and their [Italian] neighbors prevented any observations they might make of the latter from being incorporated into their point of view. Interrelations between Villagers and local people in this community tended to reflect rather than to mould attitudes."[122]

Italian restaurants were one of the few institutions run by Italian residents that the Villagers patronized. Yet there, too, interaction between middle-class customers and Italian staffs was largely superficial, and developing stronger relationships was discouraged. The restaurant economy, based on the exploitation of stereotypes, reinforced both the determination of Italian staffs to act according to expected behaviors and the annoyance they felt when "American" patrons attempted to approach them more closely, or, worse, to act as Italians. "Nothing earned greater scorn than to talk Italian. 'You don't like people who try to turn native.' One speakeasy proprietor . . . was so annoyed at [his patrons'] efforts in Italian that some Jewish boys on the block taught him a Yiddish phrase that would express his real sentiments toward these customers. His response to the hated '*Buon giorno*' was 'How are you, *signor*? May you drop dead, *signor*.' It delighted his neighbors to hear him call after a departing patron, 'Good-bye, *signor*. May you drop dead, *signor*.'"[123]

In multiethnic societies, as Barth argues, people whose behavior does not conform to their ethnic affiliation are typically subjected to scorn or reproach. "In such systems . . . just as both sexes ridicule the male who is feminine, and all classes punish the proletarian who puts on airs, so also can members of all ethnic groups in a poly-ethnic society act to maintain dichotomies and differences."[124] In the staged performances of the Italian restaurant, every single form of communication was mediated by and ultimately supported the mutual representation of otherness. The frustrated efforts of "American" patrons to embrace Italian culture was the flip side of the obligation to adhere to the controlling stereotype—sometimes degrading—of the Italian waiter or cook. Charlie, the owner of an Italian restaurant in East Harlem, was painfully aware of the dynamic: "He was called Charlie—and not Mr. Bucato—by everyone. . . . I think he liked to be called Charlie by the bohemians and professional people who used to haunt his place because he found something very ironic in the situation—these pigs of people calling him by the familiar, personal first name—as one does with a servant—while really Charlie considered himself a gentleman and not a pig to get drunk and throw up in a public restaurant."[125]

In the Italian restaurants of New York in the 1920s and 1930, much more developed than the synthesis of many Italian cuisines into the popular synopsis that appealed to a vast and diverse public. Against the backdrop of an increasing multicultural and cosmopolitan metropolis, where capitalism transformed even subaltern cultures into objects of consumption and leisure, Italian immigrants used their restaurants to concoct a powerful system of self-representation. Although its primary purpose was to please middle-class consumers, this representation articulated immigrants' efforts to reconcile their rural simplicity and their inherited taste for beauty; their racial distinctiveness and their whiteness; their diasporic idea of nation and their place in America.

Epilogue

Third-generation Italian American writer Helen Barolini recently looked back at the values and ideals that in the 1950s guided the suburban life of her parents, the first in their families to join the professional middle class. Barolini recalled, "In adopting American ways and the modernity of the twenties, both my parents lost the old-world family cohesiveness and unity of their parents. They had discovered a whole world outside family—family was no longer the fortress one stayed immured in; there were other attractions like business and social success, a country club and Corinthian club, material possessions." As clearly as Barolini mourned that loss, she still acknowledged that the "whole world outside the family" did not always extend to her Italian American table. "We girls learned to sew and cook in home-economics class," Barolini wrote.

> I remember learning to make Welsh rarebit, tuna fish casserole, prune whip, tomato aspic, chipped beef on toast—all things we'd never eat at home, but which I told my mother about. It turned out that she herself, once, had attempted to go Wasp in her early days of marriage by serving my father creamed chicken on waffles. Once and never more; he had certain rules: Sunday was for spaghetti with meatballs (the word *pasta* was not used and no other form of it ever appeared) and he could get testy about the tomato sauce if it was too bitter, too thin, too thick, too cooked; a chunk of iceberg lettuce to munch on was all he wanted—no mixed salad; white fish or kidney beans were served in a broth of oil and garlic; strawberries were never to be crushed as a topping for ice cream and fruit in general was not to be promiscuously mingled in a "fruit cocktail"; and only Italian bread was ever to be placed on his table. American bread, which pop disparaged as cotton batting, was reserved for our school sandwiches. "Take out the soft part," he'd command us children about Italian bread, "eat the crust, the soft part's no good."[1]

The dark, crackling crust spoke candidly to Barolini's memory of the working-class origins of her Italian American cooking. That sound and those smells symbolized the resilience, even in a suburban world of supermarkets and single-family houses, of the food culture that immigrants and their children had shaped, out of feelings of shame and inferiority, through conflicts and compromises, in places like East Harlem, the South Village, and Mulberry Street's Little Italy. Just like it had been in the 1920s and 1930s, though, the distinctiveness of Italian American food in postwar America would be the result of continuous transformations and adaptations to a changing Italian America and American culture. In the 1950s, many Italians began leaving their neighborhoods and, while still overrepresented among the ranks of the working class, quickly moved upward economically in the following decades, as college graduates and homeowners. From 1950 to 1970, the population of first- and second-generation Italians in New York City dropped by 36 percent, or more than 357,000. Language loyalty was disappearing as quickly as the immigrant generation itself. And the new immigrant families who arrived after the loosening of immigration restriction in 1965 came from a different Italy.

Despite all this, Italian immigrant food culture sustained itself, but it was also transformed, as a cultural sphere that once again proved resilient to loss—but open to change. Its persistence in the life of Italian America and larger society can be grounded in different related dynamics. During these decades of social, cultural, economic, and political change within the Italian American community, Italian immigrant food became big business, both for local, independent, Italian American firms catering to an ethnic clientele and for aggressively growing national corporations. The once "dangerous" trattorias of Little Italy were transformed into comfortably middle-class attractions, and dining on spaghetti and meatballs at a restaurant run by a black-mustached cook became so common, and desirable, an experience that the consumption of difference through food would reach unprecedented popularity. Italian food became a culture that could be packaged for a mass consumer market, like the cans of spaghetti in tomato sauce that started appearing in the 1930s.

Pizza is a vivid example of this continuing influence of an Italian working-class lifestyle and food culture in American life during the 1950s and 1960s. Before World War II, most non-Italians were completely unfamiliar with pizza, which a 1930 guide to dining in New York described as "an inch-thick, potato pan-cake, sprinkled with Parmesan cheese and stewed tomatoes."[2] In 1947, the *New York Times* Sunday magazine claimed that pizza, a favorite in New York's Little Italies, "could be as popular a snack as the hamburger, if only the Americans knew more about it," and provided a recipe.[3] In the 1950s, a national market for pizza was created almost overnight by inventive Italian American cooks and entrepreneurs who finessed the familiar culinary triangle (dough, tomato sauce, cheese) popularized in spaghetti dishes. They opened modernized "pizza parlors" outside Little Italy, exploited new forms of leisure and consumption, and profited from a growing circulation of Italian tastes and imaginaries, often brought by GIs returning from occupied Italy.[4] Blending narratives of tradition with modern production methods, Italian American food entrepreneurs had reworked the Neapolitan street food into an American staple. "In New Jersey a belt-line assembles pizza as if they were General Motors tanks," an article reported in 1956. The success of pizza was made possible by "the American way of life, the free enterprise system and the capitalistic interplay of supply and demand."[5]

Although it was not until the 1980s that corporate food giants systematically started snapping up independent Italian food businesses as a way to "diversify" their product lines, the industrialization of Italian food endangered its ability to proclaim a real sense of ethnic identity. Suddenly, Italian foods came from everywhere—and nowhere. Pizza made by New Jersey's Nino Food Products and shipped by the thousands each week to Ohio, Illinois, and Michigan, was "a real international pie: plum tomatoes from California, olive oil from Castelvetrano in Sicily, and pure black pepper from the Pacific area."[6] Italian foods of all kinds were becoming common items on the shelves of supermarkets across America. Still, even during this golden age of mass markets, Italian food continued to embody values of solidarity and commensality that were increasingly important to a white ethnic America anxious about its place in the social, cultural, and political changes of the 1960s. While "traditional" foodways were sources of longing and nostalgia for white ethnics, they were appreciated by the liberal middle class as sources of authenticity and informality. In a popular 1969 commercial for the Italian American–owned Prince Spaghetti Company, twelve-year Anthony Martignetti runs home past the markets, bocce courts, and tenement houses in the Italian North End of Boston to a warm, nurturing, heavily matriarchal atmosphere of good food and family. "Prince Spaghetti—Share It with Your Family," the closing caption reads.

By this time, Italian American domestic foodways were undergoing yet another round of changes. While the meal formats were de-ethnicized on some weekdays with such "American" dishes as platters of cold cuts and a red-meat or chicken course with vegetables, rich "Italian" food was widely served on Sundays and other festive occasions. Lasagna, homemade macaroni in Italian "gravy," meatballs, stuffed beef, and fish prepared according to regional and family preferences were among the popular dishes of holiday Italian menus that further ritualized and emphasized tradition, heritage, and cultural difference.[7] After World War II, the Italian American diet was being "standardized" on its own terms, through an increasing availability of mass-produced Italian food and, for the first time, cookbooks designed for Italian American home cooks. As an antidote to the loss of orally transmitted culinary knowledge, Italian American housewives of the second generation widely purchased—or, as often, were given as wedding gifts—cookbooks like Ada Boni's *The Talisman Italian Cookbook* or Maria LoPinto's *The Art of Italian Cooking*.[8] While the former was the translation of a classic manual by a bourgeois Roman woman aimed at struggling middle-class Italian housewives and the latter was the work of a daughter of immigrants, both functioned as guides to cooking and being Italian for postwar Italian American women. The books offered an introduction to real Italian eating, cooking, and drinking—as if the reader lived in Rome, not New York or Long Island.

Transnational flows of cooking styles, tastes, and products grew in significance in the 1970s and 1980s, as the meanings of Italian American food were reworked in the neoliberal landscape of deindustrialization, globalization, and a postmodern culture in which "the self" was created through consumption and where cultural difference became just another commodity. A new group of middle-class Italian immigrants to New York City, many of whom had never cooked in Italy, started to reshape Italian food in America by detaching it from its immigrant origins and relocating it within the "authentic" traditions of Italian regional cuisine. As cookbook writers, cooking instructors, chefs, and, later, TV hosts, people like Marcella Hazan, Giuliano Bugialli, Franco Romagnoli, Pino Luongo, and Lidia Bastianich were welcomed by a culture industry eager to let them popularize real Italian food among a growing cosmopolitan bourgeoisie who were avid consumers of ethnic cuisines. Sometimes called northern Italian cuisine to differentiate it from the down-market red-sauce clichés of immigrants, this new template for Italian eating introduced ingredients like pesto, balsamic vinegar, and focaccia to the Italian American larder and translated macaroni and spaghetti into "pasta."[9] At the same time, at a more grassroots level, a post-1965 wave of southern Italian immigrants opened new food stores, importing businesses, and restaurants in urban as well as reconstituted Italian suburban communities. They reinvigorated dormant foods and food cultures with fresh ingredients and reengaged traditions, often to the surprise of older Italian Americans.

By the 1970s, financially secure third-generation Italian Americans interested in "rediscovering their roots" in a post–civil rights era of identity politics also became avid consumers of these real Italian cuisines and beneficiaries of the appealing new image of Italian food and culture. But they also looked back to the humbler food that was the heritage of their grandparents' immigrant generation, a dissolving legacy that now seemed a shield against the cultural, racial, and status anxieties that were challenging ethnic America.[10] By the 1980s, community cookbooks, collections of traditional family recipes, and commercial cookbooks recreating the classic restaurant dishes of Little Italy became widely popular. Nancy Verde Barr's *We Called It Macaroni*, which re-created Providence, Rhode

Island's Little Italy in memory and recipes, was a breakthrough success for its distinguished publisher. A few years later, a spiral-bound cookbook from the members of the Florida chapter of the Order Sons of Italy in America that offered a variety of straightforward and uncommodified family recipes, including some for very localized specialties, sold more than forty thousand copies in the first few years.[11] Through these cookbooks, the "old neighborhood" was revived once again as a nostalgic nonplace, a space that reconfigured itself in the geographies and historical imaginations of the Italian migrant experience in America.[12]

Since the 1990s, the "recovery" of immigrant and southern Italian foodways by descendants of immigrants has become ever more a sophisticated adventure, made possible by amazingly rich source material: serious cookbooks; the presence of a prosperous Italy, to which many second- and third-generation Italians return; and the growing availability of high-quality Italian food in supermarkets as well as in gourmet shops, in small Little Italy *salumerie* but more often in the sleek Italian American superstores that feed the newly regrouped ethnic suburbs.[13]

In the last two decades, the politics of working-class Italian American food has also been further refocused. A debate has centered on the place of food in a progressive Italian American culture long lost to public memory. Since the 1990s, some scholars, writers, and performers have sought to counter the conservative stereotype of a conservative Italian America by bringing to new light the participation of Italian men and women in labor and antifascist movements, against intolerance and bigotry in American society, and more broadly the radical legacy of the Italian immigrant experience. In this context, the work in the kitchen of immigrant women (and their daughters and granddaughters) has been recast less as an act of submission to patriarchy than as a work of care, self-assertion, and identification, relevant not only in the construction of an ethnic domestic haven but also in building community, transracial working-class solidarities, and diasporic memory.[14]

A slightly different discourse, still embryonic, has connected that same experience with the issues of food sustainability, food justice, and food sovereignty.[15] The battle of nongovernmental organizations for local and organic food, produced through fair treatment of workers, animals, and the environment, and accessible to all, has become a pivotal issue in today's global politics. The Italy-based organization Slow Food has advocated the "defense" of traditional local foods endangered by agroindustry multinationals, encouraging consumers to pay a sustaining "fair" (higher) price to farmers in order to preserve bio- and cultural diversity. As this book has shown, Italian immigrants of a century ago struggled against social and economic pressures to eat food that was meaningful and tasty to them. In doing so, they were resisting an industrial transformation of food that was unprecedented. Long before it became the political credo of (prevalently middle-class) consumers activists, immigrants privileged homemade, local, and "fresh" food and supported a large network of independent farms and food businesses, in the process creating community and place. Around their distinctive food practices, as hybrid and nontraditional as they were, Italian women and men constructed the authenticity—that is, the meaningfulness—of their entire diasporic culture.

Indeed, the continuing uses of the history of Italian American food validate the main argument of this book: from domestic kitchens to luxurious restaurants, Italian immigrants framed a food culture that, responding to the needs of their working-class world, created a nation and shaped their self-representation as a group. So convincing was this achievement that it left indelible marks in American culture and remains a powerful narrative for comparing Italian and other migrant identities.

In an influential essay, sociologist Herbert Gans defined as "symbolic ethnicity" the casual identification of third- and fourth-generation white ethnics with their European immigrant heritage, articulated mostly in the consumption of ethnic goods and leisure. Gans's model inscribes identity in (white) immigrant bodies, by suggesting that class, endogamy, and residential segregation naturally made them act and think "ethnic" without any agency on their part. In turn, when the descendants of European immigrants became indistinguishable from other "whites," they used ethnicity as an ornament with no relevance for what really counted: class and electoral politics.[16] *The Italian American Table* has worked in an opposite direction from Gans. The formation of Italian food culture in New York City was the *creative* work of mostly poor and uneducated migrant working women and men who assembled ingredients from different cultures and economies into an original material culture *and* a symbolic narrative that responded to their needs, fears, dilemmas, and ambitions. This food culture created a diasporic nation across classes, genders, and generations, and its link to the larger New York marketplace gave immigrants much more of a pathway to assimilation than scholars have described.[17] In the process of culinary invention, Italians significantly changed that marketplace, emerging as a *dominating* force within it. New York Italians invented their identities around the table and in the kitchen within a racialized human ecology, where they interacted with many "others" and many other hybrid American cultures. Translating their home- and nation-making food narratives to the wider sphere of restaurants and the food trade, Italians made a long-term contribution to transnational American culture; one that has lived long after "Little Italy" was gone. In fact, symbolic consumption—the practice that Gans describes as an empty gesture—has always been the code by which people and groups make sense of themselves and their place in society, tell who they are, where they think they come from, and what they want to become. Even in contemporary regime of consumption, the capacity of Italian food to produce and narrate meaningful identities rooted in immigrants' negotiations and struggles for recognition has continued to provide material for the construction of ethnicity and appropriation of diasporic culture in the marketplace of diversity.

One very visible example of this is an emerging "red-sauce revival," led by trained young chefs, many of them Italian Americans. On Mulberry Street in the heart of Little Italy in New York, Torrisi Italian Specialities targets foodies and hipsters with its stylish reworking of old-school dishes. With local, artisanal products, Torrisi showcases "brightly packaged products with names ending in 'o'—Stella D'oro biscotti, Polly-O ricotta, Progresso bread crumbs. 'Nothing from Italy,' declares Rich Torrisi, one of a pair of chef/owners, in a video on the restaurant's Web site. 'This is American food.'"[18] Torrisi and a raft of similar places offer artful, even playful, representations of the past (even if it is somebody else's past) as high-end heritage tourism—a process that historians have long been studying.[19]

Italian American food still conveys a lifestyle, a taste, and a *history*. Even as the ground for Italian American (and Italian) identity has shifted. The celebrity chef Mario Batali has come to define Italian cooking in America, through his enormously successful restaurants, cookbooks, television shows, and partnership in Eataly, the Italian food megastore in New York City. An Italian American from Seattle, Batali has been careful to downplay any Italian American accents in the Italy he offers his customers to, literally, eat. His Italy is a collection of middle-class luxuries, urban and rustic, that on the surface have little to do with the more diminutive pleasures of classic Italian American cooking. For his legions of followers, Batali's improvisational, playful Italian style can be consumed as a globalized brand freed from the stigma of immigration. His customers are permanent tourists in a modern, middle-class Italy. Yet Batali, like Rich Torrisi and his partner, Mario Carbone, remains an Italian American phenomenon. His adaptive energy, creativity, and carefully staged ties to traditional Italian—if not Italian American—foods and foodways reflects the legacy of generations of similar entrepreneurs. The success of this stylishly performative Italian food culture—also revealed in a recent explosion of "authentic" Neapolitan pizzerie and meticulously sourced regional *trattorias*—reflects, and depends on, generations of Italian American foodways, from its entrepreneurs to the families who became its consumers, and for whom, as Nancy Verde Barr has written, "food was always about more than eating."[20]

Notes

Abbreviations of Archival Sources

FTC	Federal Writers' Project, "Feeding the City," Municipal Archives of the City of New York
ILOHP	New York City Immigrant Labor Oral History Project, Robert F. Wagner Labor Archives, Tamiment Institute Library, New York University
INY	Federal Writers' Project, "The Italians of New York," Municipal Archives of the City of New York
LBB	Federal Writers' Project, "Let the Buyer Beware," Municipal Archives of the City of New York
LCP	Leonard Covello Papers, Pennsylvania Historical Society, Philadelphia
NYCG-LC	Federal Writers' Project, "New York City Guide," Manuscript Division, Library of Congress, Washington, DC
NYCG-MA	Federal Writers' Project, "New York City Guide," Municipal Archives of the City of New York
ONY	Federal Writers' Project, "Oddities of New York," Municipal Archives of the City of New York

Introduction

1. On *The Sopranos* as representation of Italian American life, see Regina Barreca, ed., *A Sitdown with the Sopranos: Watching Italian American Culture on T.V.'s Most Talked About Series* (New York: Palgrave, 2002).

2. Irvin L. Child, *Italian or American? The Second Generation in Conflict* (New Haven, Conn.: Yale University Press, 1943), 197; Herbert J. Gans, *The Urban Villagers: Group and Class in the Life of Italian Americans* (New York: Free Press of Glencoe, 1962), 33; Patrick J. Gallo, *Ethnic Alienation: The Italian Americans* (Rutherford, N.J.: Farleigh Dickinson University Press, 1974), 194; James Crispino, *The Assimilation of Ethnic Groups: The Italian Case* (Staten Island, N.Y.: Center for Migration Studies, 1980), 48–50; Richard Alba, *Italian Americans:*

Into the Twilight of Ethnicity (Englewood Cliffs, N.J.: Prentice-Hall, 1985), 133–34; John R. Mitrano, "I Have a Craving for Italian . . . : Food and Ethnic Identity Formation among Generation X Italian Americans," in *A Tavola: Food, Tradition and Community among Italian Americans*, ed. Edvige Giunta and Samuel Patti (New York: AIHA, 1998), 20–30.

3. Mario Puzo, "Choosing a Dream," in *The Immigrant Experience: The Anguish of Becoming American*, ed. Thomas C. Wheeler (New York: Dial Press, 1971), 39.

4. Stuart Hall, ed., *Representation: Cultural Representations and Signifying Practices* (Thousand Oaks, Calif.: Sage, 1997); Michel de Certeau, *The Practice of Everyday Life* (Berkeley: University of California Press, 1984); John Fiske, *Understanding Popular Culture* (Boston: Unwin Hyman, 1989); Dick Hebdige, *Subculture: The Meaning of Style* (New York: Routledge, 1979); Michel Maffesoli, *The Time of the Tribes: The Decline of Individualism in Mass Society* (Thousand Oaks, Calif.: Sage, 1996).

5. Werner Sollors, "Introduction: The Invention of Ethnicity," in *The Invention of Ethnicity*, ed. Werner Sollors (New York: Oxford University Press, 1989), xvi. The quotation from the Chinese laundryman is from "The Life Story of a Chinaman," in Hamilton Holt, ed., *The Life Stories of Undistinguished Americans as Told by Themselves* (New York: James Pott, 1906), 289.

6. Jack Goody, *Cooking, Cuisine and Class: A Study in Comparative Sociology* (New York: Cambridge University Press, 1996); Massimo Montanari, *Food Is Culture* (New York: Columbia University Press, 2006).

7. On consumerism and the production of transnational American culture, see Henry Yu, "How Tiger Woods Lost His Stripes: Post-Nationalist American Studies as a History of Race, Migration, and the Commodification of Culture," in *Post-Nationalist American Studies*, ed. John Carlos Rowe (Berkeley: University of California Press, 2000), 223–48; Kristin Hoganson, *Consumers' Imperium: The Global Production of American Domesticity* (Chapel Hill, N.C.: University of North Carolina Press, 2007).

8. Marie Hall Ets, *Rosa: The Life of an Italian Immigrant Woman* (Madison: University of Wisconsin Press, 1999), 172, 174.

9. John Mariani, "Food," in *The Encyclopedia of New York City*, ed. Kenneth T. Jackson (New Haven, Conn.: Yale University Press, 1995), 423.

10. Donna R. Gabaccia, *We Are What We Eat: Ethnic Food and the Making of Americans* (Cambridge, Mass.: Harvard University Press, 1998), 54.

11. Hasia R. Diner, *Hungering for America: Italian, Irish, and Jewish Foodways in the Age of Migration* (Cambridge, Mass.: Harvard University Press, 2001), 81–82.

12. Arjun Appadurai, "Disjuncture and Difference in the Global Cultural Economy," *Public Culture* 2, no. 2 (Spring 1990): 1–24; Arlene Davila, *Latinos, Inc.: The Marketing and Making of a People* (Berkeley: University of California Press, 2001); Irdepal Grewal, "Traveling Barbie: Indian Transnationality and New Consumer Subjects," *positions* 7, no. 3, (1999): 799–827; Purnima Mankekar, "'India Shopping': Indian Grocery Stores and Transnational Configurations of Belonging," *Ethnos* 67, no. 1 (March 2002): 75–97.

13. Lizabeth Cohen, *Making a New Deal: Industrial Workers in Chicago, 1919–1939* (New York: Cambridge University Press, 1990). Cohen brings as evidence of the demise of ethnic consumer subcultures during the Depression the popularity of chain stores, which replaced many independent ethnic stores in the 1930s. But chain stores usually made few

inroads in Italian working-class neighborhoods in New York City through the end of the decade (see chapter 4 of this book).

14. Scholars generally consider "lifestyle" a product of post–World War II consumerism, which allowed an expanding middle class to spend discretionary money on self-making projects; see Mike Featherstone, *Consumer Culture and Postmodernism* (Thousand Oaks, Calif.: Sage, 2007). I argue that the case of Italian American food, and, more broadly, consumer subculture, challenges this interpretation, which denies agency to working-class consumers in industrializing societies. Victoria De Grazia, also critical of the understanding of lifestyle as a middle-class privilege, notes that the concept of lifestyle (*genre de vie*) was originally coined by sociologist Maurice Halbwachs in 1912. In his pioneering work on French and American working-class consumption, Halbwachs identified the preference of workers for "forms of consumption that gave a sense of collective life, such as large midday meals, clothing and public entertainment," so that "consumption reinforced working-class subcultures." Victoria De Grazia, with Ellen Furlough, eds., *The Sex of Things: Gender and Consumption in Historical Perspective* (Berkeley: University of California Press, 1996), 153. The capacity of working-class consumers to create a class-bounded universe of taste, alternative to that of the middle class, which is inscribed in individuals during early socialization (habitus), is, of course, a central argument of Pierre Bourdieu, *Distinction: A Social Critique of the Judgment of Taste* (Cambridge, Mass.: Harvard University Press, 1987).

15. Matthew F. Jacobson, *Whiteness of a Different Color: European Immigrants and the Alchemy of Race* (Cambridge, Mass.: Harvard University Press, 1999).

16. Gerald J. Meyer, "Italian Harlem: Portrait of a Community," in *The Italians of New York: Five Centuries of Struggle and Achievement*, ed. Philip Cannistraro (New York: New York Historical Society; John D. Calandra Italian American Institute, 1999), 57–68.

17. Donna R. Gabaccia, *From Sicily to Elizabeth Street: Housing and Social Change among Italian Immigrants, 1880–1930* (Albany: State University of New York Press, 1984), 86–99; Gabaccia, "Little Italy's Decline: Immigrant Renters and Investors in a Changing City," in *The Landscape of Modernity: Essays on New York City's Built Environment, 1900–1940*, ed. Olivier Zunz and David Ward (New York: Russell Sage Foundation, 1992), 235–51.

18. Robert A. Orsi, *The Madonna of 115th Street: Faith and Community in Italian Harlem, 1880–1950* (New Haven, Conn.: Yale University Press, 1985).

19. Louise A. DeSalvo, "A Portrait of the Puttana as a Middle-Aged Woolf Scholar," in *The Dream Book: An Anthology of Writings by Italian American Women*, ed. Helen Barolini (New York: Schocken, 1985), 94.

20. Jennifer Guglielmo, *Living the Revolution: Italian Women's Resistance and Radicalism in New York City, 1880–1945* (Chapel Hill: University of North Carolina Press, 2010), 132–38.

21. David A. J. Richards, *Italian American: The Racializing of an Ethnic Identity* (New York: New York University Press, 1999).

22. Simone Cinotto, "All Things Italian: Italian American Consumers and the Commodification of Difference," *VIA: Voices in Italian Americana* 21, no. 1 (Spring 2010): 3–44.

23. See Fasanella's *Family Supper* (1972), now on permanent display in the Great Hall of the Ellis Island Immigration Museum. Pietro di Donato, *Christ in Concrete: A Novel* (New York: Bobbs-Merrill, 1939).

24. Arjun Appadurai, "The Production of Locality," in *Counterworks: Managing the Diversity of Knowledge*, ed. Richard Fardon (New York: Routledge, 1995), 204–25.

25. Robert A. Orsi, "The Religious Boundaries of an In-Between People: Street Feste and the Problem of the Dark-Skinned Other in Italian Harlem, 1920–1990," *American Quarterly* 44, no. 3 (September 1992): 329.

Chapter 1. The Contested Table

1. Virginia Yans-McLaughlin, *Family and Community: Italian Immigrants in Buffalo, 1880–1930* (Ithaca, N.Y.: Cornell University Press, 1977), 259–60. The scholarship on the Italian American family, which mostly emphasizes the strong definition of gender roles and the relative impermeability of the domestic sphere, includes A. Ann Squier and Jill S. Quadagno, "The Italian American Family," in *Ethnic Families in America: Patterns and Variations*, ed. Charles H. Mindel, Robert W. Habenstein, and Roosevelt Wright Jr. (New York: Elsevier Scientific, 1998), 109–37; Colleen Leahy Johnson, *Growing Up and Growing Old in Italian-American Families* (New Brunswick, N.J.: Rutgers University Press, 1985); Judith Smith, *Family Connections: A History of Italian and Jewish Lives in Providence, Rhode Island* (Albany: State University of New York Press, 1985). A revisionist perspective that stresses Italian immigrant women's political activism is offered by Donna R. Gabaccia and Franca Iacovetta, eds., *Women, Gender and Transnational Lives: Italian Workers of the World* (Toronto: University of Toronto Press, 2002), and Guglielmo, *Living the Revolution*.

2. Loretta Baldassar and Donna R. Gabaccia, eds., *Intimacy and Italian Migration: Gender and Domestic Lives in a Mobile World* (New York: Fordham University Press, 2011), 22.

3. Richard Gambino, *Blood of My Blood: The Dilemma of the Italian-Americans* (Garden City, N.Y.: Anchor Press, 1974), 21–22, here 17.

4. See the novels by Mary Cappello, *Night Bloom: An Italian-American Life* (Boston: Beacon Press, 1999), and Rachel Guido deVries, *Tender Warriors* (Ann Arbor, Mich.: Firebrand Books, 1996) and different essays in the following collections: Louise DeSalvo and Edvige Giunta, eds. *The Milk of Almonds: Italian American Women Writers on Food and Culture* (New York: Feminist Press at the City University of New York, 2002); Denise Nico Leto, Giovanna Capone, and Tommi Avicolli Mecca, eds., *Hey Paesan: Writing by Lesbians and Gay Men of Italian Descent* (Oakland, Calif.: Three Guineas Press, 1999); Edvige Giunta and Samuel Patti, eds., *A Tavola: Food, Tradition and Community among Italian Americans* (New York: AIHA, 1998).

5. Useful parallels can be found in the anthropological and sociological literature about the investment in food that Mexican immigrant families have made as part of their own race- and ethnicity-making process: Sylvia Ferrero, "Comida Sin Par: Consumption of Mexican Food in Los Angeles: 'Foodscapes' in a Transnational Consumer Society," in *Food Nations: Selling Taste in Consumer Societies*, ed. Warren Belasco and Philip Scranton (New York: Routledge, 2002), 194–219; Meredith Abarca, *Voices in the Kitchen: Views of Food and the World from Working-Class Mexican and Mexican American Women* (College Station: Texas A&M University Press, 2006).

6. Gans, *Urban Villagers*, 33.

7. Ronald H. Bayor, *Neighbors in Conflict: The Irish, Germans, Jews, and Italians of New York City, 1929–1941* (Baltimore: Johns Hopkins University Press, 1978); Nathan Glazer and Daniel Patrick Moynihan, *Beyond the Melting Pot: The Negroes, Puerto Ricans, Jews, Italians, and Irish of New York City* (Cambridge, Mass.: MIT Press, 1968); Roger Sanjek, *The Future of Us All: Race and Neighborhood Politics in New York City* (Ithaca, N.Y.: Cornell University Press, 1998).

8. "Mr. Rossano, First Ave., Pleasant Ave., E. 110th Street, E. 111th Street," "Blocks," box 78, folder 8, LCP.

9. Francesco Cordasco and Rocco G. Galatioto, "Ethnic Displacement in the Interstitial Community: The East Harlem (New York City) Experience," in *The Puerto Rican Experience: A Sociological Sourcebook*, ed. Francesco Cordasco and Eugene Bucchioni (Totowa, N.J.: Rowman and Littlefield, 1973), 174–77.

10. Alberto Cupelli, "Italian Life in New York's Harlem," reel 259, INY.

11. Thomas Jesse Jones, *The Sociology of a New York City Block* (New York: Columbia University Press, 1904), 100; May Case Marsh, "The Life and Work of the Churches in an Interstitial Area" (PhD diss., New York University, 1932), 356.

12. Salvatore Cimilluca, "The Natural History of East Harlem from Eighteen-Eighty to the Present Day" (MA thesis, New York University, 1931), 5; Cordasco and Galiatoto, "Ethnic Displacement," 176.

13. "Interviews on Development, Informant: Mr. Michael G. Pasca, Private Banker, 2072 First Avenue," "Interviews on Development, Informant: Reverend Father Enrico Mizzatesta, Rectory—448 East 116th St.," "Interviews on Development, Informant: Mrs. Nicoletta Felitti, Housewife, 405 East 114th St.," "Interviews on Development, Informant: Mr. Giuseppe Perricano, Retired, 321 East 112th St.," "Early Colony," all in box 93, folder 14, LCP; Marie J. Concistré, "A Study of a Decade in the Life and Education of the Adult Immigrant Community in East Harlem" (PhD diss., New York University, 1943), 273; Leonard Covello, *The Social Background of the Italo-American School Child: A Study of the Southern Italian Family Mores and Their Effect on the School Situation in Italy and America*, (Leiden: E. J. Brill, 1967), 276; Cupelli, "Italian Life."

14. Jones, *Sociology*, 26.

15. Arnold Shankman, "The Image of the Italian in the Afro-American Press," *Italian Americana* 4, no. 1 (Fall/Winter 1978): 30–49.

16. Bayor, *Neighbors in Conflict*, 5.

17. Cordasco and Galiatoto, "Ethnic Displacement," 178.

18. "East Harlem Population by Nationality, Nativity, and Color, 1930," box 78, folder 11, LCP.

19. William B. Shedd, *Italian Population in New York* (New York: Casa Italiana Educational Bureau, 1934).

20. As late as 1935, the census tract with the heaviest concentration of Italians in the neighborhood was reported as having 83 percent of its buildings without central heating, 67 percent without a tub or shower, and 55 percent without a private indoor toilet. Margaret Campbell Tilley, "The Boy Scout Movement in East Harlem" (PhD diss., New York University, 1935), 31.

21. Dorothy Reed, *Leisure Time of Girls in a "Little Italy"* (Portland, Ore., 1932), 18.

22. This period in the history of Italian Harlem is extensively described in Orsi, *Madonna of 115th Street*; and Gerald J. Meyer, *Vito Marcantonio: Radical Politician* (Albany: State University of New York Press, 1989).

23. Covello, *Social Background*, 149.

24. Ibid., 280–81.

25. Robert E. Park, "Human Migration and the Marginal Man," *American Journal of Sociology* 33, no. 6 (May 1928): 881–93.

26. Leonard Covello, "A Community Centered School and the Problem of Housing," *Educational Forum*, no. 8 (January 1943): 133–43.

27. "La seconda generazione italo-americana," box 67, folder 15, LCP.

28. Fredric M. Thrasher, *Final Report on the Jefferson Park Branch of the Boys' Club of New York* (New York: New York University, 1935), 86.

29. Reed, *Leisure Time of Girls*, 31.

30. Leonard Covello, "Language Usage in Italian Families," *Atlantica* (October 1934): 329.

31. Leonard Covello, with Guido D'Agostino, *The Heart Is the Teacher* (New York: McGraw-Hill, 1958), 196.

32. Thrasher, *Final Report*, 35–36.

33. Gerry Noel and Percy Shostac, "Italian Harlem," p. 6, box A535, NYG-LC.

34. Covello, with D'Agostino, *Heart Is the Teacher*, 132–33.

35. Paula S. Fass, *The Damned and the Beautiful: American Youth in the 1920s* (New York: Oxford University Press, 1977); David Nasaw, *Children of the City: At Work and at Play* (New York: Oxford University Press, 1986).

36. The role of consumer goods and commercial leisure in redefining the identities of second-generation Italian immigrants in New York is discussed in Elizabeth Ewen, *Immigrant Women in the Land of Dollars: Life and Culture on the Lower East Side, 1890–1925* (New York: Monthly Review Press, 1985); and Kathy Peiss, *Cheap Amusements: Working Women and Leisure in Turn-of-the-Century New York* (Philadelphia: Temple University Press, 1986).

37. "Mr. Murray Statement, Intercultural Education, Attacks," box 51, folder 12, LCP.

38. Thrasher, *Final Report*, 49.

39. Marjorie Roberts, "Italian Girls on American Soil," *Mental Hygiene* 13 (October 1929): 763.

40. Covello, "Language Usage in Italian Families," 329.

41. Ibid.

42. Helen Barolini, "Heritage Lost, Heritage Found," *Italian Americana* 16, no. 2 (Summer 1998): 127.

43. Jerre Mangione, *Mount Allegro: A Memoir of Italian American Life* (Boston: Houghton Mifflin, 1942), 228–29.

44. Archie A. Bromsen, "The Public School's Contribution to the Maladaptation of the Italian Boy," in Caroline F. Ware, *Greenwich Village, 1920–1930: A Comment on American Civilization in the Post-War Years* (New York: Houghton Mifflin, 1935), 455–61; Covello, *Social Background*, 283.

45. B.V., cited in Covello, *Social Background*, 339.

46. "Two Documents, Girl-Boy Relationships, Family," box 68, folder 8, LCP.

47. Covello, *Social Background*, 335.

48. Francesco Cordasco, *Immigrant Children in American Schools: A Classified and Annotated Bibliography of Selected Source Documents* (Fairfield, N.J.: A. M. Kelly, 1976), 27.

49. Diane Ravitch, *The Great School Wars, New York City, 1805–1973: A History of the Public Schools as Battlefields of Social Change* (New York: Basic Books, 1988), 161–80; Joel M. Roitman, *The Immigrants, the Progressives, and the Schools: Americanization and the Impact of the New Immigration upon Public Education in the United States, 1890–1920* (Stark, Kans.: De Young Press, 1996).

50. Jacobson, *Whiteness of a Different Color*; Gary Gerstle, *American Crucible: Race and Nation in the Twentieth Century* (Princeton, N.J.: Princeton University Press, 2002).

51. Maxine Seller, "The Education of the Immigrant Woman, 1900–1935," *Journal of Urban History* 4 (May 1978): 307–30.

52. John Spargo, *The Bitter Cry of the Children* (New York: Macmillan, 1906).

53. Alan M. Kraut, *Silent Travelers: Germs, Genes, and the Immigrant Menace* (Baltimore: Johns Hopkins University Press, 1994), 243–44.

54. Ravitch, *Great School Wars*, 178.

55. New York City Committee on the Physical Welfare of School Children, *Journal of the American Statistical Association* 10 (June 1907): 271–316.

56. John Higham, *Strangers in the Land: Patterns of American Nativism, 1860–1925* (New York: Atheneum, 1967), 234–63.

57. Desdemona L. Heinrich, "Dietary Habits of Elementary School Children" (PhD diss., New York University, 1932), 4.

58. Kraut, *Silent Travelers*, 243–44.

59. Heinrich, "Dietary Habits," 5.

60. Harvey A. Levenstein, *Revolution at the Table: The Transformation of the American Diet* (New York: Oxford University Press, 1988), 109–20.

61. Ravitch, *Great School Wars*, 178.

62. Selma C. Berrol, "Immigrants at School, New York City, 1898–1914" (PhD diss., City University of New York, 1967), 126–27; Thrasher, *Final Report*, 316–17; Reed, *Leisure Time of Girls*, 32–33; Lawrence A. Cremin, "The Revolution in American Secondary Education, 1893–1918," *Teachers College Record* 56, no. 6 (1955): 298.

63. Archie Bromsen, "The Italian Peg and the American Hole," "Adjustment," box 92, folder 2, LCP.

64. E. George Payne and John C. Gebhart, *Method and Measurement of Health Education: An Experiment in Public School 106, Manhattan, New York City* (New York: New York Association for Improving the Condition of the Poor, 1926), 3.

65. Ibid., 31, 33.

66. Ibid., 17–18, 28, 29–30.

67. Ibid., 31.

68. Florence Nesbitt, *Household Management* (New York: Russell Sage Foundation, 1918), 104–9; Lucy H. Gillett, *Adapting Nutrition Work to a Community* (New York: New York Association for Improving the Condition of the Poor, 1924), 10–12; Gertrude Gates

Mudge, "A Comparative Study on Italian, Polish and Negro Dietaries," *Journal of the American Dietetics Association* 1 (March 1927): 166–73.

69. Nesbitt, *Household Management*, 108–9.

70. Heinrich, "Dietary Habits," 97.

71. Ibid.

72. Ibid., 70, 84, 107.

73. Ibid., 70.

74. John C. Gebhart, *The Growth and Development of Italian Children in New York City* (New York: New York Association for Improving the Condition of the Poor, 1924), 17–18.

75. Madison Grant, *The Passing of the Great Race; or, The Racial Basis of European History* (New York: Scribner's Sons, 1921), 28–29.

76. Donna R. Gabaccia, *From the Other Side: Women, Gender, and Immigrant Life in the U.S., 1820–1990* (Bloomington: Indiana University Press, 1994), 116.

77. Covello, with D'Agostino, *Heart Is the Teacher*, 47.

78. D. di B., cited in Covello, *Social Background*, 341.

79. Fass, *Damned and the Beautiful*, 282; Roland Marchand, *Advertising the American Dream: Making Way for Modernity, 1920–1940* (Berkeley: University of California Press, 1985).

80. "New York University Motion Picture Study, Seminar, Wednesday, March 14, 1934," box 65, folder 3, LCP.

81. Thrasher, *Final Report*, 306.

82. Vito Teti, "Le culture alimentari nel Mezzogiorno continentale in età contemporanea," in *L'alimentazione*, ed. Alberto Capatti, Alberto De Bernardi, and Angelo Varni, Storia d'Italia 13 (Turin: Einaudi, 1998), 137.

83. Ibid., 149–50.

84. Genoeffa Nizzardini and Natalie F. Joffe, *Italian Food Patterns and Their Relationship to Wartime Problems of Food and Nutrition* (Washington, D.C.: National Research Council Committee on Food Habits, 1942), 11–13, 19–21.

85. Gambino, *Blood of My Blood*, 21.

86. Vincent Panella, *The Other Side: Growing Up Italian in America* (Garden City, N.Y.: Doubleday, 1979), 22.

87. Nizzardini and Joffe, *Italian Food Patterns*, 12.

88. Maria Sermolino, *Papa's Table d'Hote* (Philadelphia: J. B. Lippincott, 1952), 81.

89. Mangione, *Mount Allegro*, 25.

90. Thrasher, *Final Report*, 204.

91. Nizzardini and Joffe, *Italian Food Patterns*, 12.

92. Teti, "Le culture alimentari nel Mezzogiorno," 109–10.

93. Covello, with D'Agostino, *Heart Is the Teacher*, 24–25.

94. For an overview of the role of food in the making of home, see David Bell and Gill Valentine, *Consuming Geographies: We Are Where We Eat* (New York : Routledge, 1997), 57–88.

95. C.G., 1941, cited in Covello, *Social Background*, 315.

96. J.P., 1941, cited in Covello, *Social Background*, 322.

97. Dina Bertoni Jovine, *La scuola italiana dal 1870 ai giorni nostri* (Rome: Editori Riuniti, 1958).

98. Ida L. Hull, "Special Problems in Italian Families," *National Conference of Social Work: Addressees and Proceedings* (1924): 288–91.

99. Elizabeth H. Pleck, "A Mother's Wages: Income Earning among Married Italian and Black Women, 1896–1911," in *A Heritage of Her Own: Toward a New Social History of American Women*, ed. Nancy F. Cott and Elizabeth H. Pleck (New York: Simon and Schuster, 1979), 367–92.

100. Miriam Cohen, *Workshop to Office: Two Generations of Italian Women in New York City, 1900–1950* (Ithaca, N.Y.: Cornell University Press, 1992), 52.

101. Concistré, "Study of a Decade," 341.

102. Gambino, *Blood of My Blood*, 20.

103. "Alfred Botta, Case Record, August 20, 1932, New York Catholic Protectory," box 67, folder 8, LCP.

104. "Italian Family in America," box 67, folder 12, LCP.

105. Edward Corsi, "My Neighborhood," *Outlook*, September 16, 1925, 92; author's interview with Fred Gardaphé, November 18, 1998.

106. Joseph V. Colello, "East Harlem . . . The Way That It Was," typescript, pp. 81–83, Center for Migration Studies, Staten Island, N.Y.

107. "Miss S.—20 years. Born in Italy. Came to U.S. at Age of 7," "Girls," box 68, folder 2, LCP.

108. Covello, *Social Background*, 235–36; Michael J. Eula, "Failure of American Food Reformers among Italian Immigrants in New York City, 1891–1897," *Italian Americana* 18, no. 1 (Winter 2000): 95.

109. Lillian W. Betts, "The Italian in New York," *University Settlement Studies* 1 (1905–6): 94.

110. Lucy H. Gillett, "Factors Influencing Nutrition Work among Italians," *Journal of Home Economics* 14, no. 1 (January 1922): 16.

111. Ibid.

112. "Italo-American, Family from Apulia," "Italian Father in America," box 68, folder 10, LCP.

113. "Study of a Family," "Family in America," box 93, folder 17, LCP.

114. Lewis Hine, *An Italian Family Has Supper, East Side, New York City, 1915*, Lewis Wickes Hine: Documentary Photographs, 1905–1938, Photography Collection, Miriam and Ira D. Wallach Division of Art, Prints and Photographs, New York Public Library.

115. Michael J. Eula, *Between Peasant and Urban Villager: Italian-Americans of New Jersey and New York, 1880–1980; The Structures of Counter-Discourse* (New York: Lang, 1993), 159–94.

Chapter 2. "Sunday Dinner? You Had to Be There!"

1. Orlando Guadalupe, "My Community," box 79, folder 12, LCP.

2. Thrasher, *Final Report*, 199.

3. John R. Murati, "109th Street–110th St.–2nd Ave.–3rd Ave," "Blocks," box 78, folder 8, LCP.

4. Covello, *Social Background*, 301–11; Eula, *Between Peasant and Urban Villager*, 131–36.

5. Ware, *Greenwich Village*, 194.

6. Concistré, "Study of a Decade," 345, 349.

7. Victor J. Vicesvinci, "The Italian Pattern in a Family That I Know Well," 1941, box 67, folder 23, LCP, italics added.

8. Joseph Leopold, "Report on Italian Tradition, June 5, 1934," "The Boy and His Family," box 65, folder 2, LCP.

9. Covello, *Social Background*, 340.

10. "Life History, T.B., 1938," "Retention of Family Tradition in the 3rd Generation," box 68, folder 9, LCP.

11. Reed, *Leisure Time of Girls*, 45.

12. "Family Cohesion," "2nd Gen. H. S. Student—16+ Years Old—Parents from Sicily—20 Years in America," box 68, folder 5, LCP.

13. Marzio Barbagli, *Sotto lo stesso tetto: Mutamenti della famiglia in Italia dal XV al XX secolo* (Bologna: Il Mulino, 1984), 115–21; Giovanna Da Molin, "Family Forms and Domestic Service in Southern Italy from the Seventeenth to Nineteenth Century," *Journal of Family History* 15, no. 4 (1990): 503–27; Francesco Benigno, "The Southern Italian Family in the Early Modern Period: A Discussion of Co-Residential Patterns," *Continuity and Change* 4 (1989): 165–94.

14. Maddalena Tirabassi, "Trends of Continuity and Signs of Change among Italian Migrant Women," in *Le stelle e le strisce: Studi americani e militari in onore di Raimondo Luraghi*, ed. Valeria Gennaro Lerda (Milan: Bompiani, 1998), 291–92.

15. Gabaccia, *From Sicily to Elizabeth Street*. The process illustrated by Gabaccia has been detected for other parts of southern Italy too; see Leo Cellini, "Emigration, the Italian Family, and Changing Roles," in *The Italian Immigrant Woman in North America*, ed. Betty Boyd Caroli, Robert F. Harney, and Lydio F. Tomasi (Toronto: AIHA, 1978), 273–87.

16. Jane Schneider and Peter T. Schneider, *Classi sociali, economia e politica in Sicilia* (Soveria Mannelli: Rubettino, 1989), 143.

17. Gabaccia, *From Sicily to Elizabeth Street*, 115, 111.

18. "I progressi della famiglia italiana a New York," *Il Progresso Italo-Americano*, June 14, 1930.

19. Orsi, *Madonna of 115th Street*, 77.

20. Tony Dapolito, cited in Jeff Kisseloff, *You Must Remember This: An Oral History of Manhattan from the 1890s to World War II* (Baltimore: Johns Hopkins University Press, 2000), 445.

21. Mangione, *Mount Allegro*, 20.

22. C.P., cited in Covello, *Social Background*, 295.

23. Mangione, *Mount Allegro*, 136.

24. Covello, with D'Agostino, *Heart Is the Teacher*, 36.

25. Teti, "Le culture alimentari nel Mezzogiorno," 152.

26. C. L. Tepedino, "Italo-American Family Problems, Jan. 1941," box 93, folder 18, LCP; Concistré, "Study of a Decade," 21–43.

27. Tepedino, "Italo-American Family Problems." See also Joseph Leopold, "Friday, July 6, 1934—113th Street," box 65, folder 3, LCP.

28. Michael A. Di Giovine, "La Vigilia Italo-Americana: Revitalizing the Italian-American Family through the Christmas Eve 'Feast of the Seven Fishes,'" *Food and Foodways* 18, no. 4 (2010): 181–208. For an overview of Italian immigrant festive foodways, see Phyllis H. Williams, *South Italian Folkways in Europe and America* (New Haven, Conn.: Yale University Press, 1938). For East Harlem, see Concistré, "Study of a Decade," 21–43.

29. Joseph F. Perez, *Tales of an Italian-American Family* (New York: Gardner Press, 1991), 22.

30. "Celebrations in the U.S.," box 68, folder 7, LCP; "2nd Gen. Woman, School Teacher, Autobiogr. Essay," "Eating," box 68, folder 1, LCP; Perez, *Tales of an Italian-American Family*, 22–38, 80–82; author's interviews with Peter Rofrano and with Rose Pascale, December 7, 1998.

31. Louis Pesce, "Friends etc. in America," box 68, folder 2, LCP; "C.V., 2nd Gen. Female, College Grad," "Family (Concept of Friends) (America)," box 68, folder 4, LCP.

32. Mangione, *Mount Allegro*, 24–25.

33. "Migliaia di fedeli alla festa della Madonna del Carmine," *Il Progresso Italo-Americano*, July 17, 1938; Concistré, "Study of a Decade," 21–24; Alberto Cupelli, "Italian Life in New York's Harlem," reel 259, INY."

34. Concistré, "Study of a Decade," 311–12; Tirabassi, "Trends of Continuity," 287–88.

35. Nancy Verde Barr, *We Called It Macaroni: An American Heritage of Southern Italian Cooking* (New York: Knopf, 1994), 86.

36. Jerry Della Femina, *An Italian Grows in Brooklyn* (Boston: Little, Brown, 1978), 18.

37. Gambino, *Blood of My Blood*, 24.

38. Alexander C. Smeltzer, "Italian Customs in U.S.A.," "Customs," box 93, folder 7, LCP. For another ethnographic account of the work of accumulating social capital performed in the family by Italian American women, see Micaela Di Leonardo, "The Female World of Cards and Holidays: Women, Families and the Work of Kinship," *Signs: Journal of Women in Culture and Society* 12, no. 3 (1984): 440–53.

39. Gambino, *Blood of My Blood*, 22, italics in the original.

40. Mangione, *Mount Allegro*, 22–29, 131–43.

41. Robert Orsi, "The Fault of Memory: 'Southern Italy' in the Imagination of Immigrants and the Lives of Their Children in Italian Harlem, 1920–1945," *Journal of Family History* 15, no. 1 (March 1990): 133–47.

42. Luisa Passerini, *Storia e soggettività: Le fonti orali, la memoria* (Florence: La Nuova Italia, 1988), 106.

43. Michael Kammen, *Mystic Chords of Memory: The Transformation of Tradition in American Culture* (New York: Vintage, 1993); Benedict Anderson, *Imagined Communities: Reflections on the Origin and Spread of Nationalism* (London: Verso, 1991).

44. Donna R. Gabaccia, *Italy's Many Diasporas* (Seattle: University of Washington Press, 2000).

45. C.N., cited in Covello, *Social Background*, 271.

46. "C.G., 1st Generation, Came to America at Age of 30," "La famiglia in America," box 68, folder 4, LCP.

47. C.G., “Thrift,” box 68, folder 6, LCP.

48. Ibid.

49. Constantine M. Panunzio, *The Soul of an Immigrant* (New York: Arno Press, 1969), 19–26.

50. Linda Reeder, *Widows in White: Migration and the Transformation of Rural Italian Women, Sicily, 1880–1920* (Toronto: University of Toronto Press, 2003).

51. Concistré, “Study of a Decade,” 352.

52. Steven Mintz and Susan Kellogg, *Domestic Revolutions: A Social History of American Family Life* (New York: Basic Books, 1988), 113–19.

53. “Family,” “Person Interviewed: Man, 58 Years of Age. Came to America about 1908, Married Here. Locality—Girgenti, Sicily. Class—Landless Worker,” box 68, folder 10, LCP.

54. Concistré, “Study of a Decade,” 357.

55. A.F., 1939, cited in Covello, *Social Background*, 304.

56. Thrasher, *Final Report*, 302.

57. Mangione, *Mount Allegro*, 18–19.

58. Emanuel Carnevali, compiled and prefaced by Kay Boyle, *The Autobiography of Emanuel Carnevali* (New York: Horizon, 1967), 161.

59. Joe Vergara, *Love and Pasta: A Recollection* (New York: Harper and Row, 1968), 39.

60. C.B., cited in Covello, *Social Background*, 214–15.

61. Simone Cinotto, “Italian Americans and Public Housing in New York City, 1937–1941: Cultural Pluralism, Ethnic Maternalism, and the Welfare State,” in *Democracy and Social Rights in the Two Wests*, ed. Alice Kessler-Harris and Maurizio Vaudagna (Turin: Otto, 2009), 279–305.

62. Peter Rofrano, cited in Kisseloff, *You Must Remember This*, 357.

63. T.I., cited in Covello, *Social Background*, 200.

64. A.R., cited in Covello, *Social Background*, 304.

65. C.G., cited in Covello, *Social Background*, 265.

66. Reed, *Leisure Time of Girls*, 50, 52.

67. J. di V., cited in Covello, *Social Background*, 235–36.

68. Tepedino, “Italo-American Family Problems.”

69. Concistré, “Study of a Decade,” 346.

70. “Italo-American 42 Years Old, Came to U.S. as a Boy of 3, Father of 5 Girls, 1 Boy,” “Marriage Concepts of Italian Girls,” box 68, folder 1, LCP.

71. “2nd Generation 39 Years—Father of One Daughter and One Son—Lake Ronkonkoma,” “Italian Family and Family Traditions,” box 68, folder 1, LCP.

72. “Cultural Changes, from Life History, Vito Maglio, H.S. Grad Male,” box 68, folder 1,LCP.

73. “Attitude toward ‘American’ Pattern of Family Life,” box 68, folder 10, LCP.

74. Michael Novak, *The Rise of the Unmeltable Ethnics: Politics and Culture in the Seventies* (New York: Macmillan, 1972), 65.

75. “Second Generation’s Attitude toward Marrying Non-Italians. 2nd Generation H.S. Student, boy 16+ Years, Parents from Sicily, Poor Student, Truant,” box 68, folder 1, LCP.

76. "Endogamy among Italo-Americans. Old Man, Born near Bari, Apulia," box 68, folder 1, LCP.

77. Orsi, *Madonna of 115th Street*, 92.

78. "Classification of Nationalities by Proportions of Intermarriage; Men and Women of the 1st, 2nd, and 3rd Generations (1908–1912)," box 65, folder 22, LCP; Tillie Miller, "Intermarriage of the Italians in New York," reel 259, INY; Niles Carpenter, *Immigrants and Their Children: A Study Based on Census Statistics Relative to the Foreign Born and the Native White of Foreign or Mixed Parentage* (Washington, DC, 1927), 234–246.

79. By the late 1930s, Covello observes, "Whenever Italians marry into American stock, it occurs mostly within the boundaries of Italo-American communities. The domicile of such mixed matings does not change, and children of these couples remain till a late age in the Italian community where the impact of an Italian cultural pattern greatly effects the infiltration of American norms. With the isolation of the Italo-American community, with negligible intercourse between Italians and assimilated Americans, the rate of marrying into non-Italian groups is by necessity increasing only slowly. Conditions that would stimulate greater inter-marriage are limited." "Intermarriage," box 68, folder 3, LCP.

80. Valentine Rossilli Winsey, "A Study of the Effect of Transplantation upon Attitudes toward the United States of Southern Italians in New York City as Revealed by Survivors of the Mass-Migration, 1887–1915" (PhD diss., New York University, 1966), 162.

81. "Tony the Cleaner," "Marriage among Italo-Americans," box 68, folder 5, LCP.

82. "2nd Generation Man, 22 Years," "Dowries among Italo-Americans," box 68, folder 1, LCP.

83. "D.," "Family," box 68, folder 6, LCP.

84. Cited in Covello, *Social Background*, 347.

85. "Retention of Old Customs," "From Case Study, 1938," box 68, folder 9, LCP.

86. Nancy Carnevale, *A New Language, a New World: Italian Immigrants in the United States, 1890–1945* (Urbana: University of Illinois Press, 2009).

Chapter 3. An American Foodscape

1. Italian Americans benefited more than any other European ethnic group in New York from New Deal programs, in particular the Works Projects Administration (WPA). While 14 percent of the white population as a whole received some sort of public assistance, Italian Americans accounted for 21 percent—the highest percentage among white families and almost twice that of the Jews (12 percent), who represented at the time the largest ethnic group of the city. Beth S. Wenger, *New York Jews and the Great Depression: Uncertain Promise* (New Haven, Conn.: Yale University Press, 1996), 17. Covello's estimate from "Covello Book, Community Centered School (1938–39)," box 18, folder 2, LCP.

2. Marjorie T. Bellows, Godias J. Drolet, and Harry Goode, under the direction of Kenneth D. Widdemer, *Handbook Statistical Reference Data: Ten Year Period, 1931–1940* (New York: Neighborhood Health Development, Health Center Districts, Department of Health, City of New York, 1944), 73–75.

3. Meyer, *Vito Marcantonio*, 137.

4. Author's interview with Rose Pascale.

5. Orsi, *Madonna of 115th Street*, 54.

6. Velma Phillips and Laura Howell, "Racial and Other Differences in Dietary Customs," *Journal of Home Economics*, no. 41 (September 1920): 405; Gertrude Gates Mudge, "Italian Dietary Adjustments," *Journal of Home Economics*, no. 15 (April 1923): 183–84; Dorothy Wiehl, "The Diets of Low Income Families in New York City," *Milbank Memorial Fund Quarterly Bulletin* 11 (October 1933): 317–22; Robert Coit Chapin, *The Standard of Living among Workingmen's Families in New York City* (New York: Russell Sage Foundation, 1909), 172–79.

7. The original definition of embeddedness as the degree of interdependence of individuals in social networks is found in Mark Granovetter, "Economic Action and Social Structure: The Problem of Embeddedness," *American Journal of Sociology* 91, no. 3 (November 1985): 481–510.

8. Elizabeth Zanoni, "Returning Home in the Imaginary: Advertisements and Consumption in the Italian American Press," *VIA: Voices in Italian Americana* 21, no. 1 (Spring 2010): 45–61.

9. Robert Charles Freeman, "Exploring the Path of Community Change in East Harlem, 1870–1970: A Multifactor Approach" (PhD diss., Fordham University, 1994), 293–95; Concistré, "Study of a Decade," 233.

10. Remark made by Rev. Amedeo Riggio, Jefferson Park Methodist Episcopal Church, 1932, cited in Concistré, "Study of a Decade," 234.

11. Doreen Massey, *Place, Space, and Gender* (Minneapolis: University of Minnesota Press, 1994).

12. According to the U.S. Immigration Commission, in 1908 only 1.3 percent of families with a foreign-born southern Italian head in New York City lived in homes they owned (sample blocks from "Elizabeth Street, Spring to Houston, East Side," and "East One Hundred and Fourteenth Street, Second to First Avenue, North Side"). United States Senate, *Reports of the Immigration Commission*, vol. 26/1: *Immigrants in Cities: Study of Selected Districts in New York, Chicago, Philadelphia, Boston, Buffalo, Cleveland, and Milwaukee, with Statistics and Tables* (Washington, D.C.: U.S. Government Printing Office, 1911), 209. By 1930, a total of 53,849 families whose head of family was Italian born lived in their own homes; 144,835 rented. Few Italian homeowners lived in Manhattan: only 1,213 families as compared to 31,196 in Brooklyn, 11,012 in Queens, 7,371 in the Bronx, and 3,057 in Staten Island (Richmond). Bureau of the Census, *Fifteenth Census of the United States, 1930: Population. Special Report on Foreign Born White Families by Country of Birth of Head* (Washington, D.C.: U.S. Government Printing Office, 1933), 162–64. As late as 1949–50, few Italians in Harlem owned the homes where they lived. The percentage of owner-occupied units in "Italian" census tracts oscillated between .7 percent and 6.8 percent, for a median percentage of 3.6 percent, and with evidence of a direct relation between median income and rate of homeownership (the higher the income the higher the rate). In the same census tracts (194, 192, 188, 178, 162, and 170), a median percentage of 22.5 percent of dwelling units were reported to be without private bath or dilapidated. Freeman, "Exploring the Path," 234.

13. "I progressi della famiglia italiana a New York," *Il Progresso Italo-Americano*, June 14, 1930.

14. Mayor's Committee on City Planning of the City of New York, *East Harlem Community Study* (New York, 1937), 16, 19.

15. Cimilluca, "Natural History of East Harlem"; "East Harlem Population by Nationality, Nativity, and Color, 1930," box 78, folder 11, LCP.

16. Lorrin Thomas, *Puerto Rican Citizen: History and Political Identity in Twentieth-Century New York City* (Chicago: University Of Chicago Press, 2010); Donald Stewart, *A Short History of East Harlem* (New York: Museum of the City of New York, 1972); "East Harlem Population by Nationality, Nativity, and Color, 1930." The Puerto Rican population is problematic because in 1930 the U.S. Census classified Puerto Ricans in New York City as 77.4 percent white and an indefinite number as "Negro" in different census tracts. According to Gilbert Osofsky, "By 1930 some 45,000 Puerto Ricans resided in New York and most were heavily concentrated in East Harlem." Gilbert Osofsky, *Harlem: The Making of a Ghetto; Negro New York, 1890–1930* (New York: Harper and Row, 1971), 130. One source estimated that only 10,000 Puerto Ricans lived in East Harlem in 1937. Mayor's Committee, *East Harlem Community Study*, 17. Two years later, however, another study reported the presence of 18,000 "Spanish-speaking people" in East Harlem. Citizens' Housing Council of New York, *Harlem Housing* (New York, 1939), 1.

17. Federal Writers' Project, *New York City Guide* (New York: Random House, 1939), 267.

18. "History of East Harlem, East 108th Street, by L. Parziale; Interviewed by Mr. A. D'Aureli, October 28, 1935," "Early Community," box 65, folder 4, LCP.

19. Cimilluca, "Natural History of East Harlem," 30.

20. "Veto Vito?," *Time*, November 4, 1946, 24–25.

21. Nadia Venturini, "'Over the Years People Don't Know': Italian Americans and African Americans in Harlem in the 1930s," in *Italian Workers of the World: Labor Migration and the Formation of Multiethnic States*, ed. Donna R. Gabaccia and Fraser M. Ottanelli (Urbana: University of Illinois Press, 2001), 196.

22. Orsi, "Religious Boundaries."

23. Cited in Nelson Moe, *The View from Vesuvius: Italian Culture and the Southern Question* (Berkeley: University of California Press, 2006), 165.

24. Peter D'Agostino, "Craniums, Criminals, and the 'Cursed Race': Italian Anthropology in American Racial Thought, 1861–1924," *Comparative Studies in Society and History*, no. 44 (2002): 319–43.

25. Donna R. Gabaccia, "Race, Nation, Hyphen: Italian-Americans and American Multiculturalism in Comparative Perspective," in *Are Italians White? How Race Is Made in America*, ed. Jennifer Guglielmo and Salvatore Salerno (New York: Routledge, 2003), 44–59.

26. Cited in Robert F. Foerster, *The Italian Emigration of Our Times* (Cambridge, Mass.: Harvard University Press, 1919), 383.

27. Jacobson, *Whiteness of a Different Color*, 4, 62.

28. Malcolm X, *On Afro-American History* (New York: Pathfinder, 1990), 33.

29. Shankman, "Image of the Italian in the Afro-American Press."

30. Damian S. Mosley, "Cooking Up Heritage in Harlem," in *Gastropolis: Food and New York City*, ed. Annie Hauck-Lawson and Jonathan Deutsch (New York: Columbia University Press, 2008), 176.

31. Jacobson, *Whiteness of a Different Color*, 56–62. On the acceptance of American racism as a fundamental step in the construction of Italian American whiteness, see also Richards, *Italian American*.

32. L.V., cited in Covello, *Social Background*, 350.

33. Alfredo Niceforo, *Italiani del nord e Italiani del sud* (Turin: F. lli Bocca, 1901).

34. Cited in Alberto Capatti and Massimo Montanari, *Italian Cuisine: A Cultural History* (New York: Columbia University Press, 2003), 27.

35. "Chicken with Macaroni; Uneasiness above Harlem Bridge over 'Little Italy,'" *New York Times*, August 16, 1888, 8.

36. Gabaccia, *We Are What We Eat*, 138.

37. The biological transformative capacities of food were especially evident in the growing occupation of space of Italian American bodies. As early as 1909, Franz Boas demonstrated the inconsistency of the postulates of scientific racism by measuring the bodies of a sample of Italian immigrants to New York and highlighting the changes they underwent. Franz Boas, "Changes in the Bodily Form of Descendants of Immigrants," *American Anthropologist* 14, no. 3 (July–September 1912): 530–62.

38. Amerigo Ruggiero, *Italiani in America* (Milan: Fratelli Treves, 1937), 148–150.

39. Lawrence R. Chenault, *The Puerto Rican Migrant in New York City* (New York: Columbia University Press, 1938), 124, 77; Federal Writers' Project, *New York City Guide*, 267.

40. Kraut, *Silent Travelers*; Gerald V. O'Brien, "Indigestible Food, Conquering Hordes, and Waste Materials: Metaphors of Immigrants and the Early Immigration Restriction Debate in the United States," *Metaphor and Symbol* 18, no. 1 (2003): 33–47.

41. Bernardo Vega, *Memoirs of Bernardo Vega: A Contribution to the History of the Puerto Rican Community in New York* (New York: Monthly Review Press, 1984), 230.

42. Citizens' Housing Council of New York, "Harlem Housing," 4; Federal Writers' Project, *New York City Guide*, 267.

43. Charles E. Hewitt Jr., "Welcome Paupers and Crime: Porto Rico's Shocking Gift to the United States," *Scribner's Commentator* 7, no. 5 (March 1940): 11–17.

44. Howard A. Rusk, "The Facts Don't Rhyme; An Analysis of Irony in Lyrics Linking Puerto Rico's Breezes to Tropic Diseases," *New York Times*, September 29, 1957.

45. Cited in Kisseloff, *You Must Remember This*, 340.

46. Osofsky, *Harlem*, 152–53; Claudia Marie Calhoon, "Tuberculosis, Race, and the Delivery of Health Care in Harlem, 1922–1939," *Radical History Review*, no. 80 (Spring 2001): 101–19.

47. Osofsky, *Harlem*, 128; Cheryl L. Greenberg, *Or Does It Explode? Black Harlem in the Great Depression* (New York: Oxford University Press, 1991), 225.

48. Mosley, "Cooking Up Heritage in Harlem," 277; Tracy N. Poe, "The Origins of Soul Food in Black Urban Identity: Chicago, 1915–1947," *American Studies International* 37, no. 1 (1999): 9.

49. "2nd Gen., 36 Years Female, Parents from near Avellino," "Racial Tensions within Family Life," box 68, folder 5, LCP.

50. Thrasher, *Final Report*, 300, 296.

51. Mayor's Commission on Conditions in Harlem, *The Negro in Harlem: A Report on Social and Economic Conditions Responsible for the Outbreak of March 19, 1935* (New York, 1936), 62–63, 68–70, 72–74.

52. In 1936 blacks represented 4.7 percent of New York City population and 21 percent of individuals on the Home Relief Bureau's rolls but received only 9 percent of public jobs for the unemployed. Federal Writers' Project, Roi Ottley and William Weatherby, eds., "The Depression in Harlem," in *Hitting Home: The Great Depression in Town and Country*, ed. Bernard Sternsher (Chicago: Quadrangle Books, 1970), 110.

53. Ibid., 113, 107.

54. Greenberg, *Or Does It Explode?*, 38–39, 177–78.

55. Federal Writers' Project, *New York City Guide*, 265–68.

56. "Anonymous Letter," box 103, folder 23, LCP; Hewitt, "Welcome Paupers and Crime."

57. Chenault, *Puerto Rican Migrant*, 142–43.

58. Vega, *Memoirs of Bernardo Vega*, 151.

59. Lillian W. Betts, "The Italian in New York," *University Settlement Studies Quarterly* (October 1905–January 1906): 90–104

60. Greenberg, *Or Does It Explode?*, 43.

61. Federal Writers' Project, *New York City Guide*, 106.

62. Thomas Sugrue, "The Toughest Street in New York," *New York Herald Tribune*, January 17, 1932.

63. Clarence Woodbury, "Our Worst Slum: Can We Save It from Going Red?" *American Magazine*, September 1949, 31.

64. Peter Pascale, cited in Kisseloff, *You Must Remember This*, 354.

65. Jones, *Sociology of a New York City Block*, 100.

66. Carolina Crupi, series II, cassette 23, side A, ILOHP.

67. Covello, with D'Agostino, *Heart Is the Teacher*, 223.

68. Eric Schneider, *Vampires, Dragons, and Egyptian Kings: Youth Gangs in Postwar New York* (Princeton, N.J.: Princeton University Press, 2001), 78–105.

69. Jack Agueros, "Halfway to Dick and Jane: A Puerto Rican Pilgrimage," in *The Immigrant Experience: The Anguish of Becoming American*, ed. Thomas C. Wheeler (New York: Penguin Books, 1971), 94.

70. Maxine W. Gordon, "Race Patterns and Prejudice in Puerto Rico," *American Sociological Review* 14, no. 2 (April 1949): 294–301.

71. Author's interview with Peter Rofrano, December 7, 1998.

72. Della Femina, *An Italian Grows in Brooklyn*, 23.

73. Guadalupe, "My Community."

74. Cimilluca, "Natural History of East Harlem," 105.

75. Frederick Douglass Opie, *Hog and Hominy: Soul Food from Africa to America* (New York: Columbia University Press, 2010), 63–64.

76. Federal Writers' Project, *New York City Guide*, 265–68; Alfredo Lopez, *The Puerto Rican Papers: Notes on the Re-emergence of a Nation* (New York: Bobbs-Merrill, 1973), 26–27.

77. Terry Roth, "Street Cries and Criers of New York," American Life Histories: Manuscripts from the Federal Writers' Project, 1936–1940, Manuscript Division, Library of Congress, Washington, D.C.

78. Oswald Rivera, *Puerto Rican Cuisine in America: Nuyorican and Bodega Recipes* (Philadelphia: Running Press, 2002), xvii.

79. Mosley, "Cooking Up Heritage in Harlem," 277–82.

80. Piri Thomas, *Down These Mean Streets* (New York: Knopf, 1973), 26–31.

81. Ibid.

82. Vega, *Memoirs of Bernardo Vega*, 141–43.

83. Greenberg, *Or Does It Explode?*, 99, 126.

84. "Mob of 400 Battles the Police in Harlem; Italian Stores Raided, Man Shot in Crowd," *New York Times*, May 19, 1936: 6.

85. Shankman, "Image of the Italian," 45.

86. Nadia Venturini, *Neri e italiani ad Harlem: Gli anni Trenta e la Guerra d'Etiopia* (Genoa: Edizioni Lavoro, 1990), 81–82; Shankman, "Image of the Italian," 44.

87. "Report about the Block between 109th and 110th Streets and First Ave. and Second Ave., Felice De Cicco," "Blocks," box 78, folder 8, LCP.

88. Concistré, "Study of a Decade," 56. In 1934, only 14,700 jobs were available for residents in all East Harlem. Sixty thousand people commuted every day from the neighborhood to work. "Covello Book, Community Center School (1938–39)."

89. Jane Jacobs, *The Death and Life of Great American Cities* (New York: Vintage, 1975).

90. "Report from 112th St. to 111th St. and 2nd & 3rd Avenues, Amedeo D'Aureli," "Blocks," box 78, folder 8, LCP.

91. Colello, "East Harlem," 2.

92. Kisseloff, *You Must Remember This*, 364–65.

93. Colello, "East Harlem," 3.

94. La Guardia Memorial House, *100 Years of Service* (New York, 1998), 3; Stewart, *Short History of East Harlem*, 48.

95. "Family, L.C.," box 68, folder 10, LCP.

96. Jones, *Sociology of a New York City Block*, 111.

97. "Did you ever go out without your husband?" "Oh no, I went shopping, that's about all." (Gerra Bonaventure); "No, no, no, I was going to the store, shopping, that's all." (Lucy Sevirole); "I never went out during the day except to shop for food. My man brought my work to the house, he was a good man" (Donna Cassado). Quoted in *Women of Courage: Jewish and Italian Immigrant Women in New York*, ed. Rose Laub Coser, Laura S. Anker, and Andrew J. Perrin (Westport, Conn.: Greenwood Press, 1999), 41.

98. Vicesvinci, "Italian Pattern."

99. Kevin Lynch, *The Image of the City* (Cambridge, Mass.: MIT Press, 1960), 47–48, 78.

100. Ibid., 76.

101. "Italian Life in New York's Harlem," reel 259, INY.

102. Cimilluca, "Natural History of East Harlem," 110.

103. "Italian Market, First Avenue bet. 110th and 116th Sts., July 1940," reel 131, FTC; G. Morelli, "Italian Open Markets," reel 259, INY; Alberto Cupelli, "The Italian Open Air (Pushcart) Markets in New York City," reel 259, INY; Colello, "East Harlem," 53, 107–13.

104. Peter Pascale, cited in Kisseloff, *You Must Remember This*, 355–56.

105. Concistré, "Study of a Decade."

106. Kisseloff, *You Must Remember This*, 344–46.

107. "Older Brother in the Role of Protector of Girls, from Life Histories," box 68, folder 9, LCP; "Brother as Protector in U.S., L.H.—34," box 68, folder 5, LCP.

108. Colello, "East Harlem," 52.

109. Edward Corsi, *In the Shadow of Liberty: The Chronicle of Ellis Island* (New York: Arno Press, 1969), 3; Colello, "East Harlem," 110; Thrasher, *Final Report*, 141–42; Covello, with D'Agostino, *Heart Is the Teacher*, 34.

110. Colello, "East Harlem," 53.

111. Ibid., 28; Cimilluca, "Natural History of East Harlem," 100–101.

112. Alain Corbin, *The Foul and the Fragrant: Odor and the French Social Imagination* (Cambridge, Mass.: Harvard University Press, 1988).

113. Osofsky, *Harlem*, 82–83; Cimilluca, "Natural History of East Harlem," 99–100.

114. Noel and Shostac, "Italian Harlem," 3, 5.

115. Eddie Cantor, *My Life Is in Your Hands* (New York: Harper and Brothers, 1928), 27–28.

116. Sermolino, *Papa's Table d'Hote*, 25.

117. Lenny Del Genio, cited in Kisseloff, *You Must Remember This*, 353–54.

118. Della Femina, *Italian Grows in Brooklyn*, 22–23.

119. "Nausea of Immigrant," box 68, folder 1, LCP.

120. Orsi, *Madonna of 115th Street*.

121. Altogether, in 1950 there were 52 percent fewer first- and second-generation Italian Americans in the section of East Harlem east of Third Avenue than in 1930. Freeman, "Exploring the Path," 212. Covello was among those who left Italian Harlem shortly after World War II. Explaining to a friend his choice to move to a suburb in Westwood, New Jersey, the Italian American educator confessed, "Living in the city had become a most impossible situation." "Letter to Miss Fanny Ruddy, October 15, 1953," box 43, folder 9, LCP.

122. Joel Schwartz, *The New York Approach: Robert Moses, Urban Liberals, and Redevelopment of the Inner City* (Columbus: Ohio State University Press, 1993).

123. Daniel Bluestone, "The Pushcart Evil," in *The Landscape of Modernity: New York City, 1900–1940*, ed. David Ward and Oliver Zunz (Baltimore: Johns Hopkins University Press, 1992), 287–312; Suzanne Wasserman, "Hawkers and Gawkers: Peddling and Markets in New York City," in *Gastropolis: Food and New York City*, ed. Annie Hauck-Lawson and Jonathan Deutsch (New York: Columbia University Press, 2008), 153–73. The most important primary sources for the history of open markets in New York are New York City Pushcart Commission, *Report of the Mayor's Pushcart Commission* (New York, 1906); and United States Agricultural Economics Bureau in cooperation with the New York Port Authority, *Push Cart Markets in New York City* (Washington, D.C., 1925).

124. Osofsky, *Harlem*, 82.

125. Cimilluca, "Natural History of East Harlem," 110–11.

126. Richard Plunz, *A History of Housing in New York City* (New York: Columbia University Press, 1990), 245; Concistré, "Study of a Decade," 56. "When the market moved to the Bronx it put a lot of little guys out of business. . . . They all felt that they had become the victims of a political plot by an ambitious mayor"; Colello, "East Harlem," 112–13. A

few weeks after the market closure, one of Covello's students reported the following picture of the area: "On the 1st Ave. side there are stores and lofts. The section was a market place and they are almost all vacant. These apt. houses all around the block have all Italian inhabitants, all of the South of Italy, and are partially occupied. The section looks very poor. The buildings are in very bad condition. No children play in the streets. The side of the East River Water Front is in construction for a highway [Franklin D. Roosevelt Drive]." "First Ave.—East River Waterfront—E. 107th St.—E. 106th St., Louis V. Diodato, Dec. 23, 1935," "Blocks," box 78, folder 8, LCP.

127. Bluestone, "Pushcart Evil," 293.

128. "Modern Market to Replace Carts; Morgan to Ask $125,000 to Build 400 Enclosed Stalls under Park Av. Tracks; An Aid to Sanitation," *New York Times*, June 27, 1934; "Mayor Opens Cart Market; La Guardia Marches with Jostling Crowd; Some Complaints Heard; He Calls Park Ave. Mart Better for Food Peddlers," *New York Times*, May 4, 1936.

129. Covello, with D'Agostino, *Heart Is the Teacher*, 251.

130. Jonathan Randal, "The Harlem Italians: Little Italy Is Kept Alive by Former Residents Who Keep Coming Back," *New York Times*, March 30, 1966, 12.

131. Cinotto, "Italian Americans and Public Housing"; Plunz, *History of Housing*, 233, 243–45, 268.

132. East Harlem Small Business Survey and Planning Committee, "Proposed Agenda Re Material to Be Submitted to Councilman John J. Merli, Chairman of the City Council's Relocation Committee at Public Hearing, January 16, 1956"; East Harlem Merchants Association, "Proposed Agenda Re Supplementary Report to the Special Committee of the City Council of N.Y.C. on Relocation of Tenants and Dislocation of Small Business: Public Meeting, February 28, 1957," typescripts, New York City Municipal Archives.

133. Robert W. Peebles, "Interview with Leonard Covello," *Urban Review* 3, no. 3 (January 1969): 16; Orsi, *Madonna of 115th Street*, 45–49.

134. Maria Fischetti, series II, cassette 22, side A, ILOHP.

135. Sarah Garland, "A Return to East Harlem for the Dance of the Giglio," *New York Times*, September 5, 2006, B6.

136. Michael Stern, "East Harlem's Little Italy Gets Tinier Each Day," *New York Times*, October 15, 1968, 49.

137. Samuel G. Freedman, "Flock Returns Anew to East Harlem Madonna," *New York Times*, July 17, 1986, B1.

Chapter 4. The American Business of Italian Food

1. Antonio Gramsci, "Americanism and Fordism," in *An Antonio Gramsci Reader: Selected Writings, 1916–1935*, ed. David Forgacs (New York: Schocken, 2000); Marshall Berman, *All That Is Solid Melts into Air: The Experience of Modernity* (New York: Simon and Schuster, 1982).

2. Sollors, "Introduction: The Invention of Ethnicity," ix–xx.

3. Between 1900 and 1914, 3,125,308 Italians immigrated to the United States. Massimo Livi Bacci, *L'immigrazione e l'assimilazione degli italiani negli Stati Uniti secondo le statistiche demografiche americane* (Milan: Giuffrè, 1961), 7–8.

4. Foerster, *Italian Emigration of Our Times*, 338.

5. Michael La Sorte, "Vengo per Fare l'America: The Sojourner Businessman," in *New Explorations in Italian American Studies*, ed. Richard Juliani and Sandra Juliani (Staten Island, N.Y.: AIHA, 1994), 93.

6. Charlotte Adams, "Italian Life in New York," *Harper's Weekly*, April 1881, 676.

7. *Gli italiani negli Stati Uniti d'America* (New York: Italian American Directory, 1906), 68.

8. Mary Sherman, "Manufacturing Foods in the Tenements," *Charities and the Commons*, no. 16 (1906): 669.

9. *Gli italiani negli Stati Uniti d'America*, 75.

10. Joseph H. Adams, *In the Italian Quarter of New York* (New York: Congregational Home Missionary Society, 1903), microfilm, Pennsylvania Historical Society, Philadelphia.

11. Sherman, "Manufacturing Foods in the Tenements," 670.

12. "Italian Cultural Heritage," "Family Control & Unity," box 67, folder 7, LCP.

13. Williams, *South Italian Folkways*, 52; Colello, "East Harlem," 99; Mangione, *Mount Allegro*, 138.

14. Faith Moors Williams, *The Food Manufacturing Industries in New York and Its Environs: Present Trends and Probable Future Developments* (New York: Regional Plan of New York and Its Environs, 1924), 28.

15. *Gli italiani negli Stati Uniti d'America*, 75.

16. Alberto Cupelli, "The Italians in the Wholesale Food Industries," reel 260, INY.

17. *Gli italiani negli Stati Uniti d'America*, 404.

18. Sherman, "Manufacturing Foods in the Tenements," 670.

19. Louise C. Odencrantz, *Italian Women in Industry* (New York: Russell Sage Foundation, 1919), 83, 49.

20. Foerster, *Italian Emigration of Our Times*, 337.

21. Thomas Kessner, *The Golden Door: Italian and Jewish Immigrant Mobility in New York City, 1880–1915* (New York: Oxford University Press, 1977), 51–52, 55, 196n13.

22. New York City Pushcart Commission, *Report of the Mayor's Pushcart Commission* (New York, 1906), 17.

23. Giuseppe Selvaggi, *The Rise of the Mafia in New York: From 1896 through World War II* (New York: Bobbs-Merrill, 1978), 29.

24. Department of Public Markets, Weight and Measures of the City of New York, *Annual Report for the Year 1935* (New York, 1936), 16–24.

25. William Seabrook, *These Foreigners* (New York: Harcourt, Brace, 1938), 157; Ruggiero, *Italiani in America*, 146; Rocco Brindisi, "The Italian and Public Health," *Charities* 12, no. 18 (May 1904): 483–86; F. J. Panetta, "Food Habits," box 65, folder 15, LCP; "History of Broccoli; Broccoli Rabe, Vegetables, Misc. Leaf," reel 135, FTC; H. Moran, "New York City's Vegetables Next in Importance," reel 134, FTC.

26. Sophonisba Preston Breckinridge, *New Homes for Old: The Acculturation of Immigrant Groups into American Society* (New York: Transaction, 1921), 128.

27. Federal Writers' Project, *The Italians of New York* (New York: Random House, 1938), 71.

28. S. Michelson, "Metropolitan Farming and the Italian," reel 259, INY.

29. Scrittori del Federal Writers' Project della Work Projects Administration di New York City, *Gli Italiani di New York* (New York: Labor Press, 1939), 170.

30. Adams, *In the Italian Quarter.*

31. Regarding wine grapes, see Ausonio Franzoni, *Gli interessi italiani in New York* (Rome: Tipografia dell'Unione Coop. Editrice, 1908).

32. "Retail Food Stores Statistics and Data," reel 132, FTC.

33. Levenstein, *Revolution at the Table*, 30–31.

34. Susan Strasser, *Satisfaction Guaranteed: The Making of the American Mass Market* (Washington, D.C.: Smithsonian Institution Press, 1995), 6.

35. Levenstein, *Revolution at the Table*, 37.

36. Ruth Schwartz Cowan, *A Social History of American Technology* (New York: Oxford University Press, 1997), 170.

37. Levenstein, *Revolution at the Table*, 30–43.

38. Goody, *Cooking, Cuisine, and Class*, 169.

39. Susan Strasser, *Never Done: A History of American Housework* (New York: Pantheon Books, 1982), 253.

40. Gabaccia, *We Are What We Eat*, 61–62; Cohen, *Making a New Deal*, 101–20; Levenstein, *Revolution at the Table*, 167–72.

41. Stefano Somogyi, "L'alimentazione nell'Italia unita," in *Storia d'Italia Einaudi* (Turin: Einaudi, 1973), 839–87.

42. Vito Teti, "La cucina calabrese è un'invenzione americana?," *I viaggi di Erodoto* 6, no. 14 (1991): 66–67.

43. Piero Bevilacqua, "Emigrazione transoceanica e mutamenti dell'alimentazione contadina calabrese fra Otto e Novecento," *Quaderni storici*, no. 47 (1981): 520–55.

44. Teti, "Le culture alimentari nel Mezzogiorno," 91.

45. "Life Story of an Italian Bootblack," in Holt, *Life Stories of Undistinguished Americans*, 35.

46. Author's interview with Peter Rofrano.

47. Phillips and Howell, "Racial and Other Differences," 405.

48. Mudge, "Italian Dietary Adjustments," 183–84. See also Wiehl, "Diets of Low Income Families," 317–22.

49. Sidney Mintz, *Sweetness and Power: The Place of Sugar in Modern History* (New York: Penguin, 1986).

50. Federal Writers' Project, *Italians of New York*, 47.

51. Covello, with D'Agostino, *Heart Is the Teacher*, 23–24.

52. Gillett, "Factors Influencing Nutrition Work," 17.

53. Charlotte Gower Chapman, *Milocca: A Sicilian Village* (Cambridge, Mass.: Schenkman, 1971), 39; Nizzardini and Joffe, *Italian Food Patterns*, 11.

54. Lucy H. Gillett, "The Great Need for Information on Racial Dietary Customs," *Journal of Home Economics* 14 (June 1922): 260.

55. Williams, *South Italian Folkways*, 62.

56. Antonio Mangano, "The Italian Colonies of New York City," in *Italians in the City: Health and Related Social Needs*, ed. Francesco Cordasco (New York: Arno Press, 1975), 21.

57. Bevilacqua, "Emigrazione transoceanica e mutamenti dell'alimentazione," 523.

58. Michael Parenti, "The Blessing of Private Enterprise: A Personal Reminiscence," in *Studies in Italian American Social History: Essays in Honor of Leonard Covello*, ed. Francesco Cordasco (Totowa, N.J.: Rowman and Littlefield, 1975), 81.

59. Chapman, *Milocca*, 40; Mangione, *Mount Allegro*, 111–12.

60. Covello, with D'Agostino, *Heart Is the Teacher*, 24.

61. Emilio Sereni, "I napoletani da mangiafoglia a mangiamaccheroni: Note di storia dell'alimentazione nel Mezzogiorno," in *Terra nuova e buoi rossi: E altri saggi per una storia dell'agricoltura europea* (Turin: Einaudi, 1981), 362–63.

62. David Gentilcore, *Pomodoro! A History of the Tomato in Italy* (New York: Columbia University, 2010).

63. Chapman, *Milocca*, 40; Vito Teti, *Il pane, la beffa e la festa: Cultura alimentare e ideologia dell'alimentazione nelle classi subalterne* (Rimini: Guaraldi, 1976), 284–85.

64. Foerster, *Italian Emigration of Our Times*, 337–40, 467–68.

65. Odencrantz, *Italian Women in Industry*, 198.

66. Ewen, *Immigrant Women*, 27.

67. Bevilacqua, "Emigrazione transoceanica e mutamenti dell'alimentazione," 544.

68. Cinotto, "All Things Italian."

69. Winifred S. Gibbs, "Dietetics in Italian Tenements," *Public Health Nurse Quarterly* 6, no. 1 (1914): 43–46.

70. Enrico C. Sartorio, *Social and Religious Life of Italians in America* (Boston: Christopher, 1918), 57–58.

71. Levenstein, *Revolution at the Table*, 147–53.

72. Giuseppe Pitrè, *La vita in Palermo cento e più anni fa* (Palermo: A. Reber, 1898), 365; Nizzardini and Joffe, *Italian Food Patterns*, 11, 20; Teti, "Le culture alimentari nel Mezzogiorno," 95.

73. Levenstein, *Revolution at the Table*, 154–55.

74. Gillett, "Factors Influencing Nutrition Work," 17–19.

75. The sample of New York families studied by Gertrude Gates Mudge in the early 1920s spent an average 15 percent of their food budget for milk and cheese against the 20 percent suggested by NYAICP experts. Since the latter lamented that too large a share of the food budget was spent on cheese (especially imported), it is likely that little money was spent on milk. Mudge, "Italian Dietary Adjustments," 183. In a 1917–18 study conducted by researchers working at Teachers College, Columbia University, the recommended daily intake of calcium was 0.67 grams. The families receiving a daily intake of calcium below the recommended standard were so distributed: Italian 48 percent, Jewish 68 percent, Negro 63 percent, Miscellaneous 33 percent. Phillips and Howell, "Racial and Other Differences," 408.

76. Colello, "East Harlem," 79.

77. John Spargo, "Common Sense of the Milk Question," *Charities and the Commons*, no. 20 (1908): 595.

78. Mudge, "Italian Dietary Adjustments," 184.

79. Ravitch, *Great School Wars*, 161–80.

80. Celena Baxter, "Sicilian Family Life," *Family* 14 (May 1933): 86; Charlotte Raymond, *Food Customs from Abroad* (Boston: Massachusetts Department of Public Health, 1935);

Williams, *South Italian Folkways*, 63; "La pubblicità al latte nello stato di New York," *La Rivista Commerciale Italo-Americana*, January 16, 1935, 11–12.

81. Gillett, "Factors Influencing Nutrition Work," 16.

82. "Charts, Maps, Tables," box 92, folder 20, LCP.

83. "Inability to Speak English—Foreign Born Population. 10 Years Old and Over. Sex, Age, Literacy & Country of Birth, for Cities of 500,000 and More, 1930. New York, NY," box 97, folder 14, LCP.

84. Covello, "Language Usage in Italian Families."

85. Della Femina, *Italian Grows in Brooklyn*, 15–16.

86. Lawrence Veiller, "New Ideas in Social Work: Posters and Tuberculosis," *Charities and the Commons*, no. 20 (1908): 563–64.

87. "Average Amount per Capita Shown by Italian Immigrants during the Years 1899–1903 and 1904–1910. Also Amount Shown by Immigrants from All Other Countries, Based on Report by U.S. Commissioner of Immigration, 1911, vol. 3, pp. 35, 358," box 92, folder 20, LCP.

88. Cohen, *Workshop to Office*, 42–43.

89. Gino Speranza, "How It Feels to Be a Problem," *Charities*, no. 12 (1904): 457–63.

90. Kessner, *Golden Door*, 162, 167.

91. Livi Bacci, *L'immigrazione*, 11–27.

92. Kessner, *Golden Door*, 28.

93. Antonio Stella, "Condizioni igieniche e sanitarie degli Italiani nelle città del Nord-America: Il deperimento della stirpe; L'alimentazione," in *Gli Italiani negli Stati Uniti d'America*, 119.

94. Frank J. Sheridan, "Salari, ore di lavoro, consumi e risparmi degli Italiani negli Stati Uniti," in *Gl'Italiani negli Stati Uniti*, ed. Frank J. Sheridan, Napoleone Colajanni, and Emily Fogg Meade (Rome: Biblioteca della Rivista popolare, 1909), 18–21.

95. "La mensa dell'emigrato," in *Gl'Italiani negli Stati Uniti*, 158.

96. Breckinridge, *New Homes for Old*, 128–29.

97. Ibid., 127.

98. Odencrantz, *Italian Women in Industry*, 198.

99. Colello, "East Harlem," 80.

100. "Chain Stores and Turnover," *Macaroni Journal* 6, no. 6 (October 15, 1924); Strasser, *Satisfaction Guaranteed*, 222–29; Cohen, *Making a New Deal*, 106–9.

101. See, for a different context, Martin Bruegel, "How the French Learned to Eat Canned Food, 1809–1930s," *Food Nations: Selling Taste in Consumer Societies*, ed. Warren J. Belasco and Philip Scranton (New York: Routledge, 2002), 113–30.

102. Author's interview with Peter Rofrano.

103. A study of the food habits of Italians in the Mulberry District during the Depression notes, "[Although] canned foods are not used because there is an aversion of long standing to them, the popular canned tomato paste is an exception." Dorothy L. Bovee and Jean Downes, "The Influence of Nutrition Education in Families of the Mulberry Area of New York City," *Milbank Memorial Fund Quarterly* 19, no. 2 (1941): 123.

104. Vicesvinci, "Italian Patterns"; Ware, *Greenwich Village*, 416; Nizzardini and Joffe, *Italian Food Patterns*, 10, 18; Williams, *South Italian Folkways*, 65–66.

105. Della Femina, *Italian Grows in Brooklyn*, 19–20.

106. Claude Fischler, "Food, Self and Identity," *Social Science Information* 27, no. 2 (1988): 288–91.

107. Nizzardini and Joffe, *Italian Food Patterns*, 21–22.

108. "Food Habits," box 68, folder 2, LCP.

109. Colello, "East Harlem," 9.

110. Gambino, *Blood of My Blood*, 22; Williams, *South Italian Folkways*, 64.

111. Vergara, *Love and Pasta*, 34–35.

112. "Italian Cultural Heritage—Social Heritage," box 67, folder 11, LCP.

113. Nicholas Morabito, "Some Old World Customs and Mores," People in Our Community," box 79, folder 12, LCP; Jones, *Sociology of a New York City Block*, 110; Colello, "East Harlem," 105; author's interview with Rose Pascale.

114. Colello, "East Harlem," 41, 96; Breckinridge, *New Homes for Old*, 59.

115. Glazer and Moynihan, *Beyond the Melting Pot*, 185.

116. Gans, *Urban Villagers*, 183.

117. Kessner, *Golden Door*, 167.

118. S. Michelson, "Wealth of the Italians of New York," reel 260, INY.

119. Cupelli, "Italians in the Wholesale Food Industries."

120. *Gli italiani negli Stati Uniti d'America*, 68.

121. N. S. Shapiro, "Field Report, Production of Macaroni Products, Cereal and Grain Products, Macaronis," reel 134, FTC.

122. *Gli italiani negli Stati Uniti d'America*, 68–69, 264.

123. Cupelli, "Italians in the Wholesale Food Industries."

124. Williams, *Food Manufacturing Industries*, 48.

125. Cupelli, "Italians in the Wholesale Food Industries"; Ario Flamma, *Italiani di America* (New York: Cocce Brothers, 1936), 290.

126. Cupelli, "Italians in the Wholesale Food Industries"; Market Research Department of the *New York Times, A Study of Macaroni-Spaghetti in the New York City Market* (New York, June 1938).

127. "Maccheroni in pacchetti," *Il Commerciante Italiano*, October 10, 1936.

128. John Bodnar, *The Transplanted: A History of Immigrants in Urban America* (Bloomington: Indiana University Press, 1985), 138–39, 142–43.

129. Italian American pasta manufacturer Thomas A. Cuneo recalled that, while before World War I all business correspondence in the industry was written in Italian, ten years later only English was used. Giuseppe Prezzolini, *Spaghetti Dinner* (New York: Abelard-Schuman, 1955), 49.

130. Flamma, *Italiani di America*, 290.

131. Cupelli, "Italians in the Wholesale Food Industries"; Flamma, *Italiani di America*, 218.

132. Flamma, *Italiani di America*, 8.

133. Ibid., 298.

134. Orsi, *Madonna of 115th Street*, 2.

135. Concistré, "Study of a Decade," 57.

136. Stefano Luconi, "Not Only *A Tavola*: Radio Broadcasting and Patterns of Ethnic Consumption among the Italian Americans in the Interwar Years," in *A Tavola*, 58–67; Christopher Newton, "From 'The Prince Macaroni Hour' to 'Car Talk': An Evolution in Italian-American Radio," *Italian Americana* 14, no. 3 (Winter 1996): 5–15.

137. Seabrook, *These Foreigners*, 155–56.

138. Concistré, "Study of a Decade," 419; "Ronzoni Using Radio," *Macaroni Journal* 14, no. 5 (October 15, 1932): 29; La Rosa ad, *Il Progresso Italo-Americano*, March 27, 1937.

139. La Rosa ad, *Il Progresso Italo-Americano*, November 23, 1930.

140. Market Research Department of the *New York Times*, *Study of Macaroni-Spaghetti*.

141. "Curb That Volume Craze," *Macaroni Journal* 14, no. 1 (May 15, 1932); "Industry Pays a Penalty," *Macaroni Journal* 14, no. 5 (September 15, 1932).

142. "Per non morire . . . Terzo memento ai signori che dirigono l'industria dei maccheroni," *Il Progresso Italo-Americano*, July 1, 1936.

143. "Frauds and How to Guard against Them," reel 123, LBB.

144. Federal Security Agency, "Federal Food, Drug and Cosmetic Act," part 16, no. 21, issued August 1939.

145. "Cereal and Grain Products, Macaronis," reel 134, FTC; Market Research Department of the *New York Times*, *Study of Macaroni-Spaghetti*.

146. John W. Briggs, *An Italian Passage: Immigrants to Three Immigrant Cities, 1890–1930* (New Haven, Conn.: Yale University Press, 1978), 167.

147. Concistré, "Study of a Decade," 57.

148. "Importanti dati statistici riguardanti la popolazione italiana di New York," *Voice of Italy*, January 23, 1937.

149. "Greater New York Italian-American Market," *Macaroni Journal* 14, no. 12 (April 15, 1933): 10.

150. "La produzione americana di generi alimentari tipo italiano," *La Rivista Commerciale Italo-Americana*, March 12, 1938, 9.

151. "Tomato Products," reel 142, FTC.

152. Simone Cinotto, *Soft Soil, Black Grapes: The Birth of Italian Winemaking in California* (New York: New York University Press, 2012). See also Donna R. Gabaccia, "Ethnicity in the Business World: Italians in American Food Industries," *Italian American Review* 6, no. 2 (Autumn/Winter, 1997/1998): 1–19.

153. Sebastian Fichera, "Entrepreneurial Behavior in an Immigrant Colony: The Economic Experience of San Francisco's Italian-Americans, 1850–1940," *Studi Emigrazione* 32, no. 118 (1995): 338.

154. "History of the Organization and Progress of the Italian-Swiss Colony, Asti, Sonoma Co., Cal.," Asti, Calif., 1903(?), p.18, Bancroft Library, University of California, Berkeley.

155. Cinotto, *Soft Soil, Black Grapes*.

156. "History of the Organization," 11–17.

157. Cinotto, *Soft Soil, Black Grapes*.

158. *La Rivista Commerciale Italo-Americana*, April 16, 1935, 18.

159. Ruth Teiser and Catherine Harroun, *Winemaking in California: The Account in Words and Pictures of the Golden State's Two-Century-Long Adventure with Wine* (New York: McGraw-Hill, 1983), 177.

160. "Consumo di vini negli Stati Uniti," *La Rivista Commerciale Italo-Americana*, February 16, 1937, 13.

161. Teiser and Harroun, *Winemaking in California*, 177–83.

162. Fruit Industries ad, *Il Progresso Italo-Americano*, September 8, 1929.

163. Teiser and Harroun, *Winemaking in California*, 200–202.

164. Scrittori del Federal Writers' Project, *Gli Italiani di New York*, 184.

165. "La produzione americana," 11.

166. Loyal Durand Jr., "Italian Cheese Production in the American Dairy Region," *Economic Geography* 24 (July 1948): 217–30.

167. Ibid., 224.

168. Marilyn Halter, *Shopping for Identity: The Marketing of Ethnicity* (New York: Schocken, 2002); Warren Belasco, "Ethnic Fast Foods: The Corporate Melting Pot," *Food and Foodways* 1, no. 2 (1987): 1–30.

169. "Spaghetti Houses," *Macaroni Journal* 6, no. 4 (August 15, 1924): 9.

170. Goody, *Cooking, Cuisine, and Class*, 169.

171. Douglas Collins, *America's Favorite Food: The Story of Campbell Soup Company* (New York: Abrams, 1994), 100–104; Harvey A. Levenstein, "The American Response to Italian Food, 1880–1930" *Food and Foodways* 1, no. 1 (1985): 4–5.

172. "Una breve cronistoria della National Macaroni Manufacturers Association: Come sorse e come si sviluppò l'associazione," *Il Commerciante Italiano*, October 10, 1936.

173. Pasta-consumption statistics from "Spaghetti Liked by Italians," *Macaroni Journal* 13, no. 11 (March 15, 1932): 8.

174. "America's Part in Macaroni Improvement," *Macaroni Journal* 13, no. 11 (March 15, 1932): 8.

175. "Italian Plants Modern and Sanitary," *Macaroni Journal* 13, no. 12 (April 15, 1932): 12.

176. Levenstein, "American Response to Italian Food," 15–17; Gabaccia, *We Are What We Eat*, 136–39.

177. Cecil L. Griel, *I problemi della madre in un paese nuovo* (New York: National Board of the Young Women's Christian Associations, 1927[?]), 68.

178. Bureau of Consumers' Service, Department of Markets, Frances Foley Gannon, Director, "Radio Talk, April 3, 1941," reel 134, FTC.

179. "Macaroni for Home Relief," *Macaroni Journal* Vol. 13, no. 11 (March 15, 1932): 8.

180. D. R. Hodgdon, "Macaroni as Body and Health Builder in Great Favor," *Macaroni Journal* 14, no. 5 (September 15, 1932): 24.

181. James Riordan, "Americans Getting Macaroni Appetite," *Macaroni Journal* 10, no. 2 (June 15, 1928).

182. "Macaroni: An Economic Dish for Successful Wives," *Macaroni Journal* 14, no. 7 (November 15, 1932): 14; "Macaroni Is a Most Delicious and Nourishing Food," *Macaroni Journal* 14, no. 5 (September 15, 1932).

183. Collins, *America's Favorite Food*, 177, 104; Levenstein, "American Response to Italian Food," 16.

184. Lawrence Di Stasi, *Dream Streets: The Big Book of Italian American Culture* (New York: Abrams, 1994), 72–73.

185. Belasco, "Ethnic Fast Foods," 12–13.

Chapter 5. "Buy Italian!"

1. Philip V. Cannistraro, "Fascism and Italian Americans," in *Perspectives in Italian Immigration and Ethnicity*, ed. Silvio M. Tomasi (New York: Center for Migration Studies, 1977), 51.

2. Mark I. Choate, *Emigrant Nation: The Making of Italy Abroad* (Cambridge, Mass.: Harvard University Press, 2008), 72.

3. Mark I. Choate, "Sending States' Transnational Interventions in Politics, Culture, and Economics: The Historical Example of Italy," *International Migration Review* 41, no. 3 (Fall 2007): 728–68.

4. Robert E. Park and Herbert A. Miller, *Old World Traits Transplanted* (New York: Henry Holt, 1921), 149.

5. Foerster, *Italian Emigration of Our Times*, 339.

6. Alejandro Portes, Luis Eduardo Guarnizo, and William J. Haller, "Transnational Entrepreneurs: An Alternative Form of Immigrant Economic Adaptation," *American Sociological Review* 67, no. 2 (April 2002): 278–98; Ewa Morawska, "Immigrant Transnational Entrepreneurs in New York: Three Varieties and Their Correlates," *International Journal of Entrepreneurial Behaviour and Research* 10, no. 5 (2004): 325–48.

7. Piero Meldini, "L'emergere delle cucine regionali: L'Italia," in *Storia dell'alimentazione*, ed. Jean-Louis Flandrin and Massimo Montanari (Rome: Laterza, 1997), 658–64. Meldini convincingly argues that Pellegrino Artusi's cookbook *The Science in the Kitchen and the Art of Eating Well* (1st ed. 1881), generally considered the foundational text of Italian national cuisine, is more precisely a collection of some of the regional dishes that in the newly unified country stemmed from the local culinary encounters of the "low" and the "high."

8. Victoria De Grazia, *The Culture of Consent: Mass Organization of Leisure in Fascist Italy* (Cambridge: Cambridge University Press, 1981), 94–126, 187–224.

9. Capatti and Montanari, *Italian Cuisine*, 30.

10. Bodnar, *Transplanted*, 138–40; John E. Zucchi, "Paesani or Italiani? Local and National Loyalties in an Italian Immigrant Community," in *The Family and Community Life of Italian Americans*, ed. Richard Juliani (New York: AIHA, 1983), 152–53.

11. George E. Pozzetta, "The Italians of New York, 1890–1914" (PhD diss., University of North Carolina, 1971).

12. John Bodnar, *Remaking America: Public Memory, Commemoration, and Patriotism in the Twentieth Century* (Princeton, N.J.: Princeton University Press, 1991), 77.

13. Sermolino, *Papa's Table d'Hote*, 232–35.

14. Richard Alba, *Italian Americans: Into the Twilight of Ethnicity* (Englewood Cliffs, N.J.: Prentice-Hall, 1985), 74–75; Philip V. Cannistraro, "The Duce and the Prominenti: Fascism and the Crisis of Italian American Leadership," *Altreitalie*, no. 31 (July–December 2005): 76–86.

15. William F. Whyte, *Street Corner Society: The Social Structure of an Italian Slum* (Chicago: University of Chicago Press, 1943), 274.

16. Tim Edensor, *National Identity, Popular Culture and Everyday Life* (New York: Berg, 2002), 109–13.

17. Flamma, *Italiani di America*, 197–98; Scrittori del Federal Writers' Project, *Gli Italiani di New York*, 183.

18. Flamma, *Italiani di America*, 118; G. Morelli, "Occupazioni e professioni degli italiani," reel 259, INY.

19. *Gli italiani negli Stati Uniti d'America*, 462–64; Morelli, "Occupazioni e professioni degli italiani."

20. Flamma, *Italiani di America*, 100.

21. Ibid., 288.

22. Ibid., 154, 266.

23. Philip V. Cannistraro, "Fascism and Italian-Americans in Detroit, 1933–1935," *International Migration Review* 9, no. 1 (Spring 1975): 34; John P. Diggins, *Mussolini and Fascism: The View from America* (Princeton, N.J.: Princeton University Press, 1972), 100; Morris Schonbach, *Native American Fascism during the 1930s and 1940s: A Study of Its Roots, Its Growth and Its Decline* (New York: Garland, 1985), 80; Gabriella Facondo, *Socialismo italiano esule negli USA, 1930–1942* (Foggia: Bastogi, 1993), 33.

24. Camera di Commercio Italiana in New York, *Nel Cinquantenario della Camera di Commercio Italiana in New York, 1887–1937* (New York, 1937), 66.

25. By the mid-1890s, in New York imported pasta sold at about eight cents a pound wholesale and sixteen cents retail. An average laborer earned about seven dollars a week. Harvey A. Levenstein and Joseph Conlin, "The Food Habits of Italian Immigrants in America: An Examination of the Persistence of a Food Culture and the Rise of 'Fast Food' in America," in *Dominant Symbols in Popular Culture*, ed. Ray Browne et al. (Bowling Green, Ohio: Bowling Green Popular Culture Press, 1990), 233.

26. Phillips and Howell, "Racial and Other Differences," 397.

27. Gillett, *Factors Influencing Nutrition Work*, 17.

28. Camera di Commercio Italiana in New York, *Nel Cinquantenario*, 66.

29. Ibid., 64–65.

30. "La produzione delle paste alimentari negli Stati Uniti," *La Rivista Commerciale Italo-Americana*, February 9, 1929.

31. "Il pastificio americano," *La Rivista Commerciale Italo-Americana*, March 23, 1929; "L'industria americana delle paste alimentari," *Il Progresso Italo-Americano*, December 27, 1930.

32. Ad in *Il Progresso Italo-Americano*, September 7, 1930.

33. Camera di Commercio Italiana in New York, *Nel Cinquantenario*, 78.

34. Strasser, *Satisfaction Guaranteed*, 169.

35. Pietro Petri, "A Talk on Sicilian Specialties," *Italian-American Review*, February 4, 1922.

36. "Il commercio dei prodotti alimentari negli Stati Uniti," *La Rivista Commerciale Italo-Americana*, April 1, 1935, 9.

37. Ad in *Il Progresso Italo-Americano*, January 4, 1935.

38. Committee on Ways and Means, House of Representatives, "Hearings on General Tariff Revision; Brief Presented by the Italian Chamber of Commerce in New York," *La Rivista Commerciale Italo-Americana*, March 2, 1929.

39. "La nuova tariffa americana e i principali prodotti italiani," *Il Progresso Italo-Americano*, September 1, 1929.

40. "Penetrazione americana dei generi alimentari italiani," *La Rivista Commerciale Italo-Americana*, June 29, 1929.

41. "Quello che fanno gli altri," *La Rivista Commerciale Italo-Americana*, May 1, 1935, 12; "Ronzoni Using Radio," 29.

42. *La Rivista Commerciale Italo-Americana*, November 16, 1935, 13–14.

43. *La Rivista Commerciale Italo-Americana*, December 1, 1935, 16.

44. *La Rivista Commerciale Italo-Americana*, December 16, 1935, 13.

45. *La Rivista Commerciale Italo-Americana*, November 16, 1935, 9.

46. *La Rivista Commerciale Italo-Americana*, May 16, 1936, 10.

47. Levenstein and Conlin, "Food Habits of Italian Immigrants," 234.

48. "Consumo dell'olio d'oliva negli Stati Uniti," *La Rivista Commerciale Italo-Americana*, November 23, 1929, 10.

49. W. R. M. Wharton, "The Olive Oil Industry and the Federal Food and Drugs Act: The Olive Oil Association of America Yearbook 1936," reel 122, LBB.

50. Ibid.

51. Ibid.

52. "Prodotti italiani e sostituti nel mercato dei generi alimentari," *Il Commerciante Italiano*, August 1, 1934.

53. Camera di Commercio Italiana in New York, *Nel Cinquantenario*, 82.

54. "Digest of Radio Address by the Hon. Alex Pisciotta: Olive Oil, December 10, 1938," reel 122, LBB.

55. "A. Pisciotta, March 4, 1939," reel 122, LBB; "Le frodi al pubblico perpetrate da disonesti rivenditori d'olio," *Il Progresso Italo-Americano*, January 28, 1940.

56. Goody, *Cooking, Cuisine, and Class*, 172–73; Strasser, *Satisfaction Guaranteed*.

57. Harold Gastwirt, *Fraud, Corruption and Holiness: The Controversy over the Supervision of Jewish Dietary Practices in New York City, 1881–1940* (Port Washington, N.Y.: Kennikat Press, 1974).

58. Walter Benjamin, "The Work of Art in the Age of Mechanical Reproduction," in *Illuminations: Essays and Reflections*, ed. Hannah Arendt (New York: Schocken, 1969), 217–52.

59. "Frauds and How to Guard against Them," reel 123, LBB.

60. Camera di Commercio Italiana in New York, *Nel cinquantenario*, 81–82.

61. *Il Commerciante Italiano*, August 1, 1934.

62. Mary Douglas and Baron Isherwood, *The World of Goods: Towards an Anthropology of Consumption* (New York: Routledge, 1996); Featherstone, *Consumer Culture and Postmodernism*; George Ritzer, *Enchanting a Disenchanted World* (Thousand Oaks, Calif.: Pine Forge Press, 2005).

63. Roland Barthes, "Pour une psycho-sociologie de l'alimentation contemporaine," *Annales ESC* 16 (1961): 977–86; Roland Barthes, "Rhetoric of the Image," in *Visual Culture: The Reader*, ed. Jessica Evans and Stuart Hall (Thousand Oaks, Calif.: Sage, 1999), 51–60.

64. Ida L. Hull, "Special Problems in Italian Families," in *National Conference of Social Work: Addressees and Proceedings* (New York, 1924).

65. "S'incomincia, Signori!" *Il Commerciante Italiano*, September 16, 1934.

66. "Prodotti americani e prodotti italiani," *Il Commerciante Italiano*, January 19, 1935.

67. "Memoriale del Rag. Cav. Carlo Bertolaia sul Commercio di Prodotti Alimentari Italiani," *La Rivista Commerciale Italo-Americana*, June 1, 1937, 10.

68. "Pensiamo a noi per un poco!," *Il Prodotto Italiano*, June 6, 1940.

69. "Little Italy Sours on Duce and War; Pictures, Plaques and Busts Disappear from Mulberry Bend as Losses Rise; Food Shortages Hurt; Premier Blamed as Imports of Staples Cease; He Talks Too Much for Youngsters," *New York Times*, February 9, 1941.

70. George E. Pozzetta and Gary R. Mormino, "The Politics of Christopher Columbus and World War II," *Altreitalie*, no. 17 (1998): 9.

71. "Venite, mostriamo ad Adolfo che egli ha commesso il suo più grande sbaglio," ad in *Il Progresso Italo-Americano*, October 12, 1942.

Chapter 6. Serving Ethnicity

1. As late as the turn of the twentieth century, reporters, writers, and other commentators used the notion of "Little Italy" to indicate the Italian section of East Harlem in uptown Manhattan. The even more populous Italian enclave delimited by Broadway, the Bowery, East Houston, and Canal Streets was normally referred to as the Mulberry District. Only with the emergence of urban tourism in the second and third decades of the century was the Little Italy designation—matching the neighboring Chinatown and Jewish ghetto, with which it made up a glamorous ethnic tourist package—attached to the first area of Italian settlement in downtown Manhattan. Not incidentally, the Little Italy name slipped away from the peripheral Harlem at the very moment in which "Harlem" became a formula evoking a black neighborhood and, to white middle-class visitors, the promise of experiencing black culture and sexuality. Donna Gabaccia, "Inventing Little Italy," *Journal of the Gilded Age and Progressive Era* 6, no. 1 (2007): 7–41.

2. Hunter and Denver, "Tony Moneta," "Foreign Restaurants," reel 144, FTC.

3. Rian James, *Dining in New York* (New York: John Day, 1930), 60.

4. Federal Writers' Project, *Italians of New York*, 181.

5. Quoted in E. Digby Baltzell, *The Protestant Establishment: Aristocracy and Caste in America* (New York: Vintage Books, 1965), 30.

6. Kessner, *Golden Door*, 28–30.

7. Elizabeth Frazer, "Our Foreign Cities: New York," *Saturday Evening Post*, June 16, 1923, 6–7; Foerster, *Italian Emigration of Our Times*, 385.

8. Michael La Sorte, *La Merica: Images of Italian Greenhorn Experience* (Philadelphia: Temple University Press, 1985), 136.

9. Donald Tricarico, *The Italians of Greenwich Village: The Social Structure and Transformation of an Ethnic Community* (New York: Center for Migration Studies, 1984).

10. A. Ritchie, "The Italians of Bleecker Street," reel 40, ONY.

11. F. J. Panetta, "Food Habits," box 65, folder 15, LCP.

12. F. De Cicco, "Food Habits," box 67, folder 25, LCP.

13. George Pozzetta, "The Mulberry District of New York City: The Years before World War One," in *Little Italies in North America*, ed. Robert F. Harney and J. Vincenza Scarpaci (Toronto: AIHA, 1981): 7–40.

14. Amedeo D'Aureli, "N.Y.C. East Harlem," box 66, folder 9, LCP.

15. Levenstein, *Revolution at the Table*, 16–17; William Grimes, *Appetite City: A Culinary History of New York* (New York: North Point Press, 2009).

16. Lewis A. Erenberg, *Steppin' Out: New York Nightlife and the Transformation of American Culture, 1890–1930*, (Chicago: University of Chicago Press, 1984). On the broader cultural change that allowed for the rise of turn-of-the-twentieth-century American consumerism, see William Leach, *Land of Desire: Merchants, Power and the Rise of a New American Culture* (New York: Pantheon, 1993); Jackson Lears, *Fables of Abundance: A Cultural History of Advertising in America* (New York: Basic Books, 1994); Susan Porter Benson, *Counter Cultures: Saleswomen, Managers, and Customers in American Department Stores, 1890–1940* (Urbana: University of Illinois Press, 1986); Elaine S. Abelson, *When Ladies Go A-Thieving: Middle-Class Shoplifters in the Victorian Department Store* (New York: Oxford University Press, 1989).

17. Chad C. Heap, *Slumming: Sexual and Racial Encounters in American Nightlife, 1885–1940* (Chicago: University of Chicago Press, 2009), 183.

18. Sermolino, *Papa's Table d'Hote*, 14.

19. Rich Beard and Leslie Cohen Berlowitz, *Greenwich Village: Culture and Counterculture* (New Brunswick, N.J.: Rutgers University Press, 1993), 294.

20. Ritchie, "Italians of Bleecker Street"; Harry DeSteese, "Downtown Restaurants," reel 29, NYCG-MA; Beard and Berlowitz, *Greenwich Village*, 160; George Chauncey, *Gay New York: Gender, Urban Culture, and the Making of the Gay Male World, 1890–1940* (New York: Basic Books, 1994), 239–40.

21. Levenstein, *Revolution at the Table*, 185–86.

22. Sermolino, *Papa's Table d'Hote*, 15.

23. Edith M. Barber, "Delicious Italian Food at Its Source," *Better Homes and Gardens*, October 1930, 24.

24. "A typical Gonfarone's menu, at any time during the first decade of the twentieth century, might have read as follows: Assorted Antipasto; Minestrone; Spaghetti with Meat or Tomato Sauce; Boiled Salmon with Caper Sauce; Sweetbread with Mushroom Patty; Broiled Spring Chicken or Roast Prime Ribs of Beef; Brussels Sprouts, Spinach; Boiled or Mashed Potatoes; Green Salad; Biscuit Tortoni or Spumoni; Fresh Fruit, Assorted Cheese; Demi-tasse. This formidable list represented not a choice of items, but a list of all the food a customer could have on a weekday night for fifty cents, including a pint of California red wine." Sermolino, *Papa's Table d'Hote*, 125–26.

25. Barber, "Delicious Italian Food."

26. Sermolino, *Papa's Table d'Hote*, 124.

27. Ibid., 126.

28. Ibid., 124.

29. "Family Solidarity (Economic, Education), from Life History, Armando D'Amato, 1938," box 68, folder 1, LCP.

30. Winnie Lem, "Daughters, Duty and Deference in the Franco-Chinese Restaurant," in *The Restaurants Book: Ethnographies of Where We Eat*, ed. David Beriss and David Sutton (Oxford: Berg, 2007), 133–50.

31. Gabaccia, *We Are What We Eat*, 120.

32. See the essays in David Beriss and David Sutton, eds., *The Restaurants Book: Ethnographies of Where We Eat* (Oxford: Berg, 2007); Gary Alan Fine, "Occupation Aesthetics: How Trade School Students Learn to Cook," *Urban Life* 14, no. 1 (1985): 3–31; Gordon Marshall, "The Workplace Culture of a Licensed Restaurant," *Theory, Culture and Society*, no. 1 (1986): 33–47; Yen Peterson and Laura D. Birg, "Top Hat: The Chef as Creative Occupation," *Free Inquiry in Creative Sociology*, no. 16 (1988): 67–72.

33. Sermolino, *Papa's Table d'Hote*, 126.

34. Ibid.

35. *Gli italiani negli Stati Uniti d'America*, 75.

36. Carnevali, *Autobiography of Emanuel Carnevali*, 77.

37. Bartolomeo Vanzetti, *The Story of a Proletarian Life* (Boston: Sacco-Vanzetti Defense Committee, 1923), 9–10.

38. Ibid., 13.

39. G. Morelli, "Italo-Americans in Industry in New York," reel 259, INY.

40. Margaret Case Harriman, "Two Waiters and a Chef: Colony Restaurant," *New Yorker*, June 1, 1935, 20.

41. Giovanni G. Schiavo, *Four Centuries of Italian American History* (New York: Vigo Press, 1952), 394.

42. Levenstein, *Revolution at the Table*, 184–87; Humbert S. Nelli, *The Business of Crime: Italians and Syndicate Crime in the United States* (New York: Oxford University Press, 1976), 146–47.

43. Michael A. Lerner, *Dry Manhattan: Prohibition in New York City* (Cambridge, Mass.: Harvard University Press, 2007).

44. Michael Di Liberto, "Wine Time in East Harlem," *New York Times*, November 8, 1931, SM9.

45. Allon Schoener, *New York: An Illustrated History of the People* (New York: W. W. Norton., 1998), 250.

46. Ware, *Greenwich Village*, 60.

47. Ibid., 57.

48. Morabito, "Some Old World Customs and Mores"; Frazer, "Our Foreign Cities."

49. Katherine Young, *My Old New York Neighborhoods* (New York: Profile Press, 1979), 14.

50. Ware, *Greenwich Village*, 61–62.

51. "Document on File in the Boys' Club Study," cited in Cimilluca, "Natural History of East Harlem," 12.

52. Chauncey, *Gay New York*, 239–40, 82.

53. Erenberg, *Steppin' Out*, 253; Heap, *Slumming*, 57–70; Kevin J. Mumford, *Interzones: Black/White Sex Districts in Chicago and New York in the Early Twentieth Century* (New York: Columbia University Press, 1997), 133–54.

54. Harry Zahm, "Italian Restaurants and Foods in New York," reel 259, INY.

55. Young, *My Old New York Neighborhoods*, 19.

56. Beard and Berlowitz, *Greenwich Village*, 155–56.

57. Federal Writers' Project, *Italians of New York*, 206.

58. Sermolino, *Papa's Table d'Hote*, 15.

59. Giorgio Bertellini, *Italy in Early American Cinema: Race, Landscape, and the Picturesque* (Bloomington: Indiana University Press, 2010), 19–68.

60. D'Agostino, "Craniums, Criminals, and the Cursed Race."

61. Joseph P. Cosco, *Imagining Italians: The Clash of Romance and Race in American Perceptions, 1880–1910* (Albany: State University of New York Press, 2003), 21–60.

62. Bertellini, *Italy in Early American Cinema*, 165–235.

63. Susan Kalčik, "Ethnic Foodways in America: Symbol and the Performance of Identity," in *Ethnic and Regional Foodways in the United States*, ed. Linda Keller Brown and Kay Mussell, (Knoxville: University of Tennessee Press, 1984), 37. See also Lisa Heldke, *Exotic Appetites: Ruminations of a Food Adventurer* (New York: Routledge, 2003), 1–60.

64. Jacobson, *Whiteness of a Different Color*, 203–23.

65. Covello, *Social Background*, 280–81.

66. Jacob A. Riis, *How the Other Half Lives: Studies among the Tenements of New York* (New York: Charles Scribner's Sons, 1890), 29.

67. Ibid., 44.

68. Harry Roskolenko, *The Time That Was Then: The Lower East Side, 1900–1914: An Intimate Chronicle* (New York: Dial Press, 1971), 98.

69. Charlotte Kimball, "An Outline of Amusements among Italians in New York," *Charities*, no. 5 (August 18, 1900): 5.

70. Jacob A. Riis, "Feast-Days in Little Italy," *Century Magazine*, August 1899, 491–99; "Quaint Italian Customs of Summer Festal Days; With Music, Gifts and Feasting the Denizens of Little Italy Pay Their Devotion to the Saints; Curious Phases of the Celebrations," *New York Times*, July 12, 1903, 30; "Little Italy's Fete Day; Feast of Our Lady of Mount Carmel Celebrated; Many Thousands Take Part; Houses Too Cramped to Shelter Guests from Other Cities; Scenes in Church and Street," *New York Times*, July 17, 1900, 12; "Feast of Mount Carmel; Little Italy, in Holiday Garb, Observes the Festal Day; Continuous Procession and Many Prayers for Pope Leo; Fireworks Strings of Lanterns, and Confetti in the Streets," *New York Times*, July 17, 1903, 2; "Thousands Do Homage to Our Lady of Carmel; Gorgeous Festival in Honor of Italian Patron Saint; Little Italy's Gala Day; Masses and Monster Parade; Rich Gifts at Shrine; Bills Pinned on Silken Banner," *New York Times*, July 17, 1904, 17; "Little Italy Honors Lady of Mt. Carmel; Tons of Candles Burned on Her Altars; Streets a Riot of Color; Residents of the Quarter, in Holiday Attire, Keep Open House," *New York Times*, July 17, 1906, 2; "Religion of Lucky Pieces, Witches and the Evil Eye," *World Outlook*, October 1917, 24–25; Giuseppe Cautela, "Italian Funeral," *American Mercury*, October 1928, 200–206.

71. Mario Maffi, *Gateway to the Promised Land: Ethnic Cultures on New York's Lower East Side* (Amsterdam: Rodopi, 1994), 280.

72. Featherstone, *Consumer Culture and Postmodernism*, 23.

73. Konrad Bercovici, *Around the World in New York* (New York: Century, 1924), 125–28.

74. In her study of the leisure time of Italian Harlem girls, Dorothy Reed notes that during gangster movie screenings young Italian Americans loudly took the gangster's side: "There is one characteristic typical of these Italian child audiences which has been

noted by observations at various movies by social workers and patrolmen in the area. Enthusiastic applause greets the success of the villain and the downfall of any 'cop' or representative of 'the Law.' Is it at all indicative?" Reed, *Leisure Time of Girls*, 32.

75. Daniel S. Golden, "Pasta or Paradigm: The Place of Italian-American Women in Popular Film," *Explorations in Ethnic Studies* 2 (January 1979): 4.

76. Bercovici, *Around the World in New York*, 128.

77. Alessandro Carrera, "Folk Music and Popular Song from the Nineteenth Century to the 1990s," in *The Cambridge Companion to Modern Italian Culture*, ed. Zygmunt Guido Baranski and Rebecca J. West (Cambridge: Cambridge University Press, 2001), 326.

78. Anna Maria Martellone, "La rappresentazione dell'identità italo-americana: Teatro e feste nelle Little Italy statunitensi," in *La chioma della vittoria: Scritti sull'identità degli italiani dall'Unità alla seconda Repubblica*, ed. Sergio Bertelli (Florence: Ponte alle Grazie, 1997), 377–84.

79. Kessner, *Golden Door*, 33. Several biographies of Italian musicians in New York in the 1930s appear in Flamma, *Italiani di America*.

80. Adams, "Italian Life in New York," 683–84.

81. Harry DeSteese, "Foreign Restaurants," reel 29, NYCG-MA.

82. Di Stasi, *Dream Streets*, 100.

83. *Corriere della Sera*, December 5, 1954, quoted in Prezzolini, *Spaghetti Dinner*, 41.

84. Ritchie, "Italians of Bleecker Street."

85. Di Stasi, *Dream Streets*, 100.

86. Grace S. Selden, "Vegetable Victories," *Good Housekeeping*, October 1918, 50.

87. Elizabeth G. Palmer, "All Ready, Let's Go! Italian Dinner," *Woman's Home Companion*, September 1935, 60–61.

88. Schoener, *New York*, 229.

89. Gene Leone, *Leone's Italian Cookbook* (New York: Harper and Row, 1967), 1–7; DeSteese, "Foreign Restaurants"; Ritchie, "Italians of Bleecker Street."

90. DeSteese, "Foreign Restaurants."

91. Grimes, *Appetite City*, 125.

92. DeSteese, "Downtown Restaurants."

93. Hunter, Denver, "Tony Moneta."

94. Levenstein, *Revolution at the Table*, 190.

95. James, *Dining in New York*, 121; DeSteese, "Downtown Restaurants."

96. H. Clere, "San Remo Restaurant, Bleecker and MacDougal Streets," "Eating Out—Foreign Restaurants," reel 144, FTC.

97. Barber, "Delicious Italian Food."

98. Sermolino, *Papa's Table d'Hote*, 134.

99. Zahm, "Italian Restaurants."

100. DeSteese, "Foreign Restaurants."

101. Samuel Ornitz, *Allrightniks Row: Haunch, Paunch and Jowl; An Anonymous Autobiography* (New York: Boni and Liveright, 1923), 139–40.

102. Douglas and Isherwood, *World of Goods*.

103. Appadurai, "Disjuncture and Difference."

104. Yu, "How Tiger Woods Lost His Stripes."

105. Food studies scholar Krishnendu Ray, who has examined the treatment of the "cuisines of the others" in the press over the last two centuries, argues that both Chinese and Italian restaurants very similarly attracted most attention from newspapers and magazines when the respective immigration flows were at their lowest (for Chinese before the 1960s and for Italians in the 1920s and 1930s). Krishnendu Ray, "A Taste for Ethnic Difference: American Gustatory Imagination in a Globalizing World," in *Globalization, Food and Social Identities in the Asia Pacific Region*, ed. James Farrer (Tokyo: Sophia University Institute of Comparative Culture, 2010), http://tinyurl.com/b77440a; and Ray, "Nation and Cuisine: The Evidence from American Newspapers ca. 1830–2003," *Food and Foodways* 16, no. 4 (October 2008): 259–97.

106. Stuart M. Emery, "Chinatown Is Chinatown Still; A Midnight Visit to the Quarter Where East Is Still the East in the West," *New York Times*, September 7, 1924, SM7. On the history of Chinese restaurants in New York before World War II, see Hanna Miller, "Identity Takeout: How American Jews Made Chinese Food Their Ethnic Cuisine," *Journal of Popular Culture* 39, no. 3 (2006): 430–65.

107. Ann Douglas, *Terrible Honesty: Mongrel Manhattan in the 1920s* (New York: Farrar, Straus and Giroux, 1996); Erenberg, *Steppin' Out*; Mumford, *Interzones*; Heap, *Slumming*.

108. Betty Fussell, "Hail to the Garlic Revolution," http://www.sallybernstein.com/food/columns/fussell/garlic.htm.

109. Erenberg, *Steppin' Out*, 252–59.

110. James, *Dining in New York*, 205.

111. E. Altieri, "N.Y.C. East Harlem," box 66, folder 6, LCP.

112. Federal Writers' Project, *New York City Guide*, 26.

113. Zahm, "Italian Restaurants."

114. Vergara, *Love and Pasta*, 47.

115. Amy Bernardy, *Italia randagia attraverso gli Stati Uniti* (Turin: Bocca, 1913), 58–59.

116. Pier Antonio Quarantotti Gambini, *Neve a Manhattan* (Rome: Fazi, 1998), 143.

117. In a study conducted at Princeton University in 1932 in which students were asked to choose characteristics they would associate with different racial and ethnic groups, "Artistic," "Impulsive," "Emotional," "Short-Tempered," and "Musical" well outdistanced all others when it came to Italians. Gustave M. Gilbert, "Stereotype Persistence and Change among College Students," *Journal of Abnormal and Social Psychology* 46 (1951): 245–54.

118. Quoted in La Sorte, *La Merica*, 147.

119. Sermolino, *Papa's Table d'Hote*, 71.

120. Fredrik Barth, *Ethnic Groups and Boundaries: The Social Organization of Culture Difference* (Prospect Heights, Ill.: Waveland Press, 1998), 19.

121. Ibid., 16.

122. Ware, *Greenwich Village*, 115.

123. Ibid., 118–19.

124. Barth, *Ethnic Groups and Boundaries*, 18.

125. "What Makes Life Interesting in East Harlem," box 67, folder 21, LCP.

Epilogue

1. Helen Barolini, *A Circular Journey* (New York: Fordham University Press, 2006), 24–25.

2. James, *Dining in New York*, 33.

3. Jane Nickerson, "Hot, Hearty Pizza," *New York Times*, May 25, 1947, SM42–43.

4. Richard Gehman, "Crazy about Pizza; Call It Tomato Pie, Pizza Pie or Just Plain Pizza, This Delectable, Pungent Italian Concoction Is Giving the Hot Dog a Run for the Money as the Favorite American Snack," *Saturday Evening Post*, November 30, 1957, 32–60.

5. Herbert Mitgang, "Pizza a la Mode; In Many Variations Italy's Famous Pie Now Rivals the Hot Dog in Popularity," *New York Times*, February 12, 1956, SM64–66.

6. Herbert Mitgang, "For the Love of Pizza; An Old Italian Treat Is Sweeping the Nation; It's a Meal-in-a-Dish So Succulent, Composers Have Written Songs about It," *Collier's*, March 7, 1953, 67–70.

7. Judith G. Goode, Karen Curtis, and Janet Theophano, "Meal Formats, Meal Cycles, and Menu Negotiation in the Maintenance of an Italian-American Community," in *Food in the Social Order: Studies of Food and Festivities in Three American Communities*, ed. Mary Douglas (New York: Russell Sage Foundation, 1984), 143–218.

8. Ada Boni, *The Talisman Italian Cookbook* (New York: Crown, 1950); Maria LoPinto, *The Art of Italian Cooking* (New York: Doubleday, 1948).

9. Marcella Hazan, *The Classic Italian Cook Book: The Art of Italian Cooking and the Italian Art of Eating* (Boston: Atlantic Monthly Press, 1973); Giuliano Bugialli, *The Fine Art of Italian Cooking* (New York: Times Books, 1977); Margaret and G. Franco Romagnoli, *The Romagnoli's Table: Italian Family Recipes* (Boston: Little, Brown, 1974); Pino Luongo and Andrew Friedman, *Dirty Dishes: A Restaurateur's Story of Passion, Pain, and Pasta* (New York: Bloomsbury USA, 2008); Lidia Bastianich, *La Cucina di Lidia: Distinctive Regional Cuisine from the North of Italy* (New York: Doubleday, 1990).

10. Matthew F. Jacobson, *Roots Too: White Ethnic Revival in Post–Civil Rights America* (Cambridge, Mass.: Harvard University Press, 2006).

11. Verde Barr, *We Called It Macaroni*; Order Sons of Italy in America Florida, *Preserving Our Italian Heritage* (Memphis: Wimmer, 1991). For New York City's examples of community cookbooks based on restaurants, see Vincent Schiavelli, *Bruculinu, America: Remembrances of Sicilian-American Brooklyn, Told in Stories and Recipes* (Boston: Houghton Mifflin Harcourt, 1998); Frank Pellegrino, *Rao's Cookbook: Over 100 Years of Italian Home Cooking* (New York: Random House, 1998); Ann Volkwein, *The Arthur Avenue Cookbook: Recipes and Memories from the Real Little Italy* (New York: Ecco, 2004).

12. Donna Gabaccia, "Food, Recipes, Cookbooks, and Italian-American Life," in *American Woman, Italian Style: Italian Americana's Best Writings on Women*, ed. Carol Bonomo Albright and Christine Palamidessi Moore (New York: Fordham University Press, 2011), 121–55.

13. Italian Americans busy in the construction of their diasporic identity even consumed refined cookbooks on Italian regional cuisines, usually by non-Italian lovers of all things Italian, such as Arthur Schwartz, *Naples at Table: Cooking in Campania* (New

York: Harper Collins, 1998); Nancy Harmon Jenkins, *Flavors of Puglia: Traditional Recipes from the Heel of Italy's Boot* (New York: Broadway Books, 1997); Fred Plotkin, *Recipes from Paradise: Life and Food on the Italian Riviera* (Boston: Little Brown, 1997); Lynne Rossetto Kasper, *The Splendid Table: Recipes from Emilia-Romagna, the Heartland of Northern Italian Food* (New York: William Morrow Cookbooks, 1992). Regarding the ethnic suburbs, see Joshua M. Zeitz, *White Ethnic New York: Jews, Catholics, and the Shaping of Postwar Politics* (Chapel Hill: University of North Carolina Press, 2007).

14. DeSalvo and Giunta, *Milk of Almonds*; Guglielmo, *Living the Revolution*, 132–38. See also Caroline Waldron Merithew, "Domesticating the Diaspora: Remembering the Life of Katie DeRorre," in *Intimacy and Italian Migration: Gender and Domestic Lives in a Mobile World*, ed. Loretta Baldassar and Donna R. Gabaccia (New York: Fordham University Press, 2011), 69–83.

15. See the program of the conference "Mangia Piano: The Internationalization of Italian Local Foodways," Montclair State University, March 6–7, 2012.

16. Herbert J. Gans, "Symbolic Ethnicity: The Future of Ethnic Groups and Cultures in America," *Ethnic and Racial Studies* 2, no. 1 (1979): 1–20.

17. Ewen, *Immigrant Women*; Peiss, *Cheap Amusements*; Andrew R. Heinze, *Adapting to Abundance: Jewish Immigrants, Mass Consumption, and the Search for American Identity* (New York: Columbia University Press, 1992).

18. Lila Byock, "Torrisi Italian Specialties," *New Yorker*, August 2, 2010, http://tinyurl.com/27gebam.

19. David Lowenthal, *The Past Is a Foreign Country* (Cambridge: Cambridge University Press, 1985); Raphael Samuel, *Theaters of Memory* (New York: Verso, 1994).

20. Verde Barr, *We Called It Macaroni*, v.

Index

SIMONE CINOTTO teaches history at the University of Gastronomic Sciences, Pollenzo, Italy, where he is the director of the Master's Program in Food Culture and Communications: Food, Place, and Identity. He is the author of *Soft Soil, Black Grapes: The Birth of Italian Winemaking in California*.

The University of Illinois Press
is a founding member of the
Association of American University Presses.

Composed in 10.5/13 Adobe Minion Pro
by Lisa Connery
at the University of Illinois Press
Manufactured by Thomson-Shore, Inc.

University of Illinois Press
1325 South Oak Street
Champaign, IL 61820-6903
www.press.uillinois.edu